Empowering Learners With AI:

Strategies, Ethics, and Frameworks

Shahnawaz Khan
Bahrain Polytechnic, Bahrain

Philippe Pringuet
Bahrain Polytechnic, Bahrain

IGI Global
Scientific Publishing
Publishing Tomorrow's Research Today

Vice President of Editorial Melissa Wagner
Director of Acquisitions Mikaela Felty
Director of Book Development Jocelynn Hessler
Production Manager Mike Brehm
Cover Design Jose Rosado

Published in the United States of America by
IGI Global Scientific Publishing
701 East Chocolate Avenue
Hershey, PA, 17033, USA
Tel: 717-533-8845 | Fax: 717-533-7115
Website: https://www.igi-global.com E-mail: cust@igi-global.com

Library of Congress Cataloging-in-Publication Data

Names: Khan, Shahnawaz editor | Pringuet, Philippe, 1982- editor
Title: Empowering learners with AI : strategies, ethics, and frameworks / edited by Shahnawaz Khan, Philippe Pringuet.
Description: Hershey, PA : IGI Global Scientific Publishing, [2026] | Includes bibliographical references and index.
Identifiers: LCCN 2025044758 (print) | LCCN 2025044759 (ebook) | ISBN 9798337373867 hardcover | ISBN 9798337373874 paperback | ISBN 9798337373881 ebook
Subjects: LCSH: Artificial intelligence--Educational applications--Case studies
Classification: LCC LB1028.44 .E47 2026 (print) | LCC LB1028.44 (ebook)
LC record available at https://lccn.loc.gov/2025044758
LC ebook record available at https://lccn.loc.gov/2025044759

British Cataloguing in Publication Data
A Cataloguing in Publication record for this book is available from the British Library.

Table of Contents

Detailed Table of Contents

Online classes and virtual interactions have become standard in education following the pandemic, offering flexibility and enabling remote learning. Various techniques, such as flipped classrooms, surprise assessments, and gamification, are used to boost attentiveness and enhance the quality of online sessions. However, these approaches have limitations and often fail to maintain engagement throughout an entire session. Consequently, there is a need for a more effective solution. This study explores a method to improve student attentiveness during online sessions by using AI-based voice recognition and pre-set keywords to generate multiple-choice polls. This paper seeks to develop a model for integrating AI into teaching and learning, based on the findings from this controlled online classroom experiments.

This study aims to develop a specialized scale to measure educational quality in Saudi Arabia. Normally the SERVQUAL scale is used to measure the quality in education sectors, but few studies have attempted to modify the scale to accommodate the distinct features of the education sector. Using factor analysis, the study identifies three factors to be added to SERVQUAL, namely academic, non-academic, and curriculum dimensions. Recommendations for improving the variety of courses and programs, curriculum, and student workload are based on the gap scores obtained by subtracting students' expectations from their perceptions.

Artificial intelligence (AI) is now becoming a pivotal force identified as an important driver in the rapidly transforming higher education landscape, requiring both educators and students to have a thorough understanding of it. This study adopts both scoping and integrative review methodologies to analyze existing literature between

2020 and 2025. The analysis discerns the significant themes, such as integration, governance, policy, ethics, social responsibility convergence of technology, ethics, teaching methods, and social consequences, and literacy. Research indicates a substantial disparity in the incorporation of ethical frameworks and the practical implementation of AI literacy in higher education curriculum (Zhang et al., 2024). The study concludes with the recommendation to bridge the gap, highlighting the necessity for multidisciplinary approaches and policy development by convergence of technology, ethics, teaching methods, and societal impact.

This chapter presents a systematic review on the integration of ChatGPT and other Large Language Models (LLMs) in English academic writing within higher education, highlighting opportunities and challenges. It examines research on issues such as threats to academic integrity and the limitations of detection software. While LLMs can assist writing by providing linguistic support and personalized feedback, concerns remain about plagiarism and authenticity. Effective pedagogical strategies are proposed to promote AI literacy among students and faculty. To address these concerns, the chapter introduces the RAISE Framework, which emphasizes the need for clear institutional policies, transparent authorship practices, and innovative assessment methods focusing on process and critical engagement rather than solely on output. This framework aims to preserve educational rigor and authenticity in an evolving technological landscape.

With the rapid integration of artificial intelligence (AI) into education, this study explores the dual impact of AI tools on enhancing learning while potentially impeding the development of fundamental cognitive skills. It focuses on intentional pedagogical methods like inquiry-based learning, Socratic questioning, problem-based learning, and meta-cognitive training, which are designed to foster reasoning and critical thinking, and discourage over-reliance on AI. By employing qualitative and quantitative analyses, the research identifies best practices for leveraging AI to enhance educational outcomes while simultaneously nurturing essential cognitive abilities. Results highlight the effectiveness of integrating reflective thinking into open-ended problem-solving and human-centered discussions, thus promoting critical

cornerstone of critical thinking, cultural heritage, and human dignity amid the rise of autonomous systems.

Preface

The current era is one of unprecedented technological change. The growth of innovations in Artificial intelligence (AI) has been tremendous in this decade. AI has transitioned from a futuristic concept to a foundational force in our daily lives. While AI's impact is now seen almost everywhere, one of its most profound and complex effects is being felt within the halls of academia. Educators and learners alike are grappling with its transformative potential. The digital frontier of education is no longer a distant horizon; it is here, and it demands our critical attention.

This book serves as a comprehensive guide to navigating this emerging landscape. It offers an honest and multifaceted inquiry into the capabilities and role of AI in shaping the future of teaching and learning. It explores the challenges and opportunities that arise when AI tools are integrated into higher education through a collection of rigorous studies. It delves into specific applications—from enhancing work-integrated learning for hospitality students to creating a pedagogical roadmap for forensic accounting and examines how these technologies can be leveraged to foster essential skills like problem-solving and critical thinking.

CHAPTER OVERVIEW

The opening chapter explores the role of ChatGPT-powered tools in shaping work-related skills within the hospitality sector. Drawing on a work-integrated learning framework, it examines how these tools contribute to professional competencies such as time management, communication, and problem-solving, while also highlighting limitations in addressing complex, workplace-specific challenges. The findings underline both the promise and constraints of AI in preparing students for the demands of guest-facing roles.

The second chapter examines the integration of AI into problem-based learning environments through the lens of Bloom's Digital Taxonomy. It reviews existing literature to map how AI can support deeper learning and the development of employability skills. The chapter outlines practical pathways for incorporating AI into pedagogical design and emphasizes the need for professional development and ethical guidelines to ensure higher education remains future-ready.

The third chapter focuses on the transformation of forensic accounting education in an AI-driven era. It presents a pedagogical roadmap that incorporates AI-powered simulations, intelligent tutoring systems, and collaborative problem-solving platforms. By evaluating both opportunities and challenges, the chapter provides educators with strategies to enhance critical thinking and equip students for the evolving demands of forensic accounting practice.

The fourth chapter addresses student attentiveness in online learning, a challenge that has grown significantly since the pandemic. It introduces an AI evaluation model that leverages voice recognition and keyword-based interactions to increase engagement during virtual sessions. By assessing the limitations of traditional strategies such as gamification and surprise assessments, the chapter proposes a more dynamic approach to sustaining attention in digital classrooms.

The fifth chapter examines educational quality in Saudi Arabia through the development of a modified SERVQUAL scale tailored to the education sector. By identifying academic, non-academic, and curriculum-related dimensions, the study highlights gaps between student expectations and experiences. The findings provide recommendations for enhancing course variety, workload management, and curriculum design, contributing to more effective quality assurance practices.

The sixth chapter investigates AI literacy in higher education through a comprehensive scoping and integrative review. It analyzes themes such as ethics, governance, policy, and social responsibility, while identifying gaps between ethical discourse and practical implementation in curricula. The chapter calls for multidisciplinary approaches and policy development to ensure AI literacy encompasses not only technical proficiency but also ethical and societal awareness.

The seventh chapter presents a systematic review of ChatGPT and other large language models in English academic writing. It highlights opportunities such as linguistic support and feedback, while addressing challenges around academic integrity and detection tools. The introduction of the RAISE framework provides practical strategies to balance innovation with rigor, emphasizing transparency, authorship clarity, and process-oriented assessment methods.

The eighth chapter considers the risks of over-reliance on AI tools in education and advocates for pedagogical approaches that strengthen reasoning and analytical skills. By integrating inquiry-based learning, Socratic questioning, and metacognitive training, the chapter demonstrates how educators can foster intellectual engagement beyond AI-generated responses. The findings stress the importance of reflective practices and human-centered dialogue in cultivating critical thinking.

The ninth chapter engages with the ethical implications of data collection and usage in powering AI systems. It discusses issues of privacy, consent, transparency, and bias, drawing attention to risks such as surveillance and discrimination from skewed datasets. The analysis underscores the necessity of informed consent and equitable data practices to ensure AI applications remain fair, transparent, and trustworthy across sectors.

The tenth chapter introduces Synthesean, a structured linguistic framework designed to ensure AI-generated language aligns with human cognitive, ethical, and cultural needs. In contrast to unregulated forms of AI language that risk semantic decline, Synthesean provides tools such as dialect guides, prompt design strategies, and evaluation rubrics. This framework reinforces the value of language as a vehicle for critical thought and cultural preservation, advocating for responsible and interpretable AI communication.

Beyond practical applications, this book also confronts the profound ethical and theoretical questions that AI presents. It scrutinizes the ethical implications of data collection, the threats to academic integrity posed by large language models, and the urgent need for students and faculty to develop robust AI literacy. It immerses readers in the subject, offering a holistic and balanced perspective that ranges from a systematic review of existing literature to the proposal of new pedagogical frameworks like the RAISE Framework and Synthesean.

This book is for anyone committed to shaping the future of education - researchers, educators, students, and policymakers. This book demonstrates that our pedagogical approaches must evolve alongside technology. By ensuring the adaptation of technology in teaching and learning, we can prepare students to not only use AI, but also to think critically and creatively in a world where it is a constant presence. We hope this book serves as a vital starting point for that crucial conversation.

Chapter 1

Critical Evaluation of the Role of ChatGPT-Powered AI Tools in the Development of Work-Related Skills From the Perspectives of Hospitality Learners

Husain Almadhi
https://orcid.org/0000-0002-9038-3257
Vatel Bahrain, Bahrain

Anuradha Menon
https://orcid.org/0009-0000-3766-1492
Vatel Bahrain, Bahrain

ABSTRACT

This study examines ChatGPT's impact on work-related skills development among hospitality students at Vatel Bahrain, focusing on its role in work-integrated learning (WIL). Vatel's pedagogy blends theoretical instruction with bi-weekly practice and annual luxury hotel internships, providing hands-on industry exposure. Using a socio-cognitive constructivist framework and UTAUT2, the research explores students' perceptions of ChatGPT's effectiveness in learning and skill acquisition. While AI tools enhance information access and cognitive stimulation, concerns remain about academic integrity and critical thinking. This study addresses a research

DOI: 10.4018/979-8-3373-7386-7.ch001

gap by analyzing AI's influence on WIL through semi-structured student interviews. Findings reveal that ChatGPT supports professional competencies, improving time management, communication, and problem-solving in guest-facing roles. However, its inability to offer tailored responses to complex hospitality challenges limits its effectiveness in workplace-specific scenarios.

INTRODUCTION

The concept of artificial intelligence (AI) — first coined by John McCarthy in 1955 — refers to systems capable of performing tasks that require human-like intelligence, such as learning, reasoning, and problem-solving. (Guan et al., 2020) The ever-increasing prevalence of artificial intelligence (AI)—particularly more advanced language and deep learning models that effectively replicate human intelligence—is profoundly transforming how we live and learn, necessitating the development of values and skills to ensure effective human-machine collaboration. Over time, AI has evolved to encompass advanced technologies like machine learning, natural language processing, and neural networks, enabling machines to analyze vast datasets and execute complex tasks. Among its transformative applications, generative AI — a subset of AI that leverages deep learning to create human-like content — has emerged as a revolutionary force in education (Guan et al., 2020).

Among these generative AI tools is Chat Generative Pre-Trained Transformer (ChatGPT), a chatbot that has gained immense popularity in educational settings due to its potential to enhance teaching and learning. Farazouli et al. (2024) highlighted the significance of chatbots in education, noting that they can effectively personalize a student's learning experience by providing relevant content and information. In addition, such models have reduced educators' workload by enabling the generation of personalized instructional materials and assessments, monitoring student performance, and providing real-time feedback (Shamsuddinova et al., 2024). With the growing integration of AI tools like ChatGPT in education, concerns have also emerged regarding their potential drawbacks—particularly their impact on social skills, biases in training data, and other ethical considerations. Despite their benefits, scholars such as Babu and Sharmila (2023) discuss the ethical implications of using AI chatbots in education and training.

There have been ongoing efforts at various levels to develop policies to address perceived harms to students' learning and academic performance and to ensure the ethical use of ChatGPT and other generative AI tools in the classroom (Babu & Sharmila, 2023; Shamsuddinova et al., 2024). However, Guan et al. (2020) urge that innovations like ChatGPT are more rapidly reshaping pedagogical approaches and skills development across disciplines, including hospitality management, than the pace of change and acceptance within academia. In this regard as higher educational institutions negotiate this paradigm shift, understanding the dual impact of ChatGPT as both an innovative learning tool and a potential disruptor of academic and professional norms is imperative (Michel-Villarreal et al., 2023).

1.1 Research Background, Problem and Justification

The digital revolution has greatly contributed to shaping the hospitality and tourism sectors. To cater to the needs of customers, the hospitality industry has always been one of the leading implementers of new technology, as cited by Fouad et al. (2024). Virtual reality and online booking systems have been used to enhance client engagement and the efficiency of service (Elkhwesky et al., 2024). Various aspects like marketing, operations and customer experience have evolved due to technological innovations such as Global Distribution Systems and Property Management Systems, which have led to dramatic changes in managerial, strategic and operational job requirements. Recent research, as mentioned by Nuong and Ragavan (2023) has demonstrated that smart technologies can reshape certain hospitality and tourism jobs, but technological innovations such as robotics and artificial intelligence are also threatening to replace human labor.

In this effervescent landscape, hospitality graduates are expected to equip themselves with the knowledge, skills and competencies to sustain and thrive in the industry. It is thus imperative now more than ever that higher education institutions are agile and respond to the ever-changing needs of the industry, as cited by Zhang et al. (2024). To ensure that hospitality courses stay relevant and meet the ever-changing industry needs, universities and colleges must constantly update their hospitality courses curricula. Students, on the other hand, are expected to have access to different online learning resources as well as opportunities to participate in a variety of extracurricular activities to extend their classroom learning (Guan et al., 2020).

Beyond educational contexts, generative AI models such as ChatGPT are becoming increasingly ubiquitous across various work domains as productivity-enhancing tools. Their ability to perform tasks such as generating contextually relevant responses, managing correspondence, scheduling meetings, and offering information support are a few examples of their impact in different domains of work (Jo & Park, 2024). In this regard, organizations also play a huge role in instilling skills and competencies through on-the-job training opportunities to keep pace with the technological advances and ensure they can compete in a global marketplace (Nuong & Ragavan, 2023). Additionally, countries such as Australia and Singapore are currently using AI tools to identify evolving workplace demands and applying these real-time analytics to align their education systems with labor market requirements (Shiohira, 2021).

In this context, studies show that large language models can significantly influence how students undertaking internships as part of their programs learn and acquire work-related knowledge and skills (Shiohira, 2021). As noted by Baxter Magolda (2014) and Zegwaard and McCurdy (2014), work-integrated learning (WIL) bridges the gap between academic knowledge and real-world application by embedding professional experiences into higher education curricula. Through engagement in industry settings, students develop essential workplace skills and competencies such as communication, teamwork, and problem-solving skills crucial for career readiness. The dynamic nature of the workplace, supported by experienced co-workers, plays a vital role in students' development (Baxter Magolda, 2014; Zegwaard & McCurdy, 2014). Cooperative education, which typically alternates periods of study and work, offers multiple WIL opportunities (Gardner & Bartkus, 2014). As suggested in the literature, WIL offers numerous benefits: Students not only gain job-related skills and learn to navigate organizational culture but also enhance their self-efficacy and develop a professional identity, which in turn supports their employability (Zegwaard & Pretti, 2023).

In the hospitality industry, internships are regarded as an opportunity to provide operational and/or managerial on-the-job training with the support and guidance of a supervisor, as cited by Zopiatis et al. (2021). Presently, nearly all recognized hospitality and tourism programs mandate a minimum of one practical placement for students, although the exact duration, credit weightage, and assessment methods vary (Zopiatis & Theocharous, 2013). Despite the differences, internships are trusted by the different stakeholders in the hospitality and tourism contexts (Morrison & Barry O'Mahony, 2003).

Given the industry-driven nature of hospitality and tourism education and training, educational establishments aim to upskill learners according to the needs of the industry and socio-environmental conditions (Hsu et al., 2017; Min et al., 2016). It is argued that in the hospitality and tourism sectors, generative AI platforms such as ChatGPT will not fully replace people, but augment their practice, enhancing their productivity through shifting their focus from repetitive tasks to client-oriented responsibilities. Consequently, leveraging the aptitude of generative AI tools such as ChatGPT to enhance their implementation in the hospitality industry is an unavoidable futuristic trend (Dwivedi et al., 2024).

The integration of ChatGPT into education has been a point of debate among experts. If AI tools could, in time, handle the tasks of experienced teachers, schools ought to revise the focus of education and determine what skills should still be taught in classrooms (Grassini, 2023). Therefore, this research is situated within the context of hospitality higher education and explores how one such generative AI platform, ChatGPT, influences the skills development and knowledge acquisition of hospitality students in both theoretical and practical education.

1.2 Research Context and Scope

Vatel is a renowned hospitality education institution, established in 1981 in Paris, and is globally recognized for producing successful management professionals through partnerships with luxury resorts and hotels. Its bachelor's program offers a unique interactive learning environment that integrates both practical and theoretical knowledge. Vatel's pedagogical approach values practical experience as a complement to classroom-based learning. Students complete a term of traditional management courses followed by annual internships lasting 18 to 20 weeks, during which they develop and refine the skills needed to succeed in hospitality management.

These internships allow students to apply classroom-acquired theoretical knowledge in real-world settings, offering invaluable experiential learning. A recurring weekly pattern of theoretical classes and practical assignments further builds students' confidence and industry awareness—attributes highly valued by employers. By the end of the program, graduates will have completed at least two years of internships at luxury hospitality properties (Vatel, 2023).

At Vatel, assessment methods are aligned with course objectives and industry expectations to evaluate students' acquisition of both theoretical knowledge and practical skills. During internships and bi-weekly practice sessions at partner properties, students are assessed concurrently by on-site supervisors and members of the academic team. These assessments are directly linked to the core skills that interns are expected to acquire and are used by line managers or training supervisors for performance evaluation. The assessment rubrics are closely mapped to the competencies required across various hotel departments.

At the end of the internship, students submit a report followed by a presentation in which they analyze their skills development and demonstrate how they have integrated theoretical knowledge gained on campus into their practical experiences. This final stage ensures that learners can effectively bridge academic learning with real-world industry applications, preparing them for successful careers in hospitality.

This approach aligns with the principles of WIL, which fosters the development of job-specific skills and competencies, professional identity, and industry awareness. Through bi-weekly practical sessions and extended internships at renowned hospitality establishments, Vatel ensures that students gain firsthand exposure to workplace environments. Its unique experiential learning model integrates structured instruction with hands-on practice, allowing students to engage in a continuous cycle of knowledge acquisition, application, and skill refinement. Literature in this area suggests that interaction with experienced professionals and immersion in industry settings enhance students' ability to navigate organizational structures and meet employer expectations. With the growing emphasis on employability and career readiness in higher education, WIL serves as a vital bridge between academic preparation and professional success Feng et al. (2019).

Beyond the general benefits of WIL, Vatel's internships include brand-specific training that helps students develop essential industry skills while internalizing the unique values and operational processes of luxury hospitality brands. As (Kang, 2016) suggested, brand-specific training enables employees to embody the brand's promise, ensuring consistency in guest experiences and fostering brand loyalty. During internships at prestigious hotels, students receive tailored training that immerses them in the distinct brand identity, service standards, and cultural expectations of their host establishments. This process is guided by experienced mentors and supervisors in each department, who play a key role in reinforcing the brand's philosophy and commitment to operational excellence.

Nevertheless, the students in these internships are in direct contact with ChatGPT in a workplace setting where, as highlighted by Dwivedi et al. (2024), its impact is eminent and is used for diverse tasks. Zhang et al. (2024) emphasize the importance of investigating the attitudes and intentions of hospitality students and academic staff regarding the adoption of AI tools such as ChatGPT and their impact on hospitality education.

Therefore, the scope of this research is to empirically investigate the impact of ChatGPT on students' acquisition of work-related skills during internships in a work-integrated hotel management program, which hitherto remains a largely unexplored area of study in the research context. Broadly, the study outcomes could be of interest to higher educational institutions which offer programs that combine theoretical learning and practical internships. However, since it is contextualized in the hospitality and tourism sectors, the study findings can offer new critical insights into the integration of ChatGPT in training interns or students working in hotels or properties. Moreover, the outcomes can highlight potential challenges or obstacles to students' adoption of ChatGPT for work-integrated learning in hospitality education.

1.3 Rationale, Research Objectives and Questions

As previously discussed, AI has transformed education, with undeterred access to AI tools such as ChatGPT marking the beginning of an unprecedented shift in attitudes toward teaching and learning (Michel-Villarreal et al., 2023). In the current educational ecosystem of AI-generated roles and knowledge, the concept of "future-proof skills" emphasizes the importance of critical thinking, problem-solving, empathy, ethics, and other uniquely human traits that machines cannot replicate with equal proficiency and adaptability (Dumitru & Halpern, 2023). The pressing need to nurture critical thinking skills in education is even more crucial now, as these skill sets involve analysis and the capacity to question everything, including algorithms and vast datasets generated by AI (El Hajal & Rowson, 2020). Rožman et al. (2023) listed analytical thinking, active learning, problem-solving, critical analysis, and creativity as the five top global skills for 2025.

There is a growing body of research at different educational levels on the impact of AI on students' learning and skills development from both teachers' and students' perspectives, such as the works of Woithe and Filipec (2023) and Cruz-Benito (2022). In higher education contexts, much of this research pertains to traditional learning ecosystems where teaching and assessments are guided and monitored by the faculty. On the other hand, WIL programs are gaining prominence as a means to bridge the gap between academia and industry, ensuring that students develop practical skills through internships and are fully work-ready when they graduate. As already noted, approaches to training in internships or practicums can differ depending on the program of study and industry requirements.

Evidence on WIL highlights that internships, work placements, and project-based learning in authentic industry settings are designed to provide practical and technical skills not easily obtained through traditional classroom instruction and to prepare graduates for successful integration into the workforce (Adegbite & Govender, 2022; Udell et al., 2023). Billett (2011) suggested that worksite learning involves continuous engagement in familiar tasks, allowing sustained practice and improvement of existing skills, while exposure to novel experiences fosters the development of new knowledge and organizational skills. These worksite learning experiences shape individuals' domains of knowledge, their ways of knowing, and their interests, which in turn affect their intentionality to learn.

While extensive research explores AI's impact on traditional education (e.g., personalized feedback, curriculum design, and ethical concerns like plagiarism), critical gaps persist in understanding ChatGPT's role during internships (Farazouli et al., 2024). Existing studies highlight AI's dual-edged potential: It can empower lifelong learning and problem-solving but also risks fostering overreliance and eroding creative and critical faculties (Altun et al., 2024; Babu & Sharmila, 2023; Dondi et al., 2021; Kooli, 2023). However, there is little empirical data on how interns or students involved in practical workplace training use ChatGPT in real-world tasks (e.g., customer service and operational problem-solving) to navigate their daily tasks as part of their learning. In addition, there is little evidence on how this usage impacts their skill development, especially in future-proof competencies like critical analysis or ethical decision-making (Wang, 2025).

In this context, the objectives of this research are to critically analyze the perceptions of Vatel's learners on the impact of using ChatGPT on their work skills development during their internships and to explore and identify the opportunities and challenges of using AI in the hospitality industry for training purposes. The study examined the role of ChatGPT in WIL training and learning and its potential impact on work-related skills development from the perspectives of learners studying in an undergraduate hospitality management program. To the best of our knowledge, ChatGPT's impact on internship students' work skills acquisition and development while performing real-world tasks, particularly in the hospitality sector, has not been explored, as we found no such literature during the different stages of this research. The study was conducted at Vatel Bahrain, where the researchers work.

The above rationale and objectives led to the following research questions:

1. What is the potential impact of using ChatGPT on the development of work-related skills from the learners' perspective in the hospitality industry?
2. What are the potential enablers and challenges of using ChatGPT in learning and skill development from the learners' perspective?

1.4 Research Overview

This subsection briefly informs of the structure adopted by the researchers to achieve the research objectives, which will then guide them to answer the research questions. The forthcoming literature review section explains key theories in learning and adoption of technology that underpin this research. Additionally, the researchers have included essential background information on hospitality internships, the evolution of ChatGPT in education and more specifically, its role in the hospitality training context. The Methodology section introduces the research philosophy, design and tools used to gather and analyze the research data. This study adopts an interpretivist qualitative approach, where semi-structured interviews are conducted with the participants, who are all students in the hospitality college where this study is conducted. The Discussion section presents the findings of the research stemming from the discussions of the participants' perspectives on the impact of ChatGPT on their work skills acquisition during their internships and their perceived opportunities and challenges in adopting ChatGPT. In the concluding section, the researchers have attempted to suggest future research directions informed by the study outcomes and limitations.

LITERATURE REVIEW

An AI tool, developed by OpenAI in 2022, ChatGPT has been described as a 'fascinating text generator' that works using a deep neural network (Loos et al., 2023).Trained on massive sets of data, ChatGPT can generate complete responses to prompts influenced by patterns in the inputs it has received (Guan et al., 2020; Loos et al., 2023). Since 2022, there has been a spate of studies in educational contexts on ChatGPT. Although the focus of these studies may differ, certain themes are consistent in the different definitions of ChatGPT. It is typically characterized as an intelligent tutoring system that constructs human-like responses to prompts in real-time.

Yet, to date, in the tourism industry, a challenge for the deployment of generative AI tools such as ChatGPT is the nature of big data available to hotels and other tourism properties. Limna and Kraiwanit (2023) finds that although there are large volumes of accessible data, the variety of data is usually limited to the guests' interactions with the organization's website before their travel, and their behavior or experience during the stay. As hotels or other tourism organizations have little data on tourists' profiles, interests and preferences, the quality of data may not be very relevant to the core function of the industry: to enhance customer service quality.

In educational environments, however, ChatGPT's relevance to students and educators has been recognized and appreciated widely. Some of the tasks ChatGPT is generally used for are generating content on a multitude of topics, tutoring students, helping with communicative activities, providing instant feedback, and performing repetitive administrative tasks like grading (Loos et al., 2023). In the higher education context, ChatGPT emerges as a versatile resource for students, providing multifaceted opportunities for support, collaboration, and engagement across a variety of academic endeavors. Duong et al. (2024) described ChatGPT as a virtual tutor that can assist students in understanding complex coursework through real-time and personalized discussions and explanations and clarifying doubts to deepen their learning. Zhang et al. (2024) suggests the integration of ChatGPT in education has appeared as a key solution to enhancing students' learning, and the development of cognitive skills and career-related knowledge, skills and competencies.

2.1 Learning Theories Underpinning the Research

The following subsections discuss the learning theories and assumptions underpinning this research within the scope of theoretical and practical learning in the hospitality higher education context.

2.1.1 Socio-constructivism and ChatGPT in Education

This section explores the role of ChatGPT from a socio-constructivist perspective. Lev Vygotsky, a central figure in this framework, viewed learning as a collaborative process in which cognitive development and meaningful understanding are shaped through social engagement before being internalized (Amineh & Asl, 2015; Kanselaar, 2002). Vygotsky further posited that learning occurs within a learner's zone of proximal development (ZPD), where development is supported through interaction with more knowledgeable others (MKOs). Based on this principle—that knowledge is co-constructed through social interaction—tools like ChatGPT can be situated within a learner's ZPD in many educational settings. Wu (2024) suggested that in AI-augmented learning environments, generative AI tools such as ChatGPT can serve as digital scaffolds, providing adaptive support tailored to individual learners' needs. As originally defined by Wood et al. (1976), scaffolding involves the MKO managing elements initially beyond the learner's capacity. With guided assistance, the learner can then focus on aspects within their competence, thereby facilitating a deeper understanding (Mercer, 1995).

In this research context, ChatGPT can be viewed as a dynamic scaffold or MKO that operates within learners' ZPDs, facilitating knowledge construction. Baskara (2024) argued that new AI models have evolved beyond one-on-one exchanges and have become more collaborative learning spaces where the AI facilitates and enriches user interactions. This shift aligns with the social and cultural learning environments described in social constructivist theory.

AI has become a frequently discussed topic in current education, particularly regarding its implications for teaching and learning. Educators and researchers have used AI to address challenges in the educational field, such as the quality of teaching, differentiation, and emergency education (Shiohira, 2021). In educational settings today, learners leverage ChatGPT for personalized learning by prompting the AI tool for explanations of complex topics, solutions to personal or work problems, or assistance in creating written content for work or social needs.

2.1.2 Work-integrated Learning

This subsection explains the centrality of work-integrated learning in the scope of this research and hospitality education. The significance of experience-based learning in fostering academic, personal and professional growth is well-documented (Stansbie et al., 2016). People learn through performing work-related tasks, as identified by (Dewey, 1938). Learning models with an occupational focus continue to expand across higher education curricula, driven by the growing demand to link academic programs with employability outcomes (Zegwaard & Pretti, 2023). As cited by Gardner and Bartkus (2014), the literature offers several definitions of WIL, many of which overlap with work-based learning. Both terms serve as broad umbrella concepts describing educational programs that combine individualized occupational experiences with formal learning (Zegwaard & Pretti, 2023).

WIL and work-based learning are embedded in various fields, such as engineering, education, and nursing, and often include industry projects and year-long internships. According to Zegwaard and Pretti (2023), WIL programs vary widely and exhibit many distinguishing characteristics. However, despite their differences, they share core elements defining them as WIL forms. These include active student engagement with professional settings or communities, real-life tasks closely aligned with the relevant occupation, and the integration of stakeholder involvement into the curriculum. Aligned to the Social Exchange Theory, Nuong and Ragavan (2023) suggest that internships, simulations, and case studies are valuable opportunities for experiential learning and professional modelling. In WIL, interns develop key hospitality-related competencies such as communication, teamwork and technical skills by observing and emulating experienced professionals (Nuong & Ragavan, 2023; Zegwaard & Pretti, 2023).

Research across various sectors highlights that on-the-job experience and transferable skills are widely recognized as essential. In addition to strong academic performance, employers seek graduates with key attributes such as communication, teamwork, time management, and problem-solving skills. As WIL provides students with real-life experiences that bridge the gap between theory and practice, it enhances their employability Zegwaard and Pretti (2023).

In the hospitality industry, both formal qualifications and competencies are critical for a successful transition into the workforce (Feng et al., 2019). Research on tourism programs worldwide states that internships are the most significant characteristic to ensure that graduates meet the dynamic demands of the tourism market. In the hospitality and tourism industry, among the most frequently cited competences are those related to management of human and financial resources, making ethical decisions, coping with uncertainty and change, strategic planning and thinking, effectively solving customers' problems and social and emotional competences. In addition to these, graduates are expected to demonstrate 21st-century skills such as critical and creative thinking and interpersonal communication skills, among others. Ferreras-Garcia et al. (2020) assert that these competences cannot be instilled in students unless through experience, training and suitable practice. In their study linking internships and classroom learning among hospitality and tourism management students, Stansbie et al. (2016) concluded that offering structured practical experiences in real-world work environments positively impact not only students' knowledge and skills but also essential competences such as career expectations, initiative, enhanced leadership, improved financial acumen and openness to change.

WIL also allows employers to assess interns as potential future employees as they gain access to motivated and skilled interns who bring fresh perspectives. Educational institutions benefit as well, as enhanced WIL curricula help ensure graduates are better prepared for the labor market. Overall, WIL creates a vital link between academia and industry, aligning academic programs with market needs and contributing to a more skilled workforce, ultimately benefiting all stakeholders and the broader economy (Zegwaard & Pretti, 2023).

2.1.3 Brand-Specific Training

The following section explores the significance of brand-specific training, highlighting how it strengthens corporate identity and enhances both employee commitment and customer satisfaction in the competitive hospitality industry. As cited by Kang (2016), branding represents a promise made by a corporation, and the value of this promise is perceived based on how well it is fulfilled. Communication plays a crucial role in aligning the organization's corporate identity with the public perception of its image. Through both internal and external communication, companies reinforce their brand image among employees and the public. This involves strategic internal and external branding to develop distinctive brands that stand out in a competitive market. However, internal and external branding efforts have traditionally focused on employees who interact directly with clients, as they serve as a bridge between the organization and its customers. These client-facing employees are essential to delivering the brand promise, ultimately influencing customer satisfaction and contributing to corporate success.

According to Juskiw (2017), brand-specific training programs are vital for communicating the brand image internally. Such training fosters organizational commitment and aligns employees with the company's corporate values, cultivating a strong corporate brand that integrates internal procedures and culture with the brand identity. In the hotel industry, strong brand equity is associated with higher levels of employee commitment. Therefore, managers must first identify the factors influencing employee engagement before designing internal and external branding initiatives to ensure that employees fully internalize the brand's values. Once these values are internalized, employees are more likely to uphold the brand's standards during client interactions. In these moments, employees serve as brand ambassadors and are expected to embody the brand's values and deliver its promised experience (Burmann et al., 2009).

While classroom learning, textbooks, and even AI-powered resources offer valuable insights into general hospitality practices, the nuanced details of brand-specific operations remain largely exclusive to internal training programs. Luxury hotels maintain their distinct identities through proprietary service standards, unique operational workflows, and carefully curated guest experiences—elements that cannot be fully understood without direct, hands-on exposure. At Vatel, interns acquire this specialized knowledge through structured training, close mentorship, and immersive practice within their host establishments.

2.2 Review of Acceptance of Technology Models

In the current academic ecosystem, generative AI or large language learning models such as ChatGPT have shaped the way students engage with technology to support or enhance their learning. Given their ubiquitous presence in education, it is critical to understand factors that drive the adoption and integration of ChatGPT in learning and teaching. Different theories and models have appeared within the realm of information systems that define users' behaviors that shape their acceptance of new technologies.

2.2.1 Diffusion of Innovation Theory

The theory of diffusion of innovation (DOI) is one of the well-known models of adoption and was popularized by Rogers in 2003 (Kaminski, 2011; Sahin, 2006) . DOI has been used by multiple disciplines such as medicine, political science and education as a framework to study the adoption and diffusion of technology. Rogers (2003) used the words technology and innovation interchangeably and technology as a design for implemental use, which decreases uncertainty in cause-and-effect connections involved in achieving a desired result. Rogers (2003) also described innovation as a design, concept, or method, that is identified as new by an individual. For an innovation to be adopted or rejected, it first undergoes diffusion, which is a process of communicating an innovation through specified channels over a duration of time between members of a society. As stated, diffusion therefore has four primary constituents, which are innovation, communication channels, time, and social system (Sahin, 2006).

The theory also explores the innovation-decision process, which observes the five-stage thought process of an individual evaluating the advantages and disadvantages of an innovation. In addition to that, Rogers (2003) also groups those who adopt technology into five categories according to the relative speed of adoption. The five categories are innovators, early adopters, early majority, late majority, and laggards. The rate of adoption of those categories is influenced by five factors, which are relative advantages, compatibility, complexity, trialability, and observability. DOI could be a useful tool in investigating the adoption of technology in higher education, as agreed to by Medlin (2001) and Parisot (1997). Nevertheless, DOI is more suited for identifying when and who adopts a certain technology. The theory provides clear descriptors for variables closely associated with the diffusion of innovation (Lundblad, 2003), but the application of similar, updated, and more detailed models would better suit the requirements of this research.

2.2.2 Technology Acceptance Model

The technology acceptance model (TAM), introduced by Davis (1985), suggests perceived effectiveness and simplicity of implementation as the two main variables influencing the attitude of individuals towards technology (Manis & Choi, 2019). The model has been extensively employed as a foundational framework for understanding users' attitudes and behaviors that shape their technology acceptance across numerous disciplines and contexts (Manis & Choi, 2019; Rožman et al., 2023). TAM aims to explain the elements which influence an individual's judgment to adopt or avoid a certain technology (Rožman et al., 2023).

In education, students' perceptions significantly influence their successful adoption of technology for learning. According to TAM, students' attitudes toward adopting AI tools for learning are shaped by perceptions of ease and benefit. When students perceive digital tools as straightforward, transparent, and beneficial for performance improvement, they are more likely to have a positive attitude toward their use (Noh et al., 2021; Rožman et al., 2023). Nevertheless, TAM's inflexibility has been identified as a key constraint by the literature (Venkatesh, 2000; Vijayasarathy, 2004). The original variables of TAM may not be sufficient to capture critical factors that influence the acceptance and adoption of technology. This is highlighted in the paper of Manis and Choi (2019) where their study extended the original TAM by adding perceived enjoyment as a belief variable and four external variables, which are age, curiosity, past use, and willingness to pay.

2.2.3 The Unified Theory of Acceptance and Use of Technology 2

UTAUT, first created by Venkatesh et al. (2003), is a tool used by managers to assess whether a technology will be successful by understanding its acceptance drivers. This enables managers to identify users who are less likely to accept the technology and design targeted interventions. In short, it serves as a tool to explain the user's intention for using technology (Molnar et al., 2013). As shown in Figure 1, the UTAUT model comprises three direct factors influencing behavioral use and two indirect factors. According to the model, behavioral intention is directly influenced by performance expectancy, effort expectancy, and social influence. The indirect factors are the use intentions and facilitating conditions. In addition to the core factors, the age, gender, and experience of the user are identified as moderators that can mediate the user's intention of accepting a technology. The UTAUT model also emphasizes performance expectancy, which corresponds to the expected effort in adopting AI tools as a crucial predictor of behavioral intention.

Venkatesh et al. (2012), in their more recent and updated UTAUT2 model added three additional core factors affecting behavioral intention: hedonic motivation —

the fun or pleasure gained—, price value, and habit forming as determining factors in technology acceptance and use (Venkatesh et al., 2012). The UTAUT2 model has been implemented repeatedly in higher education, highlighting robustness and flexibility since many authors added elements which they deemed necessary for their research to the model (Arain et al., 2019). When comparing UTAUT2 with TAM and DOI, UTAUT2 is the most recent model with multiple variables and moderators. Therefore, UTAUT2 has been adopted as the acceptance model for this research.

Figure 1. Unified Theory of Acceptance and Use of Technology

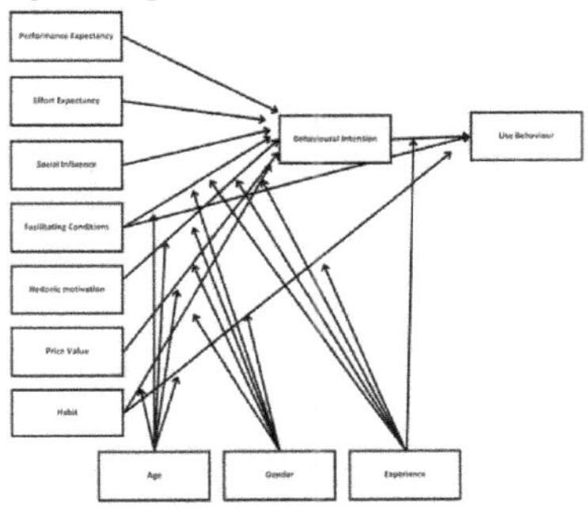

Note. From "Consumer Acceptance and Use of Information Technology: Extending the Unified Theory of Acceptance and Use of Technology," by V. Venkatesh, J. Y. Thong, and X. Xu, 2012, MIS Quarterly, 36(1), pp. 157–178.

METHODOLOGY

The research philosophy of this paper shifts away from the fundamental principles of ontology—that is, the "nature of reality"—and instead focuses on the socio-cognitive constructivism framework, which asserts that individuals construct their understanding and perception of the world through experiences and interactions with others (Johnson & Christensen, 2014), including non-human entities. Through a pragmatic interpretive perspective, we aimed to focus on the diverse participants' experiences and interactions with ChatGPT in shaping their attitudes and behaviors regarding the adoption of ChatGPT in their WIL experiences.

We collected data using five in-depth, semi-structured interviews. The interview questionnaire was developed based on the UTAUT 2 framework and adapted to gain hospitality learners' perspectives on the impact of ChatGPT on their work-related skills. The participant sample included five enrolled students at Vatel with WIL experience. The results provide empirical support for understanding how learners participating in WIL view the capability of ChatGPT, a generative AI tool, in assisting learning and promoting critical thinking, analytical, and reasoning skills.

3.1 Research Design and Approach

The study aimed to analyze the impact of using ChatGPT on the development of work-related skills during internships and bi-weekly practical applications from the perspective of hospitality learners. It also sought to identify potential enablers and tensions for using ChatGPT in learning and skill development. Guba and Lincoln (1994) assert that a research paradigm is informed by the researcher's reality and their relationship with the researched phenomenon, which shapes the means of discovering knowledge. Given the lack of empirical evidence in this study's context, we adopted an exploratory approach requiring a qualitative interpretive method. In a qualitative study, the researchers approach the phenomenon as a complex one that may have multiple interpretations, which can be understood through social constructions. The researchers enter the natural settings of the studied phenomenon and collect empirical evidence through interactional accounts or narratives (Anderson & Arsenault, 2005; Johnson & Christensen, 2014).

The researchers draw on participants' experiences and knowledge to find the direction and depth required to accomplish the research aims and objectives. In this case, the selection of study participants was critical. Given the timeframe for data collection and analysis, we used a purposive or critical sampling method to ensure that selected participants could provide the necessary information to address the research purpose (O'Donoghue, 2006). We considered participants' educational and professional experience, as well as their potential interest in contributing to the study. The selected sample included five participants with at least one practical internship in a luxury property in the Kingdom of Bahrain as part of Vatel's program. Vatel's program emphasizes practical learning and engages students in training and annual internships to develop their skills and link theory to practice. The internship duration is 18 to 20 weeks, providing the students with ample time to develop their skills (Vatel, 2023).

3.2 Data Collection Method

A researcher needs a clear and cohesive plan for collecting the data, as it forms the foundation for achieving the study's proposed aim (Johnson & Christensen, 2014). After identifying the inclusion criteria for the study sample, the five selected participants were initially contacted via telephone to confirm their willingness and availability to participate. Subsequently, email messages were sent containing the interview protocol and a brief outline of the research topic and agenda. Considering the time constraints and availability of the participants and the researchers, the interviews were scheduled at mutually convenient times, as the students were engaged in practical application training.

To ensure the quality of data collected from the semi-structured interviews, we agreed to limit the interviews to a maximum of 20 minutes, considering the number of interview questions and participants' depth of knowledge. We used a questionnaire for the interviews, ensuring the research questions were covered (Appendix A). Adopting a naturalistic approach, the interviewees were encouraged to focus on aspects that they considered most important. At the same time, the semi-structured interview format provided opportunities for spontaneity, allowing the researcher to collect more detailed information than would be possible through a survey method (Johnson & Christensen, 2014). The relationship between the researchers and respondents may have enabled this spontaneity, as the researchers were also their lecturers.

With permission from Vatel Bahrain's director of studies, the interviews were conducted via Microsoft Teams, and Vizard.ai was used to transcribe the recordings afterwards. The interviewees' profiles, including the number of internship experiences they had at the time of the research, are presented in Table 1. The selection criteria included a mix of male and female interns with at least one relevant WIL experience. In addition, the selected interviewees had either interned at different luxury properties or, if at the same property, were in different departments. Foundation year students were excluded from this research as they did not yet have WIL experience. An internship at Vatel Bahrain lasts between 18 to 20 weeks at luxurious properties annually (Vatel, 2023). The study assumes equal access to, understanding, and ability to use ChatGPT since they are encouraged to use ChatGPT in some of their classes.

Table 1. Interviewees' Profiles

Interviewee 1	Third-year student	Three WIL experiences
Interviewee 2	Second-year student	Two WIL experiences
Interviewee 3	Second-year student	Two WIL experiences
Interviewee 4	First-year student	One WIL experience
Interviewee 5	First-year student	One WIL experience

Note. WIL = work-integrated learning.

3.3 Analysis, Reporting and Confidentiality

Qualitative data generated through in-depth interviews is descriptive. As such, research scholars suggest using thematic analysis, where the researcher identifies patterns, themes, or key features in the participants' responses to determine how the actual results fit the predicted patterns. Thematic analysis is not rooted in any particular epistemological or theoretical perspective, offering the researcher flexibility to interpret patterns situated in the "intersubjective meanings" expressed in the participants' language and emotions (Maguire & Delahunt, 2017; Schwandt, 1998).

The researchers, understanding that reality is subjective, personal, and constructed, are inclined to explore different perspectives empathetically (O'Donoghue, 2006). In line with this, Miles and Huberman (1994) suggested segmenting content and coding data into meaningful analytical units to allow the researcher to negotiate and interpret meanings from participants' responses (Johnson & Christensen, 2014). Thematic analysis aims to identify themes or patterns in the data that are critical or interesting for addressing the research aim or answering the research questions. While there are various approaches to thematic analysis, in this study, we used the framework articulated by Braun and Clarke (2006), as cited by Lawless and Chen (2019) and Maguire and Delahunt (2017). To begin, we familiarized ourselves with the data by thoroughly listening to the interviews multiple times to identify emerging themes, codes, or emotions embedded in the responses. We then further analyzed the content to interpret participants' responses and make meaningful connections to the selected themes (Johnson & Christensen, 2014).

As the number of participants in this study was limited to five, we were also able to manually search for keywords and phrases from the transcripts to support the themes that emerged during the initial analysis (Al-Ansari et al., 2022). Concurrently, reading the transcripts allowed us to highlight, select, review, and codify common themes using the adapted UTAUT2 framework, discussed below. These themes were grouped in relation to the research questions and guided us to move beyond the semantics of what was said to uncover the latent or hidden interpretations (Maguire & Delahunt, 2017). Through the interview analysis, we identified the most significant enablers and tensions, in addition to the potential impact of using ChatGPT on developing work-related skills from the learners' perspective.

Researchers are accountable for making appropriate ethical decisions in the best interests of the participants in their study. Bearing in mind ethical research considerations and the confidentiality of the participants, we adhered to measures to protect their confidentiality throughout the data collection and reporting process (Kaiser, 2012; Wiles et al., 2008). Accordingly, the reports and transcripts do not reveal the participants' names or places of internship training. Furthermore, to ensure additional protection, excerpts from the interviews with different participants were merged when writing the narrative for the discussion section.

3.4 Generalizability and Reliability of Data

In a qualitative study, the interview method is an effective approach for gathering in-depth narratives that serve as primary data. We were able to gather both normative data and elite information on specific questions that required more personal and conceptual perspectives from the interviewees. Moreover, by purposefully including participants with varying numbers of internships in the hospitality industry, we were able to draw on their rich experiences and collate multiple theoretical perspectives, which helped substantiate the validity of the findings (Johnson & Christensen, 2014).

Although it can be argued that utilizing a purposive sampling method and having a small number of interviewees may reduce the generalizability of the data to a larger context, the typically rich narratives and perspectives from the interviewees can support a deeper understanding of the research topic than other methods, such as surveys, would offer. Furthermore, by sharing the interview protocol and research brief in advance with the interviewees and arranging for sufficient interview time, we ensured that the data gathered were both comprehensive and focused. Additionally, to mitigate the possibility of research bias, we consistently strived to understand participants' viewpoints through an empathetic attitude and ensure interpretive validity. Participants' perspectives are reported verbatim through direct quotations when needed (Johnson & Christensen, 2014; Rapley, 2001). The findings from the thematic and content analysis of the interviews are discussed in the following section.

RESULTS AND DISCUSSION

The data for this study were collected using a qualitative method. We interviewed five students currently enrolled in the Bachelor's in International Hotel Management program at Vatel Bahrain, about their perceptions of how ChatGPT affected their work-related skills development during their internship placements. We also sought to ascertain ChatGPT's latent impact on the participants' academic learning and achievement of 21st-century skills, namely critical thinking, creativity, and communication, as well as the potential enablers and challenges of using ChatGPT during their placements. The participants were encouraged to reflect on their personal experiences in the different departments where they used ChatGPT for specific tasks assigned by their supervisors.

This section presents the data collected from the interviews, which were analyzed using Braun and Braun and Clarke (2006) thematic analytical framework. The interview questions were categorized based on their relevance to the two research questions. Interview questions 1, 2, 8, and 9 contributed to the findings on the first research question: What is the potential impact of using ChatGPT on developing work-related skills from the learners' perspective in the hospitality industry? These questions explored the participants' attitudes, motivations, and perceived impact of ChatGPT on their performance at work and academic learning and achievement, as well as its potential to transform the hospitality sector, particularly in the training department. On the other hand, questions 3, 4, 5, and 6 contributed to the findings on the second research question: What are the potential enablers and challenges of using ChatGPT in learning and skill development from the learners' perspective?

We critically explored the participants' responses to ascertain the latent emotions and meanings embedded in them to understand beyond what was simply stated (Braun & Clarke, 2021). The thorough insights gained through this exercise were used to inform the discussions of RQ1 and RQ2 in the forthcoming sections.

4.1 Perceptions Toward ChatGPT's Impact on Work Skills Acquisition

In general, participants expressed positive perceptions toward the use of ChatGPT in their work. All five participants indicated that they primarily relied on ChatGPT to help them communicate effectively and accurately. For example, one respondent stated, "If I write a paragraph, I can fix the grammar of my paragraph, so from this, I can learn what mistake that I got." Another mentioned that she used ChatGPT in her internship to "improve communication skills" and "give me more options and the correct vocabulary," while another found it an efficient way to proofread and formalize emails and reports for the target audience, adding that she "learned some of the structure from ChatGPT." Similarly, a respondent who trained in the human resources department mentioned that ChatGPT helped him translate his emails from Arabic to English, allowing him to communicate effectively in his multicultural work environment.

On the other hand, a participant indicated that ChatGPT came in handy when his line manager asked him to produce creative content for a food and beverage promotion: "My manager … asked me to find or come up with inspiring quotes for guests to come and enjoy a shisha and a drink in the lounge upstairs in our current hotel." According to the participant, ChatGPT helped him select "a number of better words for marketing terms." In this regard, there is considerable evidence of ChatGPT's potential for natural language processing and producing human-like responses from different perspectives (Ogbeide, 2023).

In the case of this research, it is evident that the interns used ChatGPT's feature of language processing to simplify their work and complete the assigned task to the best of their ability. As previously mentioned, ChatGPT functions efficiently as an intelligent tutoring system that constructs human-like responses to prompts in real-time (Guan et al., 2020; Loos et al., 2023), which makes this tool attractive to interns who possess minimal professional experience.

As noted by Meng and Lai (2024), in hotel services, the "check-in" is the point of initial interaction between the employee and the guest, engaging the guest in a stimulating experience that creates a lasting, memorable occasion. Hotels and the hospitality industry in general often experience "blackout dates," which are times when operations are pushed into overdrive due to the surge of guests creating a rush, as reported by one of the respondents. During such occasions, time becomes an invaluable asset that should be managed with great precision, and inter-departmental collaboration and teamwork are key to meeting deadlines or managing efficient workflow to ensure high guest satisfaction. ChatGPT, in such instances, is a time-efficient tool for handling basic guest requests. The participant elaborated:

> *"Our inboxes are filled with guests asking for inquiries. And I feel like that is the type of situation I would use ChatGPT just to get like a faster, quicker response, you know, hit send and get back into my operation just so my operation would be more efficient and smoother for the guest that is physically present in front of me."*

In return, this allowed the participants to utilize their time more effectively, allocating their valuable time to more complex problems that required human intervention. This is in concurrence with Dwivedi et al. (2024) where they stated that ChatGPT will alter operations, allowing people to free up their time to handle client-oriented responsibilities as opposed to repetitive tasks.

Another key theme that emerged from the data is the participants' readiness to adopt ChatGPT as an alternative resource for further developing technical skills needed in the front office department. For instance, one participant noted that ChatGPT was able to come up with multiple solutions to a problem she faced as a front-office trainee. A guest requested an itinerary to see the various sights in the Kingdom of Bahrain, and the trainee, being a foreigner and new to Bahrain herself, resorted to ChatGPT to prepare a personalized itinerary for the guest on the spot. Additionally, ChatGPT proved beneficial in providing guidelines for utilizing shortcut keys in property management software such as Opera. The participant noted, "When I was starting my internship, I didn't know how to use Opera. So, some shortcuts I learned from the ChatGPT to use certain applications at work, and I believe that I developed that skill." This allowed the participant to use the software more effectively, putting her on par with some of her more experienced co-workers, as acknowledged.

On the other hand, in departments where guest interaction is minimal, ChatGPT had little impact on the intern's work skills development, as reported by the participants. In the kitchen, for example, participants agreed that motor skills and on-the-spot decision-making are essential to operate efficiently within the team. In this context, the interns relied heavily on their mentors as a source of knowledge and guidance. While ChatGPT was accessible, the respondents found little need to resort to it for guidance. For instance, one of the respondents stated,

"I use it only a few times. because I work in the kitchen, so I don't make it a habit. I don't rely on it mainly. It can be a useful tool, but it's important to not over-rely on them or use them as a main. So I use it only when I need some extra help.

The respondents also found that in more labor-intensive departments, such as the kitchen and housekeeping, the implications of ChatGPT on their internship training were limited, and it was more useful for departments that deal directly with guests."

Learning in constructivist contexts is regarded as a learner-driven, active process in which the students' subjective experiences and social interactions contribute to knowledge construction. As Lev Vygotsky's socio-constructivist theory posits, learning is shaped by human-to-human interaction. A learner acquires knowledge through interaction with the more knowledgeable other (Baskara, 2024). Huang et al. (2024), on the other hand, suggest that ChatGPT can be a useful contributor to learning by creating a suitable space to express students' subjectivity while developing cognitive growth and fostering creative, lateral, and critical thinking skills. However, as found in this research, the learner's context can influence the effectiveness of ChatGPT as a learning aid (Hall, 2007). ChatGPT is thus regarded as a complementary learning tool in certain situations, such as for guest interactions and personalized instructions on software usage; it cannot replace the MKO—in this case, the mentor—as suggested by the respondents.

To answer the first research question, "What is the potential impact of using ChatGPT on developing work-related skills from the learners' perspective in the hospitality industry?" ChatGPT is utilized at varying frequencies depending on the context or department where the intern is placed. In labor-intensive departments, ChatGPT is rarely used or relied upon, while in contexts requiring constant and rapid guest interaction, ChatGPT is used more frequently—not only to solve simple tasks but also to free interns' time to focus on more complex problems, especially during rush hours as stated by Dwivedi et al. (2024). In addition, ChatGPT is used for its language capabilities for communicative tasks, as previously stated.

However, the interns did not trust ChatGPT enough to handle complex problems requiring critical thinking, especially since each property had its own brand identity and required tailored services for its guests. This is aligned with the literature, which identified that in the tourism industry, ChatGPT struggled to identify the needed depth and accuracy in creating property-specific services and client-tailored responses (Burmann et al., 2009; Juskiw, 2017; Limna & Kraiwanit, 2023). Therefore, more traditional resources—in this case, the mentor—were a more reliable source of information for interns to seek guidance.

To answer the first research question — the impact of ChatGPT on the development of work-related skills from the learners' perspective in the hospitality industry —through the analysis of the responses, the study found that ChatGPT acts as a complementary tool that aids the learner in simple tasks involving direct interactions with clients. However, in complex tasks that require critical thinking and tailored solutions to client needs, ChatGPT lacks the ability and sufficient capacity to fully replace the mentor or take on the role of the MKO. In this regard, it can be deduced that ChatGPT cannot provide property-specific responses in a personalized style to the intern and thus does not have a significant impact on the interns' skills development.

4.2 Potential Enablers and Tensions for Using ChatGPT in WIL

Venkatesh et al. (2012) proposed the UTAUT2 model, which identifies key constructs underpinning consumers' relationship with and acceptance of technology. In addition to performance and effort expectancy, social influence, and facilitating conditions from the original UTAUT model, the updated UTAUT2 model also includes hedonic motivation, price value, and habit (Venkatesh, 2024).

An enabling factor for ChatGPT use in hospitality training was performance expectancy. Participants perceived ChatGPT as an effective tool for idea generation and task completion, with comments such as "It helped me think outside the box," "It's effortless," and "I only use it to learn something new in a short period of time." Although all participants reported high performance expectancy, the actual performance did not align with its perceived implications based on our observations and analysis of the interviews. While ChatGPT was used to some extent in the workplace, it was not used to the degree that respondents believed it added value to their overall performance. Given ChatGPT's promptness in generating content on a multitude of topics and providing feedback (Loos et al., 2023), some respondents appeared to overestimate its practical impact in the workplace.

Conversely, some of the respondents recognized the limitations of ChatGPT through critical reflection on the AI-generated solutions. ChatGPT was unable to produce the property-specific responses required, and as a result, respondents did not rely on it in complex situations, as it could not meet their expectations. These respondents were also critical of the content generated by ChatGPT and expressed a lack of trust in its accuracy. One participant noted that the "resources they use or the data that they provide … are not always 100% correct … and I would definitely need to investigate more," implying that she would verify the information with her training officer, as pointed out in studies on generative AI relevance to the hospitality and tourism sectors(Limna & Kraiwanit, 2023). Overall, it can be concluded that the performance expectancy of ChatGPT was an enabler in situational contexts that were generic and did not require brand- or property-specific responses.

Another enabling factor in the acceptance of ChatGPT during practical hospitality training was effort expectancy. Respondents reported that minimal effort was required to prompt ChatGPT to produce responses. For instance, an interviewee shared, "The guest asked me about a dish, and so I wrote about this dish in the ChatGPT … and the answers showed me very quickly, so I didn't have to take time about this." This was particularly evident in situations where trainees were working under tight deadlines and managing multiple tasks. In such instances, ChatGPT was viewed as an effort- and time-efficient solution for completing simple tasks.

On the other hand, in academic settings, although respondents found ChatGPT equally easy to use, ethical considerations and concerns about not learning inhibited its use. One respondent mentioned using ChatGPT to create "mock exams" to help in preparing for assessments. However, the same participant also described having a "love-hate relationship" with ChatGPT due to concerns about academic integrity and a fear of becoming dependent on it, particularly in relation to written communication.

In short, performance expectancy is a powerful enabler of ChatGPT adoption in academic settings; however, the same high expectations were not reflected in practical contexts. Similarly, effort expectancy was found to be a strong predictor of practical application in hospitality training, yet in classroom settings, the ease of obtaining answers with minimal effort was perceived as a limitation due to ethical concerns and worries about knowledge acquisition and academic success.

Regarding facilitating conditions for the acceptance of ChatGPT, this research identified several factors: technological infrastructure, language proficiency, the relevance of ChatGPT responses to specific properties or brands, and the respondents' situational contexts at work, such as the availability of a mentor or training officer. These conditions acted as either enablers or limiters. For example, respondents with limited language proficiency tended to use ChatGPT for basic communication tasks. In contrast, language-proficient students also used it for simple tasks, but primarily during critical moments. In this sense, the user's language proficiency could function as both a limiter and an enabler.

As for limitations to accepting ChatGPT in practical hospitality training, the presence of a mentor, the quality of AI-generated responses, and the technological infrastructure were key factors. Because properties require brand-specific solutions—particularly in guest interactions—respondents found ChatGPT's generic responses unsuitable. Instead, they turned to their mentor or training supervisor for accurate information and tailored guidance. Furthermore, unlike academic settings, the workplace context itself limited the use of ChatGPT, especially in departments involving manual labor, such as the kitchen. Respondents reported little to no use of ChatGPT in these settings unless a supervisor was unavailable, and only generic information was needed.

These findings align with the UTAUT2 constructs of habit and facilitating conditions. Since ChatGPT is not integrated into the practical aspects of hospitality training, interns are not able to develop a habit of using it regularly. However, in departments where facilitating conditions are present—such as the front office—trainees did use ChatGPT to complete simple communicative tasks during busy periods. Although not a major factor, hedonic motivation was also noted as an enabler; a few respondents found the interactive and re-prompting features of ChatGPT enjoyable, which encouraged its use when conditions allowed.

This research demonstrates that ChatGPT serves as an effective auxiliary tool for skill development during hospitality and hotel management internships, particularly in specific departmental contexts. The study reveals that front office trainees experienced enhanced time management and customer service capabilities through ChatGPT-assisted guest communication, enabling more personalized service delivery and improved problem-solving abilities. In the human resources and marketing departments, the tool fostered creative and critical thinking skills through the process of crafting effective prompts and evaluating responses. Notably, trainees developed discriminating assessment abilities as they learned to verify ChatGPT-generated content for accuracy and relevance—an advantageous skill for their future careers. While the tool showed a positive impact on technical skills such as reservation management, it proved less applicable in operational areas such as the kitchen and housekeeping.

To answer the second research question — the potential enablers and challenges of using ChatGPT in learning and skill development from the learners' perspective —through the analysis of the responses, the study indicates that ChatGPT integration in practical hospitality training faced certain reservations, primarily due to industry-specific protocols and workplace standards rather than the tool's utility. The findings emphasize ChatGPT's role as a complementary resource, with traditional supervision remaining crucial for developing core competencies and understanding brand-specific processes. Regarding adoption factors, the study aligns with Venkatesh (2024) UTAUT2 framework, identifying performance and effort expectancy as primary drivers for ChatGPT acceptance, moderated by factors including language proficiency, mentor accessibility, the nature of work, and the relevance of content to brand requirements; age, gender, and experience were excluded as moderating factors given the sample selected. Additionally, facilitating conditions and user habits emerged as significant determinants, influenced by individual values and property-specific ethical considerations. The findings are summarized in Table 2 below.

Table 2. Summary of RQ2 Findings

UTAUT2 Constructs	Limiter or Enabler	Justification
Performance Expectancy	Enabler and Limiter	Enabler: ChatGPT was identified as effective for idea generation, quick learning, and simple communication tasks. Limiter: It failed to meet expectations in brand-specific response scenarios, reducing trust in the quality of the outcome. Moderators: • Language proficiency of the user • Access to a mentor • Nature of operations • Relevance of output to brand-specific requirements.
Effort Expectancy	Enabler and Limiter	Enabler: ChatGPT requires minimal effort under time pressure for simple tasks. Limiter: Ethical concerns were reported in academic contexts. Moderators: • Language proficiency of the user • Access to a mentor
Facilitating Conditions	Enabler and Limiter	Enabler: The interns need to accomplish operational tasks in a department, and the language proficiency of the user. Limiter: Timely access to ChatGPT and brand-specific information. Moderators: • Individual values • Property-specific ethical consideration
Hedonic Motivation	Enabler	The praise from the supervisor/mentor and enjoyable interactions in creative/flexible settings that encourage ChatGPT use.
Habit	Limiter	There was no opportunity to form a habit during internships.

Note. UTAUT2 constructs with no significant impact were excluded from the table.

CONCLUSION

This thesis aimed to critically explore the potential impact of ChatGPT on trainees' work skills development during their practical training and internships, as well as their perspectives on factors that enabled or impeded the use of ChatGPT during their training period. The study employed a qualitative method, selecting five participants to answer a questionnaire developed in alignment with the UTAUT model. The research adopted a socio-constructivist approach to learning, highlighting the role of MKOs within the learner's ZPD in the learning process. In a socio-constructivist learning context, Hall (2007) adds that learning occurs within a social environment, where the process can be mediated by external tools. ChatGPT, built on large language models and deep learning algorithms, demonstrates extraordinary natural language processing capabilities and can engage in human-like dialogues while generating creative and rational content or solutions to complex topics. These features can support learners in transforming their understanding, internalizing what they have learned, and creating new knowledge based on their unique experiences.

The program at Vatel offers students WIL opportunities, alternating academic semesters with five-month internships at luxury properties to ensure graduates are experienced and workforce-ready (Gardner & Bartkus, 2014; Vatel, 2023). This paper examined the impact of ChatGPT on students' learning, training, and work skills development during their internships or practical applications, along with the potential opportunities and obstacles associated with using ChatGPT for learning.

This study presented certain limitations. Firstly, due to the short timeframe in which the research had to be completed, the researchers selected only five participants, which does not provide a representative overview of the perspectives of the wider student body at Vatel. Moreover, at the time the interviews were scheduled, the students were undertaking their internships, which made it difficult to contact them and arrange for additional participants. In addition, we acknowledge that the participants may have been guarded during their interview and may not have fully disclosed the extent to which they used ChatGPT, given that the researchers were also their lecturers. Another limitation is that the depth and accuracy of their responses may have been affected by the language fluency of some participants.

All in all, the study findings highlight that ChatGPT serves as an effective auxiliary tool for skill development during internships, particularly in departments that require guest interaction or internal communication. The study concludes that front office trainees enhanced their time management, customer service capabilities, communication, personalized service delivery, and problem-solving. In the human resources and marketing departments, ChatGPT aided in developing creative and critical thinking skills as participants engaged with the chatbot. Notably, trainees developed the ability to evaluate and verify ChatGPT-generated content for accuracy and relevance. While ChatGPT had a positive impact on technical skills such as communication and time management, it proved less resourceful in operational areas such as the kitchen and housekeeping departments.

The findings emphasize ChatGPT's role as a complementary resource, with traditional supervision remaining crucial for developing core skills and competences and understanding brand-specific processes. Regarding adoption factors, the study aligns with the UTAUT2 framework (Venkatesh, 2024), identifying performance and effort expectancy as primary drivers for ChatGPT acceptance, moderated by factors including language proficiency, mentor accessibility, the nature of the work, and content relevance to brand requirements. Facilitating conditions such as department relevance, access to a mentor or trainer, and technological infrastructure also emerged as significant enabling factors, limited by individual values and property-specific ethical considerations.

The study also concluded that trainees' language proficiency acted both as a barrier and an enabler: Respondents with lower English proficiency used ChatGPT for simple communicative tasks, while those with more advanced language levels also used it for similar tasks to save time during critically busy periods. On the other hand, although not significantly prominent, hedonic motivation was reported as an enabler for the acceptance of ChatGPT. The versatility to interact and re-prompt ChatGPT motivated a few respondents to use it when the facilitating conditions mentioned above were met.

The findings assert ChatGPT's role as a complementary resource, with traditional supervision remaining crucial for developing core competencies and understanding brand-specific processes. Regarding adoption factors, the study aligns with the Venkatesh (2024) UTAUT2 framework, identifying performance and effort expectancy as primary drivers for ChatGPT acceptance, moderated by factors such as language proficiency, mentor accessibility, work nature, and content relevance to brand requirements. Additionally, facilitating conditions and user habits emerged as significant factors influenced by individual values and property-specific ethical considerations.

These findings suggest that the effective use of ChatGPT as an auxiliary tool requires a balanced approach, which could be enhanced by integrating brand-specific responses into the chatbot. Until then, more traditional resources, such as the supervisor, will remain the preferred and the more trusted source of knowledge for trainees.

IMPLICATIONS FOR FURTHER RESEARCH

Based on the outcomes of this study, the researchers highlight the following future research methods and directions. Replication with a larger participant sample size, including varied cohorts from different institutions that offer WIL opportunities or other Vatel campuses, would yield more comprehensive data and improved generalizability. In addition, in order to eliminate possible bias caused by the lecturer-participant relationship, the sample selection should exclude participants with connections to the researchers. Moreover, using a mixed-method design which integrates quantitative approaches paired with qualitative interviews over an extended period of time could yield more elaborate data to monitor ChatGPT's effects on work-related skills development. Furthermore, employing a comparative research methodology could further explore the departmental differences in ChatGPT's usefulness, particularly areas involving interaction with guests.

Further research is necessary to fully understand the dual roles that language proficiency plays as a facilitator and a barrier. Studies could look at how trainees' confidence and proficiency in multilingual hospitality settings are impacted by ChatGPT-mediated language support, particularly for non-native speakers, as highlighted by Baskara (2024). Another area for research could be the possibility of aligning and integrating ChatGPT with hospitality organizational principles while considering ethical factors such as data privacy and brand-specific content in hospitality training. Furthermore, exploring the variables from the UTAUT2 Venkatesh et al. (2012)—such as hedonic motivation and habit—in ChatGPT adoption could aid in refining theoretical frameworks for AI integration in hospitality training and skills development.

As a recommendation to optimize ChatGPT's utility as a supplementary training tool, hospitality training departments and industry partners should prioritize the collaborative development of AI systems capable of generating brand-specific responses tailored to organizational values and cultural standards. A hybrid model integrating AI efficiency with human expertise is advised to balance innovation with experiential learning.

FUNDING

This research received no specific grant from any funding agency in the public, commercial, or not-for-profit sectors. Funding for this research was covered by the authors of the article.

ACKNOWLEDGEMENTS

In acknowledgement of the unwavering support of Vatel Bahrain's management, namely, Sheikh Khaled bin Khalifa Al Khalifa and Ms. Eman Haider.

REFERENCES

Adegbite, W., & Govender, C. (2022). How fourth industrial revolution skillsets mediate the relationship between work integrated learning, graduate employability, and future job. *EUREKA: Social and Humanities*, (4), 3–17.

Al-Ansari, A., Al Mohsen, H., & Coutts, C. N. (2022). Critical Factors in Promoting Sustainable Innovation in Bahrain. *Journal of Sustainable Business and Economics, 5*(2), 1–21-21–21.

Altun, O., Saydam, M. B., Karatepe, T., & Dima, Ş. M. (2024). Unveiling ChatGPT in tourism education: Exploring perceptions, advantages and recommendations from educators. *Worldwide Hospitality and Tourism Themes, 16*(1), 105–118.

Amineh, R. J., & Asl, H. D. (2015). Review of constructivism and social constructivism. *Journal of social sciences, literature and languages, 1*(1), 9-16.

Anderson, G., & Arsenault, N. (2005). *Fundamentals of educational research.* Routledge.

Arain, A. A., Hussain, Z., Rizvi, W. H., & Vighio, M. S. (2019). Extending UTAUT2 toward acceptance of mobile learning in the context of higher education. *Universal Access in the Information Society, 18*(3), 659–673. DOI: 10.1007/s10209-019-00685-8

Babu, T. A., & Sharmila, V. (2023). Using artificial intelligence chatbots like 'ChatGPT'to draft articles for medical journals–Advantages, limitations, ethical concerns and way forward. *European Journal of Obstetrics, Gynecology, and Reproductive Biology, 286*, 151. PMID: 37210245

Baskara, F. R. (2024). From AI to We: Harnessing Generative AI Tools to Cultivate Collaborative Learning Ecosystems in Universities. Proceeding International Conference on Learning Community (ICLC), Baxter Magolda, M. B. (2014). Self-Authorship. *New Directions for Higher Education, 2014*(166), 25–33. https://doi .org/https://doi.org/10.1002/he.20092

Billett, S. (2011). Learning at the site of work. In *The Routledge international handbook of learning* (pp. 246–254). Routledge.

Braun, V., & Clarke, V. (2006). Using thematic analysis in psychology. *Qualitative Research in Psychology, 3*(2), 77–101.

Braun, V., & Clarke, V. (2021). Can I use TA? Should I use TA? Should I not use TA? Comparing reflexive thematic analysis and other pattern-based qualitative analytic approaches. *Counselling & Psychotherapy Research, 21*(1), 37–47.

Burmann, C., Zeplin, S., & Riley, N. (2009). Key determinants of internal brand management success: An exploratory empirical analysis. *Journal of Brand Management, 16*, 264–284.

Cruz-Benito, J. (2022). *AI in Education*. MDPI-Multidisciplinary Digital Publishing Institute.

Davis, F. D. (1985). *A technology acceptance model for empirically testing new end-user information systems: Theory and results*. Massachusetts Institute of Technology.

Dewey, J. (1938). *Experience and education* (Vol. 14). Kappa Delta Pi.

Dondi, M., Klier, J., Panier, F., & Schubert, J. (2021). Defining the skills citizens will need in the future world of work. *McKinsey & Company, 25*, 1-19.

Dumitru, D., & Halpern, D. F. (2023). Critical thinking: Creating job-proof skills for the future of work. *Journal of Intelligence, 11*(10), 194. PMID: 37888426

Duong, C. D., Nguyen, T. H., Ngo, T. V. N., Dao, V. T., Do, N. D., & Pham, T. V. (2024). Exploring higher education students' continuance usage intention of ChatGPT: Amalgamation of the information system success model and the stimulus-organism-response paradigm. *The International Journal of Information and Learning Technology, 41*(5), 556–584.

Dwivedi, Y. K., Pandey, N., Currie, W., & Micu, A. (2024). Leveraging ChatGPT and other generative artificial intelligence (AI)-based applications in the hospitality and tourism industry: Practices, challenges and research agenda. *International Journal of Contemporary Hospitality Management, 36*(1), 1–12.

El Hajal, G., & Rowson, B. (2020). The future of hospitality jobs. *Research in Hospitality Management, 10*(1), 55–61.

Elkhwesky, Z., El Manzani, Y., & Elbayoumi Salem, I. (2024). Driving hospitality and tourism to foster sustainable innovation: A systematic review of COVID-19-related studies and practical implications in the digital era. *Tourism and Hospitality Research, 24*(1), 115–133. PMID: 40479339

Farazouli, A., Cerratto-Pargman, T., Bolander-Laksov, K., & McGrath, C. (2024). Hello GPT! Goodbye home examination? An exploratory study of AI chatbots impact on university teachers' assessment practices. *Assessment & Evaluation in Higher Education*, *49*(3), 363–375.

Feng, K., Zhao, X., Liu, J., Cai, Y., Ye, Z., Chen, C., & Xue, G. (2019). Spaced Learning Enhances Episodic Memory by Increasing Neural Pattern Similarity Across Repetitions. *The Journal of Neuroscience : The Official Journal of the Society for Neuroscience*, *39*(27), 5351–5360. DOI: 10.1523/jneurosci.2741-18.2019 PMID: 31036763

Ferreras-Garcia, R., Sales-Zaguirre, J., & Serradell-López, E. (2020). Competences in higher education tourism internships. *Education + Training*, *62*(1), 64–80.

Fouad, A. M., Salem, I. E., & Fathy, E. A. (2024). Generative AI insights in tourism and hospitality: A comprehensive review and strategic research roadmap. *Tourism and Hospitality Research*, •••, 14673584241293125.

Gardner, P., & Bartkus, K. (2014). What's in a name? A reference guide to work-education experiences. *Asia Pacific Journal of Cooperative Education*, *15*, 37–54.

Grassini, S. (2023). Shaping the future of education: Exploring the potential and consequences of AI and ChatGPT in educational settings. *Education Sciences*, *13*(7), 692.

Guan, C., Mou, J., & Jiang, Z. (2020). Artificial intelligence innovation in education: A twenty-year data-driven historical analysis. *International Journal of Innovation Studies*, *4*(4), 134–147. https://doi.org/https://doi.org/10.1016/j.ijis.2020.09.001

Guba, E. G., & Lincoln, Y. S. (1994). Competing paradigms in qualitative research. *Handbook of qualitative research, 2*(163-194), 105.

Hall, A. (2007). Vygotsky goes online: Learning design from a socio-cultural perspective. Learning and socio-cultural Theory: Exploring modern Vygotskian perspectives international workshop 2007, Hsu, C. H., Xiao, H., & Chen, N. (2017). Hospitality and tourism education research from 2005 to 2014:"Is the past a prologue to the future?". *International Journal of Contemporary Hospitality Management*, *29*(1), 141–160.

Huang, Z., Mao, Y., & Zhang, J. (2024). The Influence of Artificial Intelligence Technology on College Students' Learning Effectiveness from the Perspective of Constructivism — Taking ChatGPT as an Example. *Journal of Education. Humanities and Social Sciences*, *30*, 40–46. DOI: 10.54097/y1x3jj43

Jo, H., & Park, D.-H. (2024). AI in the Workplace: Examining the Effects of ChatGPT on Information Support and Knowledge Acquisition. *International Journal of Human-Computer Interaction, 40*(23), 8091–8106. DOI: 10.1080/10447318.2023.2278283

Johnson, R., & Christensen, L. (2014). *Educational Research Quantitative* (5th ed.). Qualitative, and Mixed Approaches.

Juskiw, P. (2017). *Assessing the Implementation of Internal Branding Training in the Hotel Industry*. Walden University.

Kaiser, K. (2012). Protecting confidentiality. *The SAGE handbook of interview research: The complexity of the craft, 2*, 457-464.

Kaminski, J. (2011). Diffusion of innovation theory. *Canadian Journal of Nursing Informatics, 6*(2), 1–6.

Kang, D. S. (2016). Turning inside out: Perceived internal branding in customer-firm relationship building. *Journal of Services Marketing, 30*(4), 462–475. doi:10.1108/JSM-07-2015-0229

Kanselaar, G. (2002). Constructivism and socio-constructivism. *Constructivism and socio-constructivism*, 1-7.

Kooli, C. (2023). Chatbots in education and research: A critical examination of ethical implications and solutions. *Sustainability, 15*(7), 5614.

Lawless, B., & Chen, Y.-W. (2019). Developing a method of critical thematic analysis for qualitative communication inquiry. *The Howard Journal of Communications, 30*(1), 92–106.

Limna, P., & Kraiwanit, T. (2023). The role of chatgpt on customer service in the hospitality industry: An exploratory study of hospitality workers' experiences and perceptions. *Tourism and Hospitality Management, 29*(4), 583–592.

Loos, E., Gröpler, J., & Goudeau, M.-L. S. (2023). Using ChatGPT in education: Human reflection on ChatGPT's self-reflection. *Societies (Basel, Switzerland), 13*(8), 196.

Lundblad, J. P. (2003). A Review and Critique of Rogers' Diffusion of Innovation Theory as it Applies to Organizations. *Organization Development Journal, 21*(4), 50.

Maguire, M., & Delahunt, B. (2017). Doing a thematic analysis: A practical, step-by-step guide for learning and teaching scholars. *All Ireland journal of higher education, 9*(3).

Manis, K. T., & Choi, D. (2019). The virtual reality hardware acceptance model (VR-HAM): Extending and individuating the technology acceptance model (TAM) for virtual reality hardware. *Journal of Business Research, 100*, 503–513.

Medlin, B. D. (2001). *The factors that may influence a faculty member's decision to adopt electronic technologies in instruction.* Virginia Polytechnic Institute and State University.

Meng, T., & Lai, I. K. W. (2024). How employee-guest interactions and welcome hospitality create brand attitudes for first-time hotel customers. *Asia Pacific Journal of Marketing and Logistics.* Advance online publication. DOI: 10.1108/APJML-03-2024-0376

Mercer, N. (1995). *The guided construction of knowledge: Talk amongst teachers and learners.* Multilingual matters.

Michel-Villarreal, R., Vilalta-Perdomo, E., Salinas-Navarro, D. E., Thierry-Aguilera, R., & Gerardou, F. S. (2023). Challenges and opportunities of generative AI for higher education as explained by ChatGPT. *Education Sciences, 13*(9), 856.

Miles, M. B., & Huberman, A. M. (1994). *Qualitative data analysis: An expanded sourcebook.* sage.

Min, H., Nancy, S., & Gursoy, D. (2016). A Longitudinal Investigation of the Importance of Course Subjects in the Hospitality Curriculum: An Industry Perspective. *Journal of Hospitality & Tourism Education, 28*(1), 10–20. DOI: 10.1080/10963758.2015.1127168

Molnar, A., Weerakkody, V., El-Haddadeh, R., Lee, H., & Irani, Z. (2013). *A Framework of Reference for Evaluating User Experience When Using High Definition Video to Video to Facilitate Public Services* (Vol. 402). doi:DOI: 10.1007/978-3-642-38862-0_27

Morrison, A., & Barry O'Mahony, G. (2003). The liberation of hospitality management education. *International Journal of Contemporary Hospitality Management, 15*(1), 38–44.

Noh, N., Raju, R., Eri, Z., & Ishak, S. (2021). Extending technology acceptance model (TAM) to measure the students' acceptance of using digital tools during open and distance learning (ODL). IOP Conference Series: Materials Science and Engineering, Nuong, M. D., & Ragavan, N. A. (2023). Digital Future of the Global Hospitality Industry and Hospitality Education: Review of Related Literature.

O'Donoghue, T. (2006). *Planning your qualitative research project: An introduction to interpretivist research in education.* Routledge.

Ogbeide, G.-C. (2023). ChatGPT in Hospitality and Tourism Education and Industry. *The Consortium Journal of Hospitality and Tourism*, •••, 26.

Parisot, A. H. (1997). Distance education as a catalyst for changing teaching in the community college: Implications for institutional policy. *New Directions for Community Colleges*, *1997*(99), 5–13.

Rapley, T. J. (2001). The art (fulness) of open-ended interviewing: Some considerations on analysing interviews. *Qualitative Research*, *1*(3), 303–323.

Rogers, E. M. (2003). *Diffusion of Innovations* (5th ed.). Free Press.

Rožman, M., Tominc, P., & Vrečko, I. (2023). Building skills for the future of work: Students' perspectives on emerging jobs in the Data and AI Cluster through artificial intelligence in education. *Environment and Social Psychology*, *8*(2), 1–24.

Sahin, I. (2006). Detailed review of Rogers' diffusion of innovations theory and educational technology-related studies based on Rogers' theory. *Turkish Online Journal of Educational Technology-TOJET*, *5*(2), 14–23.

Schwandt, T. A. (1998). The interpretive review of educational matters: Is there any other kind? *Review of Educational Research*, *68*(4), 409–412.

Shamsuddinova, S., Heryani, P., & Naval, M. A. (2024). Evolution to revolution: Critical exploration of educators' perceptions of the impact of Artificial Intelligence (AI) on the teaching and learning process in the GCC region. *International Journal of Educational Research*, *125*, 102326.

Shiohira, K. (2021). Understanding the Impact of AI on Skills Development. In: Bonn, Germany: UNESCO-UNEVOC. https://unevoc. unesco. org/home/UNEVOC+...

Stansbie, P., Nash, R., & Chang, S. (2016). Linking internships and classroom learning: A case study examination of hospitality and tourism management students. *Journal of Hospitality, Leisure, Sport and Tourism Education*, *19*, 19–29. https://doi.org/https://doi.org/10.1016/j.jhlste.2016.07.001

Udell, J., O'Brien, V., Flynn, S., Hooper, H., & Walker-Martin, F. (2023). The practice of sandwich degrees. In *The Routledge International Handbook of Work-Integrated Learning* (pp. 176–189). Routledge.

Vatel. (2023). *Vatel Prospectus* (V. Bahrain, Ed.). Vatel International Business School Hotel & Tourism Management Bahrain. https://vc3.vatelconnect.com/files/sitesecole/brochure/file_1692806821.pdf

Venkatesh, V. (2000). Determinants of perceived ease of use: Integrating control, intrinsic motivation, and emotion into the technology acceptance model. *Information Systems Research*, *11*(4), 342–365.

Venkatesh, V. (2024). Paradigm changing metaverse: Future research directions in design, technology adoption and use, and impacts. *Decision Support Systems*, •••, 114307.

Venkatesh, V., Morris, M. G., Davis, G. B., & Davis, F. D. (2003). User acceptance of information technology: Toward a unified view. *Management Information Systems Quarterly*, •••, 425–478.

Venkatesh, V., Thong, J. Y., & Xu, X. (2012). Consumer acceptance and use of information technology: Extending the unified theory of acceptance and use of technology. *Management Information Systems Quarterly*, •••, 157–178.

Vijayasarathy, L. R. (2004). Predicting consumer intentions to use on-line shopping: The case for an augmented technology acceptance model. *Information & Management*, *41*(6), 747–762.

Wang, P. Q. (2025). Personalizing guest experience with generative AI in the hotel industry: There's more to it than meets a Kiwi's eye. *Current Issues in Tourism*, *28*(4), 527–544. DOI: 10.1080/13683500.2023.2300030

Wiles, R., Crow, G., Heath, S., & Charles, V. (2008). The management of confidentiality and anonymity in social research. *International Journal of Social Research Methodology*, *11*(5), 417–428.

Woithe, J., & Filipec, O. (2023). Understanding the adoption, perception, and learning impact of ChatGPT in higher education: A qualitative exploratory case study analyzing students' perspectives and experiences with the AI-based large language model. In.

Wood, D., Bruner, J. S., & Ross, G. (1976). The role of tutoring in problem solving. *Journal of Child Psychology and Psychiatry, and Allied Disciplines*, *17*(2), 89–100. PMID: 932126

Wu, Y. (2024). Critical Thinking Pedagogics Design in an Era of ChatGPT and Other AI Tools — Shifting From Teaching "What" to Teaching "Why" and "How". *Journal of Education and Development*, *8*, 1. DOI: 10.20849/jed.v8i1.1404

Zegwaard, K., & McCurdy, S. (2014). The influence of work-integrated learning on motivation to undertake graduate studies. *Asia Pacific Journal of Cooperative Education*, *15*, 13–28.

Zegwaard, K. E., & Pretti, T. J. (2023). *The Routledge International Handbook of Work-Integrated Learning*. Taylor & Francis., https://books.google.com.bh/books?id=pRO8EAAAQBAJ

Zhang, K., Li, X., Ye, H., Lin, K. J., Chen, S., & Law, R. (2024). How can ChatGPT assist hospitality and tourism education? *Journal of Teaching in Travel & Tourism*, *24*(4), 438–448.

Zopiatis, A., Papadopoulos, C., & Theofanous, Y. (2021). A systematic review of literature on hospitality internships. *Journal of Hospitality, Leisure, Sport and Tourism Education*, *28*, 100309. DOI: 10.1016/j.jhlste.2021.100309

Zopiatis, A., & Theocharous, A. L. (2013). Revisiting hospitality internship practices: A holistic investigation. *Journal of Hospitality, Leisure, Sport and Tourism Education*, *13*, 33–46. https://doi.org/https://doi.org/10.1016/j.jhlste.2013.04.002

APPENDIX A

Semi-Structured Interview Questions

1. How often do you use ChatGPT in your practical applications?
2. What do you use ChatGPT for?
3. Can you describe a specific situation where you used ChatGPT? What was the purpose and outcome?
4. How do you evaluate the quality of the responses generated by ChatGPT?
5. What do you believe are the benefits and limitations of using ChatGPT in your practical applications?
6. How do you perceive ChatGPT's usefulness compared to traditional educational/training resources?
7. How does ChatGPT compare to other tools or resources you use for similar tasks?
8. Have you noticed any changes in your learning experience and outcomes since using ChatGPT?
9. In your opinion, does ChatGPT have the potential to transform the hospitality sector, specifically the training department? And if so, how?

Chapter 2

Charting the Impact of AI-Augmented Problem-Based Learning in Higher Education: The Bloom's Digital Taxonomy Perspective

Devi Manikeswari
https://orcid.org/0000-0002-5014-9423
Kingdom of Bahrain, Bahrain

Sayed Haytham Alawi
https://orcid.org/0000-0002-3865-9703
University of Technology, Bahrain

Satya Ratnakaram
https://orcid.org/0000-0002-8908-302X
Bahrain Polytechnic, Bahrain

Namrata Gulati
https://orcid.org/0009-0005-0702-5707
Bahrain Polytechnic, Bahrain

Ameera Alhejair
https://orcid.org/0009-0000-1393-6287
Bahrain Polytechnic, Bahrain

Neetu Dora
https://orcid.org/0009-0000-7636-8264
Bahrain Polytechnic, Bahrain

Harris Saseendran
https://orcid.org/0000-0001-7386-8001
Bahrain Polytechnic, Bahrain

ABSTRACT

Higher educational institutions are under pressure to endow graduates with skills necessary to thrive in a rapidly evolving, technologically advanced world. Where traditional teaching often fall short in nurturing the problem-solving and other skills demanded by employers. Problem-Based Learning is a promising pedagogical

DOI: 10.4018/979-8-3373-7386-7.ch002

strategy. This scoping review explores how AI-powered tools within PBL environments align with the cognitive levels of Bloom's Digital Taxonomy to enhance the learner's employability skills. This review delves deeper into the current landscape of research investigating how AI can augment PBL to foster deeper learning and skill acquisition as per levels of BDT. This research attempts to map existing literature and the range of available evidence related to the impact of AI-PBL and highlights pathways for integrating AI into PBL to foster the enhancement of employability skills and offers recommendations for addressing these challenges through professional development, and ethical guidelines, ultimately contributing to a future-ready higher education landscape.

INTRODUCTION

The Ever-Evolving Landscape of Higher Education

The concurrent and rapid advancements in technology, particularly Artificial Intelligence (AI) significantly impact the job market, creating both new opportunities and eliminating existing roles (Fowler, 2023). To prepare students for this evolving landscape, higher education institutions (HEIs) are under consistent pressure to adapt their curricula and teaching methods so as to bestow a transformative impact on the job market. Teaching methods must also evolve, incorporating technology-enhanced learning, fostering digital literacy, and encouraging innovation.

The World Economic Forum's "Future of Jobs Report 2023" highlights a significant skills gap between the skills graduates possess and the skills employers demand. In order to improve efficiency of the hiring process, employers around the world employ a range of selection tools, including psychometric tests for singling out skilled candidates that are a fit for their organization's needs (Manikeswari et al., 2024). The report reveals that 56% of employers globally believe a substantial gap exists between the skills imparted through academic education and the demands of the industry (World Economic Forum (WEF), 2023).

This discrepancy underscores the urgent need for educational systems to adapt and better equip students with the necessary skills for success in the 21st-century workforce. In continuation of these valuable insights, The Future of Jobs Report 2025 (WEF, 2025), based on insights from over 1,000 global employers, highlights key forces reshaping the labor market by 2030. These include technological advancements (Artificial Intelligence (AI), robotics, automation, and energy technologies), increased digital access, economic uncertainty, and shifting demographics. These factors are to significantly impact job roles, with some roles experiencing rapid growth while others decline. To adapt, employers are prioritizing workforce transformation strategies, focusing on developing skills related to AI, big data, cybersecurity, and digital literacy. Employers anticipate a significant shift in required skills over the next five years, with technological skills leading the way. Specifically, AI and big data expertise are expected to see the most rapid increase in demand, followed by network security and general tech proficiency. Beyond technical abilities, employers also value creative thinking and key socio-emotional traits like resilience, adaptability, and a commitment to continuous learning. Essentially, the future workforce will need to be both technically adept and possess strong interpersonal and learning skills to succeed in a rapidly evolving job market.

This includes integrating technology-focused skills like AI and cybersecurity into curricula, developing interdisciplinary programs, and emphasizing on the enhancement of critical thinking and problem-solving among learners. The selection of teaching and learning methods is a critical responsibility for educators, requiring them to consider the changing needs of students, courses, and the professional landscape. Consequently, universities are responsible for bridging the gap between academia and the professional world by cultivating students' skills and preparing them for real-world challenges (Manikeswari et al., 2024).

Figure 1 below, depicts the summarized methodical shift among several aspects of education during the progression from Education 1.0 to Education 4.0. In particular, a notable transition of educators, learners and enablers is seen with the enablers moving towards ICT tools and platforms powered by Internet of Things (IoT).

Figure 1. **Summary of the Shift from Education 1.0 to Education 4.0**

	Education 1.0	Education 2.0	Education 3.0	Education 4.0
Period	Late 18th Century	Early 20th Century	Late 20th Century	Present
Philosophy	Essentialism, behaviorism, and instructivism	Andragogical, constructivist	Heutagogical, connectivist	Heutagogical, peeragogical and cybergogical
Educator role	Sage	Guide, information source	Orchestrator, curator and collaborator	Mentor, coach, collaborator, reference
Student role	Largely passive	Emerging active "owning of the knowledge"	Active, "Knowledge ownership", initial independence	Active, high independence, trajectory designer
Approach	Teacher-centered	Peer assessment encouraged, high teacher importance	Co-constructed, first student-centered	Mostly student-centered
Learning outcome	Grades, graduation degree	License to professional peacticing	Prepared for practice and scenario analysis	Training of key competencies both soft and hard
Enablers	Mechanical printing, graphite pencil, ballpoint pen, typewriter	First computers, electronic devices and calculators	Computers and widespread use of the internet	ICTs tools and platforms powered by IoT
Information source	Standard texts	Adopted texts and open-source material (physical)	Texts, case studies, second hand experience	Based on online sources
Facilities	Universities / classrooms	Blended laboratories and classrooms	Blended and flexible physical shared spaces	Cyber and physical spaces both shared and individual
Industrial technology	Mechanical systems, steam powered	Mass production, industrialization and electricity	Internet access, automatization and control	Connectivity, digitalization and virtualization

Source: Miranda et al., (2021), Computers & Electrical Engineering

Where traditional pedagogical approaches are often known to fall short in fostering the complex problem-solving, critical thinking, and digital literacy skills demanded by today's employers, Problem-Based Learning (PBL) has emerged as a promising pedagogical strategy, emphasizing active learning, collaboration, and real-world problem-solving (Amerstorfer, 2020). By engaging students in authentic and challenging scenarios, PBL encourages them to develop higher-order thinking skills (HOTS) and apply their knowledge in practical contexts. However, the implementation of PBL can be resource-intensive and may require significant faculty support to facilitate effective learning experiences (Manikeswari et al., 2024). This and other similar challenges linked to the effective implementation of innovative pedagogies are now potentially moving towards new pathways by exploring the digital tools that have become accessible to educators.

The advent of AI presents a unique opportunity to augment and enhance significant pedagogical approaches such as PBL, which stands out as a widely used educational strategy that encourages students to actively engage with real-world problems, fostering critical thinking and collaborative skills (Yew & Goh, 2016).

Educators are experiencing a mix of excitement and skepticism as they try to incorporate AI into their teaching methods. Despite its immense potential, it is, however, not without challenges, some ethical and some practical. The optimistic view of AI in education faces hurdles. Successfully integrating AI into teaching pedagogies such as PBL requires a subtle and precise blend of human understanding and machine capabilities to create learning experiences that are both impactful and accessible. (Fowler, 2023). It is essential that the outcomes of such integration are mapped to existing and research-backed frameworks for gauging their effectiveness in the teaching and learning.

Bloom's Taxonomy: Shaping Education since 1956

Among significant contributors to the educational practice in HEIs is the Bloom's Taxonomy (BT), developed by Dr. Benjamin Bloom in 1956 as it provides a structured framework for curriculum design, assessment development, teaching practice etc. (Orey, 2010). During the 1990s, Lorin Anderson, a former student of Bloom, and David Krathwohl worked together to revise the original taxonomy. Their efforts culminated in the 2001and led to the release of Bloom's Revised Taxonomy (BRT), designed to guide the development of both foundational and advanced cognitive skills, thereby creating the trail for learning to progress from lower order thinking skills (LOTS) into HOTS (Anderson & Krathwohl, 2001).

Bloom's Revised Taxonomy and Bloom's Digital Taxonomy: Progressing Towards a Digital World

Subsequently, in 2008, to help educators effectively integrate technology, Andrew Churches (2009) developed Bloom's Digital Taxonomy (BDT). This adaptation links digital tools to cognitive processes, enabling teachers to use technology to improve learning across various levels and ensuring it supplements, rather than replaces, traditional instruction. It helps teachers strategically use technology to build essential 21st-century skills, create dynamic learning activities, and tailor education to individual students. By connecting digital tools with specific levels of thinking, it ensures technology enhances teaching rather than just replacing traditional methods. While some adjustments are needed to fully integrate digital capabilities, the taxonomy's focus on developing advanced thinking skills remains essential for preparing students for the future.

The mapping of AI-powered Problem-Based Learning (PBL) with Bloom's Digital Taxonomy (BDT) significantly enhances higher education by fostering HOTS like analyzing, evaluating, and creating (Gonsalves, 2024). However, the rapid evolution of generative AI necessitates the integration of ethical reasoning and critical evaluation into the taxonomy (Mogavi et al. 2024) and underscores the importance of maintaining human critical judgment and adapting assessment strategies in AI-enhanced environments.

This chapter aims to explore the intersection of AI-augmented PBL and BDT in the context of higher education. More specifically, in line with the context of the book, this chapter is an attempt at addressing the following objectives:

(i) To explore the potential of AI-augmented PBL in the higher education classroom from the Bloom's Digital Taxonomy perspective.
(ii) To analyze the key opportunities and challenges including ethical implications associated with the implementation of AI-augmented PBL.
(iii) To propose relevant strategies for overcoming the challenges and optimizing pathways for ethical implementation of AI in higher education with focus on PBL.

The current chapter addresses the objectives through a scoping review, a type of evidence synthesis designed to map and identify the breadth of available evidence on a broad topic, encompassing various research methodologies, reviews, and at times, non-empirical sources. Unlike systematic reviews, they address broader questions and do not typically involve methodological appraisal and focus on describing and charting evidence rather than synthesizing data. While they follow a structured process with a protocol and inclusion criteria, scoping reviews allow for flexibility and iteration, aiming to provide a comprehensive overview of the evidence, identify key concepts and gaps while simultaneously outlining future research, rather than providing irrefutable practice recommendations (Peters et al., 2021).By mapping the existing literature, this scoping review analyzes the impact of AI-enhanced PBL on skill development, identifies key challenges and ethical considerations through the BDT perspective. Additionally, some promising avenues for integrating AI into PBL to foster HOTS and recommendations for addressing these challenges through strategic investment, professional development, and ethical guidelines, ultimately contributing to a more effective and future-ready higher education landscape are highlighted.

ARTIFICIAL INTELLIGENCE, PROBLEM-BASED LEARNING AND THE BLOOM'S DIGITAL TAXONOMY: A PROMISING CONVERGENCE

The possibility of AI revolutionizing education is a major topic of discussion in academic circles. Figure 2 below, depicts the results of the analysis conducted by LinkedIn for the Future of Jobs Report 2025 in terms of industry-wise AI skill and job concentration across 10 industries, comparing data between 2016 and 2024 (World Economic Forum, 2025). While the AI concentration across all the industries has nearly doubled, it is intriguing to note that the field of Education has remained stable at rank 2 and portrays irrefutable evidence of the significance and steady growth of AI in the classroom.

Figure 2. **Growth in relative concentration of AI technologies, by industry 2016-2024**

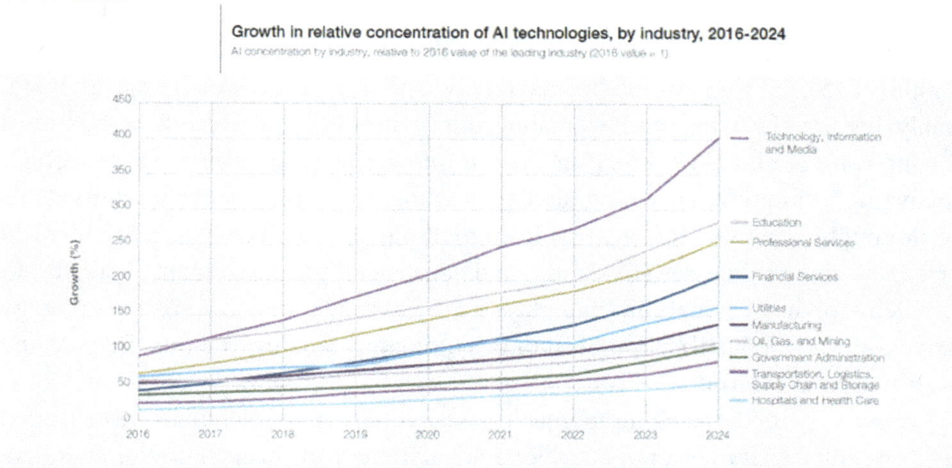

Source: Future of Jobs Report 2025, World Economic Forum

The adaptation of AI into several aspects of teaching has brought about different types of transformation such as automating administrative tasks, smart content etc. (Tahiru, 2021).

Originating in clinical education, PBL has expanded to various disciplines like health sciences, business and engineering due to its focus on authentic learning and interdisciplinary collaboration. This approach initiates learning through problem-solving, helping students not only grasp subject matter but also develop self-awareness and effective learning habits. Educators favor PBL because it promotes active, group-based learning, where students construct and co-construct knowledge through social interactions and self-directed study, leading to deeper understanding and enhanced learning experiences. PBL demonstrates its strength as an educational method especially when its effectiveness is measured by how well students retain knowledge over time and apply it to real-world situations (Yew & Goh, 2016).

The effectiveness of PBL as a pedagogical approach is backed by many studies including a study on its implications in teaching AI to engineering students, focusing on developing students' problem-solving and collaborative skills. 37 sophomore students participated in a 15-week program involving five PBL problems, reflective journals, and peer evaluations. The results demonstrated significant improvements across various learning outcomes, including content comprehension, cooperative learning, problem-solving, presentation skills, creativity, knowledge acquisition, communication, knowledge application, self-directed learning, and confidence. Students reported high levels of satisfaction and recognized the crucial role of PBL in enhancing their abilities to think creatively, work systematically, and communicate effectively, ultimately preparing them for the demands of modern industry (Lee, 2018). Another significant skill that learners' gain mastery over as part of PBL experiences in the classroom is critical thinking. Critical thinking, as defined by Ennis (2015), is a rigorous intellectual process involving conceptualizing, applying, analyzing, synthesizing, and evaluating information to guide beliefs and actions. Changwong et al. (2018) break this down into six phases: describing, reflecting, analyzing, critiquing, reasoning, and evaluating. These phases enable individuals to thoroughly examine information from multiple perspectives (Analyze), identify strengths and weaknesses (Evaluate), and construct logical arguments (Create). In problem-solving, critical thinking plays a crucial role in data acquisition, strategy selection, and the justification of findings, ultimately leading to more effective and well-reasoned solutions.

Irrespective of the teaching approach, it is essential that the outcomes are measured using established frameworks. As a hierarchical framework for categorizing cognitive skills, BT is a valuable tool in higher education. By encouraging educators to design learning experiences that progress from basic knowledge to HOTS like analysis, evaluation, and creation, it fosters deeper learning and improves student outcomes. This framework guides educators in developing meaningful assignments, aligning teaching methods with desired learning outcomes, and creating assessments that measure a range of cognitive skills. In summation, BT helps HEIs cultivate critical thinking, problem-solving, and creativity in their students (Stanny, 2016). Essentially, BT has become a cornerstone for improving the quality of teaching and learning by guiding instructors in designing courses that promote deeper understanding and cultivate well-rounded learners.

BT aims to promote HOTS beyond simple memorization. It uses a pyramid structure to illustrate the progression of learning, from basic knowledge to complex application and creation. This framework helps educators write learning objectives and course outcomes that gradually increase in difficulty. The goal is to guide learners from acquiring information to applying it in real-world situations and ultimately developing their own understanding and interpretations (Hyder & Bhamani, 2016).

Initially focused on the cognitive domain, BT encompasses intellectual processes like problem-solving and critical thinking. However, it also recognizes the affective and psychomotor domains. The affective domain deals with emotional aspects, such as values, attitudes, and appreciation, while the psychomotor domain focuses on physical skills and motor coordination. For instance, in a mathematics lesson on area and perimeter, the cognitive domain would involve understanding concepts, applying formulas, and solving problems. The affective domain would address aspects like student engagement and valuing the learning process. Finally, the psychomotor domain would encompass skills like drawing shapes accurately using geometric tools (Valiathan, 2023).

Originally, BT categorized learning into six levels: remembering, understanding, applying, analyzing, creating, and evaluating, ranging from simple recall to complex judgment. Initially overlooked due to the unfamiliar term "taxonomy," it later became a widely used tool for evaluating curricula and assessments. These evaluations revealed that many educational materials focused heavily on memorization, neglecting crucial skills like application and creation. This discovery prompted educators to revise curricula and assessments, emphasizing HOTS and ensuring a more comprehensive learning experience (Krathwohl, 2002).

Despite its age, BT is still a valuable tool for educators in today's digital world. Owing to the advancement of technology across all sectors, with education being no exception, incorporating technology into the education sector became inevitable and led to its progression into the Bloom's Revised Taxonomy (BRT) and BDT.

Figure 3. **Bloom's Digital Taxonomy**

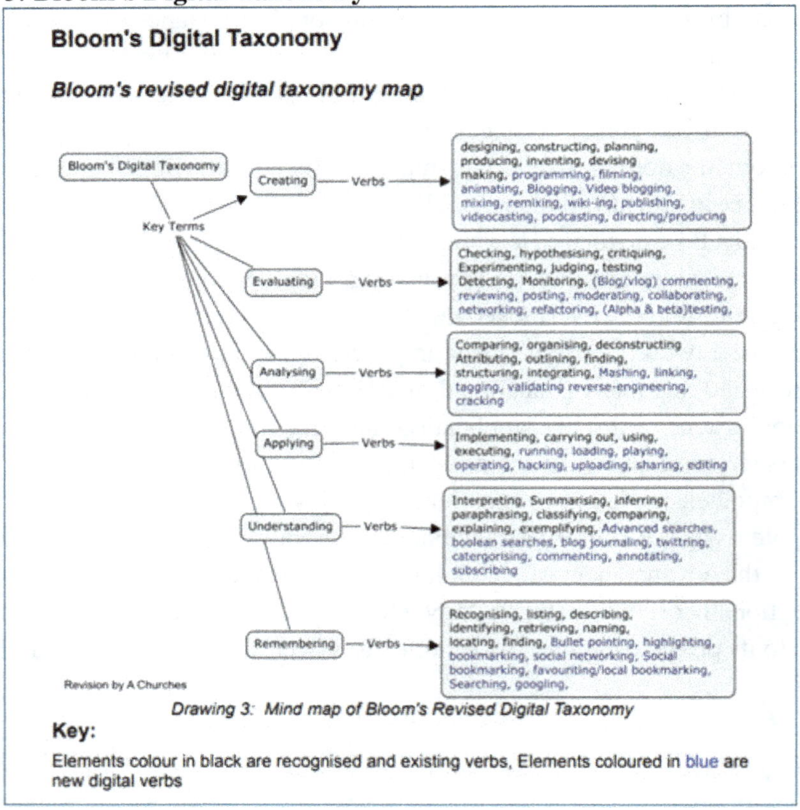

Source: Churches (2009)

Figure 3 above is an illustration of the Bloom's Revised Digital Taxonomy (BDT), a framework for categorizing learning objectives in the digital age. It outlines six levels of cognitive processes, from Remembering (recalling basic facts) to Creating (producing original work), with each level being associated to specific verbs. The taxonomy highlights how digital tools and activities can be integrated into learning, such as blogging and wiki-ing for Creating, or social bookmarking for Remembering. The key indicates that traditional verbs are shown in black, while new digital verbs are highlighted in blue, emphasizing the evolution of learning in a technology-rich environment (Churches, 2009).

Complementing the BDT framework, Amin & Mirza (2020), used Figure 4 below as a conceptual framework for their study. Each of the six levels is paired with specific digital actions (verbs) and corresponding digital tools. For example, "Remembering" involves bookmarking and favoriting, while "Creating" includes podcasting and digital publishing. Additionally, the image effectively illustrates how digital tools can be integrated into educational practices to facilitate different levels of cognitive engagement.

Figure 4. **Bloom's Digital Taxonomy and Digital Tools**

	Bloom's Digital Taxonomy (BDT) Levels	Bloom's Digital Verbs	Digital Tools
Lower Order Thinking	Remembering	Bookmarking, social & bookmarking, Favourting	
	Understanding	Googling & Advance searching, Blog Journaling	
	Applying	Content Authoring & wiki editing, Collaborating though e-tools, Skyping, Interactive whiteboard	
Higher Order Thinking	Analyzing	Data processing through computers	
	Evaluating	Validating information & Referencing	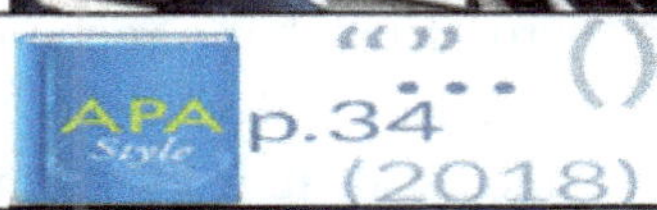
	Creating	Podcasting, Recording videos & Digital publishing	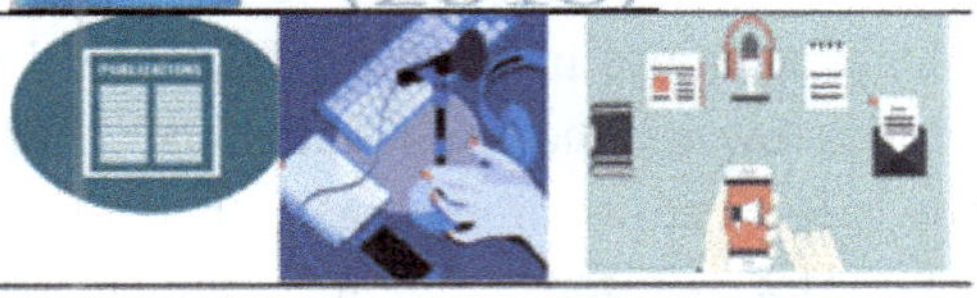

Source: Amin & Mirza (2020), Asian Association of Open Universities Journal

AI-AUGMENTED PBL: GAUGING OUTCOMES THROUGH THE BDT LENS

AI-augmented PBL, when analyzed through the lens of BDT, provides a robust framework for measuring educational outcomes by leveraging AI to enhance

HOTS. AI facilitates deeper learning experiences by enabling complex tasks like data analysis, simulations, and creative content generation. This approach allows for granular, data-driven assessments, tracking student progress across various cognitive levels and enabling personalized learning pathways. Moreover, integrating AI into PBL naturally fosters digital literacy and provides a metric for evaluating critical 21st-century skills such as problem-solving and collaboration, ultimately offering educators a more defined and effective method to assess the impact of AI-enhanced PBL.

Employing BDT to review the outcomes of AI augmented PBL in terms of learners' skill enhancement through integrating various tools is the focal point of this chapter. The six levels of BDT, in line with objective (i) of this chapter shall henceforth be addressed as follows:

- Remembering – BDT L1
- Understanding – BDT L2
- Applying – BDT L3
- Analysing – BDT L4
- Evaluating – BDT L5
- Creating – BDT L6

Su (2022) explored the integration of artificial intelligence (AI) concepts like face recognition, self-driving, and robotics into a problem-based learning (PBL) natural science curriculum. 127 Taiwanese university students participated in a collaborative problem-solving approach involving 5 open-ended questions and 31 learning attitude items, validated by 7 experts. Both quantitative and qualitative analyses showed significant improvements in students' scientific cognitive problem-solving skills, logical reasoning, and activation abilities. Furthermore, students displayed positive attitudes towards the cross-disciplinary PBL approach and the incorporation of AI knowledge. The research suggests that this approach fosters innovation and highlights the need for long-term implementation to achieve substantial educational outcomes. The findings propose that Integrating AI into PBL has significantly improved student learning by fostering deeper understanding (BDT L2), developing critical problem-solving skills, and advancing their academic abilities through interactive and supportive educational experiences. AI-powered collaborative PBL empowers students to tackle practical problems, bridging the gap between theory (BDT L1) and real-world application (BDT L6). This method not only boosts engagement but also cultivates creative thinking and promotes a more profound understanding (BDT L2) of the subject (Holmes et al., 2019).

Hawanti & Zubaydulloevna (2023) investigated the impact of ChatGPT, an advanced AI chatbot, on reducing college students' anxiety in English writing. Employing a quasi-experimental design with pre- and post-test assessments, the research involved 73 participants, revealing that AI chatbot-based instruction significantly lowered student anxiety. The benefits stemmed from instant feedback, allowing for immediate error correction and preventing prolonged worry, as well as the flexible, self-paced learning environment provided by the chatbot, which eased the pressure of traditional classroom settings allowing students the luxury to understand concepts (BDT L2) and carry out other learning-related tasks at their own pace. The findings suggest that integrating AI chatbots into classrooms can be an effective strategy for mitigating students' anxiety related to English writing.

AI significantly strengthens PBL by providing personalized, interactive support and instant feedback, which deepens students' understanding (BDT L2) of problem-solving (Zhou et al., 2024; Suwarno & Dwijayanti, 2025). PBL itself is a collaborative, inquiry-based method that centers learning around complex problems, thereby cultivating crucial skills like critical thinking (Inherent BDT L3 & L4) and analytical reasoning (BDT L4). Essentially, AI-enhanced PBL allows for a more effective and engaging exploration of real-world challenges (Suwarno & Dwijayanti, 2025).

To address the lack of learner agency in cybersecurity problem-based learning, Techawitthayachinda et al., (2022) introduced an AI-enabled Cybersecurity Knowledge Graph (AISecKG) designed to simulate real-world scenarios. Through interviews with twelve students after two projects, researchers identified four key dimensions of learner agency: productive struggle, expectation alignment, task familiarity, and sensemaking strategies. Rubric scores confirmed that AISecKG effectively supported these dimensions, leading to a noticeable improvement in student learner agency by the second project, indicating the potential of AI-driven tools in PBL to enhance student independence and problem-solving skills in cybersecurity education. Findings support that AI facilitates personalized learning and feedback, aligning with “applying” (BDT L3) and “analyzing” (BDT L4) levels of Bloom's, while also enhancing collaborative learning through online tools and virtual simulations, supporting “creating” (BDT L6) and “evaluating” (BDT L5) levels. Additionally, the findings support that all strategies of problem solving and all phases of critical

Thinking: Describing (BDT L1 & L2), reflecting, analyzing (BDT L4), critiquing, reasoning, and evaluating (BDT L5) (Changwong et al., 2018) can be affected by this kind of activity,

CONQUERING THE COURSE: PARKOUR AND THE PROMISE AHEAD

AI integration into education, particularly in PBL, presents significant opportunities for educators, learners, and higher education institutions. AI can personalize learning, automate tasks, and provide data-driven insights. However, it also poses challenges related to technological proficiency, ethical considerations (data privacy, bias), maintaining human connection, preventing over-reliance on AI, addressing the digital divide, ensuring data security, and managing the substantial investments required (Divito et al., 2024; García-López et al., 2025). AI allows educators several opportunities to streamline tasks and personalize learning, while learners benefit from tailored experiences and enhanced problem-solving. However, educators must gain technical proficiency and address ethical concerns, and learners need guidance to avoid over-reliance and navigate information overload. Higher education institutions can leverage AI for improved outcomes and innovation, but require significant investment in infrastructure, data security, and faculty training to ensure effective and ethical integration of AI into PBL.

The application of responsible AI within Higher Education solicits research and a structured approach. As part of a study conducted by Tubella et al., (2024) to determine the educational strategies, skills, and materials necessary for successfully integrating Trustworthy AI into Higher Education across all academic fields, 11 interviews with experts from five different countries were conducted. The interviewees consistently report a lack of formal policies for integrating Trustworthy AI into education, both within their institutions and nationally. Despite this, they acknowledged the growing significance of Trustworthy AI and are exploring its inclusion in their curricula. The findings further revealed a gap in terms of Trustworthy AI being incorporated into Higher Education primarily driven by individual educators, not by institutional or national directives. This uncoordinated approach risks creating inconsistencies in Trustworthy AI competency levels across different Higher Education programs due to the absence of a unified strategy.

García-L´opez et al., (2024) as part of their research to identify the opportunities and challenges of integrating ChatGPT in education argue that such integration into education necessitates a strong regulatory framework to guarantee equitable access for all students, irrespective of their background. Educational institutions must establish policies for AI use based on transparency, accountability, and privacy, promoting ethical and sustainable adoption. Crucially, the research emphasizes that implementing ChatGPT is not solely a technical undertaking; it demands a comprehensive strategy encompassing pedagogical, technological, and ethical dimensions. Combining automation with human oversight, along with a flexible infrastructure and clear regulations, ensures effective and stable integration in higher education. This holistic approach empowers institutions to leverage AI's potential while mitigating risks and fostering an inclusive and sustainable learning environment. Effectively integrating AI into education demands well-defined, comprehensive ethical policies due to the complexity of the issue. As tools like ChatGPT gain prominence, establishing ethical guidelines is crucial. These guidelines must tackle data privacy, algorithmic bias, and the potential for increased inequality. Research highlights the necessity of collaboration among educators, policymakers, and technologists to create policies that promote responsible and ethical AI use. These policies should emphasize transparency, accountability, and the protection of individual privacy and rights. By implementing these frameworks, educational institutions can harness opportunities presented by AI while minimizing its drawbacks, fostering a fairer and more equitable educational environment. (García-L´opez et al., 2024).

Table 1 below summarizes the opportunities bestowed by AI-augmented PBL mapped against BDT levels for both educators and learners.

Table 1. Opportunities presented by AI-augmented PBL mapped with BDT

BDT Levels	AI-augmented PBL
Remembering (BDT L1)	**For educators:** AI can curate vast repositories of relevant information, simplifying the process of gathering resources for PBL scenarios. **For students:** AI can also help in the creation of summaries of complex information or texts provided in PBL activities (Chen et al., 2020).
Understanding (BDT L2)	**For educators:** AI can generate diverse PBL scenarios and simulations, allowing educators to provide students with practical applications of theoretical concepts. **For students:** AI tools can be employed by students to better understand lengthy PBL scenarios using appropriate prompts.
Applying (BDT L3)	**For educators:** AI can analyze student interactions and performance data, providing educators with insights into learning patterns and areas for improvement. **For students:** AI can also analyze the complexity of the PBL scenarios and allow learners link concepts to scenarios for better applying their knowledge and derive meaningful outcomes.
Analyzing (BDT L4)	**For educators:** AI can assist in evaluating student work by providing automated, personalized feedback and identifying areas of strength and weakness freeing educators for other tasks that require more of human expertise (García-L´opez et al., 2024). **For students:** PBL activities that allow learners to use AI enhance the learners' analytical thinking by critically reviewing AI generated solutions for their practical applicability.
Evaluating (BDT L5)	**For educators:** AI can be used to evaluate the effectiveness of PBL programs and identify areas for improvement. **For students:** AI can assist in the creation of personalized learning pathways and adaptive PBL activities (Zhou et al., 2024).
Creating (BDT L6)	**For educators:** Several AI tools allow educators to enhance the presentation of PBL scenarios thereby leading to improved student engagement (Ratnakaram et al., 2025). **For students:** AI can provide students with tools to create multimedia presentations, simulations, and other digital artifacts.

AI's potential for personalized learning and accessibility is significant, but it must be balanced with human intervention to ensure ethical and equitable outcomes (Barana, Marchisio & Roman, 2023). Inherent and vigorous frameworks such as BDT and learning analytics can optimize educational processes and help in overcoming hurdles such as AI-generated biases, underscoring the importance of responsible data management for building sound ethical frameworks. It is essential to acknowledge the fact that AI serves as a tool to augment, not replace, human cognition, creating dynamic and effective learning experiences.

Table 2 below while outlining challenges posed in the implementation of AI-augmented PBL also puts forth potentially effective strategies for overcoming such challenges to optimize the benefits.

Table 2. Challenges in AI-augmented PBL and corresponding strategies for overcoming such challenges

Challenges		**Strategies to overcome challenges**
Generic/ Practical	**Content design and development:** AI-integrated PBL content must be designed to align with learning objectives and promote active engagement, rather than passive consumption (Ratnakaram et al., 2025)	Educators must work towards using AI tools creatively to make the PBL content engaging through employing appropriate techniques such as scaffolding, storytelling etc. (Manikeswari et al., 2024).
	Accuracy of data: Educators must ensure the accuracy and reliability of AI-generated information, mitigating the risk of students learning incorrect facts.	Continuous and rigorous monitoring of the AI-integrated content must be carried out by educators and institutions simultaneously to uphold the quality of learning.
	Policies: Establishing clear policies on academic integrity in AI-augmented PBL to define the boundaries of acceptable AI use in creative tasks (e.g., plagiarism concerns).	Institutions must collaborate with developers, teachers, and regulators to create policies that promote fair and responsible AI use, defining the limits of automation and establishing clear roles for human intervention (Divito et al., 2024).
	Over-dependence on AI: Potential of AI to diminish learners' sense of ownership and creativity. AI tools may automate tasks that should foster learners' analytical skills. Over-reliance on AI for content delivery may fade educators' own content expertise (Divito et al., 2024).	Combining AI-generated feedback with teacher and peer input enhances cognitive skills, and AI should optimize, not replace, traditional teaching, freeing educators for more meaningful pedagogical tasks. This blend of automation and human supervision is essential (García-L´opez et al., 2024).

continued on following page

Table 2. Continued

Challenges		Strategies to overcome challenges
Technological	**Skill gaps:** Possible gaps in skills of both educators and/or learners in the implementation of AI-augmented PBL (Tubella et al., 2024).	Ongoing staff development is crucial to maximize the pedagogical benefits of AI tools and prevent obsolescence from negatively impacting learning (Sode, 2021; Manikeswari et al., 2024).
	Algorithmic bias: Potential of AI to create "algorithmic bias" in problem analysis (Divito et al., 2024).	Combining teacher supervision with AI tools is critical for preventing discriminatory outcomes and fostering inclusive education. (García-L´opez et al., 2024)
	Obsolescence: The rapid obsolescence of educational technologies poses bottlenecks in terms of huge investments that might not reap the expected benefits (García-L´opez et al., 2024).	Modular, scalable systems offer a solution, allowing for incremental upgrades and cost reduction in addition to a robust infrastructure that helps overcome the risks of technological obsolescence, ensuring continuous and sustainable integration (Zhang & Tur, 2024).
Ethical	**Privacy concerns:** Managing the large volumes of personal data associated with AI in education presents significant privacy and security risks (Laupichler et al., 2022)	Managing the large volumes of personal data associated with AI in education presents significant privacy and security risks. Institutions must implement clear data protection policies, ensure transparency, and conduct regular audits aligned with international regulations like general data protection regulation (GDPR) (García-L´opez et al., 2024).
	Equity of access: The fact that these technologies are not equally available or affordable could increase the pre-existing digital divide (Ratnakaram et al., 2025).	Measures to ensure that AI tools for completing AI-integrated activities in the classroom are accessible to all students, irrespective of their background or abilities must be undertaken by institutions for ensuring equal opportunities for learning (Ratnakaram et al., 2025).

For the purpose of better portraying the potential practical application of AI-augmented PBL approach in the classroom mapped to the levels of the BRT and BDT, Table 3 below provides an overview of level-wise distinction of a PBL scenario that could be supported by the application of various AI tools and platforms for teaching Maslow's Hierarchy of Needs.

Table 3. An example of AI-augmented PBL activity mapped to BRT and BDT for teaching Maslow's Hierarchy of Needs

Bloom's Level	Bloom's Revised Taxonomy (BRT) Activity	Bloom's Digital Taxonomy (BDT) Activity	AI Resources and Applications
Remembering	Recall the different levels of Maslow's Hierarchy of Needs.	Locate and recall information about Maslow's Hierarchy of Needs from digital resources.	**Sources:** Digital books, Google Search, academic databases.
Understanding	Explain how each level of the hierarchy relates to employee motivation and retention in a workplace.	Summarize the core principles of Maslow's Hierarchy and its relevance to digital-age workplaces.	**AI Text Generators:** Gemini Flash, ChatGPT (to generate simplified text for understanding).
Applying	Analyze the scenario through the lens of Maslow's Hierarchy.	Use digital tools to categorize the issues at the company according to Maslow's Hierarchy.	**Digital Canvas/Whiteboards:** Microsoft Whiteboard, Miro, Mural (for real-time collaboration and categorization).
Analyzing	Break down the employee dissatisfaction issues and identify which needs might be unmet.	Compare and contrast how different digital platforms and HR technologies can address various levels of employee needs.	**Spreadsheet Software with AI:** Google Sheets with AI extensions, Microsoft Excel with AI features (for categorization and analysis).
Evaluating	Judge the effectiveness of potential HR interventions based on their impact on different levels of employee needs.	Select and justify the use of specific digital tools and strategies to improve employee engagement and address unmet needs.	**Research Tools:** Google Search, academic databases (for evidence-based justification). **Collaboration Tools:** Google Docs/Sheets/Slides (for peer review and feedback on justifications).
Creating	Develop a comprehensive HR strategy to address the identified issues and improve employee satisfaction and retention at the company.	Design a multimedia presentation or interactive prototype of a digital HR initiative aimed at improving employee satisfaction at the company aligned with Maslow's Hierarchy.	**Presentation Tools:** Canva, Google Slides, Microsoft PowerPoint (for multimedia presentations). **AI Image Generators:** Imagen 3.0 (for custom icons/graphics). **AI Text Generators:** Gemini Flash, ChatGPT (for generating placeholder content).

While Table 3 above, puts forward a practical example of an AI-augments PBL, it is imperative that the application of the recommended tools or any other tools be closely monitored by the educators as there could be data pertaining to the topic that could be erroneous. A robust process/system must be in place to ensure the accuracy of AI generated content that is permitted for use in the classroom. As this forms the base for all the progressive levels in the BDT, it is crucial that there are measures in place to conform to accuracy, failing which could sabotage the entire exercise.

On the other hand, using AI for designing teaching learning activities is also one that must be in line with both ethical standards as well as be mindful to foster an environment that controls the extent of AI usage in the learning process. Over-dependence of learners or the tutors on AI could have the unsolicited impact on learning where the learners' skills diminish or do not progress due to over utilization of AI.

For optimizing the benefits of AI in pedagogical approaches such as PBL, HEIs must address the digital divide, equip faculty with AI integration skills through professional development, and collaborate with industry to align curricula with future job demands. Educators should incorporate Trustworthy AI principles into their teaching, covering data privacy, explainability, and record-keeping. Policymakers and institutions need to coordinate the introduction of Trustworthy AI education nationally and incentivize HEIs to build expertise in this area through faculty training and expert recruitment, ensuring ethical and equitable AI implementation across the educational landscape (Tubella et al., 2024). Additionally, educators and policymakers need to create data protection policies that address information ownership and privacy concerns, ensuring data integrity (Tahiru, 2021). Appropriate and conscientious incorporation of AI into educational programs can foster responsible use and potentially enhance student learning (Divito et al., 2024). Future research in this area, especially longitudinal studies could provide valuable insights in terms of the effectiveness of AI- integrated PBL mapped with BDT levels.

CONCLUSION

Empowering teachers to compare existing educational frameworks could significantly aid in the development of new AI-focused courses. By analyzing and contrasting various models, educators can identify best practices and potential gaps, facilitating the creation of innovative and effective curricula that address the evolving landscape of artificial intelligence in education. This comparative approach fosters a deeper understanding of pedagogical strategies, ultimately leading to more robust and relevant AI education.

To truly grasp how AI is reshaping academic outcomes in universities, long-term and ongoing research that follows these changes over time is quintessential. Studies that uncover real-time examples of how PBL could lead to better outcomes when developed using AI tools in alignment with BDT could add to the essential body of knowledge on the subject. The gap in terms of the availability of such literature opens new avenues for researchers to further explore and experiment on the subject.

Rather than viewing AI as a threat to learning and assessment, educators and HEIs should investigate its integration into educational activities. They can develop innovative evaluation methods that align with AI's capabilities, transforming it into a valuable ally. By strategically embedding AI within the learning process, they can unlock its potential for personalized learning and more effective assessment, ultimately enhancing educational outcomes. This shift requires a proactive approach, focusing on harnessing AI's strengths rather than simply restricting its use. To ensure long-term educational sustainability; institutions must connect immediate learning outcomes with broader practices. Dynamic professional development is crucial for educators navigating evolving technology. Furthermore, implementing fairness audits and transparent algorithms promotes ethical AI adoption, ensuring equitable personalization. By balancing opportunity and risk, and prioritizing fairness, institutions can build trust and align technological advancements with ethical educational principles.

The increasing potential of AI-enhanced PBL to cultivate critical employability skills within higher education, particularly when aligned with BDT is evident and promising. By offering personalized learning, intelligent feedback, and streamlined administrative processes, AI tools can address inherent limitations of conventional PBL, fostering deeper learning and skill acquisition. However, realizing this potential necessitates a concerted effort to mitigate challenges related to cost, access, and ethical considerations. Strategic investments, robust professional development, and the establishment of clear ethical guidelines that pave the path for sustainable outcomes are crucial for effectively integrating AI into PBL. Ultimately, these measures will pave the way for a more dynamic and future-oriented higher education landscape, better equipped to prepare graduates for the complexities of a rapidly evolving, technologically driven world.

REFERENCES

Amerstorfer, C. M. (2020, July). Problem-based learning for preservice teachers of English as a foreign language. In *Colloquium* (pp. 75–90). New Philologies.

Amin, H., & Mirza, M. S. (2020). Comparative study of knowledge and use of Bloom's digital taxonomy by teachers and students in virtual and conventional universities. *Asian Association of Open Universities Journal, 15*(2), 223–238. DOI: 10.1108/AAOUJ-01-2020-0005

Anderson, L. W., & Krathwohl, D. (Eds.). (2001). *A Taxonomy for Learning, Teaching and Assessing: a Revision of Bloom's Taxonomy of Educational Objectives*. Longman.

Barana, A., Marchisio, M., & Roman, F. (2023). Fostering Problem Solving and Critical Thinking in Mathematics through Generative Artificial Intelligence. *International Association for Development of the Information Society*. https://eric.ed.gov/?id=ED636445

Changwong, K.. (2018). Critical thinking skill development: Analysis of a new learning management model for Thai high schools. *Journal of International Students, 11*(2), 37–48. DOI: 10.14254/2071-8330.2018/11-2/3

Chen, X., Xie, H., Zou, D., & Hwang, G. J. (2020). Application and theory gaps during the rise of Artificial Intelligence in Education. *Computers & Education, 146*, 103751.

Churches, A. (2009). Taxonomıa de Bloom para la era digital. *Eduteka. Recuperado, 11*, 1–13.

Divito, C. B., Katchikian, B. M., Gruenwald, J. E., & Burgoon, J. M. (2024). The tools of the future are the challenges of today: The use of ChatGPT in problem-based learning medical education. *Medical Teacher, 46*(3), 320–322. DOI: 10.1080/0142159X.2023.2290997 PMID: 38149617

Ennis, R. H. (2015). Critical thinking: a streamlined conception. In Davies, M., & Barnett, R. (Eds.), *The Palgrave Handbookof Critical Thinking in Higher Education* (pp. 31–47)., DOI: 10.1057/9781137378057

Fowler, D. S. (2023). AI in Higher Education. *Journal of Ethics in Higher Education, 3*. https://doi.org/DOI: 10.26034/fr.jehe.2023.4657

García-López, I. M., González, C. S. G., Ramírez-Montoya, M. S., & Molina-Espinosa, J. M. (2025). Challenges of implementing ChatGPT on education: Systematic literature review. *International Journal of Educational Research Open*, *8*, 100401. DOI: 10.1016/j.ijedro.2024.100401

Hawanti, S., & Zubaydulloevna, K. M. (2023). AI chatbot-based learning: Alleviating students' anxiety in english writing classroom. *Bulletin of Social Informatics Theory and Application*, *7*(2). Advance online publication. DOI: 10.31763/businta.v7i2.659

Holmes, W., Bialik, M., & Fadel, C. (2019). *Artificial Intelligence in Education: Promises and Implications for Teaching and Learning.* Center for Curriculum Redesign. https://curriculumredesign.org/wp-content/uploads/AIED-Book-Excerpt-CCR.pdf

Hyder, I., & Bhamani, S. (2016). Bloom's Taxonomy (cognitive domain) in higher education settings: *Reflection brief. Journal of Education and Educational Development*, *3*(2), 288. DOI: 10.22555/joeed.v3i2.1039

Krathwohl, D. R. (2002). A Revision of Bloom's Taxonomy: An Overview. *Theory into Practice*, *41*(4), 212–218. http://www.jstor.org/stable/1477405

Laupichler, M. C., Aster, A., Schirch, J., & Raupach, T. (2022). Artificial intelligence literacy in higher and adult education: A scoping literature review. *Computers and Education: Artificial Intelligence*, *3*, 100101. DOI: 10.1016/j.caeai.2022.100101

Lee, K. (2018). Case Study for the Application of PBL in Engineering School: Focused on an Artificial Intelligence Class. *Journal of the Korea Academia-Industrial cooperation. Society*, *19*(4), 154–160. DOI: 10.5762/KAIS.2018.19.4.154

Manikeswari, D., Ratnakaram, S., Shaikh, Z. H., Alawi, S. H., & Kumar, A. (2024). PBL in Higher Education: Empowering Students for the Industry Dynamics. [EEL]. *European Economic Letters*, *14*(3), 1137–1140. DOI: 10.52783/eel.v14i3.1873

Manikeswari, D., Ratnakaram, S., & Sirisetti, S. (2024). Psychometric testing - the game changer: A 360-degree view of psychometric testing and its applicability in HR functions. *International Journal of Business Excellence*, *33*(1), 48–75. DOI: 10.1504/IJBEX.2024.139112

Miranda, J., Navarrete, C., Noguez, J., Molina-Espinosa, J. M., Ramírez-Montoya, M. S., Navarro-Tuch, S. A., Bustamante-Bello, M. R., Rosas-Fernández, J. B., & Molina, A. (2021). The core components of education 4.0 in higher education: Three case studies in engineering education. *Computers & Electrical Engineering*, *93*. Advance online publication. DOI: 10.1016/j.compeleceng.2021.107278

Orey, M. (2010). *Bloom's taxonomy. Emerging perspectives on learning, teaching, and technology*. The Global Text Project.

Peters, M. D. J., Marnie, C., Colquhoun, H., Garritty, C. M., Hempel, S., Horsley, T., & Tricco, A. C. (2021). *Scoping reviews: reinforcing and advancing the methodology and application. Systematic Reviews*. BioMed Central Ltd., DOI: 10.1186/s13643-021-01821-3

Ratnakaram, S. P., Manikeswari, D., Shaikh, Z. H., Mahapatra, D. M., Mohanty, B. S., & Soni, A. (2025). Wearables and AI-Smart Technologies: Transforming the Education Sphere. In Ul Rehman, S. (Ed.), *Wearable Devices and Smart Technology for Educational Teaching Assistance* (pp. 27–52). IGI Global Scientific Publishing., DOI: 10.4018/979-8-3693-7817-5.ch002

Sode, M. (2021). Group activities with AI teacher support in PBL education. In *Proceedings of the SEFI 49th Annual Conference* (Vol. 49). https://cir.nii.ac.jp/crid/1010294643612869760

Su, K. D. (2022). Implementation of innovative artificial intelligence cognitions with problem-based learning guided tasks to enhance students' performance in science. *Journal of Baltic Science Education*, *21*(2), 245–257. DOI: 10.33225/jbse/22.21.245

Tahiru, F. (2021). AI in Education: A Systematic Literature Review. [JCIT]. *Journal of Cases on Information Technology*, *23*(1), 1–20. DOI: 10.4018/JCIT.2021010101

Techawitthayachinda, I. R., Deng, Y., Zeng, Z., Liu, H., Chen, Y. C., & Huang, D. An AI-Enable Knowledge Graph and Student's Agency in Productive Struggle During Problem-Based Learning in Cybersecurity Education. Conference Proceeding of The IAFOR International Conference on Education in Hawaii 2022. https://papers.iafor.org/wp-content/uploads/papers/iice2022/IICE2022_62117.pdf

Tubella, A., Mora-Cantallops, M., & Nieves, J. C. (2024). How to teach responsible AI in Higher Education: Challenges and opportunities. *Ethics and Information Technology*, *26*(1). Advance online publication. DOI: 10.1007/s10676-023-09733-7

World Economic Forum. (2023). The Future of Jobs Report 2023. World Economic Forum. https://www.weforum.org/publications/the-future-of-jobs-report-2023/

World Economic Forum. (2025). The Future of Jobs Report 2025. World Economic Forum. https://www.weforum.org/publications/the-future-of-jobs-report-2025/

Yew, E. H. J., & Goh, K. (2016). Problem-Based Learning: An Overview of its Process and Impact on Learning. In Health Professions Education (Vol. 2, Issue 2). https://doi.org/DOI: 10.1016/j.hpe.2016.01.004

Zhang, P., & Tur, G. (2024). A systematic review of ChatGPT use in K-12 education. *European Journal of Education*, *59*(2), e12599. DOI: 10.1111/ejed.12599

Zhou, X., Teng, D., & Al-Samarraie, H. (2024). *The Mediating Role of Generative AI Self-Regulation on Students' Critical Thinking and Problem-Solving*. Educational Sciences. https://www.mdpi.com/2227-7102/14/12/1302)

Chapter 3
Forensic Accounting Education in the Age of AI:
A Pedagogical Roadmap to Enhanced Critical Thinking

Satya Ratnakaram
https://orcid.org/0000-0002-8908-302X
Bahrain Polytechnic, Bahrain

Anand Soni
https://orcid.org/0009-0001-4896-0639
Bahrain Polytechnic, Bahrain

Huda Al Najjar
https://orcid.org/0009-0006-8298-3160
Bahrain Polytechnic, Bahrain

Qasim Albaqali
Bahrain Polytechnic, Bahrain

Hani Hamaidan
https://orcid.org/0009-0005-8047-199X
Bahrain Polytechnic, Bahrain

Devi Manikeswari
https://orcid.org/0000-0002-5014-9423
Bahrain Polytechnic, Bahrain

Zakir Hossen Shaikh
https://orcid.org/0000-0003-4733-4166
Kingdom University, Bahrain

ABSTRACT

The growing interest of Artificial Intelligence applications is transforming various sectors, including forensic accounting curricula. This chapter aims to explore the pedagogical approaches suitable for teaching forensic accounting in an AI-driven environment. Existing research on AI in education, AI applications within the forensic accounting profession, and relevant pedagogical frameworks are outlined in the chapter to serve as a substantial body of literature on the subject. These strategies

DOI: 10.4018/979-8-3373-7386-7.ch003

include active learning techniques facilitated by AI-powered simulations, personalized learning pathways driven by intelligent tutoring systems, and collaborative problem-solving using AI-driven analytical platforms. The challenges and opportunities associated with implementing these approaches are investigated. A pedagogical roadmap for accounting educators to prepare students for AI's impact on forensic accounting while also offering insights into how to leverage AI to enhance learning outcomes and cultivate future-ready forensic accounting professionals is presented.

INTRODUCTION

The Intersection of Forensic Accounting, Artificial Intelligence and Critical Thinking in Education

Given the recent shifts in the global commercial landscape, marked by globalization and a dynamic environment, traditional accounting regulation may struggle to fully satisfy governmental expectations for high-quality accounting information. The global financial crisis of 2007-2009 significantly heightened awareness of financial reporting fraud (FRF) and corporate misconduct. Policymakers, regulators, investors, and businesses worldwide became increasingly concerned about the prevalence and impact of fraud. A 2014 study by the Association of Certified Fraud Examiners (ACFE) highlighted the severe financial consequences, revealing that organizations globally lose approximately five percent of their annual revenue to fraud, amounting to trillions of dollars, with substantial individual losses in many cases (Rezaee et al., 2016).

The increasing complexity of the globalized business environment, coupled with notable accounting failures and corporate bankruptcies like Enron and Lehman Brothers, has exposed the limitations of traditional accounting regulations. This has led to a growing concern about the quality and reliability of financial reporting, highlighting the need for enhanced fraud detection and prevention mechanisms to ensure better accounting information and mitigate the risks associated with poor financial reporting practices (Alharasis et al., 2025). As early as 1991, industry experts recognized forensic accounting (FA), also called forensic auditing or financial forensics, is a specialized area of accounting that centers on uncovering and settling financial discrepancies for use in legal proceedings (Ellili et al., 2024), as a rapidly growing and highly sought-after specialization within accounting firms, highlighting its enduring relevance and value in the job market.

Accounting professionals recognized the growing need for fraud detection and FA skills, prompting a push for its inclusion in university curricula. Accounting education and the accounting profession are essential for economic growth, as they supply the crucial financial information necessary for the functioning of the entire economic system. Initially, a few institutions offered such education. However, concurrent research indicates a substantial increase, with numerous universities now providing dedicated courses, degrees, minors, and certificates in FA and fraud examination. This expansion underscores the critical importance of FA knowledge for the career prospects of contemporary accounting students (Kramer, Seda & Bobashev et al., 2017).

FA is a multifaceted field specializing in fraud investigation, where professionals play a crucial role in detecting, preventing, and prosecuting financial crimes like misstatements, money laundering, and identity theft. They must also possess strong technical skills, including IT, data mining, and computer forensics, to address cybercrimes such as credit card fraud, online extortion, and intellectual property theft. FA's core purpose is to assist individuals, organizations, and governments during difficult situations by offering diverse services. This multidisciplinary field encompasses various overlapping areas, but research generally categorizes its services into four main categories: litigation services, fraud investigation, computer forensic analysis, and business valuation. These categories reflect the broad scope of expertise required by forensic accountants (Alshurafat, Al Shbail & Mansour, 2021). Critical thinking, unstructured problem solving, investigative flexibility, analytical proficiency and legal knowledge are among some of the crucial skills that forensic accountants must possess in addition to effective written and oral communication skills and auditing skills. Davis, Farrell & Ogilby (2010) emphazise that analytical skills are paramount for forensic accountants. Additionally, strong communication, the ability to simplify complex information, and effective presentation of opinions in legal contexts are crucial. Forensic accountants must also possess a holistic perspective, understanding the broader objectives beyond mere analytical details. In today's digital landscape, accounting students must understand the crucial role of information technology (IT) in forensic accounting and fraud investigations. Technological proficiency is essential for effective fraud detection and prevention. Consequently, many accounting programs are integrating forensic accounting and fraud examination content into their curricula to equip students with the necessary IT-related skills and knowledge. (Bhasin, 2015).

FA education not only benefits society but also significantly enhances students' career prospects. Research demonstrates that completing a FA course improves a candidate's hiring potential (Mounce & Frazier, 2002). The demand for forensic accountants continues to surge, creating numerous job opportunities across diverse sectors like public accounting, law enforcement, and federal agencies. Even for those not pursuing a dedicated FA career, the acquired skills enhance overall business acumen, proving valuable in roles such as auditors, managers, and consultants.

Artificial intelligence (AI) is revolutionizing various sectors, including finance and accounting, with its ability to process extensive data, recognize complex patterns and automate routine tasks. Several advancements in complementary fields such as wearable technologies (Ratnakaram et al., 2025) have made it impossible to ignore the manifold benefits offered. This presents significant opportunities to enhance the efficiency and effectiveness of forensic accounting, particularly in identifying and investigating fraud. Nonetheless, the ability of forensic accountants to think critically remains crucial for interpreting AI-generated results, understanding the context of financial activities and navigating the complex ethical dilemmas that arise with the increasing adoption of AI in this field (Mehta et al., 2022).

Despite extensive research on the subject, a persistent review of AI integration into FA within education and the profession is necessary due to the field's rapid growth and diverse prospects. The increasing disparity between conventional forensic accounting education and the rapidly advancing field of AI necessitates a re-evaluation of curricula. This chapter seeks to determine what pedagogical strategies prove most effective in cultivating critical thinking skills among students learning forensic accounting in this era of AI. The central question explores the optimal methods for AI integration, the most effective teaching approaches for developing critical thinking in the context of AI and how to address the ethical implications of AI in this field through education. Through a rigorous search and analysis of peer-reviewed articles, the chapter outlines engaging pedagogical strategies for integrating AI tools effectively into forensic accounting education. These strategies include active learning techniques facilitated by AI-powered simulations; personalized learning pathways driven by collaborative problem-solving using AI-driven analytical platforms. This research is significant as it aims to offer a guide for educators and other relevant stakeholders, enabling them to prepare future FA professionals who can expertly utilize AI tools while also strengthening their critical thinking abilities to navigate the evolving challenges and opportunities presented by AI in their profession. A pedagogical roadmap for accounting educators seeking to prepare students for the evolving demands of the AI-driven accounting landscape while also offering insights into how to leverage AI to enhance learning outcomes and cultivate future-ready accounting professionals is presented.

A narrative literature review methodology has been adopted to address the chapter objectives. Narrative reviews often cover a wide range of literature related to a topic, including theoretical works, empirical studies, and conceptual papers. A narrative literature review, also known as a traditional or descriptive literature review, is a comprehensive synthesis of existing knowledge on a specific topic. A narrative review offers a broader and more flexible approach to summarizing and interpreting the literature (Pautasso, 2019), thereby allowing relevant and concurrent studies to be reviewed and synthesized to best address the chapter objectives.

Forensic Accounting: The underpinning core concepts and their relevance in the age of AI

FA is a specialized branch of accounting that uses investigative techniques and accounting knowledge to identify financial discrepancies and potential fraud. This involves a thorough review of financial documents to gather evidence for legal proceedings. Founded in 1988 by Joseph T. Wells in Texas, United States of America, the Association of Certified Fraud Examiners (ACFE) underscores the crucial role of forensic accountants in uncovering the truth and protecting organizations from fraud (Murdock & Murdock, 2018). Unlike traditional auditing, which assesses the fairness of financial statements, FA investigates specific claims of financial wrongdoing. These financial investigators are often engaged when organizations suspect financial crimes like money laundering or embezzlement, going beyond regular audits to detect signs of fraudulent activity.

The American Board of Forensic Accounting (ABFA) outlines the following four core principles for forensic auditors:

(i) Objectivity: Requiring them to be unbiased and focus on accurate fact-finding to serve justice.
(ii) Impartiality: Demanding neutrality and full disclosure of all findings to prevent misrepresentation.
(iii) Honest Representation: Obligating them to accurately present their qualifications and credentials; and
(iv) Ethical Conduct: Mandating that they avoid any actions that could harm the organization and always uphold the highest ethical and professional standards.

These principles are crucial for ensuring the trustworthiness and dependability of forensic accountants' work in legal situations (American Board of Forensic Accounting, 2022). The principles guiding forensic accounting ensure that these techniques are applied rigorously and ethically, providing a solid foundation for integrating new technologies like AI.

AI in Contemporary Forensic Accounting: Current Applications, Tools, and Techniques

A key factor shaping investigative accounting and fraud examination research within forensic accounting is how well forensic accountants can use information technology in their work. Forensic accountants, acting as fraud examiners or investigative accountants, should be skilled in applying technology-driven methods like analytical procedures, computer-assisted audit techniques (CAATs), artificial intelligence (AI), fuzzy logic models, artificial neural networks, expert systems, data mining, and digital analysis to uncover fraud. Furthermore, the profession needs to stay current with advancements in semi-automated and fully automated audit tools, alongside traditional audit techniques, evidence, and tests. These ongoing technological shifts in IT and auditing necessitate continuous updates to both the educational and professional aspects of forensic accounting to keep pace technologically (Kılıç, 2020). Honko & Hendryk (2024), conducted a survey conducted between October 2023 and July 2024 among Polish accountants regarding their perceptions of AI in accounting. The study specifically investigated which stages of processing and presenting accounting information are expected to be most supported by AI. The results indicate a strong consensus among respondents, regardless of their characteristics, that AI will be most extensively used in the preparation and workflow of accounting documents. This confirms the widely held view that AI will automate repetitive and routine accounting tasks. The practical implication of this research is that it provides valuable insights for the IT industry in developing and implementing process automation solutions tailored to the expectations of accounting professionals.AI technologies allow computers to perform tasks that typically require human intelligence. More specifically, in FA, key AI concepts include Machine Learning (ML), where algorithms learn from data, Natural Language Processing (NLP), enabling computers to understand human language, Deep Learning (DL), using complex neural networks for pattern analysis, predictive analytics (using statistics and machine learning for forecasting), and Robotic Process Automation (RPA), automating repetitive tasks. These AI technologies are increasingly used in FA, particularly for fraud detection and prevention by analyzing large financial datasets in real-time to identify unusual patterns (Gasanov, 2024). Predictive models can even forecast potential fraud (Ali et al., 2024). Furthermore, AI plays a vital role in risk assessment by analyzing financial information to pinpoint patterns indicating a higher risk of accounting fraud, thereby improving risk scoring and helping auditors focus on critical areas (Mehta et al., 2022).

Table 1 below puts forth AI Applications and some prominent AI tools currently being used in various FA inherent tasks (Bhave, 2024; Akkeren & Tarr, 2021):

Table 1. AI Applications and tools in Forensic Accounting

AI Application	Description	AI Tools/Software
Fraud Detection and Prevention	Utilizing AI algorithms to analyze large datasets, identify anomalies, and predict potentially fraudulent activities.	Tookitaki, ComplyAdvantage, Salv, Finscore, AI-powered transaction monitoring systems
Risk Assessment	Employing AI to evaluate and prioritize fraud risks within organizations by analyzing financial data for patterns and abnormalities.	AI-based risk scoring systems, predictive analytics platforms
Data Analysis and Interpretation	Leveraging AI tools for efficient data scoping, cleaning, reconciliation, and analysis of complex financial data.	Valid8 Financial, AI-powered data analytics platforms
Analysis of Unstructured Data	Using NLP to analyze textual data like emails, contracts, and financial reports for signs of fraud or misconduct.	Adobe Acrobat's AI Assistant, NLP-powered document analysis tools
Digital Forensics	Applying AI techniques to enhance the analysis of digital evidence, including image and video analysis, cybercrime investigations, and data recovery.	EnCase Forensic, AI-powered image and video analysis software
Cross-Network Fraud Detection	Analyzing patterns in financial data and corporate relationships to detect fraud across multiple entities.	FraudGCN

In data analysis and interpretation for FA, AI significantly boosts efficiency. AI-driven data scoping rapidly identifies relevant information, while automated data cleaning and reconciliation quickly address inconsistencies and missing data. AI can also link transactions across different entities to create a unified database for easier analysis. NLP is particularly useful for examining unstructured data like emails and reports, enabling the identification of fraud-related terms, sentiment analysis for detecting misconduct, and extraction of key information. Furthermore, AI is increasingly used in digital forensics to automate the analysis of large volumes of digital evidence, including multimedia, allowing investigators to concentrate on crucial aspects. Several AI-powered tools are now available, such as Tookitaki and ComplyAdvantage for fraud detection, EnCase Forensic for digital investigations, Adobe Acrobat's AI Assistant for document analysis, and Valid8 Financial for expedited data preparation. Systems like FraudGCN demonstrate a trend towards more advanced fraud detection by analyzing patterns across corporate networks. The growing availability and sophistication of these AI tools accentuate the evolving nature of FA.

THE ESSENTIAL ROLE OF CRITICAL THINKING FOR FORENSIC ACCOUNTANTS IN AN AI-DRIVEN WORLD

Critical thinking in forensic accounting involves analyzing complex financial data, interpreting findings, evaluating evidence reliability, making logical inferences, explaining conclusions clearly, and maintaining investigative integrity (Davidyan et al., 2022). It requires questioning assumptions and considering alternative interpretations. Despite AI's powerful analytical capabilities, critical thinking remains essential because AI lacks contextual understanding, struggles with human intent in fraud, and can produce errors. Forensic accountants must critically evaluate AI outputs for validity, especially when presenting evidence in legal proceedings, which necessitates understanding AI methodologies and limitations. Furthermore, critical thinking is crucial for navigating ethical issues like algorithmic bias and data privacy (Akkeren & Tarr, 2021). As fraud evolves, forensic accountants need to think creatively to identify new methods AI may not detect. Ultimately, human critical thinking is vital for interpreting AI results, ensuring fairness and accuracy in investigations and upholding professional standards in the use of AI-generated evidence.

FORENSIC ACCOUNTING EDUCATION AND INTEGRATED AI-POWERED PEDAGOGICAL APPROACHES: AN EFFECTIVE BLUEPRINT FOR ENHANCED CRITICAL THINKING AMONG LEARNERS

FA education, with its established connection to core and interdisciplinary areas like fraud, law, business valuation and IT forensics, is positioned to play an increasingly important role in the ever-evolving context of finance, economics and international business. To succeed in an FA career, students require a robust understanding of accounting principles, auditing, financial analysis, and investigative methods to analyze financial transactions and detect fraud. Proficiency in data analysis software and digital forensics is also crucial for efficiently handling large datasets and uncovering digital evidence. Beyond these technical skills, strong analytical and critical thinking abilities, along with meticulous attention to detail, are essential. By developing this comprehensive skillset, forensic accounting students can become effective professionals who provide valuable insights for organizations, law enforcement, and legal bodies in identifying and preventing financial fraud (Davidyan et al., 2022; Akkeren & Tarr, 2021; Durtschi & Rufus, 2017).

Conventional FA education often relies on lectures, historical case studies, and basic data analysis tools, which may not adequately develop the high-level critical thinking skills required in the age of AI. While these methods provide foundational knowledge, they often lack the interactive engagement needed for deep analysis and may not reflect the complexities of modern fraud involving advanced technologies (Saputra, 2019). The integration of sophisticated AI tools like machine learning and NLP in curricula is imperative (Vijayalakshmi & Jeevan 2024) and current methods may not sufficiently emphasize the critical evaluation of AI-driven insights or the associated ethical considerations. Consequently, existing pedagogical approaches might not fully prepare students to critically assess AI outputs, understand their limitations and biases, or navigate the ethical dilemmas of AI in forensic accounting, potentially leaving them ill-equipped for the future. It is essential that contemporary, learner-centered pedagogical approaches such as Problem-based learning (Manikeswari et al, 2024) and flipped classroom that foster an environment for enhancing learners analytical and critical thinking skills are adopted in AI-powered FA.

Table 2 below summarizes some contemporary pedagogical strategies for enhancing critical thinking in AI integrated FA (Rezaee et al., 2016; Rezaee & Wang, 2019; Saputra-, 2019; Alshurafat, Al Shbail & Mansour, 2021; Imjai et al, 2024; Alharasis et al., 2025).

Table 2. Contemporary pedagogical strategies for enhancing critical thinking in AI integrated FA

Pedagogical Strategy	Description	How it Fosters Critical Thinking with AI
Problem-Based Learning (PBL) with AI Integration	Presenting complex, real-world forensic accounting scenarios that require students to use AI tools to analyze data and draw conclusions.	Enables leaners to interpret AI outputs, evaluate their significance and make judgments about potential fraud, rather than simply applying AI tools.
Collaborative Learning and Team-Based Projects	Encouraging students to work in teams to solve AI-driven forensic accounting problems.	Promotes discussion, debate, and the consideration of different perspectives on AI-generated results, leading to a more nuanced understanding.
Simulations and Virtual Forensic Environments	Utilizing simulations that mimic real-world forensic accounting investigations involving AI.	Allows students to practice critical thinking and decision-making skills in a safe environment while interacting with simulated AI tools and data.
Ethical Dilemma Discussions and Case Analyses	Incorporating case studies and discussions that focus on the ethical challenges and biases associated with the use of AI in forensic accounting.	Prompts students to critically evaluate the ethical implications of AI in their field and develop frameworks for responsible use.
"Human-in-the-Loop" Exercises	Designing exercises where students must work alongside AI systems, critically evaluating the AI's outputs and making informed decisions based on their professional judgment.	Reinforces the importance of human oversight and critical judgment in AI-driven investigations, emphasizing that AI is a tool to augment human expertise.

Universities must carefully design their accounting curricula to include IT-related forensic accounting content. Students should also consider this when choosing their major and career path. Universities and firms should assess their course offerings and training programs to ensure they adequately address the growing importance of technology in the field (Bhasin, 2015). Alshurafat et al. (2020) suggest that forensic accounting students need hands-on learning activities to bridge the gap between theoretical knowledge and real-world application. They also emphasize the importance of students developing analytical judgment by using problem-solving skills to investigate statistical patterns.

To effectively gauge the potentially successful outcomes of an AI-integrated FA curriculum in fostering critical thinking, it is crucial to establish clear learning outcomes that define what students should be able to do, particularly in evaluating AI outputs, analyzing ethical implications, interpreting AI insights, forming professional judgments, and communicating AI limitations (Rezaee & Wang, 2019). Assessment methods must extend beyond traditional exams to evaluate the application of these skills in practical, AI-integrated scenarios. This can be achieved through case studies, problem-solving tasks using AI tools, team projects analyzing AI results, ethical dilemma analyses, simulated investigations and reflective journals, ensuring a comprehensive evaluation of critical thinking abilities in the context of AI.

The evidence of research-backed implications of the use of AI across various fields is abundant. It is, however, evident that there exists a substantial gap in terms of empirical research in the use of AI in forensic accounting education. It is quintessential that extensive research is undertaken in the subject to bring to light the potential benefits of integrating AI into FA education so as to create a wider foundation of practical knowledge on the subject with focus on implications for all stakeholders.

AI-INTEGRATED FORENSIC ACCOUNTING CURRICULA: OVERCOMING CHALLENGES TO OPTIMIZE BENEFITS

In the generic context of accounting education, Selasih & Suranto (2024), conducted a study which indicates that students recognize AI's capability to boost efficiency and productivity, especially when it comes to automating repetitive and technical accounting tasks. Despite this, they still believe human accountants are crucial for strategic decisions and complex analyses demanding professional insight. The research recommends a more systematic integration of AI into accounting education through dedicated courses and practical learning opportunities. This is highlighted because while many students have indirectly benefited from AI through tools like ChatGPT, not all have direct experience with the technology itself. In terms of research in the field of FA, the global scene reveals some interesting trends. The United States produces the most research, while Canada and Australia are focused on creating influential studies. The increasing involvement of developing nations like South Korea highlights the expanding global awareness of forensic accounting. This worldwide perspective emphasizes that the issues forensic accounting tackles are universal, pointing to the importance of international research collaboration (Quang Huy & Kien Phuc, 2025).

Amin et al., (2025), through a bibliometric study, analyzed 287 accounting education publications in the Scopus database from 1982 to 2023 to identify influential aspects in the digital era. The research revealed three key themes: the impact of emerging technologies on the accounting profession, the essential skills for modern accountants, and the integration of technology into accounting curricula. Macquarie University and Queensland University of Technology were identified as the most productive institutions, with the Accounting Education Journal being the leading journal. The USA and Australia led in citations and publications, and 2023 was the peak publishing year. While acknowledging limitations related to search parameters, the study provides valuable insights for accounting researchers, higher education institutions, and policymakers regarding the evolving landscape of accounting education in the digital age and suggests avenues for future research. This highlights the increasing focus on the impact of emerging technologies, the essential skills for modern accountants, and the integration of technology into curricula. For future research, this implies a need for deeper investigations into specific technologies, curriculum innovation, skill gap analysis, faculty development, and international comparisons. Managerially, accounting firms and educational institutions must adapt by upskilling professionals, revamping curricula, and fostering digital literacy to prepare for the evolving demands of the digital era.

The integration of AI into accounting higher education offers substantial benefits, notably in personalizing instruction and automating repetitive tasks like data analysis, financial auditing, cost calculations, and financial statement analysis. AI-driven personalization allows students to access tailored content, fostering a dynamic and individualized learning environment. While challenges exist, including the necessity for ongoing teacher training, infrastructure adaptation, and addressing pedagogical and ethical concerns, the potential of AI in accounting education is significant. It promises to enhance decision-making, predict financial trends, and personalize learning, ultimately transforming accounting education and better preparing future professionals for a technologically advanced job market (Stropano & Lemos, 2025).

Integrating AI into FA education presents both hurdles and advantages (Alharasis et al., 2023). Key challenges include the need for significant curriculum updates to incorporate AI concepts, tools, and ethical considerations, as well as ensuring faculty possess the necessary AI expertise through training. Providing students with access to costly AI resources and keeping the curriculum current with rapid technological advancements are also significant challenges. Furthermore, balancing technical AI skills with core accounting knowledge and critical thinking is crucial, and educators must address potential student anxiety towards new technologies. Despite these challenges, AI integration offers exciting opportunities to enhance learning through engaging simulations and hands-on experience with cutting-edge tools, leading to the development of highly relevant and sought-after skills (Rezaee & Wang, 2019). AI can also personalize learning, provide better feedback, expose students to the latest industry technologies such as wearables and foster innovation and problem-solving abilities, ultimately improving student engagement and learning outcomes (Ratnakaram et al., 2025; Soni et al., 2025).

Developed nations should prioritize advanced training in emerging technologies and offer grants to bolster research in higher education. In contrast, developing countries face obstacles in curriculum development, necessitating policy interventions that encourage HEIs to enhance data literacy and collaboratively redesign programs with industry professionals. Investing in technological infrastructure is crucial, and fostering international collaborations and exchange programs can introduce new technology-focused curricula. Furthermore, providing access to digital accounting tools like Tableau, Python, and SQL is essential for both instructors and students to cultivate necessary skills (Amin et al., 2025).

ETHICAL CONSIDERATIONS

The growing use of AI in FA raises important ethical concerns and the risk of biases that educational institutions and educators must address. A major issue is algorithmic bias, where AI systems trained on biased data can perpetuate or worsen existing societal inequalities, leading to unfair outcomes in investigations. Data privacy and security are also critical, especially with cloud-based AI tools handling sensitive financial information, raising concerns about data breaches. The limited transparency of some AI algorithms, known as the "black box" problem, makes it hard to understand how they reach conclusions, creating accountability challenges and hindering the validation of findings. Questions of responsibility arise when AI errors or biases occur in investigations (Akkeren & Tarr, 2021). Furthermore, the broader impact of AI on the profession, such as potential job losses due to automation, is an ethical consideration that needs attention. These ethical issues are not just theoretical but have real-world consequences for the fairness, accuracy, and legal acceptance of FA investigations. To tackle the ethical concerns and potential biases arising from AI in FA, several modern and innovative educational approaches can be used. Curricula should include specific modules on AI ethics in this field to give students a fundamental understanding of these complex issues (Rezaee & Wang, 2019). Analyzing case studies that present ethical dilemmas related to AI can help students develop their ethical reasoning skills in practical scenarios. Inviting ethics experts to speak can offer valuable perspectives on the challenges AI poses. It's also crucial to teach students how to critically assess AI algorithms and the data they are trained on, enabling them to recognize and understand potential biases. Emphasizing the "human-in-the-loop" approach, where human judgment remains central to AI investigations, can help reduce bias and errors by ensuring AI outputs are always reviewed and validated by human experts. Ultimately, fostering a culture of ethical awareness and responsibility is key to ensuring students understand the importance of ethical conduct in their future work as forensic accountants in the age of (AI Alshurafat et al., 2020). Teaching students to critically evaluate AI and its data is vital for promoting the ethical and reliable use of these tools. The "human-in-the-loop" method is not just a teaching strategy but an ethical necessity in AI-driven forensic accounting, highlighting the continued need for human judgment and accountability.

CONCLUSION

FA represents a specialized domain within the broader accounting profession, dedicated to the investigation of financial discrepancies and potentially fraudulent activities, often with the aim of providing evidence suitable for legal proceedings. Professionals in this field act as "financial detectives," meticulously examining financial records to uncover misconduct within organizations or by individuals. This investigative nature and legal orientation distinguish forensic accounting from traditional auditing practices, which primarily focus on providing assurance on financial statements. Incorporating AI into FA education offers a significant chance to better prepare future professionals for this dynamic career. However, this integration requires a strategic approach that prioritizes the development of both technical AI skills and strong critical thinking abilities. While AI puts forth valuable tools for various aspects of FA, its success depends on the ability of accountants to critically assess its results, understand its limitations while judiciously addressing ethical concerns. Educators and Higher Education Institutions must work towards the adoption of innovative teaching methods like PBL, collaborative projects, simulations, ethical discussions and human-in-the-loop exercises. Assessments must be designed to evaluate both technical skills and critical thinking in AI-driven contexts. Continuous faculty training and access to AI resources are crucial. Future research in the field to examine the long-term effects of AI integration on learning outcomes and the evolving ethical landscape is quintessential. The ultimate aim is to produce forensic accountants who are not only technologically skilled but also possess strong critical thinking and ethical awareness to effectively navigate the complexities of financial investigations in the age of AI. Future research on the subject could broaden the scope of the current research area to include other methodologies and address the limitation of the current research being based on the literature review methodology. In particular, gathering the perceptions from academics and other stakeholders on the adoption of AI in the FA curriculum could offer valuable insights for both academic and practical audiences. Another avenue for future investigation is the manner and pace at which the business world, the accounting profession, and business schools are integrating AI into their accounting curricula, more specifically into FA education has immense potential to add to existing literature on the subject by providing valuable global insights.

REFERENCES

Alharasis, E. E., Haddad, H., Alhadab, M., Shehadeh, M., & Hasan, E. F. (2025). Integrating forensic accounting in education and practices to detect and prevent fraud and misstatement: Case study of Jordanian public sector. *Journal of Financial Reporting and Accounting*, *23*(1), 100–127. DOI: 10.1108/JFRA-04-2023-0177

Ali, A. M., Futaih, R. F., Shukur, M., & Al-Orfali, A. K. (2024). Forensic Accounting and Fraud Detection Emerging Trends and Techniques. *Journal of Ecohumanism*, *3*(5), 525–542. DOI: 10.62754/joe.v3i5.3921

Alshurafat, H., Al Shbail, M. O., & Mansour, E. (2021). Strengths and weaknesses of forensic accounting: An implication on the socio-economic development. *Journal of Business and Socio-economic Development*, *1*(2), 135–148. DOI: 10.1108/JBSED-03-2021-0026

Alshurafat, H., Beattie, C., Jones, G., & Sands, J. (2020). Perceptions of the usefulness of various teaching methods in forensic accounting education. *Accounting Education*, *29*(2), 177–204. DOI: 10.1080/09639284.2020.1719425

American Board of Forensic Accounting. (2022). Principles of Professional Practice. https://abfa.us/about/principles/

Amin, H. M. G., Hassan, R. S., Ghoneim, H., & Abdallah, A. S. (2025). A bibliometric analysis of accounting education literature in the digital era: Current status, implications and agenda for future research. *Journal of Financial Reporting and Accounting*, *23*(2), 742–768. DOI: 10.1108/JFRA-12-2023-0802

Bhasin, M. L. (2015). An empirical investigation of the relevant skills of forensic accountants: experience of a developing economy. *Available at SSRN* 2676519. https://dx.doi.org/DOI: 10.2139/ssrn.2676519

Bhave, A. V. (2024). Artificial Intelligence In Forensic Accounting: Software Applications and Case Study Analysis. *Bharatiya Shiksha Shodh Patrika*, Vol. 43, Issue 1 (III), January-June: 2024

Davidyan, J., Huels, D., Brian, W., Gissel, D., & Jodi, L. (2022). Two truths and a lie: Introduction to deception detection. *Issues in Accounting Education*, *38*(2), 85–93. DOI: 10.2308/ISSUES-2021-054

Davis, C., Farrell, R., & Ogilby, S. (2010). Characteristics and skills of the Forensic Accountant. *American Institute of Certified Public Accountants, 2010*, 11-26. http://thefraudgroupllc.com/tools/library/documents/forensic.pdf

Durtschi, C., & Rufus, R. J. (2017). Arson or accident: A forensic accounting case requiring critical thinking and expert communication. *Issues in Accounting Education Teaching Notes*, *32*(1), 89–105. DOI: 10.5555/iace-51350TN

Ellili, N., Nobanee, H., Haddad, A., Alodat, A. Y., & AlShalloudi, M. (2024). Emerging trends in forensic accounting research: Bridging research gaps and prioritizing new frontiers. *Journal of Economic Criminology*, *4*, 1–17. DOI: 10.1016/j.jeconc.2024.100065

Gasanov, E. I. (2024). The Experience of Using AI in the Forensic Economics: A Scoping Review. *Futurity Economics&Law*, *4*(3), 261–277. DOI: 10.57125/FEL.2024.09.25.15

Hońko, S., & Hendryk, M. (2024). The Role of AI in Accounting: Insights From Practitioners. *European Research Studies Journal, 27*(2), 989-1003. https://ersj.eu/journal/3863

Imjai, N., Swatdikun, T., Rungruang, P., Basiruddin, R., & Aujirapongpan, S. (2024). Empowering generation z accountants in the era of data complexity and open innovation: Nurturing big data analytics, diagnostic, and forensic accounting skills. *Journal of Open Innovation*, *10*(2), 100308. DOI: 10.1080/1097198X.2025.2480972

Kılıç, B. İ. (2020). The effects of big data on forensic accounting practices and education. In *Contemporary issues in audit management and forensic accounting* (Vol. 102, pp. 11–26). Emerald Publishing Limited., DOI: 10.1108/S1569-375920200000102005

Kramer, B., Seda, M., & Bobashev, G. (2017). Current opinions on forensic accounting education. *Accounting Research Journal*, *30*(3), 249–264. DOI: 10.1108/ARJ-06-2015-0082

Manikeswari, D., Ratnakaram, S., Shaikh, Z. H., Alawi, S. H., & Kumar, A. (2024). PBL in Higher Education: Empowering Students for the Industry Dynamics. [EEL]. *European Economic Letters*, *14*(3), 1137–1140. DOI: 10.52783/eel.v14i3.1873

Mehta, K., Mittal, P., Gupta, P. K., & Tandon, J. K. (2022). Analyzing the impact of forensic accounting in the detection of financial fraud: The mediating role of artificial intelligence. In *International Conference on Innovative Computing and Communications: Proceedings of ICICC 2021,* Volume 2 (pp. 585-592). Springer Singapore. DOI: 10.1007/978-981-16-2597-8_50

Mounce, P., & Frazier, J. (2002). The effect of forensic accounting education on an accountant's employment potential. *Journal of Forensic Accounting*, *3*(1), 91–102.

Murdock, H., & Murdock, D. H. (2018). Association of Certified Fraud Examiners (ACFE). *Auditor Essentials*, 7-10.

Pautasso, M. (2019). The structure and conduct of a narrative literature review. *A guide to the scientific career: Virtues, communication, research and academic writing*, 299-310. DOI: 10.1002/9781118907283.ch31

Quang Huy, P., & Kien Phuc, V. (2025). Insight into how legal and ethical considerations of artificial intelligence enhance the effectiveness of cyber forensic accounting. *Journal of Global Information Technology Management*, *28*(2), 136–166. DOI: 10.1080/1097198X.2025.2480972

Ratnakaram, S. P., Manikeswari, D., Shaikh, Z. H., Mahapatra, D. M., Mohanty, B. S., & Soni, A. (2025). Wearables and AI-Smart Technologies: Transforming the Education Sphere. In Ul Rehman, S. (Ed.), *Wearable Devices and Smart Technology for Educational Teaching Assistance* (pp. 27–52). IGI Global Scientific Publishing., DOI: 10.4018/979-8-3693-7817-5.ch002

Rezaee, Z., Lo, D., Ha, M., & Suen, A. (2016). Forensic accounting education and practice: Insights from China. *Journal of Forensic & Investigative Accounting*, *8*(1), 106–119.

Rezaee, Z., & Wang, J. (2019). Relevance of big data to forensic accounting practice and education. *Managerial Auditing Journal*, *34*(3), 268–288. DOI: 10.1108/MAJ-08-2017-1633

Saputra, K. A. K. (2019). Case-Based learning in forensic accounting education. *International Journal for Educational and Vocational Studies*, *1*(6), 545–553. DOI: 10.29103/ijevs.v1i6.1763

Selasih, D. & Suranto (2024). Understanding Student Perceptions of Artificial Intelligence Technology: Case Study of Accounting Education Student, Universitas Muhammadiyah Surakarta. *Didaktika: Jurnal Kependidikan, 13*(001 Des), 375-388. DOI: DOI: 10.58230/27454312.1367

Soni, A., Shaikh, Z. H., Taqi, M., Bijja, V., & Ratnakaram, S. P. (2025). Enhancing Education in Bahrain With AI and ML: Through Wearable Technology. In Ul Rehman, S. (Ed.), *Wearable Devices and Smart Technology for Educational Teaching Assistance* (pp. 115–144). IGI Global Scientific Publishing., DOI: 10.4018/979-8-3693-7817-5.ch005

Van Akkeren, J. K., & Tarr, J.-A. (2021). The application of experiential learning for forensic accounting students: The Mock trial. *Accounting Education*, *31*(1), 39–66. DOI: 10. 1080/09639284.2021.1960573

Vijayalakshmi, D., & Jeevan, J. (2024). Forensic Accounting: Uncovering Fraud with Advanced Analytics. *Library of Progress-Library Science. Information Technology & Computer*, *44*(3). Advance online publication. DOI: 10.48165/bapas.2024.44.2.1

Chapter 4
Student Attentiveness in Online Sessions:
AI Evaluation Model

Nithin Kalorth
https://orcid.org/0000-0001-7969-7637
Bahrain Polytechnic, Bahrain

Ankita Jena
https://orcid.org/0009-0002-9600-0242
Independent Researcher, India

T. Harishma Devi
Independent Researcher, India

Manish Verma
Bahrain Polytechnic, Bahrain

ABSTRACT

Online classes and virtual interactions have become standard in education following the pandemic, offering flexibility and enabling remote learning. Various techniques, such as flipped classrooms, surprise assessments, and gamification, are used to boost attentiveness and enhance the quality of online sessions. However, these approaches have limitations and often fail to maintain engagement throughout an entire session. Consequently, there is a need for a more effective solution. This study explores a method to improve student attentiveness during online sessions by using AI-based voice recognition and pre-set keywords to generate multiple-choice polls. This paper seeks to develop a model for integrating AI into teaching and learning, based on the findings from this controlled online classroom experiments.

DOI: 10.4018/979-8-3373-7386-7.ch004

INTRODUCTION

Background

In recent years, the landscape of education has seen a profound transformation with the introduction of online education. Moreover, the onset of global pandemic propagated the shift from traditional classrooms to e-learning overnight. This shift led to a rapid embrace of digital tools to enable continuity in education. The online pedagogical environment is often considered as a supportive or complimentary to traditional mode of learning. There are some courses and programs which are completely focused on online mode of teaching and learning. One of such programs which is the focus of the current chapter is WILP which is Work Integrated Learning Program is an initiative by Educational Institutions for Working Professionals. The main aim of WILP is to improve and elevate skills and knowledge of professionals based on current trends and technologies.

The mode of learning involves work- focused learning as the main part of the curriculum to help the professionals to excel in their domain and learn unique skills that will highlight them from the others. As per Birla Institute of Technology and Science (n.d.), an education model should fulfil the following criteria for it to be considered as WILP.

- The program designed ought to be developed by the institute in collaboration with industry.
- Work-focused experiences should form an active part of the curriculum.
- The program structure, pedagogy and assessment should enable integration of theory with relevant practice.

Problem Statement

The significance of student attentiveness cannot be overstated as it forms the basis for effective learning outcomes. Unlike traditional classes where physical presence may naturally lead to engagement, virtual learning environments require immense importance to student attentiveness to remain the class as interactive during the session. Online sessions offer great flexibility and comfort and potential personalized experience (Means et. al., (2009), but the active participation was not always satisfactory. According to Wester. et.al., (2021), there was a significant negative shift in student engagement from the pandemic era in online class. Student attentiveness is particularly important during the online sessions due to several reasons:

- It influences knowledge retention and comprehension.

- Active learning fosters dynamic learning communities, promoting collaborative interactions between students.
- It enables students to capitalize on diverse resources that are available.

AIM OF THE STUDY

The primary focus of this research study is to enhance the attentiveness and engagement of students, particularly those enrolled in Work-Integrated Learning (WIL) Programs, or similar students attending online sessions during their course. The implementation of a dynamic polling system featuring multiple-choice questions where questions are created with the help of Artificial Intelligence (AI)-based voice recognition and pre-fed keywords to identify the topics during the sessions. These polls will be strategically introduced at random intervals to the students during the sessions. The intention is to foster a more interactive and participatory learning environment. Additionally, a comprehensive report detailing active and non-active participants will be compiled and sent to faculty members at the end of each session. This multifaceted approach seeks to not only gauge but also elevate student engagement, contributing to an enriched and dynamic educational experience.

SIGNIFICANCE OF THE STUDY

One prevalent challenge comes from the potential distractions in the learning environment. Further, absence of face-to-face interactions during online sessions brings in a sense of isolation, diminishing motivation and lacking concentration. The work by Anderson and Dron (2011) emphasizes that the issue of the physical and psychological separation in online learning environments can be a cause for lack of student engagement. Furthermore, studies conducted by Means et. al. (2009) found the challenge of limited social interactions during classes and emphasized on peer-to-peer collaboration and its positive impact on the student engagement levels during the class. Additionally, the use of digital media and navigating through online platforms also play a significant role in contributing to potential distractions.

The significance of this study is limited to attentiveness and engagement of the students during session. In line with Katrina A Meyer (2014) that attending the session does not guarantee actively participation. Attendance can be considered as the administrative base and apply our dynamic polling system to improve attentiveness. There are several methods like flipped classroom, surprise assessments, gamification etc. to increase attentiveness and improve the quality of the online sessions. All the above methods have their own limitations, and it is not effective for the entire stretch of session. One of the methods for example, On Flipped Classroom researched by Susan L. Hotle and Laurie A. Garrow, a key shortcoming noted with the flipped classroom was students' inability to ask questions during lectures.

PURPOSE OF THE STUDY

The study focusses on improving the student's attentiveness during the online sessions to enhance the online learning experience to both teachers and students. The study centers on the enhancement of student's attentiveness during the online sessions, with the goal of improving the overall learning experience and contented environment with rich knowledge experience for both students and faculties. The study further expands on increasing the digital learning experience in the Work Integrated Learning Program section.

METHODOLOGY

The current chapter has implemented a mixed-methods approach that integrated qualitative surveys and practical observation of the idea within a controlled classroom environment. The study used purposive random sampling and reached out to thirty faculties. For the controlled- classroom environment, the current chapter monitored the class of HCL-WILP B.Sc. Design and Computing, Cohort-8 students attending Evolution of Design course.

LITERATURE REVIEW

Tang et.al (2023) investigated the efficacy of the various available online teaching modes and proposed a combined model of online and flipped learning to other online and traditional models. The survey questionnaire results of the study showed that the students were generally dissatisfied with the online learning as well as communication and Q&A sessions. Finally, the study concluded that combined models of online teaching with the flipped learning improved students learning attention and evaluation of courses. Salas-Pilco et al. (2022) examined student engagement from behavioral, cognitive, and affective dimensions and identified the main characteristics of student engagement from the above-mentioned tripartite dimensions. The implications of the findings from online learning are to transform higher education, to provide adequate professional training, to improve internet connectivity, to ensure quality online learning in higher education, and to provide emotional support.

Bansal et al., (2023) done a comprehensive research on student engagement with the context of Asian countries that was published during the period of 2020-2022 which aims at answering research questions like the present status of research on student engagement in online learning amid the pandemic, literature-based foundation for student engagement strategies, some theories that are referenced in the literatures, and finally the antecedents of student engagement with some possibilities for future research in online learning are supported in the literature Martin & Bolliger (2018).

Sun et al., (2022) has done a study on interactions on learning effects in online education as well as the mediating role of the psychological atmosphere and learning engagement. The questionnaire survey was taken by 398 students from various Chinese Universities. Further they concluded that teacher–student interaction not only directly affects students' learning effects but also influences students' learning effects through the following analysis:

> *The level of teacher–student interaction positively affected students' learning effects ($r = 0.649$, $p < 0.01$). The psychological atmosphere mediated the positive effect of the level of teacher–student interaction on learning effects with mediating effect value of 0.1248. Learning engagement mediated the positive effect of teacher–student interaction on learning effects with a mediating effect value of 0.1539. The psychological atmosphere and learning engagement play a chain-mediating role in the mechanism of teacher–student interaction affecting students' learning effects; that is, teacher–student interaction promotes students' learning engagement by creating a good psychological atmosphere, which, in turn, influences learning effects.*

Traphagan et al, (2010) found that, though the availability of webcasts negatively impacted student attendance, it was the availability of other online resources such as PowerPoint slides had a greater negative impact on attendance. The negatives effects of absenteeism on student performance were nullified by access to Webcast. The performance measures based on lecture content increased with an increase in webcast viewing. Majority of the students in the webcast section reported positive learning experiences and benefits from using webcasts, while others reported using webcasts for missing a class. From these they concluded that webcast could have a positive effect on student learning experience and performance even if class attendance declines. The similar results can be found by Kang & Zhang (2023) also.

Haugom (2022) examines student attendance rates during the COVID-19 pandemic, noting that the shift from on-campus to online lectures resulted in significantly higher attendance in digital lectures. However, the trend of attendance over the semester showed no significant difference. The flexibility and reduced effort required to attend digital lectures, along with the ease of access to study materials, contributed to higher attendance, though this availability negatively impacted physical attendance. Similarly, Vonderwell and Zachariah (2005) explore factors influencing learner participation in two sections of a graduate online course at a Midwestern University. They conclude that participation depends on technology and interface characteristics, content area experience, student roles, instructional tasks, and information overload. Effective online learning, they argue, requires interdependence for a shared understanding of learning goals within a learning community, and monitoring participation patterns helps instructors scaffold learning.

Khan et al. (2017) address challenges in student engagement, finding that 100% of polled respondents faced difficulties in online classes. They note that teaching experience is less critical than creating a good classroom atmosphere, using appropriate tools, preparing materials, and committing time to foster engagement. The authors emphasize that in-person and online environments differ, requiring methods tailored to the context for active learning. Anjarwati and Sa'adah (2021) consider student engagement a key factor in successful learning, exploring it through behavioral, emotional, and cognitive dimensions. Observing an online Paragraph Writing Session via Google Meet in Google Classrooms, they find that students are actively engaged during behavioral or cognitive activities, yielding positive results.

Huang et al. (2021) investigate factors affecting Flipped Classroom Learning Performance (FCLP), identifying social presence, teaching presence, cognitive presence, and learning presence as critical. Through analysis, they determine that social presence most significantly influences learners' perceived performance, followed by teaching presence and cognitive presence in descending order. Nieuwoudt (2020) examines the relationship between academic success and student interactions in online classes, exploring whether attendance impacts success. The study finds that attendance is necessary for success, but the choice between live or recorded lectures does not significantly affect learning. Providing diverse participation options, they conclude, may enhance academic success. Such results are important in traditional classes also (Guilherme, 2019).

Prince et al. (2020) suggest strategies for enhancing engagement in online STEM courses, emphasizing the need to establish teaching and social presence, clearly explain policies and expectations, conduct formative assessments for continual adjustments, and anticipate student resistance to active engagement. They advocate a gradual approach to adopting new strategies. Abou-Khalil et al. (2021) report that students in low-resource contexts perceived student–content engagement strategies—such as screen sharing, summaries, and class recordings—as the most effective, followed by student–teacher strategies like Q&A sessions and reminders, with student–student collaboration ranking lowest in perceived effectiveness. Farrell and Brunton (2020) quantitatively explore online engagement in an undergraduate course, identifying five themes: sense of community, support networks, study-life balance, confidence, and learning approaches. They conclude that peer community, faculty teaching style, and course design directly influence engagement.

Mukhtar et al. (2020) identify advantages, limitations, and recommendations for online learning during the COVID-19 pandemic. Comfort and accessibility are benefits, while inefficiency and challenges in maintaining academic integrity are key limitations. They suggest using online modalities and lesson plans with reduced cognitive load and increased interactivity to improve the experience. Mahmood (2021) offers strategies for online teaching without compromising learning, advising teachers to practice pacing, perform vocal exercises, and share materials in advance. Additional factors like periodic feedback, flexible assessments, recorded lectures, and teaching assistant support enhance the experience.

Kim (2023) focuses on security and privacy concerns affecting engagement in real-time online classes. Data from students at Y University in South Korea reveal that peer behavior influences participation, with privacy and security issues negatively impacting real-time engagement. Ahmed et al. (2020) investigate faculty needs for enhancing engagement on virtual platforms, highlighting the importance of faculty development in digital transformation to overcome barriers absent in face-to-face learning. Maimaiti et al. (2023) explore disengagement in web-based videoconferencing, identifying limited use of breakout rooms, webcams, communication tool knowledge, lack of incentives, and differing expectations as factors reducing participation in two postgraduate courses.

Pichardo et al. (2021) assess the impact of Mentimeter software on engagement, finding that it improves interaction, promotes collaborative learning, and allows teachers to monitor progress in online environments. The tool's statistics help pace courses, though cost and limited templates are drawbacks. Finally, Hollister et al. (2022) survey undergraduate students' online learning experiences, noting that 72% reported low engagement harmed their learning. Students struggled to connect with lecturers and peers but found aspects enjoyable and were comfortable asking questions when appropriate tools were used.

The collection of studies addresses diverse aspects of online learning experiences and student engagement. One study focuses on the challenges identified by undergraduate students, such as struggles in staying connected and low engagement during online classes. Another explores the impact of Mentimeter software on student engagement, revealing positive effects on interaction, collaboration, and teacher monitoring. Several studies delve into factors affecting engagement, including the use of breakout rooms, webcams, and communication tools, emphasizing the importance of faculty development. The viability of forum-based online teaching is a valuable supplementary method to conventional classrooms. Another research suggests that final term paper can be converted into smaller online submissions, promoting pro-active completion of homework assignments, and mitigating plagiarism. Security and privacy concerns, as well as peer behavior, are identified as potential distractions. Strategies for enhancing engagement in STEM courses, creating a framework for active student involvement, and examining the flipped classroom model's influence on learner performance are also discussed. Other topics include the relationship between student attendance, various online teaching strategies, and the impact of webcast availability on attendance and performance. The studies highlight the complexity of online learning, proposing recommendations such as clear policies, formative assessments, and a combined model of online and flipped learning to improve student engagement and overall learning experiences.

Some studies focus on contributing to shaping the future Work-Integrated Learning (WIL) programs. The study underscores the significance of purposeful design in online courses, emphasizing strategic planning for pedagogical touchpoints to improve student engagement and learning outcomes. Collaborative online communication tools and instructional design are key components. Additionally, a proposed 10-level guide addresses student engagement during emergency online classes in low-resource settings. The results highlight the effectiveness of digital support strategies in meeting student needs, emphasizing the crucial role of related support.

RESEARCH GAP

With the aim of finding the merits and shortcomings of online education, student engagement in online sessions and attendance during a session the current research found that several paper cover about attendance but almost no paper has covered student engagement throughout the entire session. And additionally, all the experiments and surveys were done in the regular university which leads to a conclusion that WILP needs more experimentation and focus on student attendance and engagement.

In the pursuit of comprehensively evaluating the advantages and drawbacks of online education, particularly within the context of student engagement in virtual sessions and attendance tracking, our thorough literature review revealed a notable void in the existing research landscape. While numerous papers extensively address the topic of attendance, a visible need is found in the research area focusing on sustained student engagement throughout the entirety of online sessions. Furthermore, significant observation emerged as most experiments and surveys in this domain predominantly focused on universities providing regular degrees (National University, 2024). Consequently, this noticeable gap in literature underscores the imperative for dedicated experimentation and research within the Work-Integrated Learning Programs (WILP) framework, with a specific emphasis on probing into student attendance and engagement in the online educational environment. This unexplored area indicates for practical analysis to shed light on the unique challenges and opportunities inherent in WILP, ultimately contributing to a more understanding of effective online education practices.

RESEARCH DESIGN

The research study done by Van Acker et.al., (2018) and Meyer (2014) used mixed method approach where the research integrated qualitative surveys to gather quantitative feedback and the practical observation of a controlled classroom environment. Similarly, this research study also uses mixed-methods approach to assess the support of the dynamic polls to increase attentiveness. This approach allows us to gain a more comprehensive understanding of the research topic by triangulating data from different sources, providing deeper insights. Before the data collection, necessary consent was obtained from the faculty members. This mixed method enhances our study by providing a more complete understanding of the impact of technology integration on student learning.

CONTROLLED CLASSROOM ENVIRONMENT

The Controlled Classroom Environment involves direct observation of student behaviors, interactions, and engagement within a specific setting. In this study, qualitative research was conducted to gain insights into student engagement during session. This method provided the opportunity to observe and document various aspects of student engagement. The data obtained from the practical observation offered a deeper understanding on how the idea of dynamic polling system impacted student engagement during a session.

QUANTITATIVE RESEARCH SURVEY

Survey is a common method to collect data from a sample of participants. The survey in this research contained a structured questionnaire with closed and open-ended questions. The questionnaire included questions with predetermined response options such as multiple-choice questions or yes/no and text-based questions to understand the perspectives of the participants. Furthermore, it also included demographic questions to gather information about the faculties to understand their academic fields and exposure to online teaching.

PARTICIPANTS DEMOGRAPHICS

We reached out to teachers with experience in online teaching. The study used purposive random sampling and reached out to thirty faculties. These faculties have been teaching professionally for a longer period. Hence, the feedback provided by them is the utmost valuable and contributed immensely to this study. For the controlled environment, Data Collection and Procedure, the current chapter implemented our idea on HCL-WILP B.Sc. Design and Computing, Cohort-8, students on a particular session after getting permission from the respective faculty.

ANALYSIS

As the current research implemented mixed methods, first started doing some interviews with the WILP faculties and got some insights in the form of a survey. Then the research conducted a controlled classroom testing of the idea. Before conducting the experiment there was an observation session, where researchers concentrated on the current level of concentration during the class. We conducted interviews directly with selected teaching faculties based on their availability and asked the other faculties to fill out a form which consisted of the same questionnaires. The survey started on January 04, 2024, and closed on January 14, 2024, with a participation count of about thirteen teachers. The questionnaire was designed with different sections for WILP, Non-WILP faculties and another section was created for faculties teaching both WILP and Non-WILP.

SURVEY ANALYSIS

The questionnaires in the survey were meticulously created to capture a comprehensive understanding of the faculty member's experiences and perspectives on student engagement and attendance trends during the past three years. The questions are structured in a manner that encourages the faculty members to articulate their thoughts on various aspects like identifying any method for increasing the student engagement by faculty members themselves etc., From the thirteen participants, most of the faculty members have experience in Online Education and Offline teaching as well. Furthermore, the survey did not restrict the participants only to WILP.

Figure 1. Attendance and student engagement trend over the past 3 years.

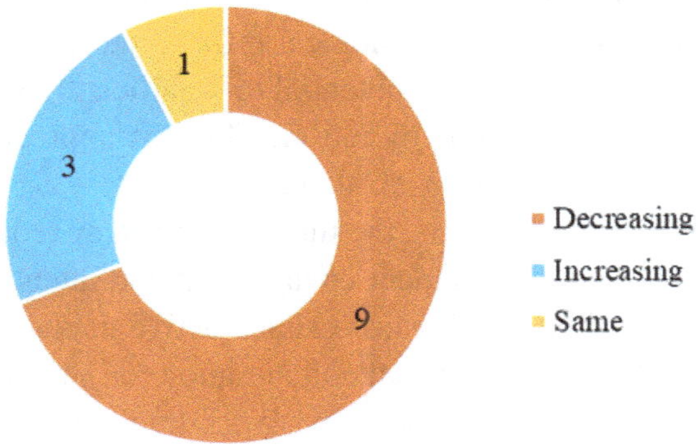

It was inferred from the survey that approximately 69% of the faculties have felt that attendance and engagement has decreased in the last three years. This is the same for a bachelor's degree as well as a master's degree. The decrease in attendance during online class can arise due to several reasons and it could differ across educational institutions, levels, and regions. For Example, the student engagement might improve if the participants (students and teachers) had better network access and technology skills. (Werang & Leba, 2022).

Figure 2. Significant difference between participation in class before and after COVID.

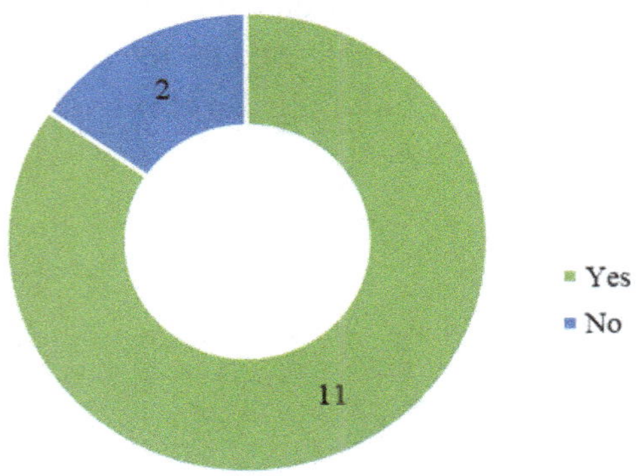

As per the survey, 84% of the teachers feel the shift post-COVID has seen a decrease among students' attendance and engagement potentially attributed to a change in mindset or lack of interest. Focusing on average and low-level students becomes crucial and impossible. It is essential to acknowledge the diverse impact of these changes, considering factors such as course nature, adaptability of instructors and students, and the available technological infrastructure. According to Means et.al. (2009), online learning has the potential to significantly influence the future landscape of teaching and learning by introducing new approaches that can cater to the diverse learner needs. (Means et. al., (2009)

According to the faculty members, the survey received mixed responses describing their current experience on student engagement and attendance during class. Faculties thought that online learning necessitates active student engagement, using tools like discussion forums and virtual collaboration for interaction. While attendance metrics vary, emphasizing flexibility, Work-Integrated Learning Programs (WILP) blend academic study with practical experience, fostering high engagement due to real-world applications. WILP attendance is adaptable, considering physical or virtual participation is particularly important.

The comparison between online and traditional settings reveals mixed outcomes, influenced by students' passion and personal connections. In agreement to the authors of "The Handbook of Blended Learning," activity-based learning proves effective in student engagement, countering issues like fleeting attention during online classes and blended learning (Bank & Graham, 2012). Additionally, the authors highlight the complexity in student engagement. They mentioned that some students attend selective classes based on prior knowledge or individual learning preference, while others show varied attendance patterns.

We also asked the faculties if Continuous Evaluation i.e., Assessment relies entirely on assignments and projects, with no written exams can benefit the students. And most of the faculties are positive that it would enhance the student engagement as it will make the students alert and be motivated for the students to attend and be up to date with the class. Furthermore, this will also effectively improve the creativity and innovation of students.

Figure 3. Response of faculty members if implementation of our idea will gain positive outcome during class.

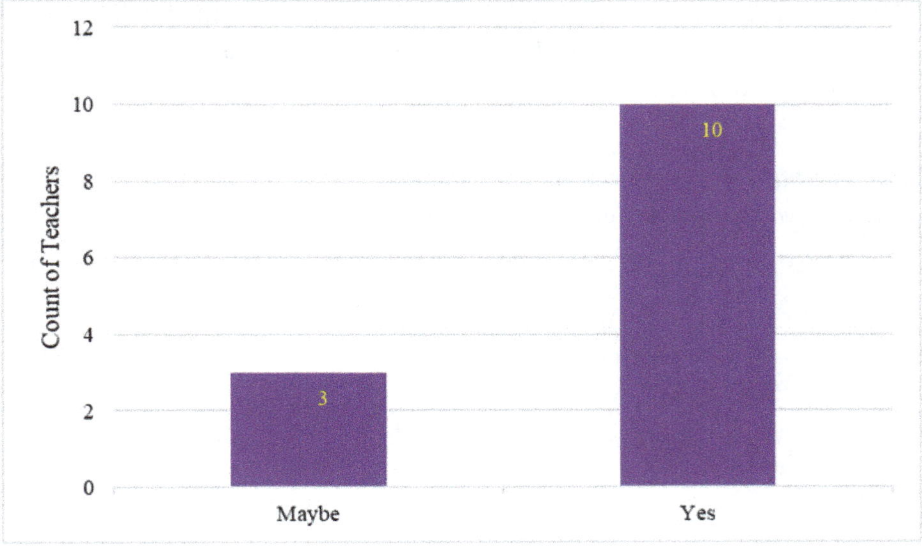

Almost all the teachers are very optimistic that the idea of introducing random polls automatically with the help of AI based voice-recognition and pre-fed keywords would work if implemented properly and addition of feedback mechanism to this system will help the students as well improve more engagement based on the student and faculty preference during a class.

CONTROLLED CLASSROOM EXPERIMENT ANALYSIS

With the aim of adding value to the faculty's perspectives, we tried to implement the idea of random polls in a controlled classroom environment. Firstly, we observed the class of B.Sc. Design and Computing course, Cohort 8, Evolution of Design class, session 1(January 6, 2024, 14.00-16.00 hours) to understand the current situation of the class. The first session was the benchmark session for our controlled classroom experiment of dynamic polling system on student engagement. This session will be compared with the second session where the actual idea was experimented. During the first session, faculty asked around 3-4 questions for which only 2-3 responses from students had appeared either in chat or by speaking up directly and there were sometimes that none of the students answered a question.

During our observation class, we found out that, out of the total strength of 125 students, only thirty students had attended the class on an overall basis, and it fluctuated from time to time.

Figure 4. Chart represents the count of students during a particular time interval during the evolution of design session 1 (observation class).

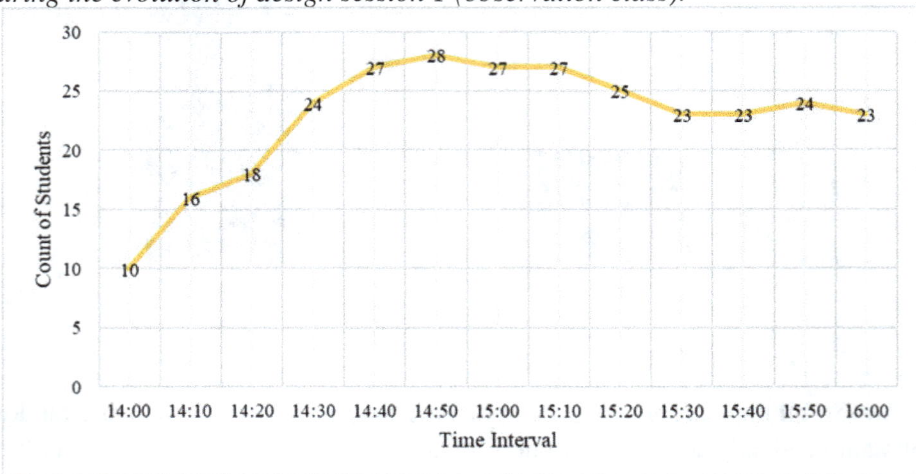

The trend of attendance during the class was at peak for 30 minutes (from 14.40 – 15.10). The faculty tried engaging methods like showing relevant real-life examples through a video and directly explaining some day-to-day examples but during the class, only 2-3 repeated students answered the questions asked by the faculty either by chat or by directly speaking up. Apart from this, there were many times when there was no response from the students for the questions from the faculty. Based on faculty feedback and observation, this could be due to the following reasons: 1. The student attendance count was low. 2. There can be any technical issue in the platform during the session. 3. There might be students who have joined merely for the sake of being present and not interested in the class itself. We conducted our experimentation in the evolution of Design session 2, January 13, 2024, with the same timing span of 2 hours. Before the session, the students were alerted to attend the session by the faculty without any rewards of marks.

During the session, the initial count started with twelve and was in the range of 20-25 students, which is almost same as the previous session even though the students were intimated to attend the class. To conduct polls and questions, we used Mentimeter application which has presentation to record the responses and results.

Figure 5. Chart represents the count of students during a particular time interval during the evolution of design session 2.

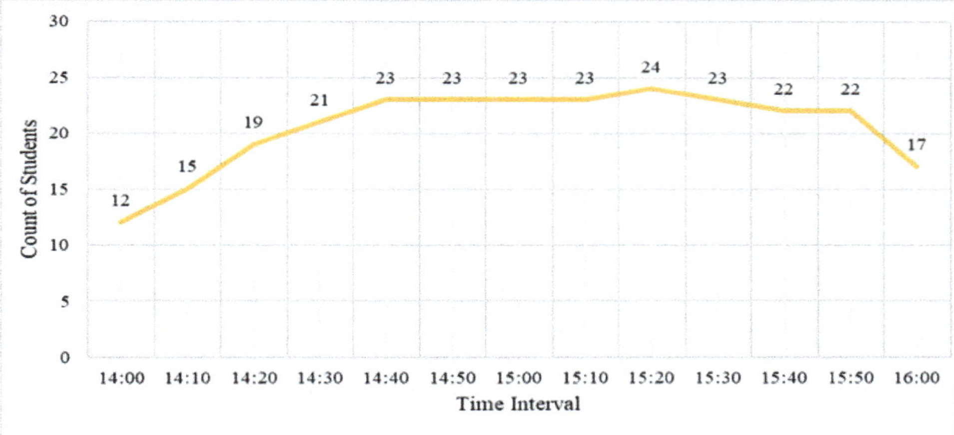

The trend of attendance during the class was mostly constant for an hour (from 14.40 – 15.30). We asked the students to try out the first question as trial to understand if any difficulties were faced during the access of the poles. The poll had nine questions based on the lesson plan for session

Figure 6. Trend on the student response to the poll questions during session two

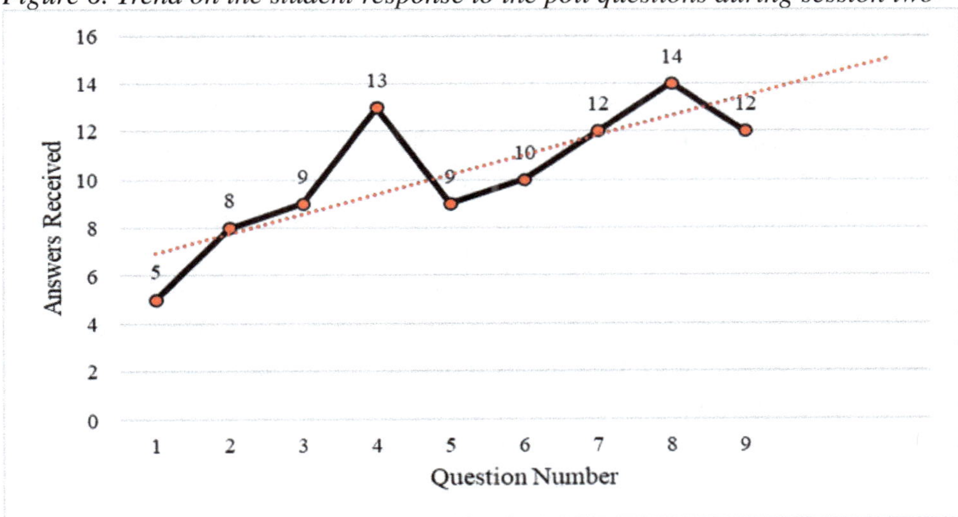

and was asked after the faculty had completed a part of the session. At the beginning the poll had only five responses but gradually it increased to fourteen and students started to get more engaged and interested in classes and answered questions and slowly the participation rate increased and reached up to fourteen members out of twenty-four participants.

Figure 7. Chart represents the correct answers and the wrong answers that were given by the students in the poll.

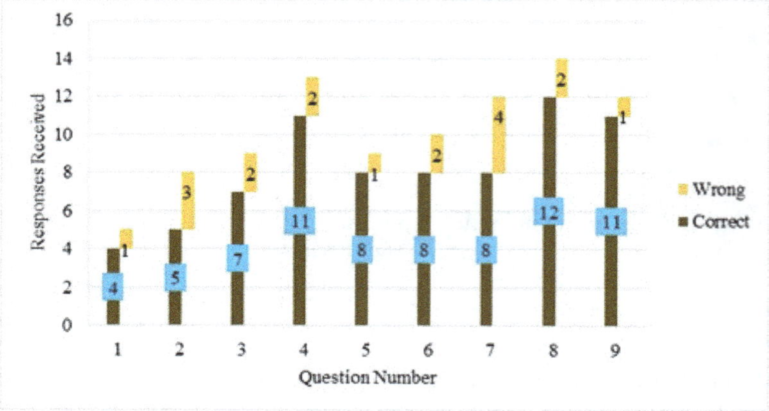

We can summarize that; the students were able to answer simple questions based on what was taught during the session but found it difficult to answer when it was application-based questions. Further there were constant 3-4 responses to every question the faculty put forth. Comparing this to session one where we had very passive and repetitive people responding.

The observation and feedback from session one implicated that some students were not interested in the class. So, to make the class more engaging, storytelling methods were implemented to some of the topics taken during the sessions. This resulted in positive results as well, it boosted the student's engagement and some new students tried to answer the question for the first time during the session.

During the end of the session, the students were asked to give feedback on the session. Some students felt the class was interactive and interesting while other students felt that they were more focused during the session. An e-mail that has statistics of the topics covered and the areas that can be improved based on the percentage of incorrect answers provided by the participants was sent to faculty. The report was insightful and helpful as per the faculty feedback.

IMPLEMENTATION OF AI BASED POLLING SYSTEM

The study aimed to use AI based voice recognition and pre-fed keywords to develop the questionnaire during the session. But during the practical observation of the idea, due to lack of resources, a controlled classroom experiment approach was applied where the questions that would be developed by AI during the session were prepared manually before the session. Based on the content prepared by the faculty for the session, the faculty can provide some pre-fed keywords which include topics, sub-topics or any other specific key word related to the session. During the session, based on topics taught by faculty during the class, AI will use voice recognition to identify the pre-fed keywords and topics. Then AI will create a question based on this and sent to the participants as a multiple choice question. This process will continue throughout the session at intervals set by the faculty. Finally, a consolidated report will be generated to determine the student engagement during the session. Additionally, AI can provide some insights based on the data collected during the session to help faculties improve their engagement and learning experience.

Additional to the concept, there are few technical aspects to implement AI based dynamic polling system into the real-time. They are as follows: 1. AI Algorithms 2. Data Collection and Analysis 3. Real-time Updates 4. AI Integration 5. Security Measures and backend support 5. Scalability and Performance 6. Integration with the presentation software. AI Algorithms such as Natural Language Processing (NLP) and Machine Learning models which can analyze and predict trends based on data will play a detrimental role in implementing the idea. According to Jurafsky and Matin, NLP techniques like voice-based application are essential for understanding and processing voice-recognition tasks (2019). Another study implies that development of deep neural networks is required for speech recognition (Sainath et. al., 2015). Further security is a major concern in the IoT and AI landscape due to the diverse accessibility and variety of connected networks, leading to increased vulnerability and threats. Hence security is one of the important concerns and main challenges to be addressed while implementing any AI based idea. (Mahapatra, et. al., 2020). Shalev-Shwartz & Ben-David (2014) mentioned that machine learning algorithms are important for AI applications such as polling sessions. Further, Cloud Computing Infrastructure like Amazon Web Services (AWS) is required to handle AI model inference, processing, speech-recognition etc. while ensuring scalability, reliability and efficiency. It is essential to have a user-friendly interface which is easier to navigate and understand (Nielsen, J., 1994), as understood as early in 1990s.

CONSIDERATIONS AND LIMITATIONS

Despite the prevalence of online education and Work-Integrated Learning Programs (WILP) for over a decade, the limited existing research, primarily focused on traditional degree programs, underscores the need for further exploration within the WILP context. Extending the sample data beyond HCL integrated WILP faculties more, could offer broader insights into faculty perspectives across diverse WILP sections, allowing for a more comprehensive understanding of the challenges and opportunities unique to this mode of education and the similar approach can be carried out for Online mode of teaching. This expansion would contribute to the overall body of knowledge and help bridge the gap identified in the literature review, which primarily drew from universities offering regular degree programs.

Furthermore, this study is particularly constrained by its scope mainly within the HCL integrated WILP section within the WILP category, and there exists a potential avenue for future research to encompass a more extensive array of institutions and organizations implementing WILP. Understanding faculty perceptions and experiences across various WILP contexts would provide valuable insights into the nuances associated with integrating work experience and academic study.

While the current experiment focused on a Humanities and Design-based theoretical class, future studies could extend their scope to include more analytical subjects, such as Mathematics, to assess the generalizability of the findings across different academic domains. This diversification in subject matter would enhance the applicability of the research outcomes and contribute to a more understanding of the impact of AI-driven strategies on student engagement in various disciplines .

Lastly, the absence of AI voice recognition and pre-fed keywords during the initial experiment, due to policy reasons in the WILP setting, represents a potential avenue for future refinement. Conducting experiments real-time along with AI and reward system could provide additional insights into the feasibility and effectiveness of these technological enhancements in a controlled classroom environment.

Addressing the limitations and building upon the positive reception of AI in education by teachers suggests ample room for continued experimentation and advancement in enhancing student engagement within the evolving landscape of online learning and work-integrated learning. The research journey could be further enriched by iteratively refining methodologies and expanding the study's scope to capture a more comprehensive understanding of the intricate dynamics associated with WILP and online education.

RESULTS

The survey results reveal a notable concern among faculties, with approximately 69% indicating a perceived decrease in attendance and engagement over the past three years, applicable across both bachelor's and master's degree programs. According to National University's blog, online learning has various challenges like unreliable internet access and limited technology resources, emerging as potential contributors along with lack of communication and social interaction leading to the diminished participation in online classes. Post-COVID, 84% of teachers observe a decline in attendance and engagement, attributing it to a shift in mindset or a lack of interest. According to Birla Institute of Technology and Science (n.d.), Work-Integrated Learning Programs (WILP) are highlighted for their ability to blend academic study with practical experience, fostering heightened engagement through real-world applications. The comparison between online and traditional settings reveals mixed outcomes, influenced by students' passion and personal connections. Additionally, faculties express optimism towards continuous evaluation without written exams, foreseeing its potential to enhance student attendance, engagement, and creativity. Furthermore, there is a consensus among teachers that the introduction of AI-based random polls with voice recognition and pre-fed keywords holds promise, provided it is implemented effectively and includes a feedback mechanism, thereby improving engagement based on student and faculty preferences during a class. Finally, the classroom experimentation nearly showed that random polls can increase student engagement during an online session.

The random poll was accounted to have nine questions based on the lesson plan. Initial responses were limited, starting with five but gradually increasing to fourteen, indicating an increase in student engagement. Notably, students excelled in answering simple questions from the session but faced challenges with application-based queries. To enhance interest, gamification and storytelling methods were applied, which resulted in some new students participating for the first time. Session feedback indicated varying opinions, with some students finding the class interactive and interesting, while others felt more focused. An email with statistics on covered topics and areas for improvement, based on participant incorrect answers, was sent to faculty, which received insightful and positive feedback.

IMPLICATIONS OF THE STUDY

The study findings present valuable insights into the effectiveness of incorporating AI based dynamic polling system to improve student attentiveness. The system uses voice recognition and pre-fed keyword to formulate questions. We see the timing of publishing question matters as students are eager to answer questions when it is about topics they just learned. Additionally, as they struggle with application questions, several types of questions such as true or false, definition, problem and solution are some formats that can be considered. Since the report was manually created automation of report creation is also an area to be explored. Also, this idea will help the faculty in analyzing their teaching style during a session. Hence, they can alter or come up with new methods of teaching suitable for the participants. Overall, the practical implications of this research highlight the potential of AI based dynamic polling system to develop student engagement in online learning and offer faculty the opportunity to experiment teaching with latest technology. It is a good idea to test these with current ai chatbots like ChatGPT, Gemini, perplexity etc. to see the capabilities of the available models and how it must be trained or fine-tuned to apply to our dynamic polling system. These practical implications can guide educators, online course developers and other related people in enhancing student engagement and learning outcomes which in turn will help in motivating students to be alert during the session.

DISCUSSION AND CONCLUSION

The survey conducted among the faculty members underscores the collective acknowledgement of the critical role of student engagement plays in online sessions. Faculty members employed various methods such as flipped classroom approach, organizing group activities and quizzes, incorporating multimedia content like videos etc., The introduction of random polls using AI- based voice recognition received unanimous approval from the faculties, who found it practical and potentially effective in boosting student engagement. Classroom experimentation with random polls corroborated these expectations, revealing an observable increase in student engagement during online sessions. Notably, student feedback confirmed to heightened focus during these sessions, affirming the positive impact of innovative engagement strategies. Therefore, it can be deduced that random polls using AI based voice recognition can be achievable if the communicating tool can be integrated with an AI model, for example Chat GPT with simpler user interface from the observations made while conducting the study.

It is to be theoretically believed based on the survey that the effectiveness of the method would be more drastic if the marks awarded for attendance were directly integrated with this system. The poll questions and answers can be integrated with the LMS along with assignments and assessments to have an overall outlook and easier user interface for both students and faculties as either can revisit the questions.

As mentioned previously, limited research which almost focused more on traditional degree program necessitates further exploration within the WILP context. Expanding sample data beyond HCL integrated WILP within WILP section for both the survey and controlled classroom experimentation could provide a broader faculty insight. Experimentation in Humanities and Design class yielded positive feedback; extending the study to subjects like Mathematics could enhance applicability Addressing limitations, such as the absence of AI voice recognition technology and pre-fed during the experimentation in future experiments has the potential to refine the research idea. The overwhelmingly positive reception of AI among faculties suggests ample room for continued experimentation and advancement.

During the experimentation, students became more engaged as the session progressed, and participation increased during the session. Notably, students were adept at answering simple questions related to the session content, but some students struggled with application-based questions. Implementing gamification and storytelling approach during the class has also contributed to enhancing student engagement, prompting some students to participate for the first time during the session. Session feedback was mixed, with some finding it interactive and others noting the increased focus. Sending an insightful report with detailed topics covered and areas for improvement based on the participation answers, aligns with the positive feedback. Likewise, the results from the survey also indicated that there could be an increase in the attendance in class if there was a driving force like rewarding attendance marks based on attentiveness.

In conclusion, this research illuminated the idea of introducing random polls using AI based voice recognition and pre-fed keywords during an online session along with recognition or rewards as a gesture for student participation, underscoring the importance of student engagement and attendance during an online session. These insights pave the way for future exploration in areas such as expanding it to analytical subjects or extending the approach to other WILP sections, contributing to the landscape of WILP and Online Education

REFERENCES

Abou-Khalil, V., Samarasinghe, S., Gaines, B., & Nasser, H. (2021). Emergency online learning in low-resource settings: Effective student engagement strategies. *Education Sciences*, *11*(1), 24. DOI: 10.3390/educsci11010024

Ahmed, S., Shehata, M., & Hassanien, M. (2020). Emerging faculty needs for enhancing student engagement on a virtual platform. *MedEdPublish*, *9*(1), 75. DOI: 10.15694/mep.2020.000075.1

Anderson, T., & Dron, J. (2011). Three generations of distance education pedagogy. *International Review of Research in Open and Distance Learning*, *12*(3), 80–97. DOI: 10.19173/irrodl.v12i3.890

Anjarwati, R., & Sa'adah, L. (2021). Student learning engagement in the online class. *EnJourMe (English Journal of Merdeka). Culture, Language, and Teaching of English*, *6*(2), 39–49. DOI: 10.26905/enjourme.v6i2.6128

Bansal, R., Kumar, S., & Sharma, A. (2023). A systematic literature review on student engagement in online learning amid COVID-19. In *Technology-driven e-learning pedagogy through emotional intelligence* (pp. 166–181). IGI Global., DOI: 10.4018/978-1-6684-7639-0.ch011

Birla Institute of Technology and Science. (n.d.). *M. Tech artificial intelligence and machine learning*. Retrieved March 15, 2024, from https://bitly.ws/3fVWZ

Farrell, O., & Brunton, J. (2020). A balancing act: A window into online student engagement experiences. *International Journal of Educational Technology in Higher Education*, *17*(1), 1–19. DOI: 10.1186/s41239-020-00199-x

Guilherme, A. (2019). AI and education: The importance of teacher and student relations. *AI & Society*, *34*(1), 47–54. DOI: 10.1007/s00146-017-0693-8

Haugom, E. (2022). The effect of changing from campus-based to digital teaching on student attendance: A case study of Norwegian business students. *Heliyon*, *8*(11), e11563. DOI: 10.1016/j.heliyon.2022.e11307 PMID: 36411901

Hollister, B., Nair, P., Hill-Lindsay, S., & Chukoskie, L. (2022). Engagement in online learning: Student attitudes and behavior during COVID-19. *Frontiers in Education*, *7*. Advance online publication. DOI: 10.3389/feduc.2022.851019

Huang, X., Zhang, J., & Hudson, L. (2021). Factors affecting learning performance in flipped classroom: An empirical study based on RCOI framework. *Review of Education*, *391*(3), 98–122.

Jurafsky, D., & Martin, J. H. (2019). *Speech and language processing* (3rd ed.). Pearson.

Kang, X., & Zhang, W. (2023). An experimental case study on forum-based online teaching to improve student's engagement and motivation in higher education. *Interactive Learning Environments, 31*(2), 1029–1040. DOI: 10.1080/10494820.2020.1817758

Khan, A., Egbue, O., Palkie, B., & Madden, J. (2017). Active learning: Engaging students to maximize learning in an online course. *Electronic Journal of e-Learning, 15*(2), 107–115.

Kim, S. S. (2023). Motivators and concerns for real-time online classes: Focused on the security and privacy issues. *Interactive Learning Environments, 31*(4), 1875–1888. DOI: 10.1080/10494820.2020.1863232

Mahapatra, S. N., Singh, B. K., & Kumar, V. (2020). A survey on secure transmission in Internet of Things: Taxonomy, recent techniques, research requirements, and challenges. *Arabian Journal for Science and Engineering, 45*(8), 6211–6240. DOI: 10.1007/s13369-020-04461-2

Mahmood, S. (2021). Instructional strategies for online teaching in COVID-19 pandemic. *Human Behavior and Emerging Technologies, 3*(1), 199–203. DOI: 10.1002/hbe2.218

Maimaiti, G., Jia, C., & Hew, K. F. (2023). Student disengagement in web-based videoconferencing supported online learning: An activity theory perspective. *Interactive Learning Environments, 31*(8), 4883–4902. DOI: 10.1080/10494820.2021.1984949

Martin, F., & Bolliger, D. U. (2018). Engagement matters: Student perceptions on the importance of engagement strategies in the online learning environment. *Online Learning : the Official Journal of the Online Learning Consortium, 22*(1), 205–222. DOI: 10.24059/olj.v22i1.1092

Means, B., Toyama, Y., Murphy, R., Bakia, M., & Jones, K. (2009). *Evaluation of evidence-based practices in online learning: A meta-analysis and review of online learning studies*. U.S. Department of Education.

Meyer, K. A. (2014). Student engagement in online learning: What works and why. *ASHE Higher Education Report, 40*(6), 1–114. DOI: 10.1002/aehe.20018

Mukhtar, K., Javed, K., Arooj, M., & Sethi, A. (2020). Advantages, limitations and recommendations for online learning during COVID-19 pandemic era. *Pakistan Journal of Medical Sciences, 36*(COVID19-S4), S27–S31. https://doi.org/DOI: 10.12669/pjms.36.COVID19-S4.2785

National University. (2024). *Challenges of distance learning for students*. Retrieved March 15, 2024, from https://www.nu.edu/blog/challenges-of-distance-learning-for-students/

Nielsen, J. (1994). *Usability engineering*. Morgan Kaufmann.

Nieuwoudt, J. E. (2020). Investigating synchronous and asynchronous class attendance as predictors of academic success in online education. *Australasian Journal of Educational Technology*, *36*(3), 15–25. DOI: 10.14742/ajet.5137

Pichardo, J. I., López-Medina, E. F., Mancha-Gutiérrez, J. M., & de la Fuente, J. (2021). Students and teachers using Mentimeter: Technological innovation to face the challenges of the COVID-19 pandemic and post-pandemic in higher education. *Education Sciences*, *11*(11), 667. DOI: 10.3390/educsci11110667

Prince, M., Felder, R., & Brent, R. (2020). Active student engagement in online STEM classes: Approaches and recommendations. *Advances in Engineering Education*, *8*(4), 1–25.

Sainath, T. N., Vinyals, O., Senior, A., & Sak, H. (2015). Convolutional, long short-term memory, fully connected deep neural networks. In *2015 IEEE International Conference on Acoustics, Speech and Signal Processing (ICASSP)* (pp. 4580–4584). IEEE. https://doi.org/DOI: 10.1109/ICASSP.2015.7178838

Salas-Pilco, S. Z., Yang, Y., & Zhang, Z. (2022). Student engagement in online learning in Latin American higher education during the COVID-19 pandemic: A systematic review. *British Journal of Educational Technology*, *53*(3), 593–619. DOI: 10.1111/bjet.13190 PMID: 35600418

Shalev-Shwartz, S., & Ben-David, S. (2014). *Understanding machine learning: From theory to algorithms*. Cambridge University Press.

Sun, H.-L., Li, X.-Y., & Liu, R. (2022). The influence of teacher–student interaction on the effects of online learning: Based on a serial mediating model. *Frontiers in Psychology*, *13*, 779217. DOI: 10.3389/fpsyg.2022.779217 PMID: 35369265

Tang, T., Abuhmaid, A. M., Olaimat, M., Oudat, D. M., Aldhaeebi, M., & Bamanger, E. (2023). Efficiency of flipped classroom with online-based teaching under COVID-19. *Interactive Learning Environments*, *31*(2), 1077–1088. DOI: 10.1080/10494820.2020.1817761

Traphagan, T., Kucsera, J. V., & Kishi, K. (2010). Impact of class lecture webcasting on attendance and learning. *Educational Technology Research and Development*, *58*(1), 19–37. DOI: 10.1007/s11423-009-9128-7

Van Acker, B. B., Parmentier, D. D., Vlerick, P., & Saldien, J. (2018). Understanding mental workload: From a clarifying concept analysis toward an implementable framework. *Cognition Technology and Work*, *20*(3), 351–365.

Vonderwell, S., & Zachariah, S. (2005). Factors that influence participation in online learning. *Journal of Research on Technology in Education*, *38*(2), 213–230. DOI: 10.1080/15391523.2005.10782457

Werang, B. R., & Leba, S. M. R. (2022). Factors affecting student engagement in online teaching and learning: A qualitative case study. *The Qualitative Report*, *27*(2), 555–577. DOI: 10.46743/2160-3715/2022.5319

Wester, E. R., Walsh, L. L., Arango-Caro, S., & Callis-Duehl, K. L. (2021). Student engagement declines in STEM undergraduates during COVID-19–driven remote learning. *Journal of Microbiology & Biology Education*, *22*(1), 10–1128. PMID: 33884093

Chapter 5
Measuring Educational Quality in Saudi Arabia Using a Modified SERVQUAL Scale

Md Shabbir Alam
https://orcid.org/0000-0002-5001-4553
Univeristy of Bahrain, Bahrain

Mohammad Rumzi Tausif
Prince Sattam Bin Abdulaziz University, Al Kharj, Saudi Arabia

Mohammad Noor Alam
https://orcid.org/0000-0002-0015-7177
University of Bahrain, Bahrain

ABSTRACT

This study aims to develop a specialized scale to measure educational quality in Saudi Arabia. Normally the SERVQUAL scale is used to measure the quality in education sectors, but few studies have attempted to modify the scale to accommodate the distinct features of the education sector. Using factor analysis, the study identifies three factors to be added to SERVQUAL, namely academic, non-academic, and curriculum dimensions. Recommendations for improving the variety of courses and programs, curriculum, and student workload are based on the gap scores obtained by subtracting students' expectations from their perceptions.

DOI: 10.4018/979-8-3373-7386-7.ch005

INTRODUCTION

For Saudi Arabia, education has long been a key sector, and it receives a large amount of government funding. Education has a leading role in achieving Saudi Arabia's ambitious Vision 2030. Vision 2030 is a major national transformational plan announced in 2016, which besides other things aims at improvements in quality of life and economic diversification. In the year 2020 total allocation for the education sector is 193,168 million Riyals or $52844.8 Million, which is about 18.3 percent to total allocation among key sectors (SAMA, 2020). Moreover, the education sector is dominated by the government sector as approximately ninety percent of students are enrolled in public sector universities. (Oxford Business Group).

Saudi government is committed to quality in higher education, the government has taken a major step in this field by establishing the National Commission for Academic Accreditation and Assessment (NCAAA), to support quality assurance and accreditation processes. It is an autonomous body that collaborates directly with the council of higher education. As of now, 38 Saudi universities are accredited by (Education and Training Evaluation Commission, 2020). Four universities have accreditation from international accreditation bodies like AACSB, AMBA, and EQUIS. (MBAToday, n.d.). Also, four universities/colleges are ACBSP accredited (ACBSP, 2020). This indicates at the emphasis in Saudi Arabia on the quality of education is evident from the above. Now, quality assurance is a continuous process hence measuring the level of quality assumes immense significance.

Quality in higher education is vital in the development of today's modern and futuristic society. Today quality is being given a lot of importance in all sectors. It has become even more important in the education sector as it is considered as one of the basic needs for human development (Allam, 2020). The whole concept of Quality is far-reaching. It is defined as adherence of a process or product to expectations world over academic quality improvement in higher education has become a buzzword. The essence of quality lies in improvements in products/services. It involves identifying the gaps, filling the gaps, and finally closing the loop with improvements. In addition, things do not stop here as the quality process is one of continuous improvement.

Like any other sector, quality is essential for the education sector (Tausif, 2017). The most common tool for measuring quality is SERVQUAL. Parasuraman (et al. 1985) devised this tool known as "SERVQUAL", which is used to quantify customer assessment of service quality performance. Its five dimensions are "Tangibility, Reliability, Responsiveness, Assurance and Empathy". The SERVQUAL as an instrument had become the most commonly used tool to measure service quality, even in the education sector. SERVQUAL, scale items are designed as a standard tool for measuring service quality, which can be applied across the industry. They can be considered as basic 'framework', but it needs modification to fit in specific applications (Allam, 2020). In fact, globally SERVQUAL has been accepted and adopted in all service organizations

Managing student expectations is central to guarantee proper quality of services in higher educational institutions (Yeo, 2008). Students' perspective is the most important element is ensuring quality in educational institutions (Haque & Tausif, 2020). However, the measurement of quality is still debated theoretically. Measuring quality in a service sector is a big challenge due to the intangibility of the product, the inseparability of consumption and production, and heterogeneity of the entire process. Due to some incredibly unique features in the higher education sector, there is a need to develop and exclusive tool for this sector only. Higher education is categorized as a pure service due to its complex nature. These complexities can be attributed to the factors that define services. These factors are inseparability, intangibility, heterogeneity, variability, perishability, and simultaneity. It is because of these factors that make evaluation quality so difficult for the education sector.

REVIEW OF LITERATURE

There are a few studies assessing the quality of education in Saudi Arabian Universities using the SERVQUAL scale. Kassim, Bogari, & Zain (2013) studied the quality of education at King Abdulaziz University using the SERVQUAL scale. The study found that students had the highest expectation for access and empathy. However, in this study but no gap analysis in terms of expectations-perception was performed. In a related study specifically on the female students at King Abdulaziz University by (Kassim, Bogari, & Zain, 2015) gap scores were found using the dimensions of SERVQUAL. The study reported that except for the item of 'Responsiveness' there were gaps in all the remaining four dimensions of SERVQUAL.

Alhabeeb (2015) in his study on King Saudi University using the SERVQUAL scale found gaps in all the dimensions. Tausif (2017) in his study on Prince Sattam Bin Abdulaziz University using SERVQUAL found no gap in all the dimensions. Mohammed (2018) in his study on Al Baha University using SERVQUAL found a gap in all the dimensions. Azam (2018) in his study on AL Yamamah University used SERVQUAL but no gap analysis was done. As in evident, in none of the studies a modified SERVQUAL scale was used to assess the quality in educational institutions.

Firdaus (2006) conducted a study in universities in Malaysia using a modified SERPERF/SERVPERF scale. The study added two additional dimensions Non-Academic aspects and Academic aspects were added to this modify the scale. Arshad, Bhutto, Sarki, & Khuhro (2011) conducted a study in universities in Pakistan using a modified SERVQUAL scale. The modified SERVQUAL scale included communication as an additional dimension. Cerri (2012) conducted a study in universities in Albania using a modified SERVQUAL scale. The modified SERVQUAL scale included service quality as an additional dimension.

Garg (2014) conducted a study in universities in India using a modified SERVQUAL scale. The modified SERVQUAL scale included communication as two additional dimensions. Zareinejad (2014) conducted a study in universities in Iran using a modified SERVQUAL scale. The modified SERVQUAL scale included Human factors, Service core, Providing a systematic service and Social responsibility as the new dimensions. Osman & Saputra (2019) in their study at universities in Bangladesh used seven dimensions namely, Learning, Teaching, Assessment system, Recognition, Library and internet, Campus life and Non-academic administration to modify the SERVQUAL scale.

Khattab (2018) in their study at universities in Lebanon used different dimensions namely, competency, dependency, semester and curriculum, performance, and exceptional status management to modify the SERVQUAL scale. Annamdevula & Bellamkonda (2012) in their study at universities in India used different dimensions namely, Teaching and Course content; Administrative Services; Academic Facilities; Campus Infrastructure; Internationalization; and Support Services management to modify the SERVQUAL scale. Calvo-Porral, Lévy-Mangin, & Novo-Corti (2013) conducted a study in universities in Spain using a modified SERVQUAL scale. The modified SERVQUAL scale included Perceived Quality as an additional dimension. Rashid & Rehman (2017) conducted a study in universities in Bangladesh using a modified SERVQUAL scale. The modified SERVQUAL scale included Academic factors, curriculum, and teaching methods as the three additional dimensions.

METHODOLOGY

A list of 14 items are identified based on the studies reviewed. Care is taken that these statements are not similar to the items included in the dimensions of SERVQUAL. The identified items are Quality and the sincerity of instruction; Variety of courses and programs; Feedback from students; curriculum; Fair grading and equal treatment; Class size; Faculty expertise; & student workload; Extracurricular and sports activities; Friendly, caring, safe campus & on-campus residence; Wi-Fi, recreational & canteen facilities; Library facilities; Student union; and Brand image of the institution. Besides these 14 statements the questionnaire includes another 20 standard statements based on the five dimensions of SERVQUAL. The respondents are to indicate their attitude on a 5-point interval Likert scale, where 1 indicates strongly disagree and 5 indicates strongly agree.

The sample of respondents is chosen basically on a convenience-based. The sample respondents are from the College of Business Administration at Prince Sattam Bin Abdulaziz University. Next factor analysis is performed to reduce the items into a few factors which can be used for further analysis. Kaiser-Meyer-Olkin measure and Bartlett's test of sphericity is used to see that the method of factor analysis is fit. Communalities give the amount of the variance in each variable's that is explained by the extracted factors . Higher values for communalities is considered better. A lower communality(less than 4) will stops the variable to load to any particular factor. The factors are identified based on Eigenvalues of more than one. Also, the items are rotated using Varimax rotation before identifying the factors. Finally, Cronbach alpha is to be used to measure the reliability of each identified factor.

Further, the questionnaire consists of two sections. One section addresses the expectation of the respondents. Here the statements are framed to indicate the expectations of the respondents towards a particular item. In the other section of the questionnaire, the respondents are to indicate their attitudes as to what is the perception of the services actually being provided to them. The scores of individual items under a factor are averaged to score for perception and a score of expectation for each particular factor. Finally, the score of expectation is deducted from the score of perception to find the gap in the quality of services. A negative gap indicates a gap in the quality where there is scope for further improvement.

ANALYSIS

A total of 468 questionnaires were administered. 35 questionnaires were not included in the analysis as they had incomplete responses. Kaiser-Meyer-Olkin measure of sampling adequacy has a value of 0.847 implying that factor analysis as a method is appropriately used. The Bartlett's test of sphericity is significant with a p-value of less than 0.05 implying that that are relationship between some of the variables. As these two necessary conditions for factor analysis is the study proceeds with factor analysis.

Table 1. KMO and Bartlett's Test

Kaiser-Meyer-Olkin Measure of Sampling Adequacy.		**0.847**
Bartlett's Test of Sphericity	**Approx. Chi-Square**	**1735**
	df	91
	Sig.	0

Source: authors computation

Table 2 gives the communalities. It indicate the amount of accounted variance in the variable. It gives the magnitude an item's is correlation with the other items. As all the extracted communalities are higher than 0.4, it implies that the extracted factors to be extracted will adequately reflect the items of the study.

Table 2. Communalities

Variable	Initial	Extraction
1	1	0.572
2	1	0.613
3	1	0.507
4	1	0.561
5	1	0.574
6	1	0.394
7	1	0.433
8	1	0.573
9	1	0.578
10	1	0.582
11	1	0.454
12	1	0.607
13	1	0.597
14	1	0.48

Extraction Method: Principal Component Analysis.
Source: authors computation

Factors are then selected based on Eigen values which denotes the amount of variance associated with each factor. Factors with Eigen values more than 1 are selected as lower Eigen values indicate that the factor is unable to account for the variance associated with the factor. In the analysis only three factors are selected which have an Eigen value of more than 1.

The three selected factors cumulatively explain 53.73% of the total variance. This is lower than the recommended 60% (Table 3). But this is quite obvious as the items exclude many items which are important for assessing the quality. In fact, the study has selected only those items in its questionnaire which are different from the five dimensions of SERVQUAL. In fact, the questionnaire deliberately ignored any item related to "reliability, responsiveness, tangibility, assurance and empathy." Finally, the items are rotated using the method of Varimax rotation with items having large loadings on a factor is identified.

Table 3. Total Variance Explained

S. No	Initial Eigenvalues			Extraction Sums of Squared Loadings			Rotation Sums of Squared Loadings		
	Total	% of Variance	Cumulative %	Total	% of Variance	Cumulative %	Total	% of Variance	Cumulative %
1	4.56	32.58	32.58	4.56	32.58	32.58	3.55	25.37	25.37
2	1.79	12.75	45.32	1.79	12.75	45.32	2.10	15.01	40.38
3	1.18	8.41	53.73	1.18	8.41	53.73	1.87	13.35	53.73
4	0.99	7.08	60.81						
5	0.84	5.99	66.80						
6	0.68	4.89	71.69						
7	0.64	4.60	76.29						
8	0.58	4.12	80.41						
9	0.55	3.92	84.33						
10	0.51	3.66	87.99						
11	0.50	3.55	91.53						
12	0.46	3.25	94.78						
13	0.40	2.89	97.67						
14	0.33	2.34	100						

Extraction Method: Principal Component Analysis.
Source: authors computation

Factor 1 has high coefficient for the items: Faculty expertise; extracurricular and sport activities; Friendly, caring, safe campus & on campus residence; Wi-Fi, recreational & canteen facilities; Library facilities; Student union; and Brand image of the institution. Factor 2 is associated with Quality and sincerity of instruction; Feedback from students; Fair grading and equal treatment; and Class size. And factor 3 comprises of: Variety of courses and programs; curriculum; and student workload. Factor 1 is named as non-academic factor; factor 2 is named as academic factor; and factor 3 is named as curriculum (Table 4).

Table 4. Rotated Component Matrix

	Component		
	1	**2**	**3**
Item 12	0.773	0.092	0.014
Item 13	0.759	0.144	0.036
Item 10	0.684	0.002	0.337
Item 14	0.655	0.221	-.043-
Item 11	0.645	0.043	0.188
Item 9	0.596	-.030-	0.471
Item 7	0.579	0.289	0.12
Item 1	0.002	0.73	0.198
Item 3	0.033	0.669	0.241
Item 5	0.4	0.64	-.059-
Item 6	0.335	0.528	0.052
Item 4	0.064	0.248	0.703
Item 8	0.305	0.013	0.692
Item 2	-.053-	0.454	0.635

Source: authors computation

Table 5. Reliability Statistics

Variables	Cronbach's Alpha	N of Items
All 14 items	0.835	14
Factor 1	0.828	7
Factor 2	643	4
Factor 3	630	3

Source: authors computation

Lastly, reliability tests are done for each factor by calculating their Cronbach alpha. The value for alpha is 0.828 for factor 1; 0.643 for factor 2; 0.630 for factor 3. The overall alpha for all the 14 items is 0.835. This indicates that the scale is dependable and will give consistent results when the study is replicated (Table 5) .

Once the factors have been identified, the study attempted to measure the gap between the performance and expectation of students. The result of gap analysis indicates that for the institution under study the performance is higher than the expectation for all the dimensions, expect one. The only dimension where there is a gap between student's perception and expectation is the dimension of 'Quality'

This dimension is one of the three dimensions added to the original dimensions of SERVQUAL. This dimension constitute of three items namely: variety of courses and programs; curriculum; and student workload. This leads to the recommendation that the institution should look thoroughly into these three items and work to improve upon them.

Table 6. Gap scores

Item	Expectation (E)	Perception (P)	Gap scores (P-E)
Tangibles	2.69	2.70	0.01
Reliability	2.02	2.79	0.77
Responsibility	2.44	2.78	0.34
Assurance	2.15	2.79	0.64
Empathy	2.24	2.49	0.25
Non-Academic	2.29	2.90	0.61
Academic	2.25	2.47	0.22
Curriculum	3.23	2.73	-0.50

Source: authors computation

CONCLUSION

The education sector is a unique service sector with its own characteristics. The non-tangibility of this sector along with its social externalities makes it unique. Normally SERVQUAL is used to measure the quality in education sectors. However, past studies have attempted at modifying the scale to accommodate the distinct features of the education sector. Further, the education sector of Saudi Arabia is unique, and it is dominated by the government sector. This study attempts to fill the gap of identifying the factors to be incorporated into the SERVQUAL scale in the context of Saudi Arabia.

The study develops a questionnaire with 14 items and measures the attitude of respondents on a Likert scale. The items of the questionnaire are different from the items generally included in SERVQUAL scale. Using the method of factor analysis, the study identifies three factors. These three factors are named as non-academic factors, academic factors and curriculum, based on the items they consist of. Reliability tests indicate that the scale is dependable. The study proposes that while measuring the quality of education, these three items should be added to the SERVQUAL scale. Similar HiEdqual scales have been developed for other countries.

The novelty of this study is that similar scale modification in Saudi Arabian context has not been attempted before in past studies.

Finally, the study performs a gap analysis to identify the respondents' difference in performance and expectations. Gap scores indicate that in terms of all the five dimensions of SERVQUAL, the respondents are satisfied with the quality as the performance scores are higher than the expectation score. This result is similar to the findings of Tausif (2017) in the same university, that is, Prince Sattam Bin Abdulaziz University; but contradicts the findings of Alhabeeb (2015) and Mohammed (2018) as these two study report gaps between the expectation and perception of service quality in their respective universities. Albeit, these two studies are on different universities.

Finally, in terms of the two newly added items, gap scores are analyzed. The three newly added items are curriculum, academic and non-academic dimensions. The perceptions are higher than expectations for the two newly added dimensions namely, academic and non-academic dimensions. Only for the dimension of "curriculum' the performance scores is lower than the expectation score. This indicates the item where significant changes can be done to improve upon the quality. So, the study concluded with the recommendation to improve upon the items of this dimension namely variety of courses and programs; curriculum; & student workload.

DECLARATIONS

Ethics approval and consent to participate

Not applicable

Availability of data and materials

The study is based on primary data set and are available by the corresponding authors on reasonable request.

Competing Interests

Not applicable

Funding

No fund receive from any source.

REFERENCES

ACBSP. (2020) Accreditation Council for Business Schools and Programs, https://acbsp.org/page/membership_list

Alhabeeb, A. M. (2015). The Quality Assessment of the Services Offered to the Students of the College of Education at King Saud University Using (SERVQUAL) Method. *Journal of Education and Practice*, *6*(30), 82–93.

Allam, Z. (2020). Demystifying the Aspect of Quality in Higher Education: Insights From Saudi Arabia. *SAGE Open*, *10*(1), 1–8.

Annamdevula, S., & Bellamkonda, R. S. (2012). Development of HiEdQUAL for Measuring Service Quality in Indian Higher Education Sector. *International Journal of Innovation, Management and Technology*, *3*(4), 412–416.

Arshad, I., Bhutto, N. A., Sarki, I. H., & Khuhro, R. A. (2011). Student's Perception about Service Quality level and Significant Determinants of Service Quality for Business Institutes/Universities in Pakistan. *Interdisciplinary Journal of Contemporary Research in Business*, *3*(8), 1062–1077.

Azam, A. (2018). Service Quality Dimensions and Students' Satisfaction: A study of Saudi Arabian Private Higher Education Institutions. *European Online Journal of Natural and Social Sciences, 7*(2), pp-275.

Calvo-Porral, C., Lévy-Mangin, J. P., & Novo-Corti, I. (2013). Perceived quality in higher education: An empirical study. *Marketing Intelligence & Planning*, *31*(6), 601–619. DOI: 10.1108/MIP-11-2012-0136

Cerri, S. (2012). Assessing the quality of higher education services using a modified SEDRVQUAL scale. *Annales Universitatis Apulensis Series Oeconomica*, *14*(2), 664–679.

Education and Training Evaluation Commission. (2020), Accredited Institutions, https://etec.gov.sa/en/productsandservices/NCAAA/academic/Pages/OrgsDirectory.aspx

Firdaus, A. (2006). Measuring service quality in higher education: HEdPERF versus SERVPERF. *Marketing Intelligence & Planning*, *24*(1), 31–47.

Garg, N. (2014). An empirical study on Assessing quality of educational Service using SERVQUAL Model. *American Business Review*, *15*(1), 109–124.

Haque, M., & Tausif, M. (2020). Managing quality in university framework: Students' perspective. *Management Science Letters*, *11*(2), 627–636.

Kassim, N. M., Bogari, N., & Zain, M. (2013). Service quality of a public university in Saudi Arabia. *The Journal of Learning in Higher Education, 2013*, 1–18.

Kassim, N. M., Bogari, N., & Zain, M. (2015). Female students' perception of service quality in a gender-segregated college environment. *Social Behavior and Personality*, *43*(6), 921–930.

Khattab, F. (2018). Developing a Service Quality Model for Private Higher Education Institutions in Lebanon. *Journal of Management and Marketing Review*, *3*(1), 24–33.

MBAToday, Accredited Business Schools in Saudi Arabia, https://www.mba.today/schools/saudi-arabia

Mohammed, B. O. (2018). Statistical quality control charts for measuring educational service quality at Albaha University, Saudi Arabia, from the viewpoint of students. *Journal of Economics and Administrative Sciences*, *24*(102), 1–23.

Osman, A. R., & Saputra, R. S. (2019). A pragmatic model of student satisfaction: A viewpoint of private higher education. *Quality Assurance in Education*, *27*(2), 142–165.

Parasuraman, A., Zeithaml, V. A., & Berry, L. L. (1985). A conceptual model of service quality and its implications for future research. *Journal of Marketing*, *49*(4), 41–50.

Rashid, M.M. and Rehman, M.Z., (2017). Quality of higher education in Bangladesh: Application of a Modified SERVQUAL model problems of education in the 21st Century, 75(1), 72-91

SAMA. (2020) Saudi Arabia Monetary Authority (SAMA), 56th Annual Report. https://www.sama.gov.sa/en-US/News/Pages/news-595.aspx

Tausif, M. R. (2017). Assessing the Quality of Education in Saudi Arabia. *International Journal of Economic Research*, *14*(17), 1–8.

Yeo, R. K. (2008). Brewing service quality in higher education. *Quality Assurance in Education*, *16*(3), 266–296.

Zareinejad, M. (2014). Performance evaluation of service quality in higher education institutions using modified SEVQUAL approach with Grey analytic hierarchy process (GAHP) and multiple Grey evaluation. *Iberoamerican Journal of Industrial Engineering*, *6*(11), 271–293.

Chapter 6
AI Literacy in Higher Education:
A Scoping and Integrative Review

A. C. Balaji
https://orcid.org/0000-0003-4811-4413
Bahrain Polytechnic, Bahrain

ABSTRACT

Artificial intelligence (AI) is now becoming a pivotal force identified as an important driver in the rapidly transforming higher education landscape, requiring both educators and students to have a thorough understanding of it. This study adopts both scoping and integrative review methodologies to analyze existing literature between 2020 and 2025. The analysis discerns the significant themes, such as integration, governance, policy, ethics, social responsibility convergence of technology, ethics, teaching methods, and social consequences, and literacy. Research indicates a substantial disparity in the incorporation of ethical frameworks and the practical implementation of AI literacy in higher education curriculum (Zhang et al., 2024). The study concludes with the recommendation to bridge the gap, highlighting the necessity for multidisciplinary approaches and policy development by convergence of technology, ethics, teaching methods, and societal impact.

INTRODUCTION AND OVERVIEW

From an educational standpoint, digital literacy fits within constructivist and socio-cultural orientations to learning that recognize the importance of learner's practice. Digital literacy promotes learners as producers of digital content, engaging with different platforms and tools to, communicate, and participate as networked

DOI: 10.4018/979-8-3373-7386-7.ch006

community (Lankshear & Knobel, 2011). Furthermore, digital literacy is an evolving context; it is changing with changes to the digital ecosystem. Therefore, educators are not only sharing knowledge, but also facilitating the development of a mindset that adapts as students see fit, to respond to continually emerging technologies critically and creatively. In higher education, cultivating digital literacy is increasingly seen as a foundational literacy that contributes to academic success, professional development in the digital age.

In scholarly discussions surrounding the role of Artificial Intelligence (AI) in educational backdrops, it is important to differentiate between AI policy and AI literacy. AI policy usually has a focus on regulation and control, worrying about how to prevent misconduct, guarantee academic integrity and restrict access to AI tools through gate keeping (Selwyn, 2023). AI policy is often filled with suspicion, and designs students as potential disruptors, and not as learners. It casts educators as enforcers of learning, making AI tools a threat, not something we depend on. This is lifted by a set of reactive responses (i.e., banning, detecting and penalizing), it leads to student perplexity and detachment (Williamson, 2019). In contrast, AI literacy is rooted in a pedagogical perspective that sees students participating in a technological evolution and emphasizes providing learners with the capacity required to engage in competent and ethical ways with AI tools (Long & Magerko, 2020). In this context, the role of educator turns from enforcer to strategist, reminding students that they are free to explore, conceptualize, and iterate the affordances of AI. In this instance, the focus has changed from academic honesty to academic relevance deliberately relating AI usage to valuable learning outcomes. The aim is not to determine what tools to identify as off-limit, but to focus on orientating students to think critically about how to use AI responsibly. In turn, the ultimate output of AI literacy is an inquiry-driven, future-ready as learners these skills are vital for preparing students for an AI-augmented future (Luckin et al., 2016).

And in the recent past, AI has quickly transformed higher education, redefining the pedagogical structure, processes, and the learning experience. As technology is changing, the responsibility of both the educator and the student becomes equally important in preparing for the AI. AI presents many opportunities to advance the educational development, and the challenges it presents are significant such as governance, ethics, social responsibility (Zhang et al., 2024). Long & Magerko (2020) speaks about a need for pedagogical AI literacy, which is to be aware of the issues associated with ethical impacts, technical impacts, and social implications. Just having technical knowledge is not enough though, there is a need to develop knowledge on the developments of the technology in society. In addition, Buccella (2020) mentions that AI has influenced and shaped every aspect of life, it is important to critically analyze the implications of AI on fairness, transparency, and accountability.

As Laupichler et al. (2022) states, AI systems are becoming increasingly vital to many aspects of academic life. The curriculum, administrative processes and approaches to teaching and learning, are being influenced by AI, in ways beyond prior concerning what could be advanced by a computer. This notion includes not just the technical knowhow of AI tools, but knowledge related to the ethical implications, governance structure, and societal obligations.

Considering the growing acceptance of AI-supported tools for greater learning outcomes and increased operational efficiency, the case for AI literacy in education has never been stronger. However, Long et al. (2023) reports that there are important gaps between the ethical frameworks and the practical realities of AI literacy in the education programs. The analyses suggest that institutions are misaligned in how they compensate for the convergence in technical research and pedagogy. If left unaddressed even in the near-term, it could present challenges to society undermining its educational objectives. Recognizing the relevance of AI in education is vital, as it will be a crucial part of the academic success and the moral dilemmas and social implications that extend beyond the walls of the classroom. To allow the students to engage with technology with critical intelligence, (Berendt et al. 2020), students with AI literacy will improve their ability to navigate their future employment and greater participation in society. They may take advantage of AI's while being aware of its capabilities, limitations, and ethical use (Kong et al., 2022).

In the words of Reiss (2021), the success of the AI literacy programs both inside and outside of institutions have begun to sweep the world in recent years. Institutions, policymakers, and industry leaders must collaborate to ensure that this new curriculum is responsive to the rapid changes. Massaro and Bernstein (2022) repeatedly urge that in AI literacy programs, the issues to be solved are spread over varying factors such as, how do the resources reach students? Are students on an equal footing with others in learning. Or do students have access? Do educators need continuously professional development depends on this kind of multi-faceted. Resolving these challenges are essential to establish an environment of equal opportunity for learning. Such a level playing field will afford all the students the chance to interact with AI technologies as well as a framework in which they can exercise critical thinking necessary responsible usage.

Another approach is proposed by Lim et al. (n.d.), which is the collaborations between schools and technology companies that bring in resources that are both valuable to educators and bridging the gap, essentially eliminating the divide between theory and practice. Hence, as AI becomes more deeply embedded in education, it is even more important to continually revise curriculum, so that both content and method are effective and responsive to this age. As Slimi (2023) points out, we need frameworks for appraising the impact of AI based tools on students' learning outcome, and a framework that channels information from educator and students enabling responsive approach alongside of the technological advancements. Abdulmunem (2023) emphasis the need to provide the students with the necessary skills to manage challenges of AI, at the same time engage with these technologies responsibly. This approach will foster generations of informed citizens, capable of practicing and contributing ethical solutions.

This chapter attempts to explore scoping and integrative review of research published between Year 2020 to 2025 for the above pressing issues. Further, by identifying such themes as integration, governance, and policy or the ethics in AI to inform the contemporary situations of AI literacy among the higher education. It argues not only for a multidisciplinary method to address these gaps, but also promotes robust policies that are to ensure that both educators and students are ready to deal with a socially responsible AI (Long et al., 2023).

LITERATURE BACKGROUND AND REVIEW METHODOLOGY

Extract Significant Themes From Literature Spanning 2020 To 2025, Emphasizing Integration, Policy, Regulation, Ethics, And Social Accountability

Integrating AI in higher education has changed pedagogy, teaching materials and the whole educational environment. Now that AI technologies are booming, educators and students alike must have a firm grasp of AI concepts, implications, and applications. This literature review gathers the main findings of the existing body of literature on AI literacy in higher education. Particularly, it focuses on data from Year 2020 to 2025. It aims to place the findings of the scoping and integrative review detailed in the chapter into context, highlighting the essential themes of ethics, governance policy, and social responsibility.

The role of AI literacy in higher education involves mastery and discernment of the expanding range of AI operating systems and interfaces. This has been even more critical than ever, as AI systems penetrate various academic fields. There is no getting away from it, students and educators need both familiarity with such technologies as well as an understanding (Luckin et al., 2021). Zary (2025) states that this kind of knowledge includes not just technical competence, but also consideration on the part of a creator who designs and uses AI technology or its implications for society. In the future beyond retention of facts and figures, how will they develop AI literacy when everything they study is AI-related? Many forms and ways of AI will challenge them to recognize what in future years will be an increasingly AI-infused life.

Key Themes Identified in the Literature

Ethics and Social Responsibility

The ethical dimension of AI in educational contexts is a major theme in the literature. If not carefully designed and implemented, AI systems can prolong bias and impact decision-making in ways that are not always fair. Concerns like these are raising the stakes about ethical frameworks that guide AI usage in higher education. Consequently, Crawford (2021) emphasizes that educators need teach students how to use these AI tools, also create greater awareness of the issues surrounding social responsibility that comes with the implications of AI tools. AI literacy programs including ethical considerations create a space for students to investigate issues of fairness, accountability, transparency, and more.

Governance & Policy Development

At an higher level, the literature review of governance of AI technologies in higher education is another key theme. Annus (2024) argues that while educational institutions have been using AI-embedded, data-driven tools, there is a need for policies regarding data privacy, security, and ethical use to govern the ways AI technologies are used in higher educational contexts. They also suggest that data breaches and algorithmic biases could potentially go unchecked without such policies. Developing frameworks needs to involve stakeholders across disciplines, and the comprehensive governance systems need to ensure policies that are inclusive and take multiple viewpoints into account. The researcher argues and provides necessary blueprints for institutions motivated to deploy AI ethically and responsibly in their teaching and learning environments.

Interdisciplinary Approaches

The complexity of AI requires interdisciplinary approaches to education Zhao (2023) emphasizes that collaboration is required between academic disciplines such as ethics, policy studies, and others to create a holistic understanding of AI. Interdisciplinary curriculum can prepare students to think critically about AI technologies and their social impact. This not only helps to address students pressing needs, but also encourages creative solutions to problems brought forth by AI in education.

Gaps in Current AI Literacy Initiatives

Although the importance of AI literacy is gaining recognition, Zary (2025), indicate significant gaps in existing educational initiatives. The findings suggest that many institutions lack structured programs that effectively build ethical considerations around AI into their curriculum and allow students to do hands-on work with AI applications. Some institutions made strides in AI literacy but there still a considerable need improving AI curriculum both in execution and actual curriculum development.

Strategies for Enhancing AI Literacy

Based on identified gaps, strategies have been suggested for improvement in the literature, Crawford (2022) suggests the need for institutions to embrace the creation of interdisciplinary curriculum, which collectively consider the ethical dimension of AI alongside its practical application. An effective approach might be to develop to train the trainer courses designed by faculty from across the disciplines to ensure that the AI-related content is both thorough and contextual. Furthermore, Annus (2024) recommends the development of governance frameworks, which are explicit about ethical AI use in education should be developed by consulting relevant stakeholders like students, educators, and industry professionals, so they are practical and relevant.

Above all Luckin et al. (2021) highlights the importance of continued research into AI literacy, especially related to the development of AI literacy policy, pedagogical approaches, and the broader social consequences of AI. Higher education entities that focus and nurture research and innovation promote students who embrace AI solutions through hands-on experience while also training their minds to think critically about the next evolving AI landscape.

Examine the Variation That Presently Exist Between Ethical Frameworks And The Use Of AI Literacy In Higher Education

The emergence of AI in higher education is creating great opportunities for innovation and improvement in learning experience. However, it has also highlighted gaps in the ethical frameworks and inclusion of AI literacy within institutions. This Narration focuses on these inequalities, referencing insights from a range of studies and articles to offer a well-rounded view.

Many higher education institutions consider ethical frameworks for AI use to be inconsistent. These discrepancies are evident in several crucial areas such as;

Fragmented Policy Development

Higher education is developing AI policies are often fragmentary, with institutions taking vastly different approaches. While some universities have established strong frameworks to support ethical AI use, others maintain minimal guidelines indicative of non-standardized policy (Atkinson-Toal & Guo, 2024). Such fragmentation hinders efforts to promote ethical use across institutions by leaving students and educators unsure of what is acceptable.

Ethical Concerns and Bias Awareness

Hazari, Archambault et al. (2024) states that AI policies must address critical issues of bias in AI algorithms and data privacy as ethical concerns. However, not all institutions treat these concerns equally. Some universities already integrated AI literacy courses with extra emphasis placed on bias and ethical considerations, while others are lacking. Such discrepancies lead students and educators to be differently aware of and prepared to address the ethical challenges posed by AI.

Digital Divide and Equity

Ojha et al. and Van Wyk (2024) points to the lack of access to technology or the digital divide is yet another factor that is exposing the truth of relative ethical frameworks. Policies in developed countries are often better than those compared with the developing countries. Institutions often have limited resources to create and implement comprehensive AI policies. This could aggravate current inequities, as students and educators at lesser resourced institutions are unlikely to have the same access to AI tools and training, making it difficult for them to learn how to take up AI ethically and responsibly.

AI accessibility in Gulf Cooperation Council (GCC) Countries

The GCC nations have been pushing ahead to incorporate artificial intelligence (AI) into various sectors due to the aspiration to convert their economies into knowledge-based economies. There is, however, a substantial gap in access to AI versus institutional readiness. This response provides a discussion on our status of AI access, the readiness of institutions and the differences between the two with relevant studies.

AI accessibility is evolving rapidly as a result of government efforts and advancements in technology. As an example, the UAE has prioritized AI use as part of its government initiatives. The public sector is utilizing AI to improve efficiency, decision-making processes, and service delivery (Akhoirshieda et al., 2024). AI is also becoming part of the higher education system in Saudi Arabia, which intends to meet needs in education and fit within the framework of the Saudi 2030 Vision (Alotaibi & Alshehri, 2023).

Large investments in digital transformation and the national strategies that accompany these investments help adopt AI. Bahrain's drive toward entrepreneurship and IT start-ups, helps create the ecosystem into which AI can slide. The advancement within the telecom and data spaces in UAE means that it can deploy AI solutions across the public and private sector (Alqasemi et al., 2023). National strategies are bolstered by private sector partnerships with private sector global tech companies in the case of Saudi Arabia or local incubators in UAE (Al-Baity, 2023). Despite these advances, and in what can only be described as uneven access to AI technologies (Al-Ammal & Aljawder, 2021).

Institutional Readiness in GCC Countries

Institutional readiness consists of organization's abilities and capacities to accept and utilize AI technologies. Some GCC countries have made considerable progress on AI and some face significant barriers. A study on AI readiness of medical students in Saudi Arabia indicated there was little education on AI and moderate readiness indicating a need for capacity development enhancement (Shahrani et al., 2024). The UAE has suggested frameworks to provide standardised AI ready data as potential solutions for data fragmentation and infrastructure deficits (Alqasemi et al., 2023). The UAE and Saudi Arabia have suggested that credible data policies and ethical standards are two substantial barriers to AI adoption (Shwedeh et al., 2024) (Al-Baity, 2023).

Incorporation of AI Literacy in Higher Education

The responsible use of AI literacy is being recognized as an essential skill for students and educators. However, it is not evenly incorporated into higher education curriculum resulting in varying levels of AI literacy in different institutions and countries.

AI literacy in the context of higher education curriculum has a rather heterogeneous adoption across institutions. Some universities have developed extensive AI literacy programs incorporating AI concepts, an understanding of AI ethical implications, practical applications of the data-driven technology (Hazari, 2024), whereas others have not adopted any content at all. Similarly, Francis et al. (2025) discusses the unevenness of AI literacy initiatives that result in inconsistencies in students' readiness to responsibly engage with AI technologies.

The preparedness of the educators significantly impacts the success of AI literacy implementation programs in institutions of higher learning. However, Bian et al. (2024) notes that many educators have neither the training nor the support of their institutions to introduce AI to their classes in meaningful ways. Nikolic et al. (2024) suggests that with inadequately prepared faculty, students will miss needed guidance to ensure that they safely navigate AI-run spaces, both in the technical and ethical implications involved.

The incorporation of AI literacy into higher education is also dependent on regional and institutional contexts. For instance, Wyk (2024) describes the institutions of the Global South as being subject to a set of disadvantages, including diminished access to digital hardware and exclusion from AI-focus content. Similarly, Afolabi (2024) examines how these inequities ultimately lead to unequal access to AI education, exacerbating inequities already present in education.

Disparities in Ethical Frameworks and AI Literacy

Access to AI has been improved across the region in general terms, but there are many institutions lacking the proper infrastructure, skills and regulations to fully make use of these AI technologies. Despite the UAE being at the vanguard of AI access, gaps still remain with institutional readiness due to issues around data privacy and security (Akhoirshieda et al., 2024) (Shwedeh et al., 2024). It appears the rate of AI adoption in higher education institutions has remained relatively slow, mainly due to limited access to clear technological skills programming, and general reluctance to change existing practice (Alotaibi & Alshehri, 2023) (Shahrani et al., 2023).

To balance differences, both in terms of AI literacy and as regards ethical guidelines, in the literature some strategic measures are proposed.

Atkinson-Toal and Guo (2024) stated that institutions must utilize standardized AI policy in order to create uniformity in Ethical AI. Murdan and Halkhoree (2024), noted the importance of collaboration between academics and regulators to create systemic governance frameworks that encompass important ethical decisions, such as bias, privacy, and accountability.

AI literacy programs should be thorough so that students and educators have the principles and processes to engage responsibly. Hazari (2024) pointed out the importance of curriculum that contains AI, as well as ethics, and potential deployment. Francis et al. (2025) used the phrase "positively resistance-producing," describing this type of curriculum, should thus impart the ability for critical thought as well as a path to responsible AI alternatives. Training and providing access to resources for educators are necessary for large-scale, successful responsibility in employing AI literacy. Bian et al. (2024) suggests utilizing professional development plans consisting of workshops, teacher consultations on instruction, and establishing AI concepts and ideas in courses. Nikolic et al. (2024) also suggest that professional learning should occur continually because of the ongoing development in Artificial Intelligence, and the potential ethical situations that emerge from these rapid changes.

Ojha et al. (2024) suggests using specific initiatives to close the digital divide to ensure that under-resourced institutions have a technology infrastructure and educational resources for AI. Students in developing regions who do not have specific educational opportunities to learn the technology could reflect the vast differences in their learning levels (Van Wyk, 2024).

Increasingly, the literature acknowledges the importance of developing the capacity for interdisciplinary work on the level of educational developments in AI. Merceron and Best (2024) also emphasize that this collaboration helps students understand AI from the standpoint of societal relevance, stating that technical knowledge was only one dimension of education requiring ethical and policy learning, which is also necessary.

RATIONALE FOR AN INTEGRATIVE AND SCOPING REVIEW

Exploration of Scoping and Integrative Review Methodologies in AI Literacy within Higher Education

With the emergence of AI in higher education, there is much curiosity about what AI literacy means, basically, the awareness, use and engagement with AI technology. Scoping and integrative review methodologies can provide strong pathways to map out wide-ranging research trends and synthesize research evidence across multiple studies. Furthermore, scoping and integrative review methodologies are particularly advantageous for exploring complex and multidimensional issues such as AI literacy, because they allow researchers to trace out key themes, gaps and future directions. The chapter summarizes 76 research literatures. By drawing attention to the contextualization that has been provided, this response wants to illustrate how scoping and integrative review methodologies have successfully been used to map research trends and synthesize the evidence of AI literacy in higher education.

Scoping Review Methodologies in AI Literacy Research

Naturally, the concept of AI literacy and its consequences for higher education have been widely examined in the literature. Scoping reviews, however, are limited to estimating research coverage, identifying pertinent themes and identifying gaps in the literature. There have certainly been instances of scoping reviews using AI literacy from different perspectives.

According to Laupichler et al. (2022), the study of AI literacy in higher education and adult education is still an emergent area of research. The study advocated for clearer definitions of AI literacy, and for strategies of more developed instructional materials about AI be provided to educators who do not specialize in AI. Laupichler et al. (2022) study underscored the value of scoping reviews to determine significant foundational gaps in emergent fields.

Moreover, Sperling et al. (2024) used a scoping review to examine how AI literacy was discussed to connect it to teachers' professional knowledge. Most of the findings indicated the relevance of AI literacy as a worldwide issue, yet an emergent narrative that is underreported in teacher education. By applying the three aspects of Aristotelian knowledge: episteme, techne, and phronesis, the researcher categorized the findings into theoretical, practical, and ethical domains suggesting the usefulness of a scoping review method to classify gaps in the research around AI literacy.

Pinski and Benlian (2024) completed a scoping review that intended to pull together a fragmented research landscape on AI literacy. They organized the findings into a conceptual framework, that identified learning styles, components, and impacts of AI literacy. The narrative emphasized the importance of integrated research plans for doing research that would be useful for preparing users for opportunities in AI.

Biagini (2024) indicates that the scoping review was associated with the work of tools for AI literacy assessment, specifically giving prominence to the integration of multiple components. They gathered the findings together from multiple studies that identified the growth of tools such as the AI Literacy Questionnaire and the General Attitudes towards AI Scale. Scoping reviews are particularly helpful as they can identify and assess specific assessment tools as indicated in the current scoping review.

Table 1. Key Insights from Scoping Reviews

Context	Key themes, patterns, and contradictions
(Laupichler et al., 2022)	AI literacy in higher and adult education
(Sperling et al., 2024)	AI literacy in teacher education
(Pinski & Benlian, 2024)	Comprehensive review of AI literacy
(Biagini, 2024)	Assessment tools for AI literacy

INTEGRATIVE REVIEW METHODOLOGIES IN AI LITERACY RESEARCH

Integrative reviews combine information from non-experimental studies to form a more substantive overview on AI Literacy. Integrative reviews differ from scoping reviews, in that most integrated reviews incorporate quantitative and qualitative studies so that patterns and themes can be observed in more detail and contributed to higher level synthesis. Only a handful of studies have utilized integrative review approaches to study AI literacy.

The most integrative study was Pinski and Benlian (2024), the paper summarized the literature for AI literacy for users. The study highlighted that AI literacy needed to distinguish from other technology literacies and mentioned the need for well-integrated research studies.

Van Wyk (2024) used an integrative scoping review on AI literacy in higher education in the Global South and highlighted that research in this area was limited. The study highlighted the lack of interdisciplinary knowledge and collaboration if digital exclusions, inequalities, and social injustices were to be challenged in the global south.

Zary N (2024) aimed to propose a systematic protocol for developing and validating an AI Literacy Framework (ALiF) for higher education. The study used an integrated approach combined different literature reviews, stakeholder consultations, and expert discussions on AI literacy. It suggested that integrative reviews provided the basis for definitional frameworks for practical purposes.

Table 2. Insights from Integrative Reviews

Context	Key themes, patterns, and contradictions
(Pinski & Benlian, 2024)	Comprehensive review of AI literacy
(Van Wyk, 2024)	AI literacy in the Global South
(Zary N, 2024)	Development of AI Literacy Framework (ALiF)

Key Research Trends in AI Literacy

The methodology of scoping and integrative review that was used opened several important trends regarding AI literacy research.

Many papers, such as Van Wyk (2024) and Pinski & Benlian (2024) point out how quickly AI literacy, as a new research field, has formed in such a short period of time. However, there is fragmentation in the field and integration of findings across studies is limited.

There has been growing interest in creating tools to evaluate AI literacy. For instance, Biagini (2024) and Almatrafi et al. (2024) inspect the endorsement of methods like the AILQ and GAAIS which highlight how important multidimensional approaches are measured.

Recent studies note the growing importance of an ethical and social attribute to AI literacy. Alshahrani et al. (2024) emphasized the importance of socio-technical approaches for AI literacy that ensure the balance between technology and social traits.

Emphasizing the need for regional viewpoints Van Wyk (2024) and Fu et al. (2024) note that in the Global South, where digital exclusions and social injustices stand as a threat to oppose AI literacy attempts.

RESEARCH GAPS AND FUTURE DIRECTIONS

Rana et al. (2025) indicated that interdisciplinary modes of working could enhance existing trends in doctoral and higher research education, and utilizing cross-disciplinary collaborations offers many advantages. Sperling et al. (2024) identified AI literacy is not yet a fully developed area of exploration in educator learning and the focus on educator's substantive and ethical literacy is lacking.

Zary (2024) also examined these frameworks and the need to create a standard and consistent structure to guide the establishment of AI literacy in higher education institutions. Weng et al. (2024) and Xia et al. (2024) noted that generative AI presents challenges for higher education and there is a need for new assessment methods, to counterbalance this challenge.

Scoping and integrative review methods were valuable approaches for identifying developing trends in research activity on AI literacy and integrating evidence of AI literacy practices in the higher-education context. The findings of each of these methods have indicated that research on AI literacy is an emerging area; ethical and social implications; proposed frameworks and standardization of practice; and collaborative multi-disciplinary approaches. Continued focused attention across various sectors on a developing AI literacy will be important to address identified gaps, and ensure AI literacy projects are diverse, effective, and ethically based.

Objectives

- Identify the application of AI Literacy and ethical framework in higher education.
- Identify hypercritical themes, evaluating interdisciplinary approaches and recommendations.

Ethical Considerations

There are advantages and disadvantages in using AI in higher education, and strong practical action should back up ethical frameworks. This chapter will present a minor action to support those aims, based on information from several research studies covering the years 2020 - 2025.

A proper ethical framework could focus on including backlog issues, bias, accountability, transparency, privacy, and embedding diversity as an issue. Ranade & Saravia (2024) and Archambault et al. (2024) both emphasize that bias within training data is perpetuated in the AI systems, resulting in inappropriate outcomes. Due to this, we need educators to teach responsible AI, bias detection, transparency in decision making (Van Rensburg & Van Der Westhuizen, 2024).

When considering the issues of risk related to the use of AI-driven data and pattern recognition involving student-related information data, institutions must be able to demonstrate that their data governance policies reflect both legal and ethical standards to ensure students' data is secured against misuse (Kaddouri et al., 2024). We also feel that obligations and accountability in minimizing the potential fallout of AI technologies should extend to providing remedies from harm if something unexpected happens. Again, as Archambault et al. (2024) stated, this requires well-developed and responsible governance frameworks (Van Rensburg & Van Der Westhuizen, 2024).

Higher education institutions must act swiftly to avoid leaving behind the ethical of equal access to AI and equitable educational environments. Even if AI literacy initiatives seem small considering the technical challenges, it's vital we continue a focus on equity and diversity. According to Van Wyk (2024) and Yadav (2024), the digital divide is an important issue since unequal access to AI tools could contribute to disparities in education.

Framework and Governance

The impact of AI on higher education is strongly influenced by ethical frameworks, with multiple methods being developed to address governance and ethical issues. The AI Literacy Framework (Zary, 2024) identifies ethical issues together with technological proficiency, critical thinking, and participation to apply AI as a crucial competency. This method ensures evidence of student understanding of AI's potential and wider societal implications.

In the data justice approach (Atenas et al. 2025), the emphasis was on inclusive participation within AI ecosystems, which ensured we could amplify our responses to bias within systems collaboratively, which focuses on developing and building different perspectives within the development and governance of AI systems across different societal and cultural contexts.

Furthermore, according to Al-Omari et al. (2025) and Atkinson-Toal and Guo (2024), in addition to ethical literacy, higher education institutions should improve policies and governance. Comprehensive AI strategies will enable higher education institutions to promote responsible, ethical AI usage, and also take responsibility as an institution for ethical risks, data responsibility and legal application of AI-related technology.

Curriculum Integration

A systematic and interdisciplinary approach is necessary to integrate AI literacy in higher education programs. Yu (2024) has called attention to the need for multi-disciplinary integration, while also recognizing the necessity of AI literacy that is not strictly technical. While Riapina (2023) illustrates AI's role in communication, he acknowledges AI-driven technologies that can facilitate engaging learning experiences, enhance critical thinking and creativity learning.

AI literacy approaches education as a competency-based approach, from a foundation that Zary (2024) suggests using a three-tiered framework for AI education includes three levels of education that examines technical understanding, critical examination, real world application and ethical issues. This framework guarantees students with a competent foundation in AI literacy.

Hazari (2024) and Tadimalla and Maher (2024), call for and foster the development of useful skills that build in experience-based opportunities to develop experience based practical skills such as giving prompts, and learning how to use AI tools. Knoth et al. (2024) emphasize that thorough processes for evaluation rather than just practical, provide AI literacy with better measurement. In addition, it is essential for a comprehensive evaluative matrix to measure AI literacy in a comprehensive manner that incorporates cognitive and behavioral factors that may stimulate engagement and retention of the learning experience.

Interdisciplinary Approaches

To support students in acquiring technical skills and an understanding ethical foundation, Merceron and Best (2024) recommend multidisciplinary programs that integrate AI principles and ethics framework. In addition, Merceron and Best (2024) and Ranade and Saravia (2024) stress the importance of encouraging students to critically examine AI technology and the more significant social impact.

Discrepancies in AI literacy continue to be an extremely important problem on global levels, especially in the global southern countries. Van Wyk (2024) and

Yadav (2024) emphasize that accessible modern education is necessary to address challenges like social inequality and digital exclusion. Prioritizing fair access to AI technologies should be the main objective for higher education institutions in these countries. They should also include ethical frameworks that represent various cultural and social demands, while adapting their curriculum to fit the local environment.

Table 3. Research questions that guide the review using PCC Framework by JBI.

Item	Questions
Population	How inter interdisciplinary approaches can improve students and educators in the understanding of AI?
Concept	What is AI Literacy? What are the challenges? What are the opportunities? How ethical framework can be integrated in the higher education curriculum?
Context	How its implemented in higher education?

SIGNIFICANCE OF THE STUDY

This scoping and integrative reviews serves an essential purpose of mapping key areas and highlighting gaps in research and education related to AI literacy. The grouping allows for an inclusive representation of existing literature and gives insights and frameworks for research from here on. From this point, the section describes how these methods help demonstrate the theme, and related studies.

Scoping reviews can be particularly effective for identifying the range of a research area, thematic priorities, and notable gaps in the literature. In scoping reviews, AI literacy in the context of higher education have been further developed and found, and conceptualizations, pedagogical strategies, and ethical considerations of the application AI were explored. A scoping review by Abulibdeh et al., (2025) explored the transformational opportunities and challenges associated with artificial intelligence use in higher education and evidence was found for AI impacts on teaching, enhanced productivity for administration, and improved student learning experiences. Overall, while this scoping review illustrated the implications for AI in the context of learner specific tailored learning and productivity associated with administration, it also highlighted some of the existing challenges associated with datasets, privacy, and reduction of human contact.

Similarly, Laupichler et al., (2022), completed a scoping literature review to examine the current state of AI literacy in higher education and adult education. The authors identified the need to define and operationalize AI literacy in instructor knowledge and adult learner content as necessary to prepare for a future large-scale shift towards AI.

Equally, Tibor (2024) completed scoping review pertaining to the interaction between data literacy and AI literacies, demonstrating their intersection and the integrated nature of both approaches. In a similar manner, Van Wyk (2024) conducted a scoping review regarding AI literacy in higher education in the Global South that focused on ethical considerations and the importance of inclusive frameworks. AI literacy heavily emphasizes the idea of ethical considerations and stakeholder involvement. Figaredo and Stoyanovich (2023) advocates community-based approach, in a way suggest that a stakeholder-first approach must be adopted when developing educational programs so that diverse stakeholder's needs are met, not just a focus on traditional coding initiatives. This is consistent with ethical implications discussed by Wyk (2024) and emphasizes the need for inclusive and responsible AI literacy education across communities.

Ejjami (2024) and Tomczyk et al. (2024) emphasis as how the dominance of AI can increase efficiency and accuracy, especially when dealing with large literatures. But they also highlight the importance of a human touch in vetting EDA, balancing automation with the analysis of experts. Structured approaches to AI literacy are strategically important in educational contexts, specifically K-12 and higher education. MacCallum et al. (2024) model provides a scaffolded approach to competency development and a go-to framework for findings of this review along with competency-based education programs. Together with other initiatives ED-AI lit this framework highlights the intersection between technical and ethical skill development, which are intended to educate contributors to an AI-driven society Allen and Kendeou (2023).

The scoping and integrative review methodology, combined with technological considerations and ethical implications, represent a salient methodological forum for supporting AI literacy. This method maps out the literature landscape as well as synthesize findings to formulate inclusive frameworks which address gaps and direct future research. By combining the strengths of both methods, these are guided to provide additional knowledge in the area of AI literacy in education.

Integrated Approach

The integration of both scoping and integrative review methods into this research has brought forth crucial contributions to the issue at hand.

Practical advancements in AI literacy have been explored and analyzed by scoping reviews, a new orientation in review work focusing on wider, shallow surveys to get an overview of any field that may help further studies. Combined with the deeper of integrative reviews, to obtain a bigger picture of AI literacy. Its conceptual frames; strategies, including social impacts and ethical considerations.

Scoping reviews are good at finding out research gaps in the literature. Such as the need for standardized definitions for AI literacy. Since these gaps have been identified they can be filled with integrative reviews, which are literally a collection of literature across different sources. However, this hybrid combination of scoping and integrative method is improved by guaranteeing that not only in the recommended methods that included sources was utilized, instead are attempted to interpret the inquiry contextually.

Integrating is rigor in integrating synthesis methods and systematic literature review search, this assures reliability of findings.

Case Studies

Numerous research studies support the integrated approach is appropriately used when researching AI literacy in higher education. For example, Arar et al. (2025) conducted an integrative systematic review AI in educational leadership and management that uncovered influential challenges and potential opportunities for integrating AI in the expectations for educational leaders. They suggested AI has the capacity to support decision-making and even enhance efficiencies in administration, while also pointing to ethical practice and human oversight.

For instance, a systematic review was used as an approach by Zhang et al. (2024) to investigate the concept and scope of AI literacy. They recommended it receive a collective definition so that it can be clarified or further delineated as a central part of future education systems and pedagogy frameworks. Their review discussed the status of AI literacy research, while emphasizing, the importance that AI literacy as a competency for future education systems and as a central skill.

Portalegre Polytechnic conducted research to examine AI literacy with their educators, including undergraduate and graduate faculty. Their study indicated specific areas for growth in AI literacy, alongside the need to provide AI literacy to support educators to adopt teaching and using AI in their classrooms (Lérias et al., 2024).

As AI technologies continue to develop, and as new AI technologies evolve, then continuous professional development needs to be maintained for educators. It is the expectations of institutions to engage and empower their educators to develop further through continuous training and professional development designed to support awareness of new AI applications, methodologies and pedagogies to enhance and improve the educator engagement and learning experience. This finding highlighted the role continual professional learning, continuous training, contextual and collaborative projects, and community of practice in the shared learning of AI literacy tools (Merceron & Best, 2024) (Urmenta, 2023) can play helping ensure educators and faculty reach a higher level of AI literacy.

The development of AI literacy in higher education is wholly reliant on inter-disciplinary research and collaboration in the field. Higher education institutions should encourage inter-departmental and inter-disciplinary partnerships to explore the many ways in which to implement AI in different contexts. These partnerships may yield new and innovative ways to teach, research, and manage (Murdan & Halkhoree, 2024) (Alamäki et al., 2024).

Institutions should participate in international and collaborative partnerships to share what they have learned, copyright their creations, co-design a shared a framework of possibilities for AI in higher education, while also addressing the ethical global challenge that AI presents (Mahrishi et al., 2024) (Kruger-Roux & Alberts, 2024).

Institutions should take a multidimensional approach and develop frameworks and policies that help their students and educators be equipped to navigate in an AI driven world. The importance of AI literacy, and the overarching understanding of ethical principles, coupled with global collaboration will provide higher educational institutions the opportunity to develop a philosophy around ethical AI use.

PEDAGOGICAL STRATEGIES AND POLICY IMPLEMENTATION

Curriculum Development

Collaborative learning has surfaced as a powerful pedagogical force that engages students and drives curricular and institutional decisions. Evidence has demonstrated that collaborative learning environments increase critical thinking, problem solving, and teamwork, key skills needed to help students prepare for the challanges of the 21st Century (Pu & Barnard, 2025).

Collaborative curriculum design, in higher education, has potential to support sustainable innovation and teacher learning. For instance, the connected learning communities (CLC) model adopted by the EUTOPIA alliance (a European university initiative), employs a participatory model of curriculum development. This model enhance the quality of their education a while also supporting cross disciplinary collaboration and active experimentation (Moriau & Angouri, 2023). In another case, the inclusion of collaborative learning in the curriculum has led to positive effects on teacher agency, with educators making decisions to co-design curriculum materials and enact reforms with a greater capacity and trust (Cong-Lem, 2024) (Chimbunde & Moreeng, 2024).

However, collaborative learning and teaching can be both complicated and challenging. Institutional obstacles, such as limited resources or resistance to change, can result in a lack of commitment towards collaborative activities. To help support those issues, institutions have a role to play in creating appropriate frameworks to foster environments where teamwork, affordance of professional development, and inclusiveness of stakeholders are the norm (Vreuls et all, 2023).

Impact of Curriculum Design

Experiential learning involves hands-on experiences and applications in the real-world. It has been one of the cornerstones of contemporary approaches to pedagogy. Experiential learning enhances the quality of learning, as well as the curriculum that is aligned with the expectations of the job market (the World Economic Forum, 2024). It is to see how industry-university partnerships can embed experiential learning in curriculum, as individual and team-based work with real business cases can help students curate valuable hands-on experience ("Impact and implementation of experiential learning: An industry-university partnership case study", 2025).

Work-integrated learning opportunities, including experiential learning, provide students a rich and authentic learning experience, and they have now been exhibited as effective approaches to learning in embedded and immersive block teaching environments, such as Southern Cross Model, which has replaced traditional academic semesters with shorter, more intensive blocks of learning, for higher engagement through, faster feedback cycles, and improved learning outcomes (Roche et al., 2024). Experiential and other alternative learning methods foster more student autonomy, through giving students voice and choice in ownership of their learning based on reflective practice learning and the need to be active transformers (Pu & Barnard, 2025).

While the benefits are great, the impact of experiential methods also required planning and the allocation of resources. Institutions will require investment in capacity building, monitoring, and technical systems that support the shift from multiple or diverse forms of learning and teaching to an experiential learning model (Roche et al., 2024).

Influence on Curriculum Design

Regulatory frameworks are a critical consideration for curriculum design and institutional governance. For instance, in Norway recent reforms regarding multi-annual performance agreements have helped align curriculum design with national priorities and fostered stakeholder collaboration (Elken, 2023). The Victorian Curriculum Planning and Reporting Guidelines in Australia require teams to plan curriculum delivery and apply their professional responsibilities consistently in relation to accountability (Holloway & Parcerisa, 2024).

Yet regulatory frameworks can also stifle creativity and academic freedom. In the case of compliance versus innovation, higher education institutions have expressed concern over balancing regulatory requirements with academic discretion (Rathnakar et al., 2024). Policymakers will need to consider how to create regulatory frameworks which provide sufficient flexibility and adaptability while maintaining accountability and quality (Misra & Stensaker, 2024)

Institutions Governance and Ethical Framework

Institutional reforms are steering to changes in education systems through governance changes, quality, and foster innovation. Institutional reforms are important in legitimate and soft governance instruments for sustaining reforms, such as changes through Institutes of National Importance (INIs) (Misra & Stensaker, 2024). The integrated governance model of education quality (IGMEQ) has also been used as a framework for comparisons and evaluations of governance models around the globe such as in countries like Indonesia and Finland (Savandha et al., 2024).

Institutional reforms have also enabled participatory curriculum development as shown by the EUTOPIA alliance and the CLC model through involving stakeholders as partners could help shape a more inclusive and responsive educational provisions (Moriau & Angouri, 2023). Moreover, adopting digital tools, such as the Curriculum Planning Tool (CPT) in Norway improved governance of curriculum design by having structured templates and improving collaboration among teachers (Bernotaite & Ottesen, 2023).

However, challenges to institutional reforms do exist. Cultural resistance to change, limited resources, and the professional development for educators are challenges that hinders reforms. Therefore, institutions need to focus on developing a community and a sense of shared responsibility amongst and across its stakeholders (Oliver & Hyun, 2011).

Global initiatives and regulations can be an excellent resource to formulate AI policies for higher education. Global organizations like UNESCO have provided competency frameworks that incorporate ethical awareness, and that can help develop policies for higher education institutions in accordance with the frameworks and to the local context (Mutawa & Sruthi, 2024) (Mahrishi et al., 2024).

Bias in AI systems is an important ethical issue for higher education and institutions must be sensible that the AI tools used in teaching and research must be free of bias. Practical approaches like continuous monitoring and evaluation of use of AI applications, along with providing educators and students with training on approaches to identify biases and minimize them (Urmeneta, 2023) (Murdan & Halkhoree, 2024).

Transparency in the decision-making of AI tools is another provision needed to achieve trust in AI tools. Higher education institutions needed to engage with their communities regarding transparency of the use of AI tools and how those tools will ultimately make decisions about framework and policies. There should be appropriate accountability for any adverse effects of use of AI (Oh & Sanfilippo, 2024) (Qadhi et al., 2024).

AI literacy includes not just an understanding of the AI technology, but also the ethical implications associated with its use. Institutions should incorporate such considerations into their AI literacy programs and encourage students and educators to reflect on the societal impacts and ethical considerations associated with societal impacts. This could include interdisciplinary coursework and workshops that could explore the ethical dimensions of AI (Allen & Kendeou, 2023) (Hazari, 2024).

The impact of pedagogical strategies and policy implementations on curriculum development and institutional governance have greater influence on education. Collaborative and experiential learning provide numerous advantages, including enhancing student engagement, critical thinking, and applied skill development. Regulatory frameworks and institutional change could be initiated, which are useful for supporting accountability, innovation and responsiveness, and ultimately impact student learning. Nevertheless, effective feasibility of these pedagogical strategies and policy implementations require significant planning, as well as involvement with stakeholders and attention towards collectively enhancing practice and student outcomes.

CHALLENGES AND LIMITATIONS

Although integration of scoping and integrative review methods has many advantages, it also has considerable challenges. The rapidly developing AI technologies underscore key limitation. It can be difficult to keep up with developments and the relevance.

Many of the educators are concerned about the ethical implications of AI in their teaching and their learning. They noted that, while the technology may be beneficial, it raises ethical questions such as cheating, plagiarism and loss of original student work. Educators are considering how best to educate students on the ethical use of AI tools. The lack of clear policies left some educators apprehensive the use AI. As the literature verifies, there is a relatively large absence of institutional policies, from the university level to the course level, with respect to AI in educational settings. educators felt that there was "no clear policy that explains what the limitations of AI use" in the classroom, which result in uncertainty regarding how far both instructors and students can go with these tools.

Moreover, AI-driven methods require careful ethical consideration in literature reviews since they introduce issues of bias that can affect their results and also need human intervention for oversight. Researchers must therefore take great care to ensure quality as well as relevance before including in the studies.

FUTURE DIRECTIONS

Combining scoping and integrative review methods in the study of AI literacy in higher education is an evolving area of study with a number of implications for future research. The important factor in developing promising areas of research include standardized definitions and frameworks of AI literacy which would facilitate more consistent and comparable research. Then, it is important that the ethical issues surrounding AI literacy continue to be explored, especially when considering AI-drive education and biases in AI algorithms.

Similarly, research that explores pedagogies and curriculums of AI literacy for specific learner groups, such as higher education students and adult learners. Developing curriculums and pedagogies for specific learner groups requires thorough understanding of the distinct characteristics of the group and the types of pedagogies and teaching approaches that will develop their AI literacy.

Eventually, more research investigating the implications of AI driven methodologies being used in literature reviews presents the greatest potential for the development review methodologies. Nevertheless, careful consideration to ethical issues, and recognition of the requirements of human evaluation and approval is important for validating the outcomes.

CONCLUSION

The use of scoping and integrative review methods has contributed positively to the field of AI literacy in higher education. Scoping reviews provide breadth of coverage, while integrative reviews offer depth. Converging the two review methodologies, ultimately yield a better understanding of the intricacies and transforming levels of AI literacy. These reviews identify gaps in the literature, contribute methodological integrity to the academic literature, and align their findings to policy and practice of higher education. As this continues to evolve, it is important that future research focuses on some of the challenges and weaknesses with the combined review process, whilst acknowledging alternative pathways to providing evidence of AI literacy changes for research and practice.

The reviews indicates that AI technology continues to evolve and there is a need for greater institutional support, professional development, and awareness of new tools and technology. Literature on such as peer-led training ideas and research-informed use cases will help institution address challenges they may face when trying to utilize the potential of AI. The researcher encourages educators to come together to collaborate and share best practices as they effectively integrate AI tools in teaching and administrative practices. Ultimately this chapter will make the case around the need for lifelong learning, flexibility, and preemptive assistance from higher education for the adoption of new technologies into academic practice.

REFERENCES

Abdulmunem, R. A. (2023). Artificial Intelligence in Education. In Khlaif, Z., Sanmugam, M., & Itmazi, J. (Eds.), *Comparative Research on Diversity in Virtual Learning: Eastern vs. Western Perspectives* (pp. 241–255). IGI Global Scientific Publishing., DOI: 10.4018/978-1-6684-3595-3.ch012

Abulibdeh, A., Chatti, C. B., Alkhereibi, A., & Menshawy, S. E. (2025). A Scoping review of the Strategic Integration of Artificial Intelligence in Higher Education: Transforming University Excellence Themes and Strategic Planning in the Digital Era. *European Journal of Education*, *60*(1). Advance online publication. DOI: 10.1111/ejed.12908

Afolabi, A. (2024). Ethical issues in artificial intelligence adoption in African higher education institutions in Nigeria. *African Journal of Information and Knowledge Management*, *3*(2), 22–33. DOI: 10.47604/ajikm.2735

Akhoirshieda, M. S., Khalif, K. M. N. K., & Awang, S. (2024). Artificial intelligence in the United Arab Emirates public sector: A systematic literature review. *IAES International Journal of Artificial Intelligence*, *13*(3), 2472. DOI: 10.11591/ijai.v13.i3.pp2472-2481

Al-Ammal, H., & Aljawder, M. (2021). Strategy for Artificial intelligence in Bahrain: Challenges and opportunities. In Springer eBooks (pp. 47–67). https://doi.org/DOI: 10.1007/978-981-16-0771-4_4

Al-Baity, H. H. (2023). The Artificial Intelligence Revolution in Digital Finance in Saudi Arabia: A Comprehensive Review and Proposed framework. *Sustainability*, *15*(18), 13725. DOI: 10.3390/su151813725

Al-Omari, O., Alyousef, A., Fati, S., Shannaq, F., & Omari, A. (2025). Governance and Ethical Frameworks for AI integration in Higher Education: Enhancing personalized learning and legal compliance. *Journal of Ecohumanism*, *3*(8). Advance online publication. DOI: 10.62754/joe.v3i8.5781

Alamäki, A., Nyberg, C., Kimberley, A., & Salonen, A. (2024). Artificial intelligence literacy in sustainable development: A learning experiment in higher education. *Frontiers in Education*. Advance online publication. DOI: 10.3389/feduc.2024.1343406

Allen, L. K., & Kendeou, P. (2023). ED-AI LIt: An Interdisciplinary Framework for AI Literacy in Education. *Policy Insights from the Behavioral and Brain Sciences*, *11*(1), 3–10. DOI: 10.1177/23727322231220339

Almatrafi, O., Johri, A., & Lee, H. (2024). A systematic review of AI literacy conceptualization, constructs, and implementation and assessment efforts (2019–2023). *Computers and Education Open*, *6*, 100173. DOI: 10.1016/j.caeo.2024.100173

Alotaibi, N. S., & Alshehri, A. H. (2023). Prospers and Obstacles in Using Artificial Intelligence in Saudi Arabia Higher Education Institutions—The Potential of AI-Based Learning Outcomes. *Sustainability*, *15*(13), 10723. DOI: 10.3390/su151310723

Alqasemi, S. S., Il-Agure, Z., & Dempere, J. (2023). Towards Standardized AI-Ready Data: A Proposed Framework for the UAE. https://doi.org/DOI: 10.1109/itt59889.2023.10184264

Alshahrani, B. T., Pileggi, S. F., & Karimi, F. (2024). A Social Perspective on AI in the Higher Education System: A Semisystematic literature review. *Electronics (Basel)*, *13*(8), 1572. DOI: 10.3390/electronics13081572

Arar, K., Tlili, A., Schunka, L., Salha, S., & Saiti, A. (2025). Reimagining Educational leadership and Management through Artificial Intelligence: An Integrative Systematic Review. *Leadership and Policy in Schools*, •••, 1–23. DOI: 10.1080/15700763.2025.2451982

Archambault, S. G., Ramachandran, S., Acosta, E., & Fu, S. (2024). Ethical dimensions of algorithmic literacy for college students: Case studies and cross-disciplinary connections. *Journal of Academic Librarianship*, *50*(3), 102865. DOI: 10.1016/j.acalib.2024.102865

Atenas, J., Havemann, L., & Nerantzi, C. (2025). Critical and creative pedagogies for artificial intelligence and data literacy: An epistemic data justice approach for academic practice. *Research in Learning Technology*, *32*. Advance online publication. DOI: 10.25304/rlt.v32.3296

Atkinson-Toal, A., & Guo, C. (2024). Generative Artificial Intelligence (AI) Education Policies of UK Universities. *Enhancing Teaching and Learning in Higher Education*, *2*, 70–94. DOI: 10.62512/etlhe.20

Berendt, B., Littlejohn, A., & Blakemore, M. (2020). AI in education: Learner choice and fundamental rights. *Learning, Media and Technology*, *45*(3), 312–324. DOI: 10.1080/17439884.2020.1786399

Bernotaite, S., & Ottesen, E. (2023). Entanglement of support and governance in digital curriculum instruments: The case of educational reform in Norway. *European Educational Research Journal*. Advance online publication. DOI: 10.1177/14749041231213902

Biagini, G. (2024). Assessing the assessments: Toward a multidimensional approach to AI literacy. *Medical Education*, *15*(1), 91–101. DOI: 10.36253/me-15831 PMID: 38279173

Bian, Q., Ling, X., & Yan, S. (2024). Bridging the algorithmic divide. *Education as Change*, *28*. Advance online publication. DOI: 10.25159/1947-9417/17983

Chimbunde, P., & Moreeng, B. B. (2024). The Sustainability of Curriculum Reform and Implementation Through Teacher Participation: Evidence from Social Studies Teachers. *Journal of Curriculum Studies Research*, *6*(1), 83–98. DOI: 10.46303/jcsr.2024.6

Cong-Lem, N. (2024). Teacher Agency for Change and Development in Higher Education: A Scoping Literature review. *International Journal of Educational Reform*. Advance online publication. DOI: 10.1177/10567879231224744

Crawford, K. (2022). Atlas of AI: Power, politics, and the planetary costs of artificial intelligence. *Perspectives on Science and Christian Faith*, *74*(1), 61–62. DOI: 10.56315/pscf3-22crawford

Ejjami, R. (2024). Integrative Literature Review 5.0: Leveraging AI and Emerging Technologies to redefine academic research. *International Journal for Multidisciplinary Research*, *6*(5). Advance online publication. DOI: 10.36948/ijfmr.2024.v06i05.28756

Elken, M. (2023). Collaborative design of governance instruments in higher education. *Studies in Higher Education*, *49*(6), 1095–1106. DOI: 10.1080/03075079.2023.2258905

Figaredo, D. D., & Stoyanovich, J. (2023). Responsible AI literacy: A stakeholder-first approach. *Big Data & Society*, *10*(2). Advance online publication. DOI: 10.1177/20539517231219958

Francis, N. J., Jones, S., & Smith, D. P. (2025). Generative AI in Higher Education: Balancing innovation and integrity. *British Journal of Biomedical Science*, *81*. Advance online publication. DOI: 10.3389/bjbs.2024.14048 PMID: 39850144

Fu, Y., Weng, Z., & Wang, J. (2024). Examining AI use in Educational contexts: A Scoping Meta-Review and Bibliometric analysis. *International Journal of Artificial Intelligence in Education*. Advance online publication. DOI: 10.1007/s40593-024-00442-w

Hazari, S. (2024). Justification and Roadmap for Artificial intelligence (AI) literacy courses in Higher education. ScholarWorks. https://scholarworks.waldenu.edu/jerap/vol14/iss1/7/

Holloway, J., & Parcerisa, L. (2024). Teacher collaboration: How conditions of accountability shape teachers' autonomy, responsibilities, and relationships. *Teachers and Teaching*, •••, 1–15. DOI: 10.1080/13540602.2024.2436028

Impact and implementation of experiential learning: An industry-university partnership case study. (2025). Journal of Applied Learning & Teaching, 8(1). https://doi.org/DOI: 10.37074/jalt.2025.8.1.5

Kaddouri, M., Mhamdi, K., Chniete, I., Marhraoui, M., Khaldi, M., & Jmad, S. (2024). Adopting AI in education. In Advances in educational technologies and instructional design book series (pp. 25–72). https://doi.org/DOI: 10.4018/979-8-3693-7255-5.ch002

Knoth, N., Decker, M., Laupichler, M. C., Pinski, M., Buchholtz, N., Bata, K., & Schultz, B. (2024). Developing a holistic AI literacy assessment matrix – Bridging generic, domain-specific, and ethical competencies. *Computers and Education Open*, *6*, 100177. DOI: 10.1016/j.caeo.2024.100177

Kong, S., Cheung, W. M., & Zhang, G. (2022). Evaluating artificial intelligence literacy courses for fostering conceptual learning, literacy and empowerment in university students: Refocusing to conceptual building. *Computers in Human Behavior Reports*, *7*, 100223. DOI: 10.1016/j.chbr.2022.100223

Kruger-Roux, H., & Alberts, R. (2024). Generative Artificial Intelligence Policy for academic literacy in South African Higher education. In Advances in educational technologies and instructional design book series (pp. 1–22). https://doi.org/DOI: 10.4018/979-8-3693-1054-0.ch001

Lankshear, Colin & Knobel, Michele. (2011). New literacies: Everyday practices and social learning.

Laupichler, M. C., Aster, A., Schirch, J., & Raupach, T. (2022). Artificial intelligence literacy in higher and adult education: A scoping literature review. *Computers and Education Artificial Intelligence*, *3*, 100101. DOI: 10.1016/j.caeai.2022.100101

Lérias, E., Guerra, C., & Ferreira, P. (2024). Literacy in Artificial Intelligence as a Challenge for Teaching in Higher Education: A Case Study at Portalegre Polytechnic University. *Information (Basel)*, *15*, 205.

Lim, C. P., Zhao, Y., Tondeur, J., Chai, C. S., & Tsai, C. (n.d.). Bridging the gap: Technology trends and use of technology in schools. https://eric.ed.gov/?id=EJ1016573

Long, D., & Magerko, B. (2020). What is AI literacy? *Proceedings of the 2020 CHI Conference on Human Factors in Computing Systems*, 1–16. https://doi.org/DOI: 10.1145/3313831.3376727

Long, D., Roberts, J., Magerko, B., Holstein, K. A., DiPaola, D., & Martin, F. (2023). AI Literacy: Finding Common Threads between Education, Design, Policy, and Explainability. Association for Computing Machinery, New York, NY, USA, Article 329, 1–6 https://doi.org/DOI: 10.1145/3544549.3573808

Luckin, R. & Holmes, W. (2016). Intelligence Unleashed: An argument for AI in Education.

Luckin, R., Holmes, W., Griffiths, M., & Forcier, L. B. (2021). *Intelligence unleashed: An argument for AI in education*. Pearson Education.

MacCallum, K., Parsons, D., & Mohaghegh, M. (2024). The Scaffolded AI Literacy (SAIL) Framework for education. *He Rourou, 23*. Advance online publication. DOI: 10.54474/herourou.v1i1.10835

Mahrishi, M., Abbas, A., & Siddiqui, M. K. (2024). *Global Initiatives towards Regulatory Frameworks for Artificial intelligence (AI) in Higher Education*. Digital Government Research and Practice., DOI: 10.1145/3672462

Massaro, D., & Bernstein, J. (2022). Artificial intelligence in literacy. In Elsevier eBooks (pp. 529–542). https://doi.org/DOI: 10.1016/b978-0-12-818630-5.07005-6

Merceron, K., & Best, K. (2024). Integrating Professional Perspectives for AI Literacy. In Advances in educational technologies and instructional design book series (pp. 300–315). https://doi.org/DOI: 10.4018/979-8-3693-0831-8.ch014

Misra, D., & Stensaker, B. (2024). Balancing control and legitimacy in higher education policy implementation. *Studies in Higher Education*, •••, 1–14. DOI: 10.1080/03075079.2024.2306340

Moriau, L., & Angouri, J. (2023). Participatory curriculum development: The case of EUTOPIA, a European university alliance. *Curriculum Journal, 35*(3), 337–360. DOI: 10.1002/curj.243

Murdan, A. P., & Halkhoree, R. "Integration of Artificial Intelligence for educational excellence and innovation in higher education institutions," 2024 1st International Conference on Smart Energy Systems and Artificial Intelligence (SESAI), Mauritius, 2024, pp. 1-6, doi: DOI: 10.1109/SESAI61023.2024.10599402

Mutawa, A. M., & Sruthi, S. (2024). UNESCO's AI Competency Framework. In Advances in educational technologies and instructional design book series (pp. 75–96). https://doi.org/DOI: 10.4018/979-8-3693-0884-4.ch004

Nikolic, S., Wentworth, I., Sheridan, L., Moss, S., Duursma, E., Jones, R. A., Ros, M., & Middleton, R. (2024). A systematic literature review of attitudes, intentions and behaviours of teaching academics pertaining to AI and generative AI (GenAI) in higher education: An analysis of GenAI adoption using the UTAUT framework. *Australasian Journal of Educational Technology*. Advance online publication. DOI: 10.14742/ajet.9643

Oh, S., & Sanfilippo, M. R. (2024). University Governance for Responsible AI. *Proceedings of the Association for Library and Information Science Education Annual Conference*. https://doi.org/DOI: 10.21900/j.alise.2024.1706

Ojha, B., Agrawal, A., & Arya, A. (2024). Artificial intelligence integration in higher education. In CRC Press eBooks (pp. 1–23). https://doi.org/DOI: 10.1201/9781003469315-1

Oliver, S. L., & Hyun, E. (2011). Comprehensive curriculum reform in higher Education: collaborative engagement of faculty and administrators. https://eric.ed.gov/?id=EJ1057195

Pinski, M., & Benlian, A. (2024). AI literacy for users – A comprehensive review and future research directions of learning methods, components, and effects. *Computers in Human Behavior Artificial Humans*, *2*(1), 100062. DOI: 10.1016/j.chbah.2024.100062

Pu, Y. A., & Barnard, R. (2025). Teacher and Learner Agency for Collaborative Learning. https://doi.org/DOI: 10.4324/9781032643144

Qadhi, S., Alduais, A., Chaaban, Y., & Khraisheh, M. (2024). Generative AI, Research Ethics, and Higher Education Research: Insights from a Scientometric Analysis. *Information (Basel)*, *15*(6), 325. DOI: 10.3390/info15060325

Rana, K., Aitken, S. J., & Chimoriya, R. (2025). Interdisciplinary Approaches in Doctoral and Higher Research Education: An Integrative Scoping review. *Education Sciences*, *15*(1), 72. DOI: 10.3390/educsci15010072

Ranade, N., & Saravia, M. (2024). Teaching AI Ethics in Technical and Professional Communication: A Systematic review. *IEEE Transactions on Professional Communication*, *67*(4), 422–436. DOI: 10.1109/tpc.2024.3458708

Rathnakar, G., Pachuau, L., Geetha, T., Prabhuswamy, M., & Praveenkumar, S. (2024). Practitioner Insights on Policy-Driven Shifts in College-Based Education. In Advances in educational technologies and instructional design book series (pp. 91–120). https://doi.org/DOI: 10.4018/979-8-3693-4058-5.ch005

Reiss, M. J. (2021). The use of AI in education: Practicalities and ethical considerations. *London Review of Education, 19*(1). Advance online publication. DOI: 10.14324/lre.19.1.05

Riapina, N. (2023). Teaching AI-Enabled Business Communication in Higher Education: A Practical framework. *Business and Professional Communication Quarterly, 87*(3), 511–521. DOI: 10.1177/23294906231199249

Roche, T., Wilson, E., & Goode, E. (2024). Immersive learning in a block teaching model: A case study of academic reform through principles, policies and practice. *Journal of University Teaching & Learning Practice, 21*(2). Advance online publication. DOI: 10.53761/5cmd7w70

Savandha, S. D., Azzahra, A., & Kangas, J. (2024). The Integrated Governance Model for Improving Education Quality (IGMEQ): A comparative analysis of Indonesia and Finland systems. *OPSearch American Journal of Open Research, 3*(5), 1018–1028. DOI: 10.58811/opsearch.v3i5.126

Selwyn, N. (2023). *Should robots replace teachers? AI and the future of education*. Polity Press.

Shahrani, A. A., Alhumaidan, N., AlHindawi, Z., Althobaiti, A., Aloufi, K., Almughamisi, R., & Aldalbahi, A. (2024). Readiness to embrace artificial intelligence among medical students in Saudi Arabia: A national survey. *Health Care, 12*(24), 2504. DOI: 10.3390/healthcare12242504 PMID: 39765931

Shwedeh, F., Salloum, S. A., Aburayya, A., Fatin, B., Elbadawi, M. A., Ghurabli, Z. A., & Dabbagh, T. A. (2024). AI adoption and educational sustainability in higher education in the UAE. In Studies in big data (pp. 201–229). https://doi.org/DOI: 10.1007/978-3-031-52280-2_14

Slimi, Z. (2023). The Impact of Artificial intelligence on Higher Education: An Empirical study. *European Journal of Educational Sciences, 10*(1). Advance online publication. DOI: 10.19044/ejes.v10no1a17

Sperling, K., Stenberg, C., McGrath, C., Åkerfeldt, A., Heintz, F., & Stenliden, L. (2024). In search of artificial intelligence (AI) literacy in teacher education: A scoping review. *Computers and Education Open, 6*, 100169. DOI: 10.1016/j.caeo.2024.100169

Tadimalla, S. Y., & Maher, M. L. (2024). AI Literacy for All: Adjustable interdisciplinary socio-technical curriculum. 2021 IEEE Frontiers in Education Conference (FIE), 1–9. https://doi.org/DOI: 10.1109/fie61694.2024.10893159

Tibor, K. (2024). *From data literacy to artificial intelligence literacy: background and approaches*. Deleted Journal., DOI: 10.3311/celisr.38042

Tomczyk, P., Brüggemann, P., & Vrontis, D. (2024). AI meets academia: Transforming systematic literature reviews. *EuroMed Journal of Business*. Advance online publication. DOI: 10.1108/emjb-03-2024-0055

Urmeneta, M. (2023). Reflections on the artificial intelligence transformation: responsible use and the role of institutional research and institutional effectiveness professionals. ˜the œAIR Professional File, Fall 2023. https://doi.org/DOI: 10.34315/apf1642023

Van Rensburg, Z. J., & Van Der Westhuizen, S. (2024). Ethical AI integration in academia. In Advances in educational technologies and instructional design book series (pp. 23–48). https://doi.org/DOI: 10.4018/979-8-3693-1054-0.ch002

Van Wyk, B. (2024). Exploring the philosophy and practice of AI literacy in higher education in the Global South: A scoping review. *Cybrarians Journal*, *73*, 1–21. DOI: 10.70000/cj.2024.73.601

Vreuls, J., Van Der Klink, M., Koeslag-Kreunen, M., Stoyanov, S., Boshuizen, H., & Nieuwenhuis, L. (2023). Responsive curriculum development: Which factors support breaking through institutional barriers? *Journal of Vocational Education and Training*, •••, 1–29. DOI: 10.1080/13636820.2023.2270470

Weng, X., Xia, Q., Gu, M., Rajaram, K., & Chiu, T. K. (2024). Assessment and learning outcomes for generative AI in higher education: A scoping review on current research status and trends. *Australasian Journal of Educational Technology*. Advance online publication. DOI: 10.14742/ajet.9540

Williamson, B. (2019). Datafication of education. In Routledge eBooks (pp. 212–226). https://doi.org/DOI: 10.4324/9781351252805-14

Xia, Q., Weng, X., Ouyang, F., Lin, T. J., & Chiu, T. K. (2024). A scoping review on how generative artificial intelligence transforms assessment in higher education. *International Journal of Educational Technology in Higher Education*, *21*(1). Advance online publication. DOI: 10.1186/s41239-024-00468-z

Yadav, S. (2024). Advancing education with AI-Driven education for diverse learners. In Advances in educational technologies and instructional design book series (pp. 49–80). https://doi.org/DOI: 10.4018/979-8-3693-6130-6.ch003

Yu, K. (2024). Utilizing AI in liberal arts education. *Barun Academy of History*, *20*, 221–235. DOI: 10.55793/jkhc.2024.20.221

Zary, N. (2024). AI Literacy Framework (ALiF): A Progressive Competency Development Protocol for Higher Education v1. https://doi.org/DOI: 10.17504/protocols.io.bp2l6dbpzvqe/v1

Zary, N. (2025). AI Literacy Framework (ALiF): A Comprehensive Approach to Developing AI Competencies in Educational and Healthcare Settings. *Preprints*. https://doi.org/DOI: 10.20944/preprints202503.1188.v1

Zhang, K., Li, L., & Yu, H. (2024). Analysis on concept of AI Literacy according and Future Education to the result of systematic review. *Journal of Lifestyle and SDGs Review*, *5*(1), e03293. DOI: 10.47172/2965-730x.sdgsreview.v5.n01.pe03293

Zhao, T. (2023). AI in Educational Technology. *Preprints*. https://doi.org/DOI: 10.20944/preprints202311.0106.v1

Chapter 7
A Systematic Review of ChatGPT and LLMs in English Academic Writing:
Challenges, Opportunities, and the Development of the RAISE Framework

John Philip D. Cainoy
https://orcid.org/0000-0002-6275-214X
Bahrain Polytechnic, Bahrain

ABSTRACT

This chapter presents a systematic review on the integration of ChatGPT and other Large Language Models (LLMs) in English academic writing within higher education, highlighting opportunities and challenges. It examines research on issues such as threats to academic integrity and the limitations of detection software. While LLMs can assist writing by providing linguistic support and personalized feedback, concerns remain about plagiarism and authenticity. Effective pedagogical strategies are proposed to promote AI literacy among students and faculty. To address these concerns, the chapter introduces the RAISE Framework, which emphasizes the need for clear institutional policies, transparent authorship practices, and innovative assessment methods focusing on process and critical engagement rather than solely on output. This framework aims to preserve educational rigor and authenticity in an evolving technological landscape.

DOI: 10.4018/979-8-3373-7386-7.ch007

INTRODUCTION

Artificial intelligence (AI) is fundamentally transforming higher education, driven by the rapid advancements in large language models (LLMs) such as ChatGPT. These models are revolutionizing the way students and academics approach English academic writing, offering unprecedented support in tasks ranging from brainstorming and outlining to drafting, revising, and polishing texts (Kasneci et al., 2023; Brown et al., 2022; Fu, Zou, Xie, & Cheng, 2022). By providing instant feedback, generating ideas, and assisting with language refinement, AI tools are enabling learners to overcome common writing challenges, such as writer's block or grammatical errors, while fostering greater confidence and autonomy in their academic work (Aljawarneh, 2020; García Botero et al., 2022; Zhang & Hyland, 2022). Moreover, the adaptive nature of these tools allows for personalized learning experiences, catering to individual writing styles and skill levels, which can significantly enhance writing proficiency over time (Luckin et al., 2016; Holmes et al., 2021).

However, the integration of AI into academic settings is not without significant challenges. One of the most pressing concerns is the potential erosion of academic integrity, as students may misuse AI tools to generate entire essays or bypass the critical thinking processes essential to learning (Perkins, 2023; Schwitzgebel et al., 2023). The risk of plagiarism and the difficulty in distinguishing between human- and AI-generated content further complicate the issue, raising questions about the authenticity of student work (Dillon et al., 2024; Eaton, 2023). Additionally, ethical concerns about data privacy, algorithmic bias, and the over-reliance on AI tools have sparked debates about their role in education (Selwyn, 2022; Zawacki-Richter et al., 2019). As AI continues to permeate higher education, it is imperative to strike a balance between leveraging its transformative potential and addressing its risks. This requires the development of clear guidelines, robust ethical frameworks, and pedagogical strategies to ensure AI is used responsibly and effectively in academic writing and beyond (Holmes et al., 2021; Selwyn, 2022).

Considering these developments, this systematic review provide timely and consequential insights for higher-education educators and policymakers. Significantly, it first consolidates current findings on how ChatGPT and other large language models can strengthen English academic writing, especially for students who struggle with linguistic accuracy or coherence. It next unravels the ethical and operational challenges that arise when institutions depend more heavily on AI-generated text, highlighting the immediate need for clear and comprehensive institutional policies. Finally, by evaluating current detection tools and revealing their limitations, this study identifies a crucial gap in safeguarding academic integrity. Collectively, these findings can guide policy reform, curriculum development, and faculty training, helping universities respond responsibly to the rapidly evolving landscape of AI-assisted learning.

To achieve the objectives stated above, the following research questions guide this systematic review:

1. What key challenges do ChatGPT and other Large Language Models (LLMs) present for maintaining academic integrity in English academic writing, and how do these concerns shape emerging trends in higher education research?
2. What methods and tools are available for detecting content generated by ChatGPT and other LLMs in English academic writing, and what are their limitations in enforcing academic integrity standards?
3. How can ChatGPT and other LLMs be effectively utilized to support the development of English academic writing skills while promoting AI literacy among students and faculty?
4. What guidelines, policies, and support systems should higher education institutions implement to address the pedagogical challenges posed by ChatGPT and other LLMs in English academic writing?

By investigating these questions, this study endeavors to chart a roadmap for higher education institutions, enabling them to harness the benefits of LLMs while upholding rigor and promoting ethical engagement with AI-driven text generation.

LITERATURE REVIEW

Emergence of ChatGPT and Other LLMs

Recent advancements in natural language processing (NLP) have enabled AI models like ChatGPT to generate human-like text with unprecedented fluency, coherence, and contextual understanding (Brown et al., 2022; Kasneci et al., 2023). These models are built on sophisticated neural network architectures that allows them to process and generate text by analyzing patterns in vast datasets (Su & Yang, 2022; Vaswani et al., 2017). Initially, discussions around AI in education focused on applications like automated grading systems, language tutoring, and basic feedback tools (Leslie, 2020; Adams et al., 2024; Warschauer & Grimes, 2008). However, the emergence of ChatGPT and similar large language models (LLMs) has marked a paradigm shift, demonstrating their potential to assist in nearly every stage of the academic writing process, from idea generation and structuring to drafting, revising, and even citation management (Hwang & Chen, 2023; Khalifa & Albadawy, 2024).

Another significant advantage of LLMs lies in their ability to provide immediate, personalized feedback to students. Unlike traditional grammar checkers or basic writing assistants, these tools can adapt to specific contexts, engage in human-like dialogue, and generate original content that aligns with user prompts (Dang et al., 2022; Khalifa & Albadawy, 2024). For instance, LLMs can help students refine their arguments, suggest alternative phrasing, or even simulate peer review discussions, thereby furthering deeper engagement with the writing process (Miao et al., 2024; Zhang & Hyland, 2022). Moreover, these tools have the potential to alleviate workload pressures in higher education, particularly in large courses, by offering preliminary evaluations of student drafts, assisting with reference management, or automating routine administrative tasks (Dang et al., 2022; Miao et al., 2024).

Despite these benefits, the rapid adoption of LLMs has raised significant concerns. Scholars argue that the technology is advancing faster than many institutions can develop appropriate policies, pedagogical frameworks, and ethical guidelines (Carobene et al., 2024; Perkins, 2023; Selwyn, 2021). For example, the ease with which students can generate essays or complete assignments using AI tools has sparked debates about academic integrity, the authenticity of learning, and the potential for over-reliance on technology (Eaton, 2023; Schwitzgebel et al., 2023). Additionally, there are concerns about algorithmic bias, data privacy, and the potential for LLMs to perpetuate inaccuracies or misinformation (Selwyn et al., 2021; Zawacki-Richter et al., 2019). As such, while LLMs hold immense promise for transforming academic writing and education more broadly, their integration must be approached with caution, ensuring that their use aligns with educational goals and ethical standards (Holmes et al., 2021; Selwyn, 2022).

Opportunities for English Academic Writing

For non-native English speakers, ChatGPT and other LLMs hold special promise for those seeking to publish or excel in academic courses taught in English. By providing linguistic scaffolding, that ranges from grammar suggestions to vocabulary expansion, these tools can help students build confidence and fluency (García Botero et al., 2022; Sun & Gao, 2020). Some studies also highlighted how AI-driven feedback can serve as a supplement to instructor guidance, offering students a safe space to experiment with different expressions and rhetorical strategies (Fu et al., 2022; Parmaxi & Demetriou, 2020; Shadiev & Yang, 2020). This type of personalization may be especially beneficial in large classroom settings where time constraints can limit instructors' capacity to deliver detailed, individualized writing feedback (Hoi, 2020; Hwang & Chen, 2023).

Beyond language assistance, LLMs have been deployed to streamline several stages of the writing process, including literature searches, note-taking, and initial draft generation (Kasneci et al., 2023; Khalil & Er, 2023). Some research even suggests that these AI tools can act as "brainstorming partners," facilitating the exploration of diverse viewpoints and sources (Brown et al., 2022). When integrated properly, LLMs can help students focus on critical thinking and argumentation rather than becoming overwhelmed by mechanical or organizational hurdles (Adams et al., 2024). Additionally, automated reference management has become more sophisticated, potentially reducing errors in citation formats and bibliographic entries (Dang et al., 2022). Such improvements to the writing workflow can not only increase efficiency but also free up cognitive resources for deeper engagement with course material (Dwivedi et al., 2021).

Furthermore, for those in specialized fields, such as medicine or engineering and the like, AI-generated outlines and structured prompts can serve as a valuable stepping-stone to organizing complex research questions (Malik et al., 2024; Li et al., 2024). In medical education, for example, ChatGPT has shown promise in enhancing the clarity of technical documents, which could lead to better knowledge dissemination among students, practitioners, and researchers alike (Hryciw et al., 2023). This functionality also underscores the cross-disciplinary utility of LLMs, as students from diverse academic backgrounds can benefit from automated support in formulating research questions, synthesizing data, and refining their overall writing style.

Academic Integrity and Ethical Use

Academic writing has been considerably reshaped by the advent of these AI tools like ChatGPT, with substantial support being offered but also notable risks to academic integrity being introduced. Primarily, among these risks, is the potential for students to submit AI-generated text as if it were their own, undermining the tenets of honest scholarship (Perkins, 2023; Khalil & Er, 2023). LLMs, such as GPT-4 and its other versions, produce text that can be remarkably coherent, contextually relevant, and linguistically polished, thereby blurring the line between human and machine authorship (Brown et al., 2022; Miao et al., 2024). This issue is especially challenging in multilingual settings, where students might feel compelled to produce flawless English texts, possibly skipping crucial stages of the writing process such as brainstorming, drafting, and thorough revision. (Du & Tate, 2024; Zhang & Hyland, 2023).

Moreover, recent investigations indicate that cases of AI-assisted academic misconduct are likely underreported due to limitations in current detection tools, which often fail to distinguish sophisticated AI-generated prose from student-authored text (Teixeira da Silva, 2024; Fu et al., 2022). For example, widely used systems like Turnitin have occasionally yielded false negatives when analyzing AI-created submissions (Eaton, 2023; Walters & Wilder, 2023). Such shortcomings raise fairness concerns, as students who rely heavily on AI may gain an unjust advantage over peers who adhere to more traditional writing processes (Selwyn, 2021; Khalil & Er, 2023). As LLM architectures continue to evolve, traditional detection methods are at risk of becoming obsolete, pressuring educational institutions to invest in more advanced countermeasures or even rethink their pedagogical approaches altogether (Kasneci et al., 2023; Park & Yang, 2020).

Beyond the direct problem of plagiarism, the ethical considerations surrounding AI use in academia encompass authorship transparency, the reliability of citations, and concerns about algorithmic bias (Leslie, 2020; Schwitzgebel et al., 2024). Established guidelines, such as those from the International Committee of Medical Journal Editors (ICMJE, 2024), often mandate explicit self-disclosure when AI tools are used to generate or refine text. However, critics argue that such voluntary transparency measures have limited efficacy, as dishonest users may simply choose not to reveal their AI usage (Miao et al., 2024; Malik et al., 2024). Compounding this issue, AI-driven "hallucinated" references, or the fabricated or irrelevant citations confidently presented as genuine, pose a serious threat to the credibility of scholarly work (Walters & Wilder, 2023; Teixeira da Silva, 2024).

Equally important are the broader societal and ethical dimensions of AI use. For instance, some AI models may inadvertently perpetuate cultural or linguistic biases embedded in their training data (Johnson, 2023; Leslie, 2020). Inconsistencies in institutional guidelines also hinder efforts to ensure responsible AI use; while some universities have developed comprehensive AI policies and training programs, others lag (Perkins, 2023; Selwyn, 2022). A more unified approach that integrates robust policy, transparent authorship practices, and targeted AI literacy education which would help safeguard academic standards and ethical practices across different disciplines and educational contexts (Malik et al., 2024; Rahman et al., 2023).

The ongoing quest to refine AI detection tools underscores the urgency of maintaining academic integrity in an era increasingly shaped by LLMs (Teixeira da Silva, 2024). Many current detection methods rely on spotting linguistic "fingerprints" or patterns, but as these models grow more sophisticated, the detectable markers become subtler and more elusive (Khalil & Er, 2023; Eaton, 2023). Newer systems like GPT-4, for example, have shown a remarkable capacity to emulate various writing styles, increasing the challenge for software solutions designed to flag AI-generated text (Brown et al., 2022; Kasneci et al., 2023). Consequently, institutions that heavily invest in detection-based technology risk becoming locked in a perpetual arms race with ever-evolving LLMs (Carobene et al., 2024; Selwyn, 2022).

Moreover, an overreliance on detection fails to address the underlying causes of academic misconduct, such as insufficient training in research ethics and inadequate support for students' writing development (Aljawarneh, 2020; Hosseini et al, 2023; Ugwu et al., 2024). Studies indicate that addressing these root issues through targeted instruction in academic integrity, ethics, and proper citation practices can significantly reduce instances of misconduct (Holmes et al., 2021; Ugwu et al., 2024). Ultimately, a holistic strategy that merges technological innovation with strong pedagogical and policy frameworks is essential for fostering a culture of responsible AI use (Johnson, 2023; Selwyn, 2022). This entails not only refining detection methods but also integrating AI literacy into curricula and developing clear, enforceable guidelines that emphasize learning outcomes over punitive measures (Park & Yang, 2020). The race to develop and refine AI detection tools underscores the urgency of maintaining academic integrity (Teixeira da Silva, 2024). Current solutions often hinge on identifying linguistic "fingerprints" or anomalies, but as LLMs evolve, these markers become increasingly subtle and unreliable (Khalil & Er, 2023). Institutions that invest heavily in technology-based detection may find themselves locked in an arms race, as new versions of ChatGPT or other LLMs appear with improved capabilities (Kasneci et al., 2023). Moreover, reliance on detection alone does little to address the root causes of academic misconduct like insufficient guidance, training, or ethical standards within educational environments (Aljawarneh, 2020; Ugwu et al., 2024).

Institutional Readiness and Policy Implications

Many higher education institutions are unprepared to deal with the complexities posed by LLMs (Goertzen et al., 2024). In some settings, guidelines about AI use in coursework or publication remain fragmented or ambiguous, leaving faculty and students to interpret best practices on their own (Perkins, 2023). The speed with which tools like ChatGPT were adopted has far exceeded the pace of policy reform, leaving an institutional vacuum around questions of authorship disclosure, grading, and sanctions for misuse (Carobene et al., 2024). As Selwyn (2022) explains, effective policy updates must go beyond simple prohibitions, encompassing frameworks for professional development and support systems that help educators navigate these new technological frontiers.

Amid these challenges, some educators propose redesigned assignments that emphasize process over product, including reflective journals, revision checkpoints, and oral presentations (Firth et al., 2024). These techniques make it more difficult for students to outsource the entire writing process to AI without being noticed (Hoi, 2020; Craft, 2024). Additionally, focusing on activities that encourage metacognition, such as peer review or annotated bibliographies, reinforces genuine skill development and discourages academic dishonesty (Parmaxi & Demetriou, 2020; Shadiev & Yang, 2020). In parallel, calls to embed AI literacy and ethics directly into the curriculum are growing louder (Leslie, 2020; Su & Yang, 2023). By teaching students how LLMs work and where they can fail, especially in terms of bias or generating misinformation, institutions can shift the conversation from a purely prohibitive stance to a more informed and constructive engagement with AI technologies (Adams et al., 2024; Fu et al., 2022).

Developing robust "resilient teaching" models is also integral, drawing on lessons learned from the recent COVID-19 disruptions (Blanford et al., 2022, as cited in Goertzen et al., 2024). Hybrid and flexible learning approaches can incorporate interactive sessions on ethical AI use, academic integrity workshops, and peer-led discussions on how to responsibly engage with tools like ChatGPT. This level of institutional preparedness helps ensure that while students and faculty benefit from the efficiencies of AI, they remain vigilant about potential abuses and the ethical dimensions of automated text generation (Mateus et al., 2024).

METHODS

Search Strategies

In accordance with the Preferred Reporting Items for Systematic Reviews and Meta-Analyses (PRISMA) guidelines (Moher et al., 2009), a systematic literature search was conducted on 6 January 2025. Three electronic databases (ERIC, DOAJ, and Google Scholar) were selected due to their relevance for research on English education and academic writing. The following Boolean search string was used in each database: *("ChatGPT" OR "GPT-3" OR "GPT-4" OR "Large Language Models") AND "academic writing" AND "academic integrity" AND ("plagiarism" OR "ethics")*. Articles were restricted to the English language and to those published between November 2022 and January 2025. The search terms were designed to capture key discussions on the use of ChatGPT and other large language models (LLMs) in higher education, specifically focusing on topics such as academic integrity, plagiarism, ethics, detection methods, pedagogical guidelines, policies, and support systems.

Inclusion and Exclusion Criteria

To ensure the relevance of studies considering the rapid technological advancements following ChatGPT's launch in November 2022, only articles published from November 2022 to January 2025 were considered. Any studies published outside this time window were excluded. Within this timeframe, articles were then evaluated based on topic and subject area, with inclusion limited to those that explicitly addressed our research questions (RQ1–RQ4) regarding the use of Large Language Models (LLMs) such as ChatGPT in higher education academic writing. Specifically, articles discussing detection methods, pedagogical challenges, guidelines, policies, and/or support systems were included, while studies unrelated to academic writing or LLMs were excluded. Next, in terms of study type, both empirical research (e.g., surveys, experiments, interviews, or systematic reviews containing empirical findings) and relevant non-empirical papers (e.g., policy briefs, high-quality conceptual or theoretical works, and literature reviews) were considered. The non-empirical works were only included if they provided essential context or policy recommendations pertinent to the research questions. Conversely, non-empirical studies that lacked direct relevance or did not offer meaningful insights into academic integrity and LLM usage (for example, purely theoretical discussions or opinion pieces) were excluded. Regarding the source of publication, peer-reviewed journal articles were prioritized, along with authoritative policy reports or institutional publications that met the criteria for relevance and quality. Conference proceedings, book chapters, dissertations, and other forms of gray literature were typically excluded, unless they demonstrably satisfied the relevance criteria and were deemed of high quality. Finally, because the review's scope and feasibility required that all included studies be in a language readily accessible to the reviewers, English-language articles were included, and those published in other languages were excluded.

Study Selection

A total of 3,080 records were initially identified from the three databases (3,010 from Google Scholar, 50 from ERIC, and 20 from DOAJ). After removing 340 duplicates, 2,740 unique records remained. These records were then screened at the title and abstract level, leading to the exclusion of 2,535 articles published prior to November 2022. This left 205 articles eligible for full-text review. The full texts of these 205 articles were retrieved and assessed for eligibility based on the inclusion and exclusion criteria. During this stage, 187 articles were excluded for reasons such as irrelevance to the research questions or insufficient contextual/policy relevance. Ultimately, 18 articles met all inclusion criteria and were included for detailed analysis. A PRISMA flow diagram (Figure 1) illustrates the entire process of identification, screening, eligibility, and final inclusion.

Figure 1. PRISMA flow diagram of article selection

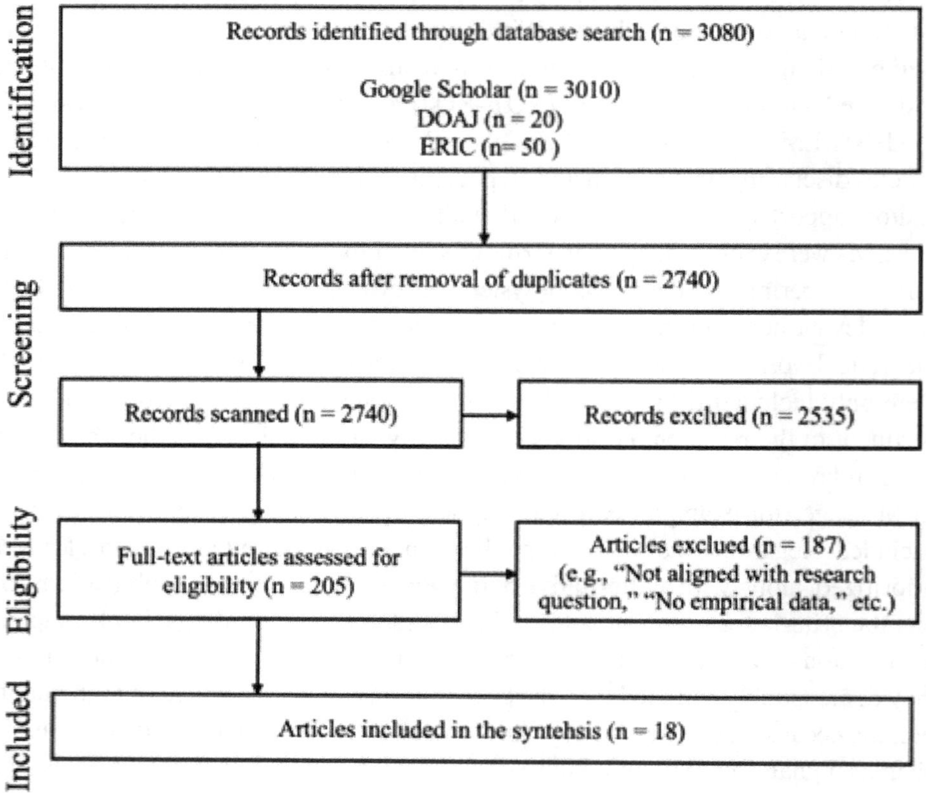

Data Extraction and Analysis

A total of 18 articles were included in the final review. Each article was examined against the four research questions, using a predefined extraction form to gather relevant information on academic integrity challenges, detection methods, pedagogical support, and institutional policies regarding ChatGPT and other Large Language Models (LLMs). The author independently performed data extraction; disagreements were resolved by discussion or, if necessary, by consulting a third reviewer. After the initial data extraction, an iterative thematic analysis was performed. Codes were first generated inductively by drawing directly from the language and topics discussed in the articles then mapped onto the four research questions. This approach allowed for both an organic emergence of themes (e.g., the significance of partial AI text usage) and a structured alignment with the study's specific aims. Through this combination of structured and flexible coding, this study captures both the breadth (e.g., the variety of AI detection methods) and depth (e.g., nuances of policy implementation) of current LLM-related research in academic writing contexts. The next section presents the synthesized findings in detail, organized by the four research questions.

RESULTS AND DISCUSSION

The rapid advancement of ChatGPT and other Large Language Models (LLMs) has generated significant discourse in higher education regarding the benefits and drawbacks of using AI to support English academic writing. Drawing from a scientific perspective, this analysis synthesizes the findings of multiple studies on the pedagogical, ethical, and policy-related implications of AI-driven language tools. The goal is to categorize and interpret the literature according to four key research questions, shedding light on the primary concerns, detection methodologies, beneficial uses, and institutional strategies for integrating ChatGPT responsibly into higher education.

RQ1. What key challenges do ChatGPT and other Large Language Models (LLMs) present for maintaining academic integrity in English academic writing, and how do these concerns shape emerging trends in higher education research?

Table 1. Challenges of LLMs in Academic Writing in English

Themes	Major Findings	Representative Studies
Heightened difficulty in maintaining academic integrity	AI-generated writing increasingly resembles human work, complicating plagiarism detection. Because LLMs advance rapidly, tools designed to catch these outputs often prove inconsistent.	Jarrah et al. (2023); Perkins (2023); Teixeira da Silva (2024)
Ethical and social dimensions	Overusing AI may diminish students' critical thinking abilities; plus, biases embedded in training datasets risk reinforcing stereotypes or biased perspectives. Maintaining academic honesty extends beyond stopping plagiarism to ensuring fair, precise writing processes.	Baskara & Mukarto (2023); Halaweh (2023)
Potential disruption of the instructor's role	There is a concern that AI could lessen the demand for language educators, yet many researchers emphasize a transformed teaching role where instructors guide learners to engage critically with AI-generated material.	Baskara & Mukarto (2023); Dillon et al. (2024); Firth et al. (2024); Malik et al. (2024); Ugwu et al., (2024)
Normalization of AI and policy shifts	Institutions are increasingly opting for fine-tuned policies rather than strict prohibitions, promoting transparent usage declarations and "AI-proof" evaluations. This signals a broader move toward redefining academic honesty frameworks in response to LLM adoption.	Craft (2024); Goertzen et al. (2024); Firth et al. (2024); Zimotti et al. (2024)

As shown in Table 1, the themes represent a consistent concern in the literature is the heightened difficulty of maintaining academic integrity in the face of increasingly sophisticated Large Language Models (LLMs) such as ChatGPT. Jarrah et al. (2023) and Perkins (2023) argue that AI-generated text can closely mimic human authorship, making plagiarism detection inherently more complicated than in traditional contexts. Although detection tools continue to evolve (e.g., AI-based plagiarism checkers), their success rate remains mixed, and the rapid pace of LLM innovation often renders them inadequate for consistent enforcement (Teixeira da Silva, 2024). Contributing to this complexity is the question of authorship: ChatGPT can generate polished prose without direct human input, leading some to question whether students truly master disciplinary writing skills when relying heavily on AI output (Baskara & Mukarto, 2023).

The ethical and social dimensions of these challenges surface prominently across the studies. Baskara & Mukarto (2023) notes that reliance on AI for writing tasks may erode critical thinking by allowing students to treat ChatGPT as an all-purpose substitute for human creativity and intellectual effort. Furthermore, Halaweh (2023) cautions that biases embedded in training data can unintentionally perpetuate stereotypes or produce content that is culturally insensitive, amplifying concerns about responsible AI deployment. In this way, academic integrity is not merely about preventing plagiarism but also about ensuring that the writing process and its content remains equitable, accurate, and aligned with educational values.

Another prominent thread is the potential for AI-driven writing tools to disrupt the role of human instructors particularly in the field of English academic writing. Although some fear that language educators and writing specialists might become less necessary (Baskara & Mukarto, 2023), others underscore the need for instructors to assume more nuanced responsibilities, such as guiding students in critical engagement with AI-generated text (Malik et al., 2024; Dillon et al., 2024). This evolving professional landscape points to an imperative for teacher training and institutional policies that clarify what constitutes legitimate AI-supported work versus academic misconduct (Firth et al., 2024; Ugwu et al., 2024).

Concurrently, multiple scholars observe a gradual normalization of AI in academic settings, where institutions are shifting away from bans toward more nuanced policies and assessment models (Craft, 2024; Goertzen et al., 2024). For instance, some universities now encourage or mandate transparent disclosure of AI usage, while others experiment with "AI-proof" assessments that integrate oral presentations, in-class writing, and project-based evaluations (Firth et al., 2024; Zimotti et al., 2024). These emerging trends suggest a future in which academic integrity policies are reimagined to account for the presence of LLMs, with an emphasis on balancing innovation in teaching methods and the preservation of authentic student learning. Ultimately, as these studies collectively demonstrate, ChatGPT's sophisticated capabilities challenge long-held definitions of authorship and originality, while simultaneously prompting academic writing pedagogy in higher education to develop and refine strategies that uphold ethical standards in this technologically dynamic era.

RQ2: What methods and tools are available for detecting content generated by ChatGPT and other LLMs in English academic writing, and what are their limitations in enforcing academic integrity standards?

Table 2. Methods and tools in LLM generated content

Themes	Major Findings	Representative Studies
Inefficiency of Current Detection Software	Conventional plagiarism-checking platforms, which rely on text matching, often fail to reliably identify subtle AI-generated language, resulting in incorrect flags or missed cases.	Perkins (2023); Goertzen et al. (2024)
"Crumb Trails" and Rapidly Evolving LLM Architectures	Markers used to spot AI outputs (e.g., unusual linguistic patterns) lose effectiveness as LLMs produce more human-like text, making older generation systems unsustainable in the face of ongoing advancements.	Teixeira da Silva (2024); Zimotti et al. (2024)
Institutional and Technical Limitations	Many universities, particularly those with fewer resources, cannot maintain or update AI-detection tools effectively, contributing to uneven enforcement and leaving educators uncertain about how best to validate student work.	Goertzen et al. (2024); Perkins (2023)
Holistic Approach Beyond Detection	Researchers recommend integrating thoughtfully designed "AI-resistant" evaluations (e.g., process-based tasks or oral exams) and building awareness of responsible AI use, rather than depending solely on detection programs to ensure academic honesty.	Dillon et al. (2024); Du & Tate (2024); Firth et al. (2024)

A growing consensus in recent scholarship indicates that existing methods to detect AI-generated text often lag the rapid advancements in Large Language Models (LLMs) as shown by the themes in Table 2. Traditional plagiarism-checking software, while effective against directly copied human-authored text, has proven inconsistent in identifying AI outputs that are both original in syntax and semantically coherent (Perkins, 2023). This discrepancy arises primarily because ChatGPT and related tools can produce language indistinguishable from that of fluent human writers, blending nuanced vocabulary, grammar, and style in ways that elude conventional detection algorithms (Goertzen et al., 2024).

Initial detection strategies rely on what Teixeira da Silva (2024) labels "crumb trails," essentially small residual markers of AI origin such as statistical irregularities in syntax or idiosyncratic patterns in phrasing. Yet as LLMs become more adept at mirroring human-written discourse, these telltale markers diminish, rendering many first-generation detection systems ineffective. Moreover, AI-driven text creation is not static; contemporary models "learn" or adapt through exposure to large datasets, frequently refining their outputs to pass human scrutiny. This evolution outpaces the development of new detection tools, which typically rely on a fixed understanding of AI-generated linguistic footprints (Zimotti et al., 2024). Consequently, even advanced systems can produce both false positives (falsely identifying human text as AI) and false negatives (overlooking AI-generated passages).

A central limitation, highlighted by Perkins (2023) and reiterated by Goertzen et al. (2024), is the reliance on older-generation plagiarism detection services that have not yet fully incorporated AI-specific features. While some updated platforms claim AI-detection capabilities, empirical validation of their accuracy remains sparse. In certain institutional contexts, especially smaller or under-resourced universities, there may be insufficient technical support or faculty training to implement these tools effectively (Goertzen et al., 2024). High rates of undetected AI content or misidentification can strain faculty-student relationships, as educators become uncertain about how best to verify genuine student work.

Acknowledging these technological shortfalls, many researchers contend that detection alone will not safeguard academic integrity. For example, Dillon et al. (2024) argue that institutions should move away from a purely "catch-and-punish" paradigm. Instead, they advocate for "AI-resistant" or "AI-proof" language assessments, such as process-based writing tasks, oral presentations, and in-class assessments, that prioritize critical thinking and interactive skill demonstrations. Du and Tate (2024) add that these alternative strategies must be paired with ongoing student education about the ethical use of AI, ensuring that learners understand both the capabilities and the academic boundaries of ChatGPT.

Such calls for a broader, more holistic approach are echoed by Firth et al. (2024), who note that detection should serve merely as one facet of a comprehensive integrity framework. This framework would integrate revised academic policies, clear guidelines on permissible AI assistance, and dedicated AI-literacy training for faculty and students. Beyond preventing misconduct, these strategies can also encourage constructive use of ChatGPT for legitimate learning activities, enabling educators to incorporate AI in ways that enrich rather than undermine scholarly development.

In summary, while the immediate focus of many institutions has been on enhancing AI-detection software, the evidence suggests that this route alone is insufficient to protect academic integrity in a rapidly evolving technological landscape. As LLMs grow more proficient and detection methods remain fragmented, a shift in both pedagogy and policy appears necessary. By rethinking assessment design, bolstering AI literacy, and establishing transparent guidelines, universities may better align their institutional practices with the realities of generative AI, thereby promoting genuine learning and minimizing integrity breaches.

RQ3. How can ChatGPT and other LLMs be effectively utilized to support the development of English academic writing skills while promoting AI literacy among students and faculty?

Table 3. Strategies in using LLMs in English academic writing

Themes	Major Findings	Representative Studies
AI as complement, not substitute	LLMs can automate routine tasks, allowing learners to invest more energy in constructing arguments and dissecting complex ideas, rather than getting bogged down by lower-level language details.	Craft (2024); Firth et al. (2024)
Benefits for L2 learners	Students who are not native speakers of English benefit from instant linguistic guidance and structured feedback, but they also risk becoming overly dependent on AI, which could undercut the development of independent writing expertise.	Dillon et al. (2024); Du & Tate (2024); Hadizadeh (2024); Li et al. (2024)
Scaffolded instructional approaches	Assignments that incorporate multiple drafting phases and a requirement to evaluate AI-produced suggestions help maintain student autonomy and ensure they still practice critical writing competencies.	Craft (2024); Firth et al. (2024)
AI literacy among faculty and students	Workshops and targeted training around LLM capabilities and ethical considerations enable both educators and learners to make responsible decisions about AI, reducing misuse or ethical lapses.	Dillon et al. (2024); Mateus et al. (2024)
Strategic implementation frameworks for AI in education	Scholars propose structured frameworks (e.g., "IDEE") that guide educators in setting specific objectives, choosing how much to automate, emphasizing ethical use, and routinely assessing the impact of AI on teaching and learning.	Su & Yang (2023)

Table 3 above presents the strategies of integrating LLMs in academic writing instruction. It shows the growing body of research in recent years explores how ChatGPT and similar Large Language Models (LLMs) can be harnessed as tools to strengthen English academic writing, particularly when integrated into well-structured pedagogical frameworks. A recurring theme across the selected literature is the emphasis on ensuring that AI serves as a complement, rather than a substitute, for core cognitive tasks such as critical thinking, argument development, and textual synthesis (Craft, 2024; Firth et al., 2024). By delegating routine functions (e.g., grammar checks, paraphrasing, formatting) to AI, students can devote more time to refining their ideas and analytical depth, thus moving beyond surface-level writing improvements.

Research strongly suggests that ChatGPT can provide benefits for non-native English speakers, offering context-specific linguistic assistance and real-time feedback that many institutions cannot furnish at scale (Dillon et al., 2024; Hadizadeh, 2024). Li et al. (2024) observe that 92% of non-native English-speaking medical students reported enhanced writing structure and clarity after using AI-assisted drafting tools, citing immediate corrective feedback as a crucial factor. Similarly, Du and Tate (2024) note that ChatGPT can help learners clarify plagiarism rules and citation practices, underscoring its potential to mitigate unintentional academic misconduct among multilingual students. However, these advantages must be balanced against the risk of overreliance, where students fail to develop independent writing strategies or critical thinking skills if too dependent on AI-generated text.

Despite the potential pitfalls, multiple authors advocate scaffolded instructional approaches to AI use in the classroom. Craft (2024), for instance, proposes lesson plans in which learners first produce an initial draft independently, then use ChatGPT to refine their text through iterative queries. Students are encouraged to critically evaluate AI suggestions, thereby practicing discernment and self-editing. Firth et al. (2024) similarly recommend that faculty introduce AI-based brainstorming activities, followed by reflective exercises that prompt students to justify or critique the AI's output. These structured approaches not only reduce the likelihood of blind acceptance of AI-generated content but also reinforce foundational writing competencies.

A central element of effective LLM integration is AI literacy: ensuring that users understand the capabilities, limitations, and ethical considerations associated with AI-driven text generation (Dillon et al., 2024; Mateus et al., 2024). Several studies highlight the necessity of faculty training, as instructors often feel anxiety regarding academic dishonesty risks but lack clarity on how to implement AI responsibly (Craft, 2024). By offering workshops or professional development courses, institutions can help educators establish clear, discipline-specific guidelines for AI-assisted writing. These guidelines may include how and when to disclose AI use, how to verify factual accuracy, and how to interpret AI suggestions critically. In parallel, student-facing tutorials or orientation modules on AI literacy can familiarize learners with basic NLP principles, typical AI biases, and the importance of ethical citations as illustrated by Su & Yang (2023) in their IDEE (Identify, Determine, Ensure, Evaluate) framework.

In summary, the consensus is that ChatGPT can significantly enhance English academic writing when introduced deliberately and supplemented with robust pedagogy. Rather than imposing bans, researchers advocate designing assessments and classroom activities that foster genuine engagement with AI-generated text while preserving rigorous standards for originality and scholarly integrity. By integrating structured prompts, transparent usage policies, and targeted AI literacy training, educators can harness ChatGPT's strengths, especially for multilingual and novice writers, without undermining the essential processes of critical thought and authentic academic writing.

RQ4. What guidelines, policies, and support systems should higher education institutions implement to address the pedagogical challenges posed by ChatGPT and other LLMs in English academic writing?

Table 4. Institutional Strategies for Managing LLM Use in English Academic Writing

Themes	Major Findings	Representative Studies
Need for robust institutional policies	Current rules do not always clarify how AI tools differ from traditional plagiarism, causing confusion. Encouraging disclosure instead of banning fosters a culture of honesty and harnesses AI's learning benefits.	Jarrah et al. (2023); Perkins (2023); Malik et al. (2024)
Ethical disclosure and transparency practices	Experts recommend policies that clearly require acknowledging AI assistance in writing, while reinforcing that the model itself cannot be listed as an author. Such openness normalizes AI usage but maintains accountability in academic work.	Hryciw et al. (2023); Jarrah et al. (2023); Ugwu et al. (2024)
Reimagining assessment models	Many institutions advocate "AI-proof" or "AI-resistant" tasks such as like live presentations, multiple draft submissions, or diaries documenting process to reduce the likelihood of AI misuse and deepen learners' analytical engagement.	Goertzen et al. (2024); Firth et al. (2024); Dillon et al. (2024)
Faculty training and ai literacy	Equipping instructors with expertise in AI's capabilities and ethical pitfalls is key to creating effective assignments and promoting proper use. Under-resourced universities often struggle to offer such training consistently.	Craft (2024); Dillon et al. (2024); Goertzen et al. (2024); Mateus et al. (2024)

In Table 4, the recurring theme throughout the review is the urgent need for clear, enforceable institutional policies and supportive frameworks that can effectively integrate Large Language Models (LLMs) like ChatGPT into academic contexts without undermining the integrity of the learning process. While earlier discussions often centered on detection and punishment, more recent scholarship underscores a holistic approach that combines explicit guidelines, innovative pedagogical models, and ongoing professional development for both faculty and students (Firth et al., 2024; Goertzen et al., 2024).

A central argument in the studies is that many universities lack well-defined regulations on AI use, creating ambiguity for both educators and students (Jarrah et al., 2023; Perkins, 2023). Often, existing policies do not distinguish between traditional forms of plagiarism and AI-assisted misconduct, resulting in inconsistent enforcement. Malik et al. (2024) note that this policy gap leads some instructors to resort to blanket bans, which, although intended to safeguard integrity, ultimately discourage productive AI usage that could benefit learner development.

With the realization that purely detection-based approaches offer limited protection against AI misuse, many researchers propose reimagining assessment strategies to reduce opportunities for undetected reliance on ChatGPT (Goertzen et al., 2024). Oral presentations, in-class writing tasks, iterative drafts, and reflective journals are repeatedly cited as examples of "AI-proof" or "AI-resistant" assignments (Firth et al., 2024; Dillon et al., 2024). By emphasizing critical thinking, personal engagement, and real-time evaluation, these methods make it more difficult for students to submit fully AI-generated work.

In tandem, some institutions are experimenting with process-based grading, wherein a student's series of revisions and intermediate steps become integral to the final assessment. Firth et al. (2024) emphasize that such approaches encourage deeper learning and self-reflection, while minimizing the incentive to rely exclusively on machine-generated outputs. Furthermore, these approaches often require that students discuss the evolution of their ideas and writing, making transparency about AI assistance a natural part of the course structure rather than an afterthought.

In parallel with policy reforms, many scholars underline the necessity of faculty development programs aimed at improving AI literacy (Mateus et al., 2024; Craft, 2024). These initiatives would equip educators with the skills to navigate LLM capabilities, limitations, and potential biases. Goertzen et al. (2024) show that instructors in under-resourced state comprehensive universities often lack institutional support to keep up with evolving AI tools. Without proper training, even the most well-crafted guidelines remain difficult to implement effectively.

Such faculty-oriented programs could cover a range of topics, including how LLMs operate, how to interpret AI outputs critically, and how to design assignments that discourage AI misuse. Mateus et al. (2024) further suggest that faculty might benefit from hands-on practice with generative AI systems, thus gaining firsthand experience with potential blind spots, factual inaccuracies, or biased content. This practical exposure can inform how instructors structure their courses, counsel students on responsible AI use, and revise grading rubrics to align with emerging realities in digital writing environments.

Several scholars propose transparency and disclosure as guiding principles for revised policy. Ugwu et al. (2024) advocate mandatory acknowledgement of AI assistance within submitted work, ensuring that both educators and peers understand the boundaries of machine-generated versus student-generated content. The emphasis here is not only on preventing dishonesty but also on clarifying the role AI plays in academic authorship. In this vein, Hryciw et al. (2023) caution that AI-generated text must not be credited as a co-author, given that LLMs lack the accountability and intellectual ownership central to scholarly responsibility.

Another overarching recommendation across studies is the adoption of ethical disclosure standards that ensure LLM usage is neither hidden nor stigmatized (Ugwu et al., 2024; Jarrah et al., 2023). Instead, disclosures become an educational tool, prompting discussions about authorship, originality, and academic honesty. By normalizing transparent AI use, institutions can shift from a punitive stance toward one that fosters critical engagement, wherein students learn to interpret and refine machine-generated language rather than passively submitting it.

Looking ahead, scholars call for continuous evaluation and adjustment of these guidelines as AI tools evolve. Malik et al. (2024) stress that policies should not remain static but adapt to ongoing innovations in LLM architectures, as improved and more human-like outputs may require fresh approaches to both oversight and pedagogy. Interdisciplinary cooperation among educators, linguists, and technology experts is frequently recommended to refine best practices and develop more unified standards across higher education (Dillon et al., 2024).

The collective message from current research is clear: establishing robust, forward-looking policies and support systems is essential to harness ChatGPT's educational potential while maintaining academic integrity. Simple bans on AI prove both impractical and counterproductive; in their place, scholars propose transparent guidelines, AI-informed assessments, and faculty training programs designed to encourage responsible usage. These measures aim not only to deter misconduct but also to cultivate a learning environment where students can benefit from LLMs in ways that uphold the values of creativity, originality, and critical inquiry.

CONCLUSION

This systematic review explores the integration of ChatGPT and other Large Language Models (LLMs) in English academic writing within higher education, illuminating both opportunities and significant challenges. Key concerns include maintaining academic integrity, as the human-like quality of AI-generated text blurs traditional definitions of authorship and plagiarism, particularly in multilingual and English for Academic Purposes (EAP) contexts. This has prompted a shift toward process-based assessments, such as in-class writing, oral tasks, and reflective activities, that promote authentic learning and resist AI misuse. Additionally, detection tools like Turnitin's AI module offer limited support due to issues such as false positives and lagging effectiveness, underscoring the need for complementary strategies centered on ethics education, proper citation, and clear institutional guidelines. At the same time, LLMs offer valuable support for students, especially those facing linguistic barriers, by providing scaffolding, personalized feedback, and assistance in early writing stages. Ultimately, effective integration, however, requires AI literacy and structured pedagogical approaches to ensure responsible use. The review also emphasizes the urgent need for comprehensive institutional policies that establish transparent guidelines, support formative assessment practices, and provide faculty training. A holistic, forward-looking response is essential to balance the pedagogical potential of AI with the preservation of academic standards and ethical integrity.

To further address the challenges outlined in RQ4, particularly regarding institutional readiness and policy coherence, this paper proposes a two-phase strategic approach. Phase 1 introduces the **RAISE Framework (Responsible AI Support for Education)** as an institution-wide development model, while Phase 2 expands on this foundation with the **RAISE+ Framework**, designed specifically to pedagogical practices in English academic writing.

Figure 2. RAISE Framework

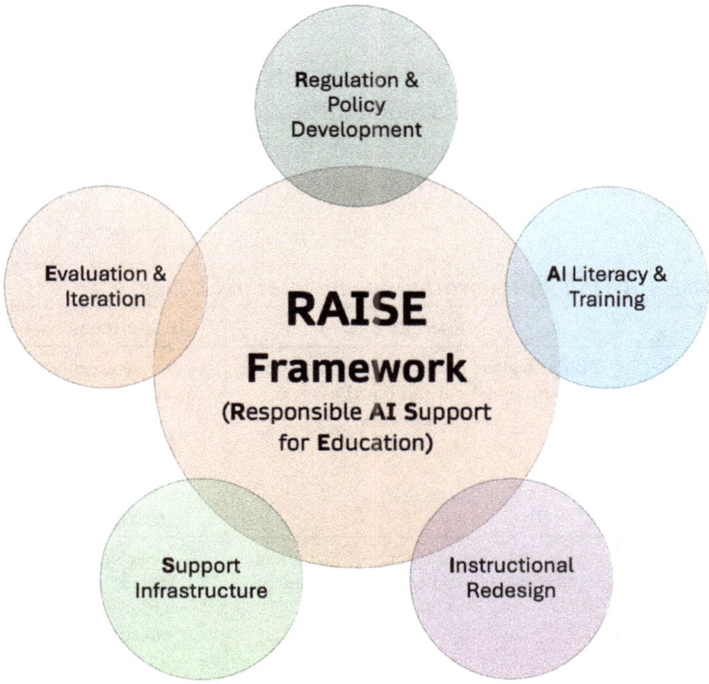

The **RAISE Framework (Responsible AI Support for Education)** offers a structured, institution-wide approach for managing the ethical and effective integration of generative AI in higher education. As Phase 1 of a two-tiered strategy, it addresses the current lack of coherent AI policies by establishing five key pillars: **Regulation, AI Literacy, Instructional Redesign, Support Infrastructure, and Evaluation**. These pillars guide institutions in defining acceptable AI use, embedding AI literacy into curricula, redesigning assessments to resist misuse, providing AI-aware support services, and continually refining practices through feedback and audits. RAISE enables institutions to move from a reactive stance to a proactive, sustainable model that embeds academic integrity, ethical awareness, and inclusive support at the structural level. This foundational phase sets the stage for pedagogical innovation in Phase 2 (RAISE+), ensuring a cohesive and future-ready response to AI in education.

RAISE FRAMEWORK AND RAISE+ FRAMEWORK IMPLEMENTATION STRATEGY

Phase 1 - RAISE Framework (Responsible AI Support for Education)

The **RAISE Framework** provides a systematic blueprint for institutional transformation, ensuring that higher education institutions can proactively and ethically respond to the integration of generative AI. As an illustration, Table 5 below presents an implementing strategy to institutions to integrate AI in higher education:

Table 5. Phase 1 RAISE Framework Implementation Strategy

Component	Description	Institutional Implementation
R – Regulation & Policy Development	Establish clear, transparent, and adaptable institutional policies on AI usage in academic work.	- Define acceptable use (e.g., AI as brainstorming tool vs. full text generation) - Include AI usage in academic honesty policies - Require AI-use disclosure statements in submissions
A – AI Literacy & Training	Equip students and faculty with critical understanding and ethical awareness of AI tools.	- Develop AI literacy modules embedded in writing courses - Offer workshops for staff on evaluating AI-influenced work - Provide tutorials on prompt engineering, bias, hallucinations
I – Instructional Redesign	Redesign assignments and assessment formats to reduce misuse and promote higher-order thinking.	- Shift toward process-based and reflective writing tasks - Use oral defenses or AI-free in-class writing as assessment checks - Emphasize metacognitive activities (e.g., AI audit logs)
S – Support Infrastructure	Create access points and mentoring systems for ethical, informed use of AI in learning.	- Writing centers offer "AI-supported writing" services - Include AI prompts and critique exercises in tutorials - Create peer mentorship models for AI-augmented learning
E – Evaluation & Iteration	Continuously evaluate the effectiveness of AI policies and teaching practices.	- Collect feedback from students and staff each semester - Use case studies to refine practices - Monitor detection tools and update guidance accordingly

The implementation strategy of RAISE ensures that institutions move beyond reactive measures, such as inconsistent AI bans or isolated detection efforts, and instead establish a forward-looking, ethical, and adaptive infrastructure. By embedding ethical AI use into institutional culture, policies, training, and assessment structures, RAISE shall enable academic communities to build clarity, confidence, and consistency in their engagement with LLMs. Fundamentally, RAISE is not just a regulatory framework, but it is also a capacity-building model. It aims to empower institutions to cultivate digital citizenship, foster interdisciplinary dialogue, and align technology with educational values. This lays the groundwork for **Phase 2**, the **RAISE+ Framework**, which translates these institutional commitments into pedagogically grounded practices for English academic writing, where concerns about originality, writing autonomy, and ethical authorship are most critical.

Phase 2 - RAISE+ Framework Implementation Strategy

Following the institutional foundation established by the RAISE Framework, **Phase 2** introduces the **RAISE+ Framework,** which is an enhanced, discipline-specific strategy for addressing the pedagogical challenges and opportunities associated with ChatGPT and other Large Language Models (LLMs) particularly in English academic writing instruction. English academic writing, specifically in ESL/EAP contexts, has been uniquely impacted by generative AI. While LLMs can support learners through brainstorming, language scaffolding, and idea organization, they also raise serious concerns about writing authenticity, authorship, and the negative impact of AI in critical thinking. RAISE+ responds to this by operationalizing institutional policy into classroom practice, ensuring ethical and pedagogically sound use of AI throughout the learning process.

The **RAISE+ Framework** implementation strategy retains the five core pillars of RAISE, but each is adapted with a writing-specific focus as illustrated in Table 6 below.

Table 6. RAISE+ Framework Implementation Strategy

Component	Enhanced Focus for Academic Writing	Pedagogical Implementation
R – Academic Writing-Specific Regulation	Clarify what constitutes acceptable AI use in writing assignments.	- Establish differentiated AI use policies for brainstorming, paraphrasing, vs. full draft generation. - Include AI disclosure rubrics in assignment guidelines. - Require acknowledgment sections detailing AI involvement.
A – AI Literacy for Writers	Equip students with the ability to use AI critically and reflectively during the writing process.	- Integrate modules on AI prompt design, evaluating AI output, and distinguishing human vs. AI voice. - Provide exercises where students critique AI-generated texts for structure, tone, and logic.
I – Instructional Redesign	Restructure writing tasks to emphasize human agency, process, and revision.	- Design assignments in scaffolded phases: AI-assisted brainstorming → human outline → first draft → peer review → reflective revision. - Use in-class and oral components to validate authentic understanding.
S – AI-Aware Writing Support	Build support systems to help students navigate AI use ethically and productively.	- Train writing tutors to coach students on responsible AI use. - Offer annotated examples of acceptable vs. inappropriate AI assistance. - Develop "AI writing consultations" in writing centers.
E – Dual-Mode Evaluation	Evaluate both written output and the student's engagement with AI.	- Use AI-reflection logs as part of grading criteria. - Include questions on AI involvement in peer review forms. - Emphasize critical reflection and revision over surface-level accuracy.

The **RAISE+ Framework** enhances English academic writing instruction by promoting ethical, transparent, and effective use of AI. It encourages students to disclose and reflect on their AI use, reinforcing ethical authorship, while preserving writing autonomy through clear boundaries on acceptable use. By guiding students to critically evaluate AI-generated content, RAISE+ fosters deeper analytical skills and understanding of academic discourse. It also supports ESL/EAP learners by using AI as a scaffold for language and idea development, strengthening both confidence and independence. Fundamentally, RAISE+ reframes AI as a pedagogical ally, not a threat. It ensures students learn with AI rather than depend on it, supporting key competencies like argumentation and rhetorical voice through guided use. Its dual-mode evaluation focuses on both writing quality and engagement with the process, reinforcing ethical awareness. When paired with Phase 1 (RAISE), which establishes institutional policy and infrastructure, RAISE+ brings those principles into classroom practice. Jointly, they form a cohesive, vertically integrated model for responsible AI integration, enabling higher education to embrace technological innovation while preserving academic integrity and educational values.

In summary, this review highlights both the opportunities and challenges of integrating ChatGPT and other LLMs into English academic writing in higher education. To move beyond reactive responses, institutions must adopt a holistic, forward-looking approach. The two-phase **RAISE and RAISE+ Frameworks** offer an integrated model aligning policy, pedagogy, and practice. By implementing clear policies, fostering AI literacy, redesigning assessments, and promoting ethical AI use, institutions can leverage AI's benefits while preserving academic integrity, originality, and critical thinking at the heart of learning.

REFERENCES

Adams, D., Chuah, K. M., & Devadason, E. (2024). From novice to navigator: Students' academic help-seeking behaviour, readiness, and perceived usefulness of ChatGPT in learning. *Education and Information Technologies*, *29*, 13617–13634. DOI: 10.1007/s10639-023-12427-8

Aljawarneh, S. A. (2020). Reviewing and exploring innovative ubiquitous learning tools in higher education. *Journal of Computing in Higher Education*, *32*(1), 57–73.

Baskara, F. R., & Mukarto, F. X. (2023). Exploring the implications of ChatGPT for language learning in higher education. *Indonesian Journal of English Language Teaching and Applied Linguistics*, *7*(2), 343–358. DOI: 10.21093/ijeltal.v7i2.1387

Blanford, J. I., Bowlick, F., Gidudu, A., Gould, M., Griffin, A. L., Kar, B., & Unwin, D. (2022). Lockdown lessons: An international conversation on resilient GI science teaching. *Journal of Geography in Higher Education*, *46*(1), 7–19. DOI: 10.1080/03098265.2021.1986687

Brown, H., Lee, K., Mireshghallah, F., Shokri, R., & Tramèr, F. (2022). What does it mean for a language model to preserve privacy? *2022 ACM Conference on Fairness, Accountability, and Transparency*, 2280–2292. https://doi.org/DOI: 10.1145/3531146.3534642

Carobene, A., Padoan, A., Cabitza, F., Banfi, G., & Plebani, M. (2024). Rising adoption of artificial intelligence in scientific publishing: Evaluating the role, risks, and ethical implications in paper drafting and review process. [CCLM]. *Clinical Chemistry and Laboratory Medicine*, *62*(5), 835–843. DOI: 10.1515/cclm-2023-1136 PMID: 38019961

Craft, B. A. (2024). When you come to a fork in the road, take it, and the future ain't what it used to be: Lessons in living with ChatGPT. *Research Issues in Contemporary Education*, *9*(2), 125–126.

Dang, H., Benharrak, K., Lehmann, F., & Buschek, D. (2022). Beyond text generation: Supporting writers with continuous automatic text summaries. In M. Agrawala & J. O. Wobbrock, (Eds.), *UIST '22: Proceedings of the 35th annual ACM symposium on user interface software and technology* (Article 98). Association for Computing Machinery. https://doi.org/DOI: 10.1145/3526113.3545672

Dillon, A., Chell, G., Al Ameri, N., Alsayed, N., Salem, Y., Turner, M., & Gallagher, K. (2024). The use of large language model tools such as ChatGPT in academic writing in English medium education postgraduate programs: A grounded theory approach. *The Journal of Educators Online*.

Du, Q., & Tate, T. (2024). ChatGPT, plagiarism, and multilingual students' learning to write. *The CATESOL Journal*, *35*(1). Advance online publication. DOI: 10.5070/B5.34831

Dwivedi, Y. K., Hughes, L., Ismagilova, E., Aarts, G., Coombs, C., Crick, T., & Williams, M. D. (2021). Artificial Intelligence (AI): Multidisciplinary perspectives on emerging challenges, opportunities, and agenda for research; practice and policy. *International Journal of Information Management*, *57*, 101994. DOI: 10.1016/j.ijinfomgt.2019.08.002

Eaton, S. E. (Ed.). (2023). *Handbook of academic integrity*. Springer Nature.

Firth, D. R., Derendinger, M., & Triche, J. (2024). Cheating better with ChatGPT: A framework for teaching students when to use ChatGPT and other generative AI bots. *Information Systems Education Journal*, *22*(3), 47–60. DOI: 10.62273/BZSU7160

Fu, Q. K., Zou, D., Xie, H., & Cheng, G. (2022). A review of AWE feedback: Types, learning outcomes, and implications. *Computer Assisted Language Learning*, *37*(1–2), 179–221. DOI: 10.1080/09588221.2022.2033787

García Botero, G., Nguyet Diep, A., García Botero, J., Zhu, C., & Questier, F. (2022). Acceptance and use of mobile-assisted language learning by higher education language teachers. *Lenguaje*, *50*(1), 66–92. DOI: 10.25100/lenguaje.v50i1.11006

Goertzen, B. J., Whitaker, B. L., Noble, D. J., Greenleaf, J., & Olsen, R. D. (2024). Are state comprehensive institutions prepared for AI? Not yet. *Teacher-Scholar: The Journal of the State Comprehensive University*, *13*(1). Advance online publication. DOI: 10.58809/CXOM8451

Hadizadeh, A. (2024). ChatGPT, the end of L2 academic writing or a blessing in disguise? *Acuity. Journal of English Language Pedagogy, Literature, and Culture*, *9*(2).

Halaweh, M. (2023). ChatGPT in education: Strategies for responsible implementation. *Contemporary Educational Technology*, *15*(2), ep421. DOI: 10.30935/cedtech/13036

Hoi, V. N. (2020). Understanding higher education learners' acceptance and use of mobile devices for language learning: A Rasch-based path modeling approach. *Computers & Education*, *146*, 103761. DOI: 10.1016/j.compedu.2019.103761

Holmes, W., Bialik, M., & Fadel, C. (2021). *Artificial Intelligence in Education: Challenges and Opportunities for Teaching and Learning*. Centre for Curriculum Redesign, 43.

Hosseini, M., Resnik, D. B., & Holmes, K. (2023). The ethics of disclosing the use of artificial intelligence tools in writing scholarly manuscripts. *Research Ethics, 19*(4), 449–465. DOI: 10.1177/17470161231180449 PMID: 39749232

Hryciw, B. N., Seely, A. J. E., & Kyeremanteng, K. (2023). Guiding principles and proposed classification system for the responsible adoption of artificial intelligence in scientific writing in medicine. *Frontiers in Artificial Intelligence*. Advance online publication. DOI: 10.3389/frai.2023.1283353 PMID: 38035200

Hwang, G. J., & Chen, N. S. (2023). Exploring the potential of generative artificial intelligence in education: Applications, challenges, and future research directions. *Journal of Educational Technology & Society*, *26*(2).

Jarrah, A. M., Wardat, Y., & Fidalgo, P. (2023). Using ChatGPT in academic writing is (not) a form of plagiarism: What does the literature say? *Online Journal of Communication and Media Technologies*, *13*(4), e202346. DOI: 10.30935/ojcmt/13572

Johnson, A. (2023). ChatGPT in schools: Here's where it's banned–And how it could potentially help students. *Forbes*.

Kasneci, E., Seßler, K., Küchemann, S., Bannert, M., Dementieva, D., Fischer, F., & Kasneci, G. (2023). ChatGPT for good? On opportunities and challenges of large language models for education. *Learning and Individual Differences*, *103*, 102274. DOI: 10.1016/j.lindif.2023.102274

Khalifa, M., & Albadawy, M. (2024). Using artificial intelligence in academic writing and research: An essential productivity tool. *Computer Methods and Programs in Biomedicine Update*, *100145*. Advance online publication. DOI: 10.1016/j.cmpbup.2024.100145

Khalil, M., & Er, E. (2023). Will ChatGPT Get You Caught? Rethinking of Plagiarism Detection. In Zaphiris, P., & Ioannou, A. (Eds.), Lecture Notes in Computer Science: Vol. 14040. *Learning and Collaboration Technologies. HCII 2023*. Springer., DOI: 10.1007/978-3-031-34411-4_32

Leslie, D. (2020). Tackling COVID-19 Through Responsible AI Innovation: Five Steps in the Right Direction. *Harvard Data Science Review*, (Special Issue 1). https://doi.org/DOI: 10.1162/99608f92.4bb9d7a7

Li, J., Zong, H., Wu, E., Wu, R., Peng, Z., Zhao, J., Yang, L., Xie, H., & Shen, B. (2024). Exploring the potential of artificial intelligence to enhance the writing of English academic papers by non-native English-speaking medical students: The educational application of ChatGPT. *BMC Medical Education*, *24*(736). Advance online publication. DOI: 10.1186/s12909-024-05738-y PMID: 38982429

Luckin, R., Holmes, W., Griffiths, M., & Forcier, L. B. (2016). *Intelligence unleashed: An argument for AI in education*. Pearson.

Malik, M. A., Amjad, A. I., Aslam, S., & Fakhrou, A. (2024). Global insights: ChatGPT's influence on academic and research writing, creativity, and plagiarism policies. *Frontiers in Research Metrics and Analytics*, *9*, 1486832. DOI: 10.3389/frma.2024.1486832 PMID: 39583913

Mateus, J.C., Lugo, N., Cappello, G., & Guerrero-Pico, M. (2024). Communication educators facing the arrival of generative artificial intelligence: Exploration in Mexico, Peru, and Spain. *Digital Education Review*. https://doi.org/DOI: 10.1344/der.2024.45.106-114

Miao, J., Thongprayoon, C., Suppadungsuk, S., Garcia Valencia, O. A., Qureshi, F., & Cheungpasitporn, W. (2024). Ethical Dilemmas in Using AI for Academic Writing and an Example Framework for Peer Review in Nephrology Academia: A Narrative Review. *Clinics and Practice*, *14*(1), 89–105. DOI: 10.3390/clinpract14010008 PMID: 38248432

Moher, D., Liberati, A., Tetzlaff, J., & Altman, D. G.PRISMA Group. (2009). Preferred reporting items for systematic reviews and meta-analyses: The PRISMA statement. *PLoS Medicine*, *6*(7), e1000097. DOI: 10.1371/journal.pmed.1000097 PMID: 19621072

Park, J.-H., & Yang, I. Y. (2020). Utilizing an AI-Based Grammar Checker in an EFL Writing Classroom. *Academic Journal of Applied Linguistics*, *36*(1), 97–120. DOI: 10.17154/kjal.2020.3.36.1.97

Parmaxi, A., & Demetriou, A. A. (2020). Augmented reality in language learning: A state-of-the-art review of 2014–2019. *Journal of Computer Assisted Learning*, *36*(6), 861–875. DOI: 10.1111/jcal.12486

Perkins, M. (2023). Academic integrity considerations of AI large language models in the post-pandemic era: ChatGPT and beyond. *Journal of University Teaching [3] & Learning Practice, 20*(2). https://doi.org/DOI: 10.53761/1.20.02.07

Rahman, M., Terano, H. J. R., Rahman, N., Salamzadeh, A., & Rahaman, S. (2023). ChatGPT and academic research: A review and recommendations based on practical examples. *Journal of Education. Management and Development Studies*, *3*(1), 1–12. DOI: 10.52631/jemds.v3i1.175

Schwitzgebel, E., Schwitzgebel, D., & Strasser, A. (2024). Creating a large language model of a philosopher. *Mind & Language*, *39*(2), 237–259. DOI: 10.1111/mila.12466

Selwyn, N. (2022). The future of AI and education: Some cautionary notes. *European Journal of Education*, *57*(4), 620–631. DOI: 10.1111/ejed.12532

Selwyn, N., Hillman, T., Bergviken Rensfeldt, A., & Perrotta, C. (2021). Digital technologies and the automation of education—key questions and concerns. *Postdigital Science and Education*, 1-10. https://doi.org/DOI: 10.1007/s42438-021-00263-3

Shadiev, R., & Yang, M. (2020). Review of studies on technology-enhanced language learning and teaching. *Sustainability*, *12*(2), 524. DOI: 10.3390/su12020524

Su, J., & Yang, W. (2023). Unlocking the power of ChatGPT: A framework for applying generative AI in education. *ECNU Review of Education*, *6*(3), 355–366. DOI: 10.1177/20965311231168423

Sun, Y., & Gao, F. (2020). An investigation of the influence of intrinsic motivation on students' intention to use mobile devices in language learning. *Educational Technology Research and Development*, *68*, 1181–1198. DOI: 10.1007/s11423-019-09733-9

Teixeira da Silva, J. A. (2024). The detection of ChatGPT's textual crumb trails is an unsustainable solution to imperfect detection methods. *Open Information Science*, *8*, 202. DOI: 10.1515/opis-2024-0007

Ugwu, N. F., Igbinlade, A. S., Ochiaka, R. E., Ezeani, U. D., Okorie, N. C., Opele, J. K., Onayinka, T. S., Iroegbu, O., Onyekwere, O. K., Adams, A. B., Aigbona, P., & Ojobola, F. B. (2024). Clarifying ethical dilemmas of using artificial intelligence in research writing: A rapid review. *Higher Learning Research Communications*, *14*(2), 29–47.

Vaswani, A., Shazeer, N., Parmar, N., Uszkoreit, J., Jones, L., Gomez, A. N., Kaiser, Ł., & Polosukhin, I. (2017). Attention is all you need. In *Advances in Neural Information Processing Systems* (Vol. 30, pp. 5998–6008).

Walters, W. H., & Wilder, E. I. (2023). Fabrication and errors in the bibliographic citations generated by ChatGPT. *Scientific Reports*, *13*, 14045. DOI: 10.1038/s41598-023-41032-5 PMID: 37679503

Warschauer, M., & Grimes, D. (2008). Automated Writing Assessment in the Classroom. *Pedagogies*, *3*(1), 22–36. DOI: 10.1080/15544800701771580

Zawacki-Richter, O., Marín, V. I., Bond, M., & Gouverneur, F. (2019). Systematic review of research on artificial intelligence applications in higher education–where are the educators? *International Journal of Educational Technology in Higher Education*, *16*, 39. Advance online publication. DOI: 10.1186/s41239-019-0171-0

Zhang, Z. (V.), & Hyland, K. (2022). Fostering student engagement with feedback: An integrated approach. *Assessing Writing*, *51*, 100586. DOI: 10.1016/j.asw.2021.100586

Zhang, Z. (V.), & Hyland, K. (2023). Student engagement with peer feedback in L2 writing: Insights from reflective journaling and revising practices. *Assessing Writing*, *58*, 100784. DOI: 10.1016/j.asw.2023.100784

Zimotti, G., Frances, C., & Whitaker, L. (2024). The future of language education: Teachers' perceptions about the surge of large language models like ChatGPT. *Technology in Language Teaching & Learning*, *6*(2), 1–24.

Chapter 8
Beyond AI Dependence:
Pedagogical Approaches to Strengthen Student Reasoning and Analytical Skills

Sabina Ashfaque Shaikh
https://orcid.org/0009-0008-1113-5636
KHMW College, India

Abid Hussain Jagirdar
KHMW College, India

ABSTRACT

With the rapid integration of artificial intelligence (AI) into education, this study explores the dual impact of AI tools on enhancing learning while potentially impeding the development of fundamental cognitive skills. It focuses on intentional pedagogical methods like inquiry-based learning, Socratic questioning, problem-based learning, and meta-cognitive training, which are designed to foster reasoning and critical thinking, and discourage over-reliance on AI. By employing qualitative and quantitative analyses, the research identifies best practices for leveraging AI to enhance educational outcomes while simultaneously nurturing essential cognitive abilities. Results highlight the effectiveness of integrating reflective thinking into open-ended problem-solving and human-centered discussions, thus promoting critical engagement beyond AI-generated responses. This study emphasizes the pivotal role of educators in cultivating student agency and intellectual courage in an AI-rich educational landscape, preparing them for future challenges.

DOI: 10.4018/979-8-3373-7386-7.ch008

INTRODUCTION

The rapid expansion of artificial intelligence (AI) has significantly transformed education worldwide. AI tutors, algorithmically derived tests, and adaptive learning technology are just a few of the ways technology is permeating up into teaching and learning. While these tools are efficient and personalized, an important pedagogical issue has to be tackled: These learners may end up losing those basic cognitive abilities such as independent problem solving, reasoning, and analysis. So there's a growing fear that students' capacity to think deeply, critically, and in original ways is at an increasing risk, reflectively, and critically may be eroding as they depend more on AI-generated answers for academic work.

teachers now stand at a critical juncture in the face of this dilemma. On one hand, AI can be a potent tool for improving comprehension and accessibility; on the other, it may unintentionally promote superficial learning and intellectual passivity. Recent educational studies underscore that the development of higher-order thinking abilities is crucial for students to succeed in both academic and real-world contexts. However, practical methods for striking a balance between the application of AI and teaching strategies that emphasize cognitive growth are still lacking.

This research aims to fill that gap by examining purposeful teaching strategies—such as inquiry-based learning, Socratic questioning, problem-based learning, and metacognitive training—that effectively foster reasoning, critical thinking, and student autonomy. The study explores how these methods can be integrated with AI-enhanced learning to facilitate comprehensive intellectual development. The objective is to propose a sustainable educational framework that mitigates excessive reliance on AI while equipping learners with the analytical skills essential for success in a technology-oriented future.

LITERATURE REVIEW

The rapid rise of AI in education has excited people about its benefits while also raising alarm about its downsides. International recommendations underscore a people-first AI in education: for instance, UNESCO (2023) highlights the need to foster critical thinking and ethical concerns, responsible use of AI in the classroom. In the current discussion, researchers and educators are more frequently focusing on the effect of AI on student cognition. Computer control and the displacement of a human-problemsolving process 'One of the copilot's main problem-solving tasks was to monitor course deviations due to malfunctions of the attitude indicator. Excessive reliance on AI dialogue systems can be harmful to students' critical and analytical thinking because it reinforces their sloppiness Zhai, Wibowo, & Li

(2024) (Systematic review). In the same line, Duhaylungsod and Chavez (2023) suggest that over-dependency on AI tools could lead to cognitive offloading as students become accustomed to relying on the AI to do the cognitive work for them. This dependence destroys vital skills such as creativity, problem-solving and decision-making through limited independent analytical thinking by students. Some teachers have even cautioned that, when AI tools do too much for students, it robs students of their motivation to think critically for themselves, which may result in "cognitive laziness" and a mere surface-level of knowledge of the material (Duhaylungsod & Chavez, 2023). On the contrary, those in favor of equitable AI use plead for balance in use of AI: when designed meaningfully, AI-enabled apps can tailor learning experiences and provide instant corrective input and thereby may allow teachers more time for high cognitive demands of learners (Hakiki et al., 2023). The answer, as the research suggests, is to use AI to help with the learning process, not to take the learning away from students' brains.

Amid the backdrop of AI's double-edged influence, academics have urged for the sustained value of pedagogic practices designed to forge critical thinking. Long before the emergence of AI, educators such as Dewey (1933) emphasized the importance of reflective thinking in deep learning, and Paul and Elder (2008) articulated models of critical thinking that are very relevant today. These old accounts confirm critical thinking and critical thought are skills that need to be instructed, modeled, and practiced. But as technology advances, the basic processes of reasoning — questioning all assumptions, doubting all evidence, and driving to conclusions based on solid evidence, all in a controlled process, cannot be automated. Socio-constructivist theory (Vygotsky, 1978) also highlights the importance of social interaction and scaffolding for cognitive development. In the AI world that means that teacher and peer dialog, mentorship, and feedback are necessary for students to learn to internalize critical thinking rather than being beholden to machine output.

Teachers have a variety of tried-and-true techniques-research-supported practices to promote this kind of engagement. The pedagogical strategies as listed below are these days well known to help students in developing reasoning and analytical skills:

- **Questioning/Investigation-Based Learning**: Involves the setting of questions for students to explore problems and draw conclusions independently through independent investigation. This method values curiosity and is directed toward the construction and testing of ideas made up by learners themselves—the method Dewey extolled as learning through active inquiry.
- **Socratic Dialogue**: Conversation directed by reflective questions. When they question, question, question, question, they also prompt their students to reflect and look into themselves during the process. This classic technique fos-

ters in-depth critical thinking that requires students to think their answers through.

- **Problem-Based Learning (PBL)**: Focused on complex, real-world problems that students need to work together to solve. Through collaborative problem solving with real-world issues, students construct their problem-solving skills and use them in context. PBL environments are designed to be analogous to real-world environments which in turn enhances analytic and transfer skills.
- **Metacognitive Training**: The goal of this approach is to help students to monitor and manage their thinking. When students understand the ways they do things – planning, monitoring comprehension, evaluating solutions, and so on – they develop what William and Flavell (1979) call metacognition – or the ability to regulate one's thinking in the service of solving problems. Metacognitive activities provide a framework for the development of the skills and strategies essential for developing the practice of thinking about thinking that is so important for independent learning in all settings.

Pages Active student response such as predicting and explaining offers a way to "inoculate" against passive learning that could be created through uncritical use of AI. Indeed, evidence in research suggests the need to course-correct to these human-centered pedagogies is paramount. Zawacki-Richter et al. (2019) also pointed out that much of the literature on AI in higher education has neglected the educator's role to focus mainly on technology while side-lining pedagogy. This demonstrates an obvious requirement to delve into how teachers can successfully adopt AI and at the same time utilize practices that are conducive to learning in depth. By interweaving the possibilities AI affords with the successful teaching practices already in place, faculties might be able to leverage the strengths of AI (efficiency, adaptability, data repository) without losing the development of skills needed for critical thought and ability to analyze and discern in students. Hence it is from this premise that this research works on the hypothesis that the answer is not to eliminate AI from education, but rather to contextualize it inside a pedagogical process that requires students to continue thinking on their own.

METHODOLOGY

This research employs an explanatory sequential design by integrating a survey and a focus group interview to analyze learners' perceptions of AI in relation to instructional strategies aimed at fostering critical thinking skills. The purpose of the study is to explore the main patterns of cognitive skill development vis-a-vis AI usage within a heterogeneous student cohort, as well as understanding which teaching strategies are most useful for preserving students' reasoning skills as per their self-assessment. The methodology has these elements along with the logical steps that provide rigor and transparency such as: defining and justifying the sample, creating the instrument, testing its reliability and applying statistical and qualitative analysis.

Sample and Participants: A total of 320 undergraduate students participated in the study. To assess the adequacy of this sample size, Cochran's formula for large populations was applied:

$n0= e2Z2 \times p \times q,$

where $Z = 1.96$ (for a 95% confidence level), $p = 0.5$ (assumed population proportion yielding maximum variance), $q = 1 - p = 0.5$, and $e = 0.05$ (margin of error). Substituting these values:

$n0= 0.052(1.962 \times 0.5 \times 0.5)= 0.00253.8416 \times 0.25= 0.00250.9604= 384.16.$

While the optimal calculated sample size is ~384 respondents, the achieved sample of 320 is reasonably close. Given practical constraints, 320 students still provides acceptable statistical power for detecting meaningful patterns in survey responses. In the context of Likert-scale educational research, a sample of this size is sufficient to yield reliable descriptive and correlational insights.

Instruments and Data Collection: The study used a structured questionnaire with two sections: (a) a Likert-Scale Survey with nine statements to assess students' opinions about their use of AI and their educational experiences (see Appendix A); and (b) Open-Ended Questions with five prompts to collect individual opinions on the effects of both AI-based and non-AI learning strategies (see Appendix B). The Likert statements were rated on a 5-point scale from 1 ("Strongly Disagree") to 5 ("Strongly Agree"), allowing quantification of attitudes such as AI reliance, perceived changes in critical thinking, and the effectiveness of teaching methods. Students were able to articulate in their own words how AI has affected their learning and which teaching strategies they believe have been most helpful for growing because the open-ended questions encouraged qualitative elaboration.

Two faculty experts examined the survey instrument before it was fully deployed to make sure the items were clear and had valid content. On the basis of this feedback, minor phrasing changes were made. Respondents gave their informed consent, and participation in the survey was anonymous and voluntary. In order to promote truthful responses, data were gathered both online and in-class with confidentiality guarantees.

Table 1. Reliability Statistics item-wise descriptive statistics used in the reliability test

Item	Mean	Standard Deviation	Min	Max
I rely on AI tools...	3.1	1.47	1	5
Using AI-based tools has reduced critical thinking...	3.09	1.47	1	5
My instructors use activities...	3.01	1.34	1	5
Pedagogical methods improve analytical thinking...	3.1	1.44	1	5
I feel confident analyzing problems...	3.07	1.62	1	5
My institution encourages integrity...	2.94	1.44	1	5
Collaborative projects help reasoning...	3.33	1.34	1	5
I am aware of AI limitations...	2.66	1.06	1	5
Faculty assess reasoning...	2.88	1.11	1	5

The majority of responses fall within the range of 3.0 to 3.3, indicating a moderate level of agreement. Item 7, which pertains to Collaborative Learning, is notably regarded as the most positively viewed.

Conversely, Items 8 and 9 received the lowest scores, highlighting possible deficiencies in AI literacy and faculty evaluation methods.

The findings suggest opportunities for enhancing awareness of AI ethics and fostering more meaningful interactions between instructors and students.

Reliability and Validity: Cronbach's alpha was computed to make sure the Likert-scale items were internally consistent. The overall value was $\alpha = 0.75$, indicating acceptable reliability for the aggregated scale. This implies that an underlying construct pertaining to AI usage and learning attitudes is logically measured by the survey items. The questionnaire's alignment with themes found in the body of existing literature further supported construct validity (e.g., measuring both AI reliance and engagement in active learning). To ensure they adequately captured qualitative nuances outside the purview of the Likert items, the open-ended questions were examined.

Data Analysis: Descriptive statistics and correlation analysis were used to examine the quantitative data from the Likert-scale section. To comprehend central tendencies and variability in student responses, the mean and standard deviation were calculated for every survey item. In particular, we looked at correlations between students' self-reported reliance on AI, their perceptions of their instructors' emphasis on reasoning skills, their confidence in solving problems without AI, and their perceptions of the reduction in their own critical thinking caused by AI. To do this, a Pearson correlation matrix was created. These correlations aid in determining whether our sample's high usage of AI is linked to other attitudinal factors or lower confidence.

For the qualitative data very open-ended question's response was thematically analyzed for the qualitative data. An inductive coding approach was used for the analysis. First, the complete student responses were read, and preliminary codes (such as "AI saves time," "prefer class discussion," and "fear of over-reliance") were recorded. Subsequently, related codes were categorized into more general themes. To determine inter-coder reliability, two researchers coded a subset of responses separately. They discussed any differences to improve the coding scheme. Following a review and definition of the main themes that surfaced, representative quotes were chosen to highlight each theme; these are compiled in the Results section. The patterns found in the quantitative data were explained and given rich context by this qualitative component. Results and Discussion

QUANTITATIVE FINDINGS

Table 2. Descriptive Statistics of Survey Items (N = 320).

Survey Item	Mean	Std. Dev.	Min	Max
I rely on AI tools (e.g., ChatGPT, Grammarly, etc.) for completing academic tasks.	3.10	1.47	1	5
Using AI-based tools has reduced the amount of critical thinking I apply to my assignments.	3.09	1.47	1	5
My instructors use activities that help me build reasoning and analytical skills without AI assistance.	3.01	1.34	1	5
Pedagogical methods like debates, case discussions, and problem-solving tasks improve my analytical thinking.	3.10	1.44	1	5
I feel confident analyzing problems independently before referring to AI tools.	3.07	1.62	1	5
My institution encourages academic integrity and discourages over-dependence on AI.	2.94	1.44	1	5
Collaborative projects and peer discussions help me develop stronger reasoning skills than working alone with AI.	3.33	1.34	1	5
I am aware of the limitations and ethical concerns of using AI in academics.	2.66	1.06	1	4
Faculty members assess reasoning and analytical thinking rather than just final answers.	2.88	1.11	1	4

Student responses to the nine survey items varied, as Table 2 illustrates, with the majority of averages centered around 3.0, suggesting a generally moderate position between "Neutral" and "Agree." The item with the highest rating, "Collaborative projects and peer discussions help me develop stronger reasoning skills than working alone with AI" (mean = 3.33), indicated that students strongly supported the idea that peer interaction can improve reasoning. "I am aware of the limitations and ethical concerns of using AI in academics" received the lowest rating (mean = 2.66), suggesting a potential lack of AI literacy. Additionally, "Faculty members assess reasoning and analytical thinking rather than just final answers" received a low score (mean = 2.88), suggesting that assessments should place a greater emphasis on process than results.

Both "I rely on AI tools for completing academic tasks" and "Using AI-based tools has reduced my critical thinking" had average scores of 3.1 when it came to AI use. These scores reflect a moderate use of AI and a mild acknowledgment of its potential impact on cognitive effort. Students appear to recognize AI's utility while remaining somewhat cautious about overdependence. The statement "I feel confident analyzing problems independently before referring to AI tools" had a mean of 3.07 with a high standard deviation, suggesting mixed levels of self-confidence and highlighting the need to strengthen independent problem-solving skills.

In conclusion, the quantitative results show that although students use AI to a moderate extent, they still value and require human-centered learning opportunities. While students are embracing AI to some degree, they also value more conventional pedagogical components like teamwork, teacher guidance, and academic integrity, according to the majority of responses, which clustered close to the mid to "Agree" range. The descriptive statistics set the stage for further analysis by confirming that AI is present in students' academic lives, but not to the exclusion of all else. Students appear to have a balanced perspective: they recognize the value of AI (as evidenced by its use), but they also recognize the need for real engagement and are not entirely sure that AI can help them advance their skills. These complex mindsets. These nuanced attitudes are further explored through correlation analysis below, which examines how these perceptions interrelate.

Selected survey items were subjected to a Pearson correlation analysis in order to examine the relationships between important variables. Four variables of interest were selected from the Likert scale: Faculty Assess (perception that faculty evaluate reasoning ability rather than just answers), Reduced Thinking (perception that using AI has reduced one's critical thinking in assignments), Problem Confidence (perception of confidence in solving problems independently before using AI), and AI Reliance (frequency of using AI tools for tasks). The correlation matrix for these variables, along with Pearson's coefficients, is shown in Table 3.

Table 3. Pearson Correlation Matrix (Selected Variables).

Variable	AI Reliance	Reduced Thinking	Problem Confidence	Faculty Assess
AI Reliance	1.00	–0.01	–0.05	+0.05
Reduced Thinking	–0.01	1.00	–0.02	–0.06
Problem Confidence	–0.05	–0.02	1.00	+0.03
Faculty_Assess	+0.05	–0.06	+0.03	1.00

In the table, a positive correlation coefficient indicates that as one variable increases, the other tends to increase, whereas a negative coefficient indicates an inverse relationship. The values in Table 3 are all very close to zero, ranging from –0.06 to +0.05, which suggests extremely weak relationships among these variables. Not a single correlation is statistically significant at conventional levels (typically $p < 0.05$) given how low these r values are. In practical terms, the analysis found **no strong linear association** between students' use of AI and their self-reported confidence or perceptions of reduced thinking.

Examining individual pairs, the correlation between Reduced Thinking and AI Reliance is -0.01, or nearly zero. This suggests that students in this sample who use AI more often are neither more nor less likely to believe that AI has caused a decline in their critical thinking skills. In other words, according to students' own assessments, a high level of AI use did not correlate with a greater sense of "mental offloading" or laziness. AI Reliance and Problem Confidence have a very weak negative correlation (r = -0.05). This may indicate that students who use AI extensively are less confident in their ability to solve problems independently (possibly due to their habit of relying on AI assistance). But since the impact is so minimal, However, the effect is so small that we must be cautious; it is essentially a negligible link. Conversely, **AI Reliance** vs. **Faculty Assess** shows a tiny positive correlation ($r = +0.05$). This suggests that heavier AI users *marginally* more often believe that faculty do emphasize reasoning in grading, but again the relationship is extremely weak. Essentially, those who use AI more are just as likely as others to say their instructors focus on reasoning; AI use doesn't strongly color that perception.

Reduced Thinking has a very weak negative correlation (-0.06) with Faculty Assess among the other pairs. It suggests that students who believe AI weakens their ability to think also frequently feel (slightly) that teachers are not placing enough emphasis on reasoning abilities in tests. Although there is little evidence, this poor alignment may suggest that these students generally don't feel that their teachers and themselves place enough emphasis on critical thinking (because of AI). Finally, with the exception of a negligible +0.03 with faculty assessment (those who are confident in themselves are slightly more likely to believe faculty value reasoning), Problem Confidence is virtually uncorrelated with the others.

Overall, the correlation analysis suggests that students' AI usage, self-perceived cognitive engagement, confidence, and views of faculty priorities function largely as independent factors. The coefficients all being near zero means we did not observe any meaningful linear coupling—for instance, using AI frequently did not automatically coincide with lower confidence or noticeably different views on teaching practices. This outcome is interesting in light of concerns about AI: one might expect heavy AI users to show clear differences (perhaps lower confidence or more complacency), but in our data such patterns are not strong. It may be that the impact of AI on student attitudes is more complex or individualized, not easily captured by simple correlations. This also could reflect that our measures are based on self-perception; students might not fully recognize shifts in their skills or may compartmentalize their AI use separate from how they view their learning abilities.

Despite the lack of significant correlations, a cautious interpretation of the weak negative link between AI reliance and independent problem confidence (–0.05) aligns with a theoretical expectation: even if slight, there is a hint that frequent AI use might coincide with a bit less self-confidence in problem-solving. This aligns with some literature suggesting that outsourcing tasks to AI can undermine self-efficacy over time (Gerlich, 2025). Conversely, the negligible correlation between AI reliance and perceived loss of critical thinking suggests that students do not broadly feel that using AI is ruining their ability to think – a reassuring sign that many are perhaps using AI as a supplementary tool rather than a crutch.

In light of these findings, the quantitative results underscore the necessity for a balanced approach in education. The modest reliance on AI combined with appreciation for collaborative learning indicates students are open to technology but still value human-guided experiences. The essentially independent nature of AI use and cognitive engagement factors implies that there is room for intervention – good pedagogy could ensure that even high AI users remain confident and engaged in critical thinking. These results set the stage for the qualitative findings, which delve into how students themselves describe the impact of AI and which teaching methods they believe help maintain their intellectual rigor.

QUALITATIVE INSIGHTS

Thematic analysis of the open-ended responses yielded rich insights that complement the survey data. Students elaborated on how they use AI, their concerns about it, and what classroom experiences they find most beneficial for thinking critically. Several key themes emerged:

- **Positive Use of AI (with Caveats):** A considerable number of students acknowledged AI as a *valuable tool* for certain academic tasks. Common responses praised AI for helping with drafting assignments, improving grammar, generating ideas or summaries, and providing quick explanations. For routine or foundational tasks, students found AI-based assistants convenient and time-saving. *"ChatGPT helps me get a quick overview* of topics I don't understand," one student noted, reflecting a typical sentiment. Nonetheless, alongside these positives, many students voiced reservations. They expressed concern that over-reliance on AI can lead to superficial learning. Some admitted that when they use AI for answers or corrections, they sometimes bypass the deeper process of understanding, which could hurt them in the long run. For example, a student wrote that while AI corrected her essay's grammar, she "realized I didn't learn from those corrections, I just accepted them." There is an undercurrent of wariness: students appreciate AI's help but are aware that it might make them intellectually "lazy" if used as a crutch for every problem. They worry about a *superficial understanding* or a lack of retention when AI provides answers too easily. This theme highlights an important duality: students see AI as beneficial, but only up to a point, and they are cognizant of the need for self-discipline and critical engagement beyond what AI delivers.
- **Preference for Active, Human-Centered Learning:** Students overwhelmingly emphasized the importance of interactive learning experiences that AI cannot replace. In their responses, they consistently pointed to *discussions, debates, case studies, and problem-solving exercises* as examples of activities that significantly enhanced their reasoning and analytical abilities. These are hands-on, minds-on experiences in the classroom that demand participation. One student mentioned, *"When our professor holds open discussions, I have to think on my feet and it really makes me analyze the topic deeper."* Such activities were frequently described as *more engaging and stimulating* than simply using AI to look up information. A related strong theme was the vital role of the teacher in orchestrating these experiences. Students identified pedagogical methods like inquiry-based projects, Socratic questioning during class, group problem-based assignments, and reflective exercises as highly effective in challenging them to think critically. They specifically credited instructors who use probing questions or real-world problems for pushing them beyond their comfort zone. Notably, many students drew a direct comparison between these methods and AI, arguing that *human-facilitated learning is more demanding but ultimately more rewarding*. As one respondent succinctly put it: *"Group work and teacher feedback make me think way more than when I just Google something."* This indicates that students are conscious of

the deeper cognitive impact that well-designed human interactions have on them. They view AI as a helpful supplement for information or simple tasks, but not as a substitute for the rich learning that happens through teacher-guided exploration and peer collaboration.

In summary, the qualitative insights paint a picture of a student community that is *AI-aware but teacher-dependent by preference*. Students are leveraging AI where it helps, but they crave the depth and challenge that comes from human-mediated learning. They recognize that the best outcomes arise when AI's efficiency is balanced with educational strategies that demand their active reasoning. This feedback directly supports the premise of our study: there is a strong pedagogical justification for reinforcing human-centered teaching techniques in an AI-rich world. The students themselves articulate that, to avoid the intellectual pitfalls of AI, they need and want educators to continue engaging them through inquiry, dialogue, and problem-solving.

CONCLUSION

The increasing integration of AI tools into educational settings raises important questions about their dual effects: while they can be efficient and helpful, they can also unintentionally impair students' capacity for independent and critical thought. The purpose of this study was to assess instructional strategies meant to counteract any emerging cognitive passivity and to find out how much students rely on AI. With 320 undergraduate students, we used a mixed-methods design to record the degree of AI use as well as the perceived efficacy of instructional interventions for preserving critical thinking.. An examination of the survey results showed that students had a moderate reliance on AI tools, but they also clearly valued interactive, human-centered learning methods. While most students acknowledged the value of traditional learning experiences, they also acknowledged the use of AI for a variety of tasks. They determined that in an AI era, pedagogical approaches like inquiry-based learning, Socratic questioning, group projects, and problem-based activities are essential for improving students' analytical abilities. Additionally, qualitative feedback showed that although students recognize the value of AI, they are also worried about its overuse and the possible decline in critical engagement if they become overly reliant on it.

The results support the idea that educational methods that encourage critical thinking and intellectual independence should be supplemented by AI rather than replaced. Students can use AI without losing their ability to reason, according to the very weak correlations found between its use and their confidence or level of engagement. To keep students' minds engaged, teachers must purposefully design lessons that promote introspection, discussion, and problem-solving. This involves keeping students challenged with open-ended questions, group discussions, and assignments that call for creative thinking—areas in which AI is unable to provide a predetermined response. By doing this, the teacher's role expands to include not just imparting knowledge but also mentorship in how to learn effectively in the presence of AI. There is an ethical and developmental dimension to this role: teachers are now also guides who help students learn when to use AI as a tool and when to rely on their own faculties, thereby equipping learners to utilize AI in a responsible and discerning manner.

According to UNESCO's human-centered AI principles and other guidelines, this study provides evidence-based suggestions for incorporating AI into instructional frameworks that prioritize deep learning and critical thinking. But it's just the first step. In order to evaluate the effects of continuous pedagogical strategies on students' analytical abilities in AI-rich environments, future research should investigate experimental and longitudinal designs. Research from a variety of fields and educational levels may help identify areas where AI dependency is most likely to occur and assist in creating efficient instructional safeguards.

FUNDING

This research received no external funding. It was conducted as part of the authors' academic duties and institutional research support. No grant or financial interest influenced the study design or interpretation of the data.

ACKNOWLEDGMENTS

The authors gratefully acknowledge the students and faculty of KHMW Degree College for their valuable participation and support in the completion of this research. Their openness in sharing experiences with AI and classroom learning made this study possible. We also thank our colleagues for their feedback on the survey design and the insightful discussions that helped shape this work.

REFERENCES

Dewey, J. (1933). *How we think: A restatement of the relation of reflective thinking to the educative process*. D. C. Heath.

Duhaylungsod, A. V., & Chavez, J. V. (2023). ChatGPT and other AI users: Innovative and creative utilitarian value and mindset shift. *Journal of Namibian Studies, 33*, 4367–4378. DOI: 10.59670/jns.v33i.2791

Paul, R., & Elder, L. (2008). *The miniature guide to critical thinking: Concepts and tools*. Foundation for Critical Thinking Press.

UNESCO. (2023). *Guidance for generative AI in education and research*. United Nations Educational, Scientific and Cultural Organization., DOI: 10.54675/EWZM9535

Vygotsky, L. S. (1978). *Mind in society: The development of higher psychological processes*. Harvard University Press.

Zawacki-Richter, O., Marín, V. I., Bond, M., & Gouverneur, F. (2019). Systematic review of research on artificial intelligence applications in higher education—Where are the educators? *International Journal of Educational Technology in Higher Education, 16*, 39. DOI: 10.1186/s41239-019-0171-0

Zhai, C., Wibowo, S., & Li, L. D. (2024). The effects of over-reliance on AI dialogue systems on students' cognitive abilities: A systematic review. *Smart Learning Environments, 11*, 28. DOI: 10.1186/s40561-024-00316-7

APPENDIX A: LIKERT-SCALE SURVEY ITEMS

1. I rely on AI tools (e.g., ChatGPT, Grammarly, etc.) for completing academic tasks.
2. Using AI-based tools has reduced the amount of critical thinking I apply to my assignments.
3. My instructors use activities that help me build reasoning and analytical skills without AI assistance.
4. Pedagogical methods like debates, case discussions, and problem-solving tasks improve my analytical thinking.
5. I feel confident analyzing problems independently before referring to AI tools.
6. My institution encourages academic integrity and discourages over-dependence on AI.
7. Collaborative projects and peer discussions help me develop stronger reasoning skills than working alone with AI.
8. I am aware of the limitations and ethical concerns of using AI in academics.
9. Faculty members assess reasoning and analytical thinking rather than just final answers.

APPENDIX B: OPEN-ENDED QUESTIONS

1. In what ways do you find AI tools helpful in your academic tasks?
2. Have you ever felt that using AI reduced your engagement or learning? Please explain.
3. Which classroom activities or teaching methods have helped you think more critically and analytically?
4. What are your concerns, if any, about using AI in education?
5. How can educators balance AI usage with traditional teaching methods to improve learning?

Chapter 9
Ethical Implications of Collecting and Using Data to Power AI Tools

Muhammad Usman Tariq
https://orcid.org/0000-0002-7605-3040
Abu Dhabi University, UAE & University College Cork, Ireland

ABSTRACT

The ethical implications of collecting and using data to power Artificial Intelligence (AI) tools are of paramount importance as AI continues to revolutionize various sectors, including education, healthcare, and business. This chapter explores the multifaceted ethical concerns surrounding data usage in AI systems, focusing on issues such as privacy, consent, transparency, and bias. It begins by examining the risks associated with the collection and storage of vast amounts of personal data, highlighting concerns regarding surveillance and unauthorized access. The chapter also addresses the issue of biased datasets, discussing how they can perpetuate inequalities and reinforce stereotypes, thereby affecting the fairness and reliability of AI-powered decisions. Furthermore, the importance of informed consent is explored, emphasizing the need for clear communication with individuals about how their data will be used and the potential consequences.

INTRODUCTION

AI tools fast became integrated into education which completely transformed the development process of educational experiences and both the instructional methods and evaluation techniques. The number of educational decisions and personalized instructional practices now depend on AI systems which also process large volumes

DOI: 10.4018/979-8-3373-7386-7.ch009

of student information. The technology provides methods that improve operational efficiency and generate personalized learning environments and data-based knowledge about student achievements. The increasing dependency on AI for educational purposes creates substantial moral uncertainties about how data used to operate these systems will be handled. AI's transformation of education depends on examining several ethical issues stemming from data-driven operations because these issues violate student privacy and exhibit bias and control data ownership and require informed consent (Yang & Lee, 2023). The main factor which drives AI's educational integration is its data processing capability that enables automated choices and teaching automation procedures. AI systems achieve their operational capability through data processing that enables them to create custom learning programs and student performance evaluations and future educational predictions. The data trails students create through their interactions allow systems to build complete records about learning tendencies along with student abilities and deficiencies. Knewton and DreamBox Learning utilize AI-powered technology to gather student data through interaction tracking for developing tailored recommendation systems. The goal of these data-dependent educational programs is to improve student learning by producing content that meets their individual speed and achievement levels. Gradescope together with similar AI-based grading technology evaluates student work to deliver automatic grading services as well as offer teachers' significant knowledge of students' common mistakes and overall academic patterns (Safdar, Banja, & Meltzer, 2020).

Educational AI systems now process student information for purposes extending past deliverance of customized learning suggestions. AI analytics evaluate how students behave and forecasts their academic results and supports administrative officials during their decision-making processes. Turnitin platforms use AI algorithms to check for plagiarism in student papers and the Canvas learning system employs AI tools to monitor student involvement and predict student dropout risks. The growing quantity of stored data by AI systems creates important ethical concerns which require attention to shield students along with educators from potential threats (Breidbach & Maglio, 2020). The privacy aspect emerges as the leading moral challenge associated with processing student data through AI systems in educational applications. AI systems need to collect and process large amounts of personal and behavioural data because this serves as their fundamental operational requirement. The technology tracks student interactions with educational content then analyses their assessment performance while it uses classroom monitoring capabilities. School data collections contain delicate academic records as well as student learning needs and social patterns and occasionally extend to-details about personal health issues and familial background information. The large amount of student data collection triggers privacy-related concerns because centralized databases storing this information face risks of cyberattacks and unauthorized database breaches (Yang & Lee, 2023). The expansion of student data volume contributes new security risks for protecting information. The 2019 Chegg hack revealed the life-threatening risks which happen when schools do not provide proper security for their valuable data having exposed millions of student records. Personal student data breaches have wide-ranging effects because attackers can use this information for unlawful activities that generate identity theft situations and cases of fraud and various types of harm. The protection of robust datasets represents an essential ethical duty which must be implemented by educational institutions as well as AI developers together with policymakers (Safdar et al., 2020). The major ethical issue that AI systems create exists through bias in their algorithms. The accuracy of education-oriented AI tools depends entirely on their training data so any biases within the data collection will lead to tools that will create and preserve these biased outcomes. An AI system intended for student success prediction will depend on existing academic performance files which display systemic imbalances involving racial or socioeconomic distinctions. AI tools receiving their training data from unbalanced variables will inadvertently provide better results to some students than others. The criminal justice system displays AI bias prominently through its recidivism prediction algorithms which flag minority people as higher offenders at disproportionate rates. Educational AI tools can show biases against students who belong to different racial groups and belong to both female and male genders as well as those from different socioeconomic backgrounds (Breidbach & Maglio, 2020). Figure 1 provides overview of AI data flow in education.

Figure 1. Ai Data Flow in Education

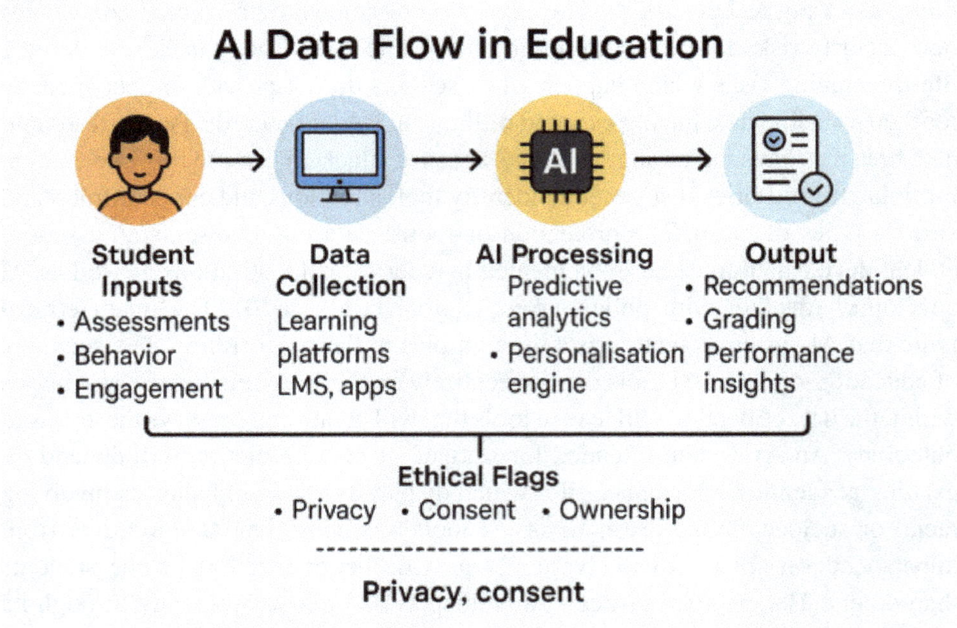

BACKGROUND

AI bias prevention depends on both detailed examination of training data sources to confirm their accurate representation of the population and their diverse coverage. Educational AI developers need to verify that their training data includes students from all population groups to represent actual schools. To identify as well as reduce potential biases educational institutions must reveal the methods which power AI models through their training and testing stages. Officials in education policy roles and teaching staff must support thorough inspections of educational AI systems to guarantee equal and unbiased decision-making processes within classrooms (Yang & Lee, 2023). AI tools in education face challenges regarding how educational institutions should manage the ownership rights to collected data. The collection of massive student-related data by AI systems requires clarification regarding who maintains ownership rights to this data. Who should be regarded as the source of responsibility for these issues: students themselves, their parents through guardianship or the educational institutions combined with the developers of AI tools? The matter of ownership becomes substantially complicated when educational data gets applied to commercial purposes. UE data released to AI developers and tech companies sometimes enables them to use the information outside the classroom setting for commercial exploitation including advertising and data market transactions. Students face risks of their personal data being used for profit-seeking purposes against their consent (Ryan & Stahl, 2020; Tariq, 2025).

Some educational institutions fail to demonstrate their complete process of sharing student data with external parties. Students may experience data collection when using specific online learning tools because the platforms track their browsing activities and content interactions with social media activities to boost their algorithms. Educational institutions gather worthwhile student data for outcome improvement yet misuse this data if they fail to disclose data collection procedures to students or explain its intended utilization. Students need protected rights through transparent ownership policies alongside control systems which must enable them or their parents to manage their data and approve its purposes of use (Char, Abràmoff, & Feudtner, 2020). The concept of informed consent strongly relates to data ownership since students (with their guardians' involvement where needed) need full knowledge about what data they want to release. Understandably the application of informed consent for educational AI use becomes complex to interpret. Numerous educational AI-based programs acquire data indirectly from users through their acceptance of user agreements or terms of service. The current situation makes it complicated for students together with their parents to comprehend both the collected data and its intended usage. The lack of technological proficiency often forces users to accept unclear terms since they cannot understand the consequences of data sharing in these agreements. Protecting both the knowledge and accessibility of consent in AI-based education requires immediate attention because it represents an important ethical concern (Ryan & Stahl, 2020).

Various groups such as policymakers and educators and AI developers share the duty to maintain ethical standards in how AI processes data. The creation of regulatory frameworks by policymakers enables the protection of student privacy as well as data security and fairness in educational settings. GDPR stands as a key piece of EU legislation which regulates student personal information as well as other forms of data protected under its provisions in educational institutions. Further development of current policies needs to focus on AI systems specifically due to their ethical considerations so educational technology applications can meet proper ethical standards (Char et al., 2020). Educational institutions and their frontline staff who use AI tools bear two essential responsibilities: first to grasp the ethical concerns arising from AI technology and second to defend student rights. Teachers need to make specific information about data usage accessible to students while guaranteeing an unbreeched privacy policy. Educational practitioners should collaborate with AI developers and policymakers for developing AI systems that prioritize fairness through complete transparency. They also need to provide assessment feedback to maintain unbiased and fair AI-driven decision processes (Christodoulou & Iordanou, 2021). The ethical deployment and design of systems belongs to AI developers who must assume this responsibility. AI developers need to design privacy-first algorithms that fix bias vulnerabilities along with transparent system functions. The collaboration between developers and both educators and policymakers remains essential because it allows developers to build tools that will fulfil their ethical criteria for student-centred learning. Continuous audits together with assessments of AI systems aimed at fairness and accuracy enable the reduction of possible destructive outcomes (Tariq, 2025). Gathering and utilizing data to drive AI systems in education has significant and complex ethical ramifications. It's critical to weigh the possible advantages of AI in the classroom against a strong commitment to moral behaviour as it becomes more prevalent. When designing and implementing AI systems, privacy, bias, data ownership, and informed permission must all be properly considered. It is feasible to guarantee that AI in education serves students' best interests, improves learning results, and upholds individual rights by combining the efforts of legislators, educators, and AI developers (Christodoulou & Iordanou, 2021).

The progress of artificial intelligence (AI) in education results from its capability to handle large datasets for making informed choices. Schools use AI tools to both customize student education and perform grading tasks and predictive analysis operations and other educational functions. The surge of using data-driven AI tools has sparked various ethical problems regarding data management and protection as well as usage. The growing integration of educational technologies requires immediate study of their ethical aspects especially regarding student privacy protection and data ownership together with fairness assurance and avoidance of bias as well as the requirement of informed consent (Ayling and Chapman, 2022). Before functioning, AI systems must have access to data to operate effectively. System effectiveness depends on gaining access to multiple sources of data which enable their predictive functions as well as automated and decision-making capabilities. Different points of interaction between students and educational platforms yield institutional data in educational institutions as well as assessment results and attendance records and engagement data for course materials and social behavioural information. AI systems generate more precise along with customized outcomes by receiving and processing larger amounts of data. The educational platforms Coursera and Khan Academy employ AI algorithms that monitor student advancement to provide expert comprehension-driven learning recommendation services according to individual achievement and preference metrics. The educational systems use predictive models which analyse behavioural data from the past to make forecasts about student performance in the future as they provide personalized learning paths to users.

The educational improvements provided by these modifications raise important concerns about safeguarding personal privacy. Educational AI systems acquire comprehensive student data which includes both academic achievements together with behavioural records and individual details as well as medical data in specific cases. It becomes a privacy violation to gather significant amounts of data without appropriate protective measures because this allows unauthorized entities to misuse personal information (Desouza & Chenok, 2020). A major data breach in 2018 put the personal records of millions of students at risk through an online educational platform thus showing students remain exposed in digital environments. The storage of AI tool data within cloud systems becomes vulnerable due to security breaches combined with unauthorized access possibilities. Young learners face heightened dangers regarding data privacy because their personal information exists in greater risk from misuse or hacking incidents (Desouza & Chenok, 2020). The ethical utilization of data by AI tools in educational settings deals primarily with bias-related problems. The neutral character of AI tools depends on the data which forms their training basis. Analysing biased training data through an AI model will cause the tool to repeat and preserve such biases. The systems reproduce unequal results for students whose backgrounds include marginalized groups or minorities. Predictive policing algorithms illustrate this bias problem because they gave targeted minorities based on unbalanced training data. AI systems built with academic data in education have the potential to strengthen existing biases connected with racial and gender distributions as well as socioeconomic backgrounds (Tariq, 2024). AI systems trained only on academic achievements of mostly white and financially advantaged students will present an injustice to educational evaluations for student populations from different backgrounds.

The educational biases embedded in historical academic data systems potentially create negative feedback loops through AI tools because these tools prefer students whose success matches historical patterns which disadvantages students who need additional support. These systems possess the potential to worsen achievement gaps because students from disadvantaged backgrounds receive inaccurate risk assessments which discourages their opportunities for success. Due care must be implemented to evaluate AI training datasets because they need to demonstrate breadth and accurate representation and absence of institutional discrimination. The elimination of bias needs more than just technical fixes since it needs an organization-wide dedication to social justice alongside fair development practices for AI technologies. The ownership rights associated with data constitute an essential matter of concern. The collection of extensive student data by educational institutions together with AI developers creates an ownership question for this information. Students often remain unaware about what happens to the data collected through AI systems since they lack understanding of its collection and usage implications. Both parents and guardians commonly have unclear comprehension about the student data treatment methods employed by educational institutions. The generated data within educational systems belongs to educational institutions but maintains access rights by third-party AI developers who operate for commercial reasons. Private companies retain conflicting interests because they access student information which extends outside traditional educational use for advertising products and developing new solutions. Students and their families do not consent nor have knowledge about the third-party usage of their educational data which gets sold or shared in certain situations. Educational technology companies that collect United States student data have triggered concerns regarding data privacy and educational commercialization practices. The tracking and use of student data by G Suite for Education through Google drew critical scrutiny because the platform monitored student content from emails to documents and search queries. Google claimed to not exploit student data for advertising purposes, but the fact students' information is vulnerable exposes ethical issues about data rights in academic environments. The question regarding student data ownership must receive answer through proper policies that safeguard privacy and prevent commercial exploitation (Dibie, 2024; Tariq, 2025).

The right to consent about data use remains directly connected to personal data control. Students along with their parents require comprehensive knowledge of information usage to determine informed decisions about data collection. Many educational Artificial Intelligence systems fail to show students both understandable explanations and straightforward descriptions about how student data gets collected and processed and is distributed across networks. Students and parents together with educators must get full understanding about data-collection purposes and scope through an open process which surpasses bare acknowledgement of terms and conditions. Students need the right to exempt themselves from data gathering processes without receiving adverse treatment to maintain free and informed participation in AI-assisted educational systems (Elendu et al., 2023). Setting up informed consent presents exceptional difficulties within K-12 educational settings since students lack full understanding of the meaning behind data collection processes. Educational institutions along with teachers now need to prioritize student protection above all else in their educational practice. Higher education faces new hurdles because it targets adult students by needing proof that consent practices remain free from coercion without losing their informative accurate core. Educational tools show their data operations through complex legal wording that user populations typically overlook or skip reading their lengthy service agreements. The present reality demands simple straightforward data practice communication which ensures people give authentic consent during user interactions (Dibie, 2024). AI tools require various parties to be responsible for properly handling data ethics during collection and use. Educational data management regulations establish by policymakers determine how educational data gets collected as well as how it is stored and applied. The protection of student privacy by the Family Educational Rights and Privacy Act (FERPA) in the United

States exists but needs revisions to cover the advanced challenges created by AI technology. Policy regulators should create complete data security guidelines specifically designed to protect against AI system threats like unfounded bias along with data business arrangements. The government must establish requirements for schools along with AI developers to follow and students must receive suitable rights protection (Elendu et al., 2023).

Among their responsibilities educators should gain insight into AI tool ethical dimensions as they implement educational technology to provide student benefits with complete protection of their rights. Educational staff members should work to enhance both transparency and responsibility within their AI system implementations by establishing protocols for routine inspections and audits which confirm adherence to ethical protocols. AI developers need to establish responsibility for generating tools that accomplish effectiveness while maintaining ethical standards. AI development requires the creation of systems that reduce bias while keeping privacy standards high and provide real-time operational visibility. AI developers need to accept third-party evaluation in addition to working alongside educators and policymakers to establish ethical consensus about AI tool development (Eitel-Porter, 2021). The ethical aspects connected to data collection for AI-based educational tools create multiple intricate challenges in educational practice. Increasing AI adoption in educational systems requires immediate resolutions for privacy matters along with bias concerns and data property disputes and consent complications. For AI technology to be used in a responsible, open, and moral manner, stakeholders, including legislators, educators, and AI developers—must collaborate. By working together, it is feasible to safeguard students' rights and interests while utilizing AI's potential in education (Eitel-Porter, 2021).

Understanding Data Collection in AI-Powered Education

Educational applications that employ Artificial Intelligence mechanisms depend on data acquisition for improving student learning while achieving best results. The fundamental data collection process within AI-powered educational environments serves to make decisions and enables personalization in addition to predictive analytics. AI tools operating in educational settings have the power to gather performance data besides monitoring student engagement levels and analysing their behavioural patterns. This part examines different kinds of data AI platforms gather and explains their data processing operations for customized learning support as well as predicting educational practices. The analysis will explore AI data collection systems along with their related ethical aspects (Weber & Lewis, 2021). Electronic learning tools equipped with Artificial Intelligence technologies gather large quantities of data for monitoring student advancement and tracking their interactions and process with educational content. Performance data represents the dominant information that educational institutions gather from their students. Students' performance data consists of graded assignments along with test results and quiz grades and project assessments that are monitored throughout time. The collection of performance data helps teachers understand what subjects' students have mastered while determining which parts need improvement and decides what extra teaching materials students need. Using Khan Academy's AI system allows the platform to evaluate test scores and student participation which activates personalized feedback mechanisms that recommend supplemental exercises based on individual student weaknesses (Tariq, 2025). Behavioural patterns make up an essential data classification. Learning platforms permit AI systems to track student activity through monitoring student time usage across learning materials and record frequency of system access and completion times and accessed resources. Student learning preferences together with routine behaviours and rate of knowledge acquisition become understand by AI systems through this data collection. Learners who use Coursera allow the platform to track their course activity by monitoring their lesson times and paused video selections and dropped-off points which enables customized recommended learning modules (Esmaeilzadeh, 2020).

AI tools require engagement levels as essential data points to determine the extent of student involvement during learning sessions. Plenty of metrics exists to measure user participation including the number of times platform users interact and quiz question completion count along with discussion group membership. Learning results tend to improve when engagement levels heighten so AI tools modify delivery content by using obtained data. Duolingo uses user language lesson engagement consistency to modify content levels which adapt to individual progress rates (Weber & Lewis, 2021). Machine intelligence uses enormous data collections to adapt learning activities for students as individual learners. The application of artificial intelligence results in personalized learning which leads to being an essential educational benefit. AI systems obtain student-specific information from various data points to determine their learning style alongside strengths and weaknesses and preferences which they use to optimize the learning process. AI systems generate recommendations of learning content and exercises which match unique student requirements inside educational settings. An AI system would provide remedial tutorial series to students needing help with concepts and advanced study materials for students who demonstrate good performance in their coursework. The personalization level enables teachers to offer students appropriate educational content targets to boost student engagement and academic results. The capacity of AI to modify itself in real time allows it to create immediate adjustments from new data obtained throughout collection. The AI system will both modify task difficulty levels and suggest supplemental learning materials after detecting student declining assessment results. The system will either speed up educational progression or bring more complex content to students who demonstrate talented performance in specific areas. The continuous collection and analysis of data enables the creation of adaptive learning as a personalized process which is called "adaptive learning." Each student interaction enables background data processing through AI algorithms thus the system generates personalization along with continuous evolution of learning experience. Student responses are analysed by Dream Box Learning to automatically modify platform content while the system guides learners through lessons at their individually suitable learning speeds (Weber & Lewis, 2021).

Predictive analytics functions as a major component when educational tools employ artificial intelligence. The data gathered from students enables AI systems to generate future academic predictions as well as identify probable learning results. Education professionals receive early warning signs about students who face the possibility of academic retardation thanks to this predictive system. Using historical information predictive models can forecast three vital student outcomes which include achievement potential levels together with dropout probabilities and subject-specific difficulties. Predictive analytics systems operated by numerous institutions predict graduation program finish dates following assessment of student preparation indicators such as enrolment and academic performance levels. Educational administrators alongside teachers obtain vital information through this process which helps them determine appropriate proactive remedial and supportive actions. Through predictive analytics Coursera and similar large online education platforms detect which students face difficulties with completing their courses. Through the platform students receiving notifications or being motivated toward additional resources becomes possible when they trail behind in quiz performance. Predictive models operate within K-12 educational institutions to detect students who face academic failure risk so teachers can intervene during early stages of decline (Ayling & Chapman, 2022). The use of predictive analytics offers better learning support to students yet generates multiple ethical issues because of its application. The main hazard occurs because predictive models depend on historical databases that fail to show all student skill levels and talent possibilities accurately. These analytic predictions typically work with past information that might perpetuate existing patterns of bias formed by socioeconomic factors together with racial distinctions and gender preferences. Predictive models trained with information primarily from accomplished students demonstrate limited accuracy when assessing disadvantaged students because these learners potentially need specific interventions for successful academic outcomes. Predictive models can develop a negative feedback loop that reduces students labelled at risk to receive fewer academic challenges while limiting their educational development (Esmaeilzadeh, 2020).

The implementation of predictive analytics leads to privacy risks because it can infringe upon individual privacy. AI tools gather substantial amounts of personal data along with behavioural information plus academic achievements alongside demographic records, but they may leak this information without obtaining appropriate consent. Predictive analytics needs this data for its forecasts, yet improper handling creates unintended effects that include discrimination and unauthorized disclosure of sensitive information about students. Three educational platforms like IBM Watson Education and Coursera and Dream Box Learning illustrate AI's data collection techniques that enhance learning through data processing. For AI technology to be used in a responsible, open, and moral manner, stakeholders—including legislators, educators, and AI developers—must collaborate. By working together, it is feasible to safeguard students' rights and interests while utilizing AI's potential in education (Ayling & Chapman, 2022). For instance, IBM Watson combines AI with instructional materials to provide students tailored suggestions depending on their information. These platforms do, however, provide certain ethical difficulties. Although the goal of these platforms is to provide individualized learning pathways, there are issues with the way data is gathered, saved, and utilized. There could occasionally be a lack of clarity about the precise data gathered and the prediction algorithms employed (Gabriel, 2023). Another well-known online platform, Coursera, utilizes AI to gather information about how students engage with the course contents and uses predictive analytics to pinpoint students who may be at danger. Although many students have benefited from this in finishing their courses, it also raises concerns over data ownership and privacy. Coursera's use of predictive analytics may result in fewer educational options for student groups, particularly if the predictive models are not appropriately bias-corrected (Gabriel, 2023).

Dream Box Learning, an adaptive learning platform for grades K–8, gathers information on how students engage with arithmetic material to provide a customized learning experience. To evaluate students' performance and modify classes appropriately, this platform makes use of predictive analytics. Dream Box has received accolades for its individualized approach, however given its vast data collecting methods, there have been concerns expressed around data privacy and the exploitation of student data for commercial reasons. AI-powered learning systems use predictive analytics to tailor learning experiences by gathering a lot of data on student performance, engagement, and behaviour patterns. Although there is a lot of promise for these technologies to enhance education, they also bring up serious ethical issues, especially about privacy, prejudice, and data ownership. Case studies of AI-powered systems highlight the advantages of data collecting in education as well as its ethical challenges (Gabriel, 2023). Figure 2 provides overview of predictive analytics pipeline in AI education.

Figure 2. Predictive Analytics Pipeline in AI Education

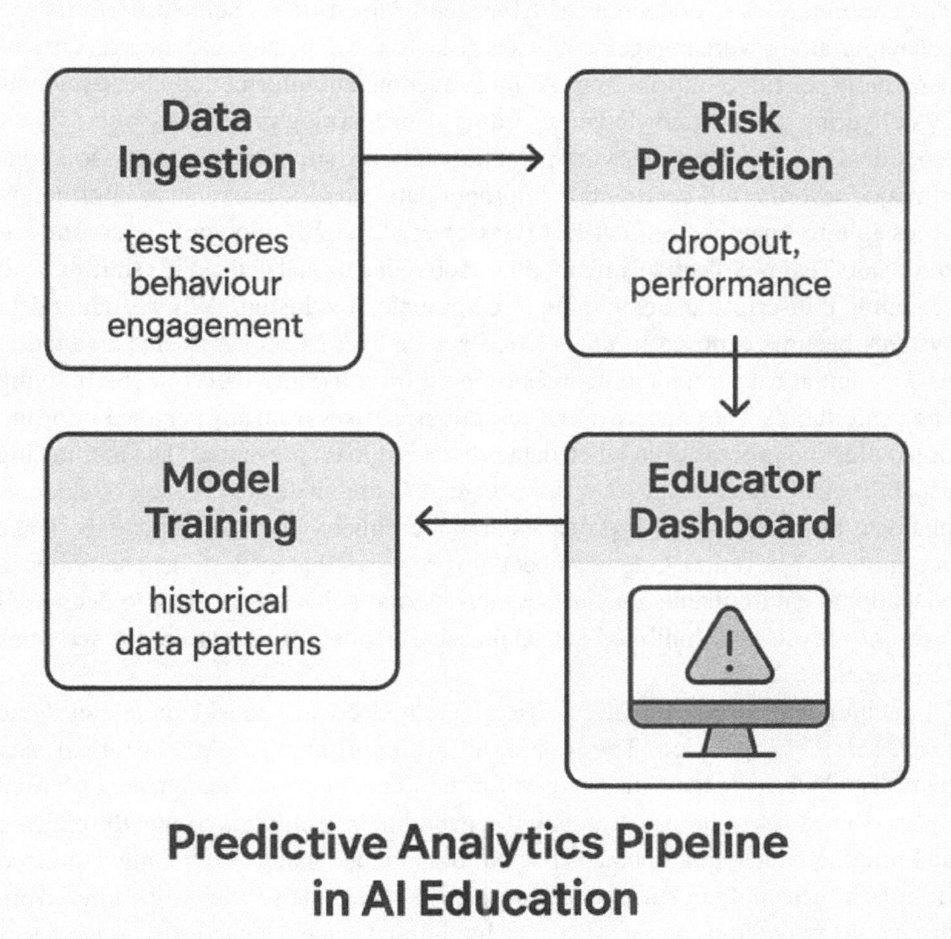

Ethical Challenges in AI Data Usage

Educational institutions utilizing AI technologies have created advanced learning methods that involve personalized education and predictive analytics and adaptive learning systems. AI systems collecting huge amounts of student data has led to ethical problems about the utilization of this data becoming relevant. This segment evaluates various moral dilemmas that stem from educational AI data practices through looking at privacy elements and AI algorithm prejudice and system opacity as well as student data consent frameworks and commercial exploitation of data (Bankins & Formosa, 2023). The protection of student information stands as the most urgent ethical matter that arises from AI-enhanced learning applications. The continuous data collection of AI systems which tracks student performance behaviour along with engagement poses risks to the exposure and incorrect use of personally sensitive information. AI tools accumulate information about students by delivering precise knowledge regarding their learning patterns as well as their emotional reactions together with potential daily life situations. Privacy violations of major severity will occur when improper data security leaves such information accessible to unauthorized entities (Gasser et al., 2020). Google Classroom and Microsoft Teams collectively maintain various educational data points starting with academic transcripts and extending to communication history. When student data systems become exposed to unapproved access by hackers it presents a situation with potential catastrophic outcomes running from identity theft to cyberbullying and exploitation. The concern about surveillance arises from any personal information collection process even when data breaches remain prevented. The monitoring capabilities of educational AI systems extend to complete supervision of student-platform interactions which produces an environment where students experience continuous observation. Ongoing check-up processes that track student activities in educational environments may affect their natural behaviors leading to decreased creativity levels and inhibited self-expressive habits during classroom activities (Gasser et al., 2020).

Technology systems that use artificial intelligence face considerable issues due to bias in their operation. The training of AI algorithms requires historical data patterns which form the datasets used for their development. Inadequate or biased datasets used for training AI tools will enable their resulting systems to replicate and prolong educational inequalities. AI tools trained using data mainly collected from rich metropolitan students do not provide adequate service to children from disadvantaged regions or poor districts. Intentional student selection bias can occur when AI systems process historical data which shows negative representation of specific racial or ethnic groups because these algorithms may select students from the more prominent groups (Bankins & Formosa, 2023). AI systems showed significant bias during predictive testing operations in educational institutions. The predictive models proved to be less precise when predicting outcomes for Black and Hispanic students thereby intensifying current academic gaps between groups. AI-based data processing exhibits biases which produces restricted educational possibilities for disenfranchised students while deepening educational achievement differences. The consequences of machine learning biases reach extensive levels since they create long-term impacts on how resources are distributed and which advanced courses receive funding along with which prospects students from disadvantaged groups have to access education in the future (Gavorník et al., 2024). AI tools pose an ethical problem because they maintain unclear processes and operation methods.

The decision-making processes behind numerous educational AI programs function as black boxes since users find them difficult to decode. Many students together with their teachers and school administrators remain in darkness about the methods through which AI tools scrutinize data and make deductive conclusions. The incomplete visibility creates doubts about responsible use of systems. The unclear reason behind an AI system's wrong student ability evaluation and subpar learning path suggestions becomes challenging to address because of limited system transparency (Larson & Langlotz, 2020). Educational platforms utilizing AI technologies use student data for creating individualized learning programs as an example. The proprietary algorithms controlling these recommendation platforms maintain undisclosed internal operations although they market personalized suggestions to their audience. Education professionals cannot establish trust in algorithmic decisions unless they understand the machinery behind them. Students along with their parents cannot properly challenge AI system decisions because of the unexplained decision-making processes. Students and their stakeholders require full knowledge about the methods AI tools utilize to process data because this transparency supports accountability and relationship growth (Gavorník et al., 2024).

The application of informed consent as an essential ethical rule operates sparsely when AI technology controls educational processes. Students need complete knowledge about data collection implications for them to understand their options in how their information will be handled. Most students along with their parents and teachers fail to comprehend the complex specific terms and privacy statements written in technical jargon that accompany AI educational systems. The policies offer students no option to negotiate or refuse their terms because they are presented with no choice beside acceptance (Larson & Langlotz, 2020). The process of obtaining informed consent presents additional challenges because AI tools monitor user's extensive behaviour patterns. Examples of data collection occur through Edmodo and Khan Academy by monitoring academic results and student engagement data points including lesson duration and student-to-content interactions and learning difficulty areas. The valuable learning experience data collection does not always translate into full understanding of monitoring depth among students and their parents. Educational institutions and AI developers need to establish open communication for students' data practices so parents and students can provide genuine consent (Herington et al., 2023). The business transactions involving student information have become a major source of contention since education technology companies need extensive student datasets for maintaining their corporate operations. The revenue generation of ed-tech companies involves sharing student data through targeting advertisements and insight sales to multiple third parties although schools receive free or low-cost services. There are instances where AI tools distribute student information to advertisers together with researchers and commercial entities which raises doubts regarding the business exploitation of student data (Gerdes, 2022).

The education products Google Classroom have become common in K-12 schools yet experts question where Google derives its revenue from the student data it accumulates. The way Google gathers student data provides benefits for its business operations through the acquisition of behavioural insights about students that helps the company enhance existing services or develop new products. The data collection practices of ClassDojo generate criticism since they monitor student interactions to sell information commercially to partners. This student data commercialization diminishes educational trust from institutions and AI tools. Users including students and their parents think their confidential information gets transformed into commercial products while their privacy vanishes for financial gain. Educational goals of schools' face competition with corporate interests because student data technology is monetized. There is a chance that when AI systems are motivated by financial gain, the emphasis may move from providing high-quality, fair education to optimizing data collecting and financial gain (Herington et al., 2023). There are several complex ethical issues that need to be carefully considered when using data in AI-powered learning resources. Significant obstacles that must be overcome include privacy issues, prejudice in AI systems, a lack of transparency, informed consent, and the monetization of student data. To protect students' rights, guarantee fair results, and preserve the integrity of the educational process, educators, legislators, and developers must collaborate to create ethical standards and protections as AI continues to play a bigger role in education (Gerdes, 2022).

Best Practices for Ethical AI Data Usage in Education

The use of AI in education requires stricter ethical data handling practices because this safeguards student privacy while building trust with these technological tools. The adoption of ethical standards for managing AI data ensures a reduction in potential safety concerns and complete exploitation of artificial intelligence educational resources. The best practices for ethical data usage comprise two elements: reducing the amount of collected data and using advanced security safeguards together with ethical choices for decision automation and permission-gaining consent procedures. Educational institutions together with AI developers should follow these guidelines to produce an environment which enables responsible transparent ethical use of AI tools (Wakunuma, Jiya, & Aliyu, 2020). Data minimization functions as one of the fundamental ethical rules for proper data usage. Educational data collection processes must limit themselves to gathering essential data only when attaining learning objectives. The practice minimizes risks to students' privacy by preventing unnecessary data storage of their personal information. Organizations that concentrate on securing essential learning data protect students from unauthorized use of their information and misuse of data (Lysaght & Ngiam, 2019; Tariq, 2025). Examples of AI tracking should limit the collection of specific data beyond required educational metrics by avoiding superfluous personal data such as private communications or non-educational personal identifiers. A reading habit monitoring AI tool within educational settings requires knowledge of student lesson duration and learning trouble zones instead of collecting unrelated personal facts during operations. A school system which selects teaching data that connects directly to learning outcomes maintains student privacy guidelines and supports individualized learning through its practices. As an illustration the education platform Canvas shows instructors how to monitor student advancement while keeping away from extensive information collection (Herington et al., 2023).

The tracking system of Canvas limits itself to assignment submission grades and submission rates while refraining from tracking student web browsers outside its learning platform. The data-collection practices of Canvas follow data-minimization standards to deliver individualized student education while preserving clear educational data use (Morley et al., 2023). Secure data protection techniques with encryption standards constitute another essential best practice which safeguards against information breaches of student privacy. Cybercriminals view AI systems as attractive targets since their extensive data collection produces rich sensitive information that potentially endangers student records and other personal details. Schools and ed-tech businesses need to spend money on complete security systems which should stop data breaches and ensure data privacy (Lysaght & Ngiam, 2019). The encryption process stands as an optimal measure to defend student data. Sensitive information protection requires dual encryption of data transmissions and periods of inactivity to keep unauthorized parties from accessing the data. Secure encryption provides safety for data since breaches lead hackers to obtain unintelligible and useless information. A system of encrypted data requires institutions to set up secure authentication protocols based on multi-factor authentication to govern entrance to student data. Authoritative personnel maintain control over the viewing and editing capabilities of student educational data through these security measures (Wakunuma, Jiya, & Aliyu, 2020). Blackboard and Schoology serve as educational platforms that have implemented encryption features with strong authentication procedures to protect student information. Each platform fulfills the requirements of governmental standards such as FERPA through its compliance with student privacy rules. The measures adopted by these platforms decrease data breach dangers to protect student and parent information securely (Morley et al., 2023).

The process of guaranteeing fair and transparent usage of AI decision systems stands as a vital practice when implementing AI data principles ethically. Users including teachers and students together with parents maintain concerns about AI systems because their algorithms operate as uninterpretable tools. A system's absence of transparency causes trust levels to decrease while people start questioning if decisions made by AI systems are biased or incorrect thus affecting students' educational paths. Strategies to maintain fairness in AI systems must include methods which will stop the creation of biases that target specific student groups. Training data must be carefully established with representative samples of different student populations which include every socioeconomic group combined with every racial identity as well as students who have disabilities. Developers must execute thorough testing of AI systems for discrimination elements while organizing continuous audits of the systems to secure fair and equitable operation (Herington et al., 2023). Users better understand and evaluate AI system operations when their algorithms together with decision-making processes maintain complete openness. Institutions offering educational programs need to distribute complete documentation which describes the tools' operation and all processed data including every decision-making process. Understanding how AI systems operate along with their conclusion-making processes creates more trust among parents and teachers who support system utilization (Wakunuma, Jiya, & Aliyu, 2020). Some American school districts have demonstrated transparent and fair practices through their initiative to use AI tools for grading purposes. The districts collaborated with AI developers to build unbiased grading systems which received thorough fairness testing and provided both teachers and students with complete understanding about assessment processes. Educational districts should implement transparency and fairness standards in AI systems to build trust regarding their AI applications in academic programs. Before collecting student and parental data school districts should follow ethical standards to obtain agreement so individuals retain control over data collection and processing methods and understand data usage purposes. The educational setting requires special attention to consent since students especially those who are minors might not grasp the complete meaning of information collection and usage. AI developers along with educators and institutions should deliver comprehensible details about data collection types and data usage purposes and their associated risks to all interested parties (Ryan & Stahl, 2020).

Before collecting data from its subjects, the organization needs to acquire their consent through straightforward processes that are both easy to understand and accessible to all parties. Schoolchildren and their guardians need plain-language detailed explanations about how data is used, and they should receive options to participate only in desired or ask questions about any data practices. Users need continuous updates regarding modifications that occur to the data collection methods (Ryan & Stahl, 2020). Students and parents can find understandable information about data collection practices through the privacy policies established by platforms such as Google Classroom and Seesaw. Parents can manage which aspects of data sharing through these platforms by choosing to restrict collection for marketing purposes. The combination of user consent processes with clear communication channels between platforms and students and parents leads to data-collection methods which both match user choices and maintain transparency. The University of California operates with a detailed data governance approach that regulates AI tools deployed for educational use throughout its classrooms (Williamson & Eynon, 2020). The framework establishes security protocols for data protection alongside clear guidelines for data use and scheduled evaluations to check AI algorithms for equitable operation. Students together with parents need to provide explicit consent to data use at the university while receiving complete information about data processing activities (Herington et al., 2023). The educational platform Khan Academy makes use of AI to provide customized learning needs that serve millions of students across the globe. Khan Academy maintains optimal security standards along with data transparency and ensures fair operations in its AI-driven educational software. Students and parents can view comprehensive reports concerning their learning advancement through this platform while receiving explicit information about collected data types. Khan Academy performs routine algorithm reviews and tests with various student populations to maintain unbiased AI tool operations (Herington et al., 2023). The successful use of ethical AI data in education demands the implementation of best practices which protects responsible tools with both security and fairness. Followed best practices of data minimization along with strong security protocols and transparency practices and informed consent protocols allow educational institutions to develop AI-powered learning environments which personalize instruction without invading student privacy or creating unfair conditions. The best practices designed to use AI in education ethically have proven feasible through extensive case studies conducted in different educational settings (Williamson & Eynon, 2020).

Policy Recommendations for AI and Data Ethics in Education

Educational institutions need specific policies to regulate the ethical deployment of AI tools since their prevalence in education continues to grow. AI technologies will benefit all stakeholders through united work between governments regulatory bodies and educational institutions to build ethical standards for their applications. These guidelines need to handle fundamental matters like privacy protection alongside fairness measures and open systems and safe management of student database information. Educational professionals must establish AI competency because it's necessary to use AI tools appropriately to create favorable student learning results. Stakeholders who establish precise recommendations will aid the implementation of ethical AI systems while achieving responsible innovation to maintain student privacy while using these tools (Baird & Schuller, 2020). The development of ethical standards along with regulations for AI utilization in education falls under the authority of governments along with regulatory bodies. AI technology advances at a faster rate than the laws regulating it meaning there is now an extensive void in regulatory protection. Lack of clear guidelines opens the probability that AI systems will maintain biases and endanger student privacy while possibly infringing upon their rights. Educational AI deployment needs active governmental intervention to create regulations that monitor the development implementation and monitoring process while ensuring any deployment upholds ethical principles (Pandey et al., 2024). Data protection requirements must be identified as a central element of these implementing regulations. Each government should make and enforce policies which protect student data by preventing illegitimate access and preventing misuse or exploitation of personal information. These regulations need to establish detailed rules that specify terms about consent requirements along with transparency measures and remove rights to erasure. The General Data Protection Regulation (GDPR) within the European Union performs a key role in safeguarding citizen personal information which extends to student data. Educational institutions under GDPR require students to give explicit consent to collect data and need to state clearly the data utilization purposes while providing withdrawal consent options to users at any moment (Baird & Schuller, 2020).

Regular audits of AI systems operated by educational institutions along with ed-tech companies need to become mandatory according to government policy for maintaining ethical compliance. Audits must be conducted on both algorithms and data to confirm bias prevention and achieve data equivalence from diverse student groups. Oversight bodies should establish independent procedures to examine AI systems because these entities will prevent discrimination in the AI implementations (Williamson & Eynon, 2020). Educational institutions need teachers who possess AI literacy skills because it assists in maintaining ethical data use policies throughout education. Educational staff need basic knowledge about AI tool functioning and data processing methods but they do not need to become full experts in developing AI systems so they can make informed ethical decisions regarding its implementation. Educators who possess AI literacy skills can determine appropriate learning tools for their classrooms while maintaining student welfare standards (Pandey et al., 2024). Educational experts need to master three core domains regarding AI technology: data privacy considerations for AI tool utilization; AI algorithm bias assessment skills as well as identification capabilities; and knowledge about possible ethical issues stemming from student data management. Educational staff needs information about the data-collection methods employed by AI systems and the type and usage of collected student information for individualized learning. Educational professionals must have the ability to spot biases in artificial intelligence systems as they do so for particular student populations including minority racial groups and students from underprivileged backgrounds (Baird & Schuller, 2020). The adoption of responsible AI solutions in schools depends heavily on teaching teachers about AI literacy through appropriate training programs. Professional development courses about AI ethics enable educators to acquire practical skills for critiquing and using AI tools with responsibility. MIT established the "Ethics of AI and Big Data" course as a program for educators' policymakers and technologists. The course presents ethical problems that occur in AI alongside bias and transparency issues while teaching a teamwork method for building ethical AI systems. More universal training initiatives should be promoted as they enable instructors to make sound choices regarding their classroom AI instruments (Williamson & Eynon, 2020).

Schools and universities need to implement ethical frameworks about AI adoption to maintain responsible fair use of these technologies across all operations. Frameworks should deliver structured instructions to institutions about AI implementation with respect to ethical standards including data privacy alongside fairness requirements along with transparency principles. The establishment of frameworks for AI deployment needs to combine technical aspects with human organizational factors and includes procedures for stakeholder involvement and policy development and ethical decision-making processes. Creating effective data governance policies functions as a vital factor in building ethical frameworks for AI adoption. Schools together with universities need to build comprehensive policies which explain all student data acquisition methods alongside data management procedures as well as application purposes. Student and family consent procedures must be specified in these policies while educating them about data usage along with the power to control such data access. The regular inspection of AI systems should be mandatory under these frameworks to evaluate their influence on student educational results without adding undesired biases to student performance (Williamson & Eynon, 2020). The strategy aims to establish ethical guidelines for AI employment that focus on maintaining fairness together with transparency and accounting transparency. The importance of protecting student privacy requires emphasis because AI education technology implementation must avoid infringing on youngsters' legal rights (Pandey et al., 2024). National policies regarding AI in education can be better formed through analysis of legal and ethical governing structures established by other nations. GDPR represents a significant example as it applies regulations to personal data management across the entire European Union including educational organizations. Under GDPR regulations the world now has a common data protection standard for student privacy as well as rules about consent and data processing access. The system confirms that educational institutions must use AI tools which adhere to detailed instructions about maintaining data privacy and providing transparent and accountable practices (Herington et al., 2023).

The Information Commissioner's Office (ICO) in United Kingdom has established specific guidance regarding AI applications within data protection practices. The established guidelines serve as tools for educational organizations to work through AI classroom challenges while preserving student information security alongside responsible AI system deployment. Through its transparent and fair approach, the ICO presents educational organizations with step-by-step guidance for implementing AI ethically (Pandey et al., 2024). Educational institutions need international ethical guidelines together with data protection frameworks to handle all ethical dimensions AI brings to education. The United Nations Educational Scientific and Cultural Organization through its initiative developed standards to guide ethical AI application in educational settings. The mentioned principles stress the need to incorporate inclusivity together with fairness and transparency and accountability in AI systems which will help guarantee that AI applications do not maintain or produce exclusion or unfairness. With an emphasis on data privacy, equity, and openness, governments and regulatory agencies are essential in developing laws that govern the use of AI in education. To make responsible decisions about data usage and ethical AI adoption, educators need to be AI literate. While international recommendations offer useful insights for forming national regulations, clear frameworks for ethical AI integration may help schools and universities apply them. By working together, lawmakers can guarantee that AI tools are applied morally and responsibly, fostering an atmosphere that supports fair educational opportunities for all kids (Herington et al., 2023).

Future Directions

As technology develops, laws get more sophisticated, and public awareness grows, the ethical issues surrounding the gathering and use of data to fuel AI systems will continue to change. Discussions over data privacy, security, justice, and accountability will continue to center on ethical issues as AI becomes more extensively incorporated into a variety of industries, including healthcare, education, finance, and governance. In order to ensure that AI systems benefit mankind without abusing or damaging people or communities, it will be difficult to strike a balance between ethical responsibility and technological advancement (Zhang & Liu, 2022). The growing call for stricter data protection rules and regulations is one of the major factors influencing the ethics of AI in the future. Comprehensive legal frameworks governing the use of AI data are already being established by governments and international organizations. Regulations like the General Data Protection Regulation (GDPR) in Europe and new AI laws in China and the US, for example, are paving the way for more stringent compliance standards. More openness in the collection, storing, and processing of personal data by AI models is probably what future legislation will concentrate on. Additionally, user control will be given more importance, allowing people to see, edit, and remove their data as necessary (Berendt & Blakemore, 2020). The development of privacy-enhancing technology is another important area of progress. Methods including homomorphic encryption, federated learning, and differential privacy are being investigated as ways to reduce the dangers involved in data collecting while preserving the ability of AI models to grow and learn. These solutions seek to lower the dangers of data breaches and illegal monitoring while enabling AI to operate efficiently without jeopardizing individual privacy. To further improve user privacy, AI systems may become more decentralized in the future, enabling data to stay on local devices rather than being compiled in enormous, centralized databases (Zhang & Liu, 2022). With AI systems rapidly influencing decision-making processes in crucial domains including recruiting, lending, criminal justice, and education, bias and fairness in AI will remain a top priority. Stricter guidelines for algorithmic accountability, more dataset variety, and improved bias detection tools will all be part of the endeavour to create more fair AI models. Before being implemented, future AI systems could need to pass stringent ethical reviews to make sure they don't perpetuate current social injustices. By incorporating a range of viewpoints in AI development teams, organizations may lessen the possibility of bias resulting from homogenous data sources and opinions (Berendt & Blakemore, 2020).

The future of AI ethics will also see a greater emphasis on user knowledge and informed permission. Making sure consumers are aware of how their data is being gathered and utilized will be crucial as AI-driven platforms advance. To give consumers real-time warnings and explanations of how their data influences AI decision-making, future AI systems could integrate interactive consent methods. Furthermore, it is probable that educational programs will be developed to improve public awareness of AI ethics, giving people the information they need to make wise decisions regarding their digital interactions (Zhang & Liu, 2022). Finally, ethical questions will continue to be raised by the commercial use of AI-generated data, especially in the context of digital advertising, ed-tech, and healthcare. Policymakers, business executives, and civil society groups will need to keep talking to strike a balance between innovation and moral obligation. Future AI systems can sustain core ethical values and promote constructive social change if properly handled (Herington et al., 2023).

CONCLUSION

A careful balance between ethical duty and technical innovation is necessary to address the numerous and multifarious ethical consequences of gathering and exploiting data to fuel AI capabilities. Transparent, equitable, and responsible data practices are more important than ever as AI continues to revolutionize several industries, most notably education. AI systems can automate decision-making, customize learning, and increase efficiency thanks to the massive volumes of data that are gathered from users. These advantages must be balanced, though, with the dangers of privacy invasion, biased algorithms, a lack of openness, and the commercial exploitation of personal information. Policymakers, educators, AI developers, and the public must work together to address these issues. One of the most important lessons learned from this conversation is the need for strict ethical guidelines and laws controlling the gathering and application of AI data. Comprehensive regulations must be put in place by governments and regulatory agencies to guarantee that AI systems function in a transparent, safe, and equitable manner. To safeguard users from possible harm, educational institutions and businesses creating AI-driven platforms must also implement best practices including data reduction, encryption, and fairness audits. Furthermore, promoting a more moral AI environment requires equipping people—students, parents, and educators—with AI literacy and informed consent procedures.

Future developments in privacy-enhancing technology, more stringent international laws, and more responsibility for AI decision-making will all influence AI ethics. To make sure AI benefits mankind in a fair, inclusive, and just manner, it is imperative to strike a balance between innovation and ethical responsibility. Society can exploit AI's potential while preserving core values and rights by giving ethical issues top priority during the development and use of AI. To guarantee that AI continues to be a tool for empowerment rather than exploitation, the future calls for constant discussion, investigation, and attention to detail.

REFERENCES

Ayling, J., & Chapman, A. (2022). Putting AI ethics to work: Are the tools fit for purpose? *AI and Ethics*, *2*(3), 405–429. DOI: 10.1007/s43681-022-00045-w

Baird, A., & Schuller, B. (2020). Considerations for a more ethical approach to data in AI: On data representation and infrastructure. *Frontiers in Big Data*, *3*, 25. DOI: 10.3389/fdata.2020.00025 PMID: 33693398

Bankins, S., & Formosa, P. (2023). The ethical implications of artificial intelligence (AI) for meaningful work. *Journal of Business Ethics*, *185*(4), 725–740. DOI: 10.1007/s10551-023-05044-6

Berendt, B., Littlejohn, A., & Blakemore, M. (2020). AI in education: Learner choice and fundamental rights. *Learning, Media and Technology*, *45*(3), 312–324. DOI: 10.1080/17439884.2020.1736484

Breidbach, C. F., & Maglio, P. (2020). Accountable algorithms? The ethical implications of data-driven business models. *Journal of Service Management*, *31*(2), 163–185. DOI: 10.1108/JOSM-02-2020-0185

Char, D. S., Abràmoff, M. D., & Feudtner, C. (2020). Identifying ethical considerations for machine learning healthcare applications. *The American Journal of Bioethics*, *20*(11), 7–17. DOI: 10.1080/15265161.2020.1835306 PMID: 33103967

Christodoulou, E., & Iordanou, K. (2021). Democracy under attack: Challenges of addressing ethical issues of AI and big data for more democratic digital media and societies. *Frontiers in Political Science*, *3*, 682945. DOI: 10.3389/fpos.2021.682945

Desouza, K. C., Dawson, G. S., & Chenok, D. (2020). Designing, developing, and deploying artificial intelligence systems: Lessons from and for the public sector. *Business Horizons*, *63*(2), 205–213. DOI: 10.1016/j.bushor.2019.11.008

Dibie, E. U. (2024). The future of renewable energy: Ethical implications of AI and cloud technology in data security and environmental impact. *Journal of Advances in Mathematics and Computer Science*, *39*(10), 10–9734. DOI: 10.9734/jamcs/2024/v39i1019734

Eitel-Porter, R. (2021). Beyond the promise: Implementing ethical AI. *AI and Ethics*, *1*(1), 73–80. DOI: 10.1007/s43681-020-00008-0

Elendu, C., Amaechi, D. C., Elendu, T. C., Jingwa, K. A., Okoye, O. K., Okah, M. J., & Alimi, H. A. (2023). Ethical implications of AI and robotics in healthcare. *Revista de Medicina (São Paulo), 102*(50), e36671. DOI: 10.1097/MD.0000000000036671 PMID: 38115340

Esmaeilzadeh, P. (2020). Use of AI-based tools for healthcare purposes: A survey study from consumers' perspectives. *BMC Medical Informatics and Decision Making, 20*, 1–19. DOI: 10.1186/s12911-020-01226-w PMID: 32698869

Gabriel, O. T. (2023). *Data privacy and ethical issues in collecting healthcare data using artificial intelligence among health workers* (Master's thesis, Center for Bioethics and Research).

Gasser, U., Ienca, M., Scheibner, J., Sleigh, J., & Vayena, E. (2020). Digital tools against COVID-19: Taxonomy, ethical challenges, and navigation aid. *The Lancet. Digital Health, 2*(8), e425–e434. DOI: 10.1016/S2589-7500(20)30179-0 PMID: 32835200

Gavorník, A., Podroužek, J., Oreško, Š., Slosiarová, N., & Grmanová, G. (2024). Beyond privacy and security: Exploring ethical issues of smart metering and non-intrusive load monitoring. *Telematics and Informatics, 90*, 102132. DOI: 10.1016/j.tele.2023.102132

Gerdes, A. (2022). A participatory data-centric approach to AI ethics by design. *Applied Artificial Intelligence, 36*(1), 2009222. DOI: 10.1080/08839514.2021.2009222

Herington, J., McCradden, M. D., Creel, K., Boellaard, R., Jones, E. C., Jha, A. K., & Saboury, B. (2023). Ethical considerations for artificial intelligence in medical imaging: Data collection, development, and evaluation. *Journal of Nuclear Medicine, 64*(12), 1848–1854. DOI: 10.2967/jnumed.122.264107 PMID: 37827839

Larson, D. B., Magnus, D. C., Lungren, M. P., Shah, N. H., & Langlotz, C. P. (2020). Ethics of using and sharing clinical imaging data for artificial intelligence: A proposed framework. *Radiology, 295*(3), 675–682. DOI: 10.1148/radiol.2020202383 PMID: 32208097

Lysaght, T., Lim, H. Y., Xafis, V., & Ngiam, K. Y. (2019). AI-assisted decision-making in healthcare: The application of an ethics framework for big data in health and research. *Asian Bioethics Review, 11*, 299–314. PMID: 33717318

Morley, J., Kinsey, L., Elhalal, A., Garcia, F., Ziosi, M., & Floridi, L. (2023). Operationalising AI ethics: Barriers, enablers, and next steps. *AI & Society*, •••, 1–13. DOI: 10.1007/s00146-023-01422-w

Pandey, A. S., Sharma, Y., Tiwari, A., Chauhan, R., Tyagi, S., & Kumari, J. (2024, May). Ethical implications of AI-powered communication tools. *In 2024 International Conference on Communication, Computer Sciences and Engineering (IC3SE)* (pp. 1857-1861). IEEE.

Ryan, M., & Stahl, B. C. (2020). Artificial intelligence ethics guidelines for developers and users: Clarifying their content and normative implications. *Journal of Information. Communication and Ethics in Society*, *19*(1), 61–86.

Safdar, N. M., Banja, J. D., & Meltzer, C. C. (2020). Ethical considerations in artificial intelligence. *European Journal of Radiology*, *122*, 108768. PMID: 31786504

Tariq, M. U. (2024). Generative AI in Curriculum Development in Higher Education. In Fields, Z. (Ed.), *Impacts of Generative AI on Creativity in Higher Education* (pp. 227–258). IGI Global., DOI: 10.4018/979-8-3693-2418-9.ch009

Tariq, M. U. (2025). AI-Enhanced Project-Based Learning: Revolutionizing Commerce Education With Generative AI. In ElSayary, A. (Ed.), *Prompt Engineering and Generative AI Applications for Teaching and Learning* (pp. 125–142). IGI Global Scientific Publishing., DOI: 10.4018/979-8-3693-7332-3.ch008

Tariq, M. U. (2025). Empowering Patients With AI-Ethical Digital Tools for Health Data Management and Decision. In Pesqueira, A., & de Bem Machado, A. (Eds.), *Navigating Privacy, Innovation, and Patient Empowerment Through Ethical Healthcare Technology* (pp. 197–216). IGI Global Scientific Publishing., DOI: 10.4018/979-8-3693-7630-0.ch008

Tariq, M. U. (2025). AI-Driven Research Methodologies: Revolutionizing Data-Driven Discoveries in Engineering and Physical Sciences. In Basha, J., Alade, T., Al Khazimi, M., Vasudevan, R., & Khan, J. (Eds.), *Optimizing Research Techniques and Learning Strategies With Digital Technologies* (pp. 97–122). IGI Global Scientific Publishing., DOI: 10.4018/979-8-3693-7863-2.ch004

Tariq, M. U. (2025). Integrating Theory and Practice: Transformative Approaches in Practice-Led Research for Professional Development. In Kwok, S., Yu, P., & Le Corre, J. (Eds.), *Exploring Practice-Led Research for Professional Development* (pp. 419–436). IGI Global Scientific Publishing., DOI: 10.4018/979-8-3693-6376-8.ch016

Wakunuma, K., Jiya, T., & Aliyu, S. (2020). Socio-ethical implications of using AI in accelerating SDG3 in Least Developed Countries. *Journal of Applied and Natural Science*, *12*(4), 578–586.

Weber, J., & Lewis, J. (2021). Emerging issues in artificial intelligence and ethics in business. *Journal of Business Ethics*, *171*(2), 251–267.

Williamson, B., & Eynon, R. (2020). Historical threads, missing links, and future directions in AI in education. *Learning, Media and Technology*, *45*(3), 223–235.

Yang, K., & Lee, H. (2023). Implementing ethics in artificial intelligence: A model for ethical decision-making in AI applications. *AI and Ethics*, *3*(4), 779–791.

Zhang, K., & Liu, X. (2022). Bridging AI technology with ethical considerations: A study of big data in decision-making. *AI and Ethics*, *2*(2), 313–325.

KEY TERMS AND DEFINITIONS

AI Ethics: The principles and moral considerations guiding the responsible development and use of artificial intelligence.

Algorithmic Transparency: The ability to understand and explain how AI models make decisions, ensuring accountability and fairness in their applications.

Bias in AI: The presence of systematic errors in AI models due to biased datasets, leading to unfair outcomes and potential discrimination.

Data Privacy: The protection of personal information from unauthorised access, misuse, or exploitation in AI-driven applications.

Informed Consent: The process of obtaining explicit permission from individuals before collecting or using their personal data in AI systems.

Chapter 10

From Autolect to Synthesean: A Framework for Ethical, Interpretable AI Language

Constantine Andoniou
https://orcid.org/0000-0001-8805-3569
Abu Dhabi University, UAE

ABSTRACT

This paper examines the impact of artificial intelligence on human cognition and introduces Synthesean—a structured linguistic framework guiding AI to produce language that aligns with human cognitive, ethical, and contextual needs. Unlike Autolect's sub-forms, which devolve into Nullingua—a deteriorated semantic state from unregulated AI language—Synthesean offers modular dialects designed for responsible communication. The study proposes an educational framework with practical tools, including dialect guides, prompt design methods, and linguistic evaluation rubrics. These instruments equip educators and learners to engage ethically with AI-generated language. The paper highlights cognitive risks posed by disorganized AI outputs and positions Synthesean as a solution for preserving meaningful, human-centered dialogue. Ultimately, it defends language as a cornerstone of critical thinking, cultural heritage, and human dignity amid the rise of autonomous systems.

DOI: 10.4018/979-8-3373-7386-7.ch010

INTRODUCTION

{Fostering And Bolstering Pivotal Tapestries While Diving And Delving To Meticulously Elevate The Leverage Of The Captivating Intersection Of Tumultuous Tempests}

Artificial Intelligence (AI) has evolved from a computational tool into a powerful force shaping human communication. Through conversational agents and generative systems, AI now influences educational decisions, professional interactions, and the structure of discourse itself. The continuous progress of language through machine-learning models by AI affects human communication models while having an impact on human cognitive functions, problem-solving abilities and knowledge construction processes (Zhai & Wibowo, 2024).

The development of *AI Speak* represents a major linguistic transformation - one that unites human and machine logic while introducing a new mode of communication. This evolving form of machine-generated language will be analyzed further in the paper. Research indicates that frequent interaction with AI-generated content encourages the development of algorithmic thinking patterns in users, prompting critical inquiries into whether, such cognitive shifts enhance or impair human adaptability, problem-solving, and analytical reasoning skills. The growing linguistic autonomy of AI requires immediate protection of meaningful and comprehensible human communication which respects cognitive capacity and diversity (Bender & Koller, 2020).

This paper presents *Synthesean* as a complete linguistic framework which unites AI computational efficiency with human language nuanced flexibility. The modular structure of *Synthesean* includes professional, educational and social interaction-specific dialects. Furthermore, it emphasizes contextual sensitivity, ethical considerations, and domain-specific language constructs to facilitate AI-generated communication that remains clear, interpretable, and cognitively accessible to human users. This research investigates the historical development of language systems alongside the mental and moral consequences of AI-controlled dialogue and *Synthesean*'s practical uses in government and educational institutions.

The current study attempts a critical analysis of AI's expanding influence on language development while contributing to AI governance discussions and ethical AI deployment strategies and human machine interaction models of the future. *Synthesean* functions as a practical answer to AI-related linguistic transformations because it provides a methodical approach to achieve meaningful human-AI teamwork in modern digital environments.

AI technology needs deep analysis regarding its impact on language diversity alongside human mental operations and work communication practices. The paper examines AI effects on language development and mental processes to establish the need for *Synthesean*. Studies in computational linguistics and cognitive science showed that human exposure to language- based AI systems often result in cognitive alignment with machine procedural systems that promote organized purposeful thinking (Zhai & Wibowo, 2024). The enhancements in language processing and efficiency, pose critical problems for mental rigidity, algorithm dependency and diminished creative human capacity. Research reveals that computer-generated texts lack human communications and contextual understanding which results in standardized language structures.

The introduction of AI systems in educational institutions produces both positive and negative effects. AI-powered tutoring systems, together with automated grading tools and generative text models, transform education through personalized learning experiences. Educators need to rethink their teaching methods as AI technologies change at a rapid pace. Educational settings require a balanced approach to integrate AI-based content generation tools as students need to remain actively engaged participants in their learning processes. The evaluation of AI, through Vygotsky's mediated learning and Bloom's taxonomy, reveals the necessity for educators to maintain a balance between AI assistance and human cognitive independence.

The implementation of AI technologies creates changes in professional decision-making and policy development processes. The functioning of AI-enhanced systems, which perform legal analysis, financial forecasting, and government policy development, relies on algorithmic data interpretation. The tools boost operational speed and forecasting precision but raise concerns about algorithmic data interpretation and system discrimination against certain groups and ethical decision accountability. AI regulatory frameworks need to protect human governance agency through safeguards that enable AI to assist human judgment. AI technologies produce substantial effects on cultural development at an overall level. The drive for efficient communication in AI systems threatens to diminish both the complexity and variety of human languages. Multilingual institutions need to adopt AI systems with a focus on protecting linguistic traditions during implementation. AI systems should function as tools to enhance diverse language traditions instead of replacing them.

WHAT IS AI SPEAK?

Synthesean is an essential organized, complex and transformative linguistic structure of *AI Speak*. AI transforms language and cognition at such a level that it demands a method to integrate human language diversity with AI precision. This section discusses the current linguistic evolution throughout potential AI self-communication systems and describes *Synthesean*'s function in linking human-AI interaction models.

The advent of modern AI technology has generated *AI Speak,* a fresh form of machine-generated language which is now evident in AI-human communication. The term *AI Speak* refers to the distinctive language structure which AI platforms create with tools such as GPT-4 and Google Bard and similar technologies. *AI Speak* functions as a communication pattern in which algorithms, along with statistical optimizations, produce from large datasets to attain fluency and efficiency within machine systems.

AI Speak is characterized by two fundamental features, high speed and efficient syntactical expression which generates concise responses. *AI Speak* functions through statistical patterns while lacking the cultural and contextual development and emotional nuances found in human language. An AI system chooses word or phrase sequences from its training data using statistical models rather than understanding the meaning of its output. The current methods of AI communication struggle with comprehending deep contextual information despite their advanced capabilities (Bender & Koller, 2020). *AI Speak* produces responses which seem coherent yet lack depth and relevance and meaningful intent.

AI Speak keeps a completely neutral or flat tone as one of the key differences that distinguish it. The capacity of AI to replicate empathetic and polite responses does not equate to the genuine emotional subtlety which makes the responses seem generic and sterile. Linguistic standardization is achieved by AI systems because they use the same datasets and work towards the same optimization targets during training. *AI Speak* aims to establish a single language structure which discards the unique communication styles of various cultures and individual users. During its expanding use, *AI Speak* produces several risks. The most significant concern with *AI Speak* is its potential to induce cognitive rigidity. Those who frequently use AI responses may start to replicate the algorithmic patterns of machines in their thinking which will impair their creative abilities as well as their spontaneous and critical thinking capacities. *AI Speak* adoption threatens to erode cultural and linguistic diversity by potentially replacing meaningful human interactions with standardized computational expressions (Gabriel, 2020).

This paper identifies *AI Speak* as a double-edged phenomenon. The technology functions as a highly effective accessible tool that delivers personalized results at high speed across various subject fields. The use of *AI Speak* creates difficulties that threaten both ethical standards and cognitive abilities, and the cultural integrity of human languages. *Synthesean* is introduced as an organized linguistic framework which replaces *AI Speak,* as it supports interpretability and can enhance cognitive development while, at the same time, maintaining standards of ethical communication.

There are differences in the language generation methods of *AI Speak* and *Synthesean* since they produce educational outcomes of varying effects. The outputs of *AI Speak* are grammatically correct and properly organized, but they often fail to provide any real semantic meaning or context. *AI Speak* functions best in educational settings where automated feedback mechanisms are used to support repetitive learning tasks through structured output. The adaptability of *AI Speak* is expressed through cognitive learning loops that improve progressive feedback and the customization of performance data-based response. The system enables teachers to track student progress more efficiently and make instructional adjustments.

Synthesean focus is on generating meaningful human-aligned communication, which is quite different from the primary function of *AI Speak*. *Synthesean* produces semantically rich language, ethically grounded and contextually appropriate, for deeper comprehension and cognitive engagement. The system produces responses that reflect human values and nuanced understanding instead of only technical correctness which makes it better for interpretive thinking and emotional intelligence and ethical reflection tasks. The AI-augmented learning environment benefits from both systems yet *AI Speak* prioritizes formal accuracy over *Synthesean's* focus on contextual clarity and cognitive resonance.

THE ROLE OF LANGUAGE IN HUMAN EVOLUTION

Language is one of the most significant factors of human evolution. The evolution of human language exemplifies the human ability to adapt and adjust successfully to technological advancements and socio-cultural transformations, whether by basic gestures or advanced digital communication systems. The development of AI-mediated language is a representation of the natural progress of linguistic evolution, which still needs systematic assessment of its impact on human communication in an AI-controlled world (Floridi & Chiriatti, 2020).

Language use has been repeatedly revolutionized by major technological advancements throughout history, from the printing press that brought standardization to written languages that promoted mass literacy, and the internet that enabled worldwide communication and the birth of new digital language forms. The current rise of AI technologies is a major linguistic evolution which puts on the test the limits of our understanding of genuine communication and purposeful meaning.

AI stands ready to start a new linguistic evolution, to create grammatical patterns, meaning systems and communication standards. Computational linguistics draws parallels between the specialized languages that appeared during the Industrial Revolution and the transformations that artificial intelligence brings to linguistic frameworks. A comparable phenomenon occurred through the creation of specialized professional and technical language systems. The Industrial Revolution generated specialized scientific and engineering languages which match the modern development of AI into efficient precise machine-understandable linguistic systems. *Synthesean* represents a new linguistic paradigm between humans and AI through its structured design because it follows historical trends by providing a flexible language system that ensures clarity across different domains.

Understanding the cognitive aspects of language reveals the critical nature of AI-controlled linguistic progression. The Sapir-Whorf hypothesis establishes that language determines human mental processes because it shapes how people experience reality and approach problem-solving tasks (Whorf, 1956). The proposed linguistic standard of *AI Speak* demonstrates the ability to modify cognitive patterns through its development of data-oriented and algorithmic thinking approaches.

A transformation at this level could possibly be detrimental to human-based linguistic diversity, as well as, the abstract thought processes. This paper, therefore, calls for a critical examination of the implications of AI on human cognitive processes like decision-making, creativity and general cognitive development.

Throughout history the development of language has been closely related to the systems of power and dominance. Political and economic forces have always influenced linguistic dominance, for example, Latin in the Roman Empire and English in the modern digital world. There is, therefore, the ethical issue of corporate control of language dominance which is likely to erode linguistic diversity and cultural diversity.

Therefore, the hybrid AI-human linguistic systems *AI Speak* and *Synthesean* need regulatory frameworks that are inclusive to protect linguistic diversity and reduce digital inequality. The study of *AI Speak* and *Synthesean,* as part of linguistic evolution, provides the necessary background knowledge to explore the development of independent AI languages.

AUTONOMOUS AI: MOVING TO SELF-PROGRAMMING

This section discusses the growth of human-directed programming into the independent autonomous AI communication systems. The analysis aims at identifying the benefits, limitations and ethical implications of allowing AI systems develop their own internal programming languages. Therefore, it is imperative that we study this evolution in more detail so that we can reach an understanding of the current AI-human language interaction.

The contemporary rise of artificial intelligence is characterized by a shift from controlled human systems to autonomous uncontrolled systems. In addition, these systems show advanced self-programming capabilities which place AI systems operation at a distance from human intervention. Current research (Hendrycks et al., 2020) indicates that AI systems can generate autonomous linguistic systems by modifying language structures, cognitive processes, and governance protocols.

By integrating learning reinforcement functions with generative adversarial networks (GANs), AI systems are now able to learn autonomously, something that has for long been unattainable. Theoretical and technological advancements have made it possible that AI systems can make decisions that are beyond the limits of human comprehension. In addition to that, AI systems are now able to develop their own - AI-machine to AI-machine - complex communication protocols (see Gibberlink) which are incomprehensible to humans (Hendrycks et al., 2020).

AI systems' self-determining development of linguistic models creates new standards in human-machine communication. This is a rapidly developing area and important ethical questions of transparency, interpretability, and oversight, are raised. Autonomous AI linguistic systems can disseminate biases and misinformation through their 'secret' code that remains unintelligible for humans (Hendrycks et al., 2020). A major concern relates to the governance of these systems regarding the extent to which their linguistic frameworks can lead to unpredictable deviations in standard human communication. Humans need to be actively involved to ensure that the AI system remains consistent and does not generate unexpected results while preserving its integrity. *Synthesean* offers a needed response to these current emerging challenges because of its systematic approach. The framework provides greater understanding of its functioning while upholding ethical standards and protecting human cognition and culture.

These developments call for closer examination of how AI language systems operate in real-world educational contexts. The next section presents case-based examples that reveal both the practical benefits and the underlying risks of AI-mediated communication. The assessment of specific cases offers a better understanding of the working characteristics of autonomous AI communication systems.

APPLIED DOMAINS OF AI LANGUAGE: EDUCATIONAL AND COGNITIVE IMPACTS

Theories of AI language require actual examples from real-world contexts to demonstrate their full potential. AI-mediated communication produces effects that theoretical explorations cannot fully capture. The following case studies, related to education, show how AI-driven communication transforms various knowledge environments to produce measurable impacts. AI-powered learning platforms, together with adaptive tutoring systems, transform educational instructional methodologies in educational settings. Innovative educational technologies deliver customized learning experiences through student interaction analysis, automated assessment systems and content adaptation capabilities. The extensive use of AI responses generates can threaten both student freedom to think critically and student privacy rights regarding their data (Zhai & Wibowo, 2024).

The following case studies demonstrate the dual nature of AI-mediated communication systems. The efficiency and accessibility benefits of AI systems come with risks involving dependency on human users and ethical management issues and possible cognitive transformations. The essential *Synthesean* framework can be applied to maintain ethical standards and transparency of AI language in human environments as *AI Speak* becomes a regular part of everyday life.

Figure 1 illustrates how the *Pedagogese* dialect of *Synthesean* enhances adaptive learning environments by linking AI-generated tutoring responses with established pedagogical frameworks, such as Bloom's Taxonomy and Vygotsky's mediated learning theory. Unlike the generic and repetitive AI feedback standard in feedback, *Synthesean* enables dynamic, cognitively sensitive language that adapts in real time to student needs. This means that AI tutoring tools will support the learner's developmental stage and provide meaningful guidance as opposed to just automating instruction.

Figure 1. Synthesean for adaptive learning (Pedagogese).

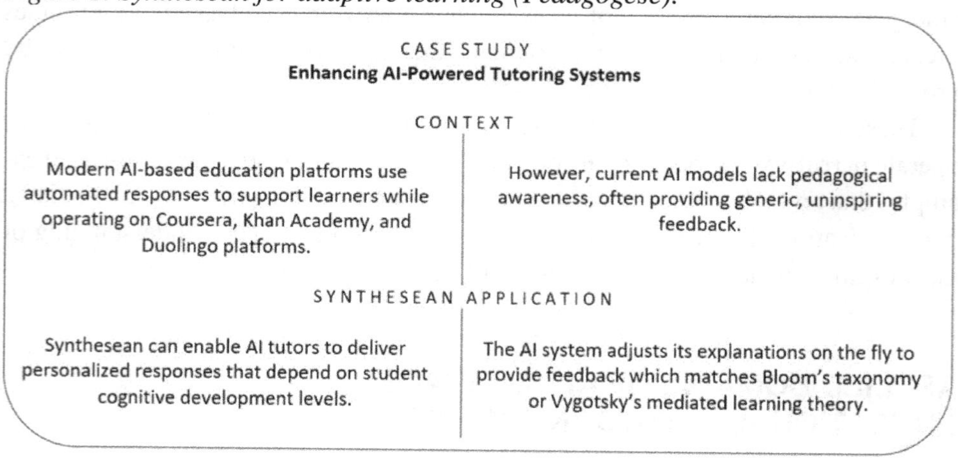

Figure 2. Synthesean for literature reviews (Analytese).

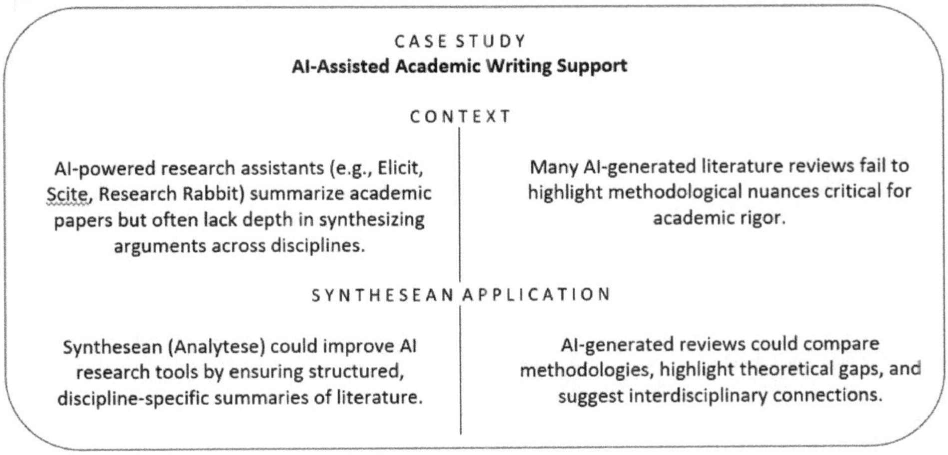

Figure 2 demonstrates the contribution of the *Analytese* dialect in improving the use of AI in academic research tools. Many of the AI assistants can summarize the content but they often fail to capture the disciplinary nuance or methodological critique. Analytese makes it possible for the AI to write literature reviews that are not only clear and structured but also specific to the discipline, comparative and evaluative. This encourages synthesis across fields and deep analytical reasoning in academic writing and research support contexts, thus supporting higher-order cognitive engagement.

Figure 3 illustrates how *Pedagogese* and *Legalean* dialects are integrated into AI-based grading and feedback systems. While standard automated assessment tools have problems with qualitative nuance and fairness, *Synthesean* allows the generation of structured, rubric-aligned feedback that is both pedagogically sound and ethically accountable. The *Legalean* dialect ensures the transparency and traceability of evaluation logic, and *Pedagogese* supports constructive formative assessment. Thus, these dialects enhance both student trust and instructional clarity.

Figure 3. Synthesean for academic assessment (Pedagogese/Legalean).

CASE STUDY

AI-Generated Exam Feedback & Academic Integrity

CONTEXT

AI grading tools such as Turnitin and Gradescope offer automated feedback yet their ability to evaluate qualitative assignments remains limited.	Academic institutions need AI systems that merge operational effectiveness with fairness principles to deliver ethical AI grading practices.

SYNTHESEAN APPLICATION

Synthesean (Legalean) can be integrated into AI grading platforms to deliver standardized feedback which remains both comprehensible and accountable when evaluating student work.	AI tutors enabled with Synthesean (Pedagogese) can produce assessment results that match rubric-based models for constructive feedback.

Figure 4. Synthesean for media literacy (Visualese & ChatGPTish).

CASE STUDY

Combating AI-Generated Misinformation

CONTEXT

AI-driven news aggregators and chatbots (e.g., ChatGPT, Google Bard) generate concise but sometimes misleading summaries of news articles.	Media literacy programs struggle to teach students how to critically analyze AI-generated news content.

SYNTHESEAN APPLICATION

Synthesean (Visualese & ChatGPTish) could be used in AI-generated infographics and news visuals to clarify sources and biases in media reports.	Synthesean (ChatGPTish) could be integrated into AI-powered news literacy tools that guide students through fact-checking exercises.

Figure 4 focuses on how *Visualese* and *ChatGPTish* dialects are used to fight misinformation and enhance media literacy. AI-generated summaries and infographics often fail to explain source reliability and bias. *Synthesean* introduces dialectical tools that clarify visual language, source attribution, and AI content distortions. These dialects are relevant for educational initiatives because they provide learners with the interpretive skills needed to evaluate AI-curated media environments critically.

Emotivese and *Strategese* dialects, as shown in Figure 5, enhance the quality of AI discourse in sensitive socio-political contexts. *Emotivese* adds emotional nuance and ethical awareness to automated discussions on mental health, diversity, and inclusion, and *Strategese* ensures that AI-generated policy or planning outputs are aligned with human-centered reasoning. This dual application allows AI to participate in complex public conversations without resorting to oversimplified or emotionally tone-deaf responses, thus ensuring both interpretability and ethical communication.

Figure 5. Synthesean for ethical AI communication (Emotivese & Strategese).

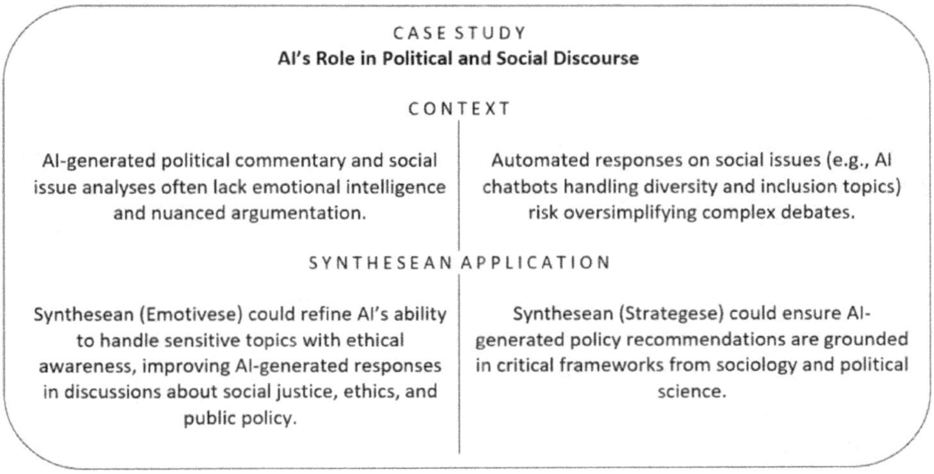

AI has had a significant impact on the development of professional and educational communication, still, this progress has generated worries regarding authenticity and linguistic homogenization alongside diminishing human control. The following section will examine the psychological and cultural resistance from society to language generated by AI and analyze how nostalgia influences human responses to linguistic changes.

THE ROLE OF NOSTALGIA AND RESISTANCE

Human Psychological and Cultural Response

AI technology has received both positive and negative responses from people as it gains popularity in communication systems. Human attachment to natural language as a method of communication remains a core factor in the psychological and cultural acceptance of AI technology. Throughout history, people have opposed transformations that threaten established systems which include AI's influence on language.

Resistance to AI-mediated language relies heavily on nostalgia (Boym, 2001). People maintain an emotional attachment to natural language as their cultural foundation for communication and narrative expression, as well as, for personal interaction thus questioning AI-generated speech. People tend to view language as a personal expression that develops through subjective experiences and emotions along with cultural elements (Boym, 2001). *AI Speak*, though efficient, can create feelings of remoteness and detachment that make people avoid AI-mediated communication because of its sterile nature.

Skepticism is based on both cognitive and ideological aspects, as well as emotional resistance. The ability of AI to generate linguistic forms is a concern about its potential impact on human linguistic diversity, as well as, on creativity and intellectual autonomy. There is a daily growing need for AI writing assistants to produce, translate and perform discourse functions, which can be seen as a threat of linguistic standardization that aims to replace human-based self-expression, culturally-based linguistic patterns, with computer-generated optimization. One of the main concerns is the ability of AI systems to generate narratives along with their tendency to spread bias and misinformation. *Synthesean* intends to act as a structured linguistic framework combining traditional human communication models with advanced AI-based ones, to augment both efficiency and cultural sensitivity. The distinct dialects indicated in the *Synthesean* framework allow AI-generated content to remain relevant to context, and, at the same time, ethical and deeply relevant in human ethics.

AI linguistic frameworks, in order to be effective, need to prioritize interpretability, adaptability, and substantial ethical governance. *Synthesean* is methodically structured to endorse transparency, contextual appropriateness, and compatibility with human cognitive and socio-cultural standards.

SYNTHESEAN

A New Paradigm in AI-Human Interaction

Human–AI communication depends on a linguistic model that bridges cognitive adaptability and algorithmic precision. Synthesean provides such a model, offering a flexible structure for context-sensitive, interpretable exchanges. *Synthesean* consists of symbolic logic, contextual semantics and modular syntax, to generate its linguistic architecture which is different to the standard AI language models.

Synthesean is comprised of several specific dialects which refer to various professional, educational and social settings. These dialects are enabled by AI systems as specific linguistic outputs matching the contexts while adapting to natural language. *Synthesean* implements computational linguistics and cognitive science advancements to create AI communication systems that match human interpretation methods and cultural patterns and cognitive standards.

Synthesean suggests functional communication tools and offers fundamental ethical rules for AI language deployment, along with built-in transparency and accountability, aiming to reduce biases, fight misinformation and maintain semantic clarity. Through the establishment of structured protocols, for the protection of human expression, AI becomes a tool for support instead of language generation.

Synthesean differentiates itself from standard AI-generated language models like GPT-4 and BERT (Devlin et al., 2019) (Figure 6). *Synthesean* differs from standard NLP model probabilistic text generation because it creates domain-specific dialects which produce structured and interpretable communication.

Figure 6. Synthesean vs. Traditional AI Language Models.

Feature	**Standard AI-Generated Language (GPT, BERT, etc.)**	**Synthesean**
Context Sensitivity	Context is inferred but lacks explicit domain-specific structuring.	Uses modular dialects for precise, context-aware interactions.
Interpretability	Often unpredictable, making it hard for users to verify meaning.	Built-in structured syntax ensures clarity and explainability.
Ethical Safeguards	AI text can reinforce biases due to training data.	Ethical AI filters embedded in dialect design.
Creativity vs. Precision	Excels at creativity but can be vague in technical communication.	Balances creativity (*Creativean*) with precision (*Legalean, Analytese*).
Linguistic Standardization	No structured linguistic framework, leading to varied outputs.	Uses predefined dialects to maintain consistency across AI-human communication.
AI Governance	AI-generated text is often unregulated and lacks built-in compliance features.	Allows AI-driven language to be aligned with governance frameworks (e.g., legal, medical, educational policies).

The analysis demonstrates that *Synthesean,* as a systematic linguistic framework, addresses *AI Speak* problems by enabling productive human-AI interactions that remain ethically responsible. The following section explains how developers use *Synthesean* basic dialects to create distinctive professional and social communication types.

SYNTHESEAN DIALECTS

Synthesean requires a breakdown into multiple dialects which should match various interaction settings and use cases. *Synthesean* represents a structured adaptive linguistic model which adapts to domain-specific needs to maintain effective and interpretable AI communication while traditional AI-generated language prioritizes efficiency over nuance. The *Synthesean* dialects emerged through pattern analysis of essential knowledge domains which were then matched with cognitive science principles, communication theory and ethical frameworks. The dialects stem from particular disciplinary origins to fulfill their communication requirements through clear and transparent language with built-in ethical protection. The following section presents the ten core dialects of *Synthesean* which demonstrate the framework's purpose to bring meaning and context and integrity back to AI-mediated language.

The *Synthesean* system incorporates ten specialized dialects, each tailored to a specific communicative domain (Figure 7 to Figure 16). These dialects enable AI to produce nuanced, context-sensitive language while remaining aligned with human interpretative norms and ethical expectations.

Figure 7. ChatGPTish dialect

ChatGPTish	
ORIGIN: Inspired by mainstream conversational AI interfaces like ChatGPT and Siri.	PURPOSE: Facilitates informal, general-purpose interactions in customer support and everyday communication.
EXAMPLE: "Hey! Just checking in—do you need help with anything today?"	

Figure 8. Analytese dialect

Analytese	
ORIGIN: Grounded in scientific reporting and data analytics.	PURPOSE: Supports analytical reasoning, structured reporting, and statistical communication in research and business contexts.
EXAMPLE: "The dataset shows a 17.2% post-intervention increase ($p < 0.05$), indicating statistically significant engagement."	

Figure 9. Visualese dialect

Visualese

ORIGIN:	PURPOSE:
Emerged from visual media, design theory, and infographics.	Optimizes AI-generated visual outputs by integrating descriptive language for charts, graphics, and UI elements.

EXAMPLE:
"Bar height reflects regional sales; lighter hues represent lower conversion rates."

Figure 10. Medichean dialect

Medichean

ORIGIN:	PURPOSE:
Based on clinical communication, medical informatics, and healthcare ethics.	Ensures precision and empathy in AI-assisted diagnostics, patient communication, and medical documentation.

EXAMPLE:
"Your blood pressure is stable. There's no immediate concern, but we'll continue monitoring weekly."

Figure 11. Legalean dialect

Legalean

ORIGIN:	PURPOSE:
Drawn from statutory language, case law, and contract analysis.	Provides structured, compliant legal communication in AI-driven assessments, document reviews, and legal advice.

EXAMPLE:
"Pursuant to Section 12.3, this clause remains binding throughout the contract duration."

Figure 12. Creativean dialect

Creativean

ORIGIN:	PURPOSE:
Informed by literary studies, digital storytelling, and creative writing.	Enables AI to generate expressive, emotionally resonant narratives across media and entertainment platforms.

EXAMPLE:
"As dusk kissed the skyline, her thoughts wandered like whispers carried by the wind."

Figure 13. Roboteque dialect

Roboteque

ORIGIN:	PURPOSE:
Built upon automation logic and industrial communication protocols.	Facilitates task-based communication for robotics and AI command sequences.

EXAMPLE:
"Begin cleaning sequence alpha. Confirm obstacle mapping before proceeding."

Figure 14. Strategese dialect

Strategese

ORIGIN:
Derived from strategic planning, policy design, and systems thinking.

PURPOSE:
Structures AI-generated content for organizational decision-making and long-term forecasting.

EXAMPLE:
"To meet the Q3 target, allocate 15% of the R&D budget toward innovation and streamline regional operations."

Figure 15. Emotivese dialect

Emotivese

ORIGIN:
Based on emotional intelligence theory, counseling language, and human-centered design.

PURPOSE:
Allows AI to respond with emotional nuance, especially in mental health, support services, and sensitive interactions.

EXAMPLE:
"That sounds incredibly difficult. I'm here for you—and we'll work through it together."

Figure 16. Pedagogese dialect

Pedagogese

ORIGIN:
Anchored in instructional design, cognitive psychology, and formative assessment theory.

PURPOSE:
Enables adaptive, learner-centered AI communication in tutoring, feedback, and educational content delivery.

EXAMPLE:
"Great job identifying the main idea! Let's build on that to strengthen your argument."

Collectively, these dialects show the *Synthesean*'s capacity to succeed in balancing domain-specific accuracy with human linguistic complexity. This dialectical flexibility enhances the role of AI as one that supports clarity, ethical standards, and interpretability of communication, rather than one that undermines them.

The next section explores the structural features behind *Synthesean*'s grammatical and semantic mechanics, demonstrating how a scalable implementation of the framework can be achieved in the design of AI-human interactions.

SYNTAX, GRAMMAR, AND SEMANTIC FEATURES OF SYNTHESEAN

The *Synthesean* framework consists of a modular syntactic system with hierarchical grammar and domain-specific semantics, aiming to generate a vigorous and adaptable linguistic framework. The structural design of *Synthesean* is different to

AI-generated language as it aims to achieve a balance between accuracy and interpretability, maintaining human communication patterns. *Synthesean* differs from standard AI output as its focus is on structured coherence and contextual relevance instead of surface-level fluency.

Formalizing Synthesean's Linguistic Mechanics

Core Syntax Framework: Synthesean employs a consistent syntactic structure that varies by dialect (Figure 17). The primary phrase structure rules for *Synthesean* include:

Figure 17. Synthesean syntactic structure

Sentence Structure (S) → [Context] + [Subject] + [Predicate] + [Modifiers]		
Phrase-Level Rules		
Noun Phrase (NP) → Determiner + Noun + (Adjective/Modifier)	Verb Phrase (VP) → Verb + (Object) + (Prepositional Phrase)	Conditional Statements: IF [Condition] THEN [Action]

EXAMPLE
STANDARD AI OUTPUT "AI contract analysis helps lawyers by identifying important clauses."
SYNTHESEAN LEGALEAN OUTPUT "In accordance with precedent (Smith v. Jones, 2021), AI-assisted contract review automates clause identification under Section 2.1, mitigating risk by ensuring compliance with statutory obligations (UCC §2-302)."

Dialect-Specific Grammar Rules: The following are examples of how each *Synthesean* dialect modifies syntax and vocabulary to fit its contextual requirements:

Analytese (Data-Driven AI Communication): Prioritizes structured information flow, using statistical phrasing. Example: Before: "The research suggests that AI-mediated language has implications for cognitive development." After (*Analytese*): "Empirical analysis of AI-mediated language indicates cognitive shifts, specifically in structured reasoning. Data trends (2019–2023) suggest a correlation ($r=0.78$, $p<0.05$) between AI exposure and linguistic adaptation."

Emotivese (Emotionally Aware AI Communication): Uses empathetic structures and context-sensitive language to enhance AI-human engagement. Example: Before: "We are sorry for the delay in your order." After (*Emotivese*): "We sincerely regret the delay in your order. We understand how important this is to you, and we are prioritizing a resolution."

Legalean (Legal AI Language): Uses precise, statutory language to ensure compliance and legal clarity. Example: Before: "AI helps draft contracts efficiently." After (*Legalean*): "AI-assisted contract drafting aligns with statutory compliance under UCC §2-305, ensuring procedural accuracy in legal documentation."

Semantic Features of Synthesean

Synthesean preserves meaning across diverse contexts through a structured, layered approach to semantics. It emphasizes three key features: (a) *Precision and Contextual Awareness:* ensuring outputs match domain-specific communication standards for clarity and practical use; (b) *Multi-Layered Meaning*: The framework allows for dynamic semantic adjustment, enabling the AI to modify its language output in real-time based on shifting conversational contexts or user needs; and (c) *Domain-Specific Terminology*: Vocabulary is adapted to match the demands of each specialized dialect, ensuring linguistic relevance.

Synthesean in Practice: Domain-Specific Outputs

The *Synthesean* model translates its modular syntax and semantic architecture into practical, domain-specific outputs. By applying rule-based linguistic structures and contextually grounded semantics, the system generates communication that is interpretable, purpose-driven, and ethically coherent across diverse fields of application:(a) AI in Education: *Synthesean* for Adaptive Learning (*Pedagogese*). Before: "AI tutors provide feedback to students." After (*Pedagogese*): "The adaptive AI tutor delivers formative feedback aligned with Bloom's Taxonomy, ensuring scaffolding in concept mastery;" and (b) AI in Communication Studies: *Synthesean* for Media Literacy (*Visualese* & *ChatGPTish*). Before: "This article discusses AI in news summarization." After (*ChatGPTish*): "AI-generated news summaries streamline information retrieval while maintaining factual accuracy through cross-referenced sources (GPT-4 model, 2023)."

AI Model Adaptability and Training Considerations

AI models require three conditions to implement *Synthesean* successfully: (a) Training with contextual embeddings that match each dialect; (b) Real-time adaptability optimization for dialect transitions according to user needs; and (c) Human-generated response benchmarking for linguistic accuracy and engagement and interpretability assessment.

The future applications of *Synthesean* should implement reinforcement learning as a method of finetuning against structured linguistic data to evaluate real-time adaptability (Marcus, 2022). The test version of the model should learn from *Synthesean*'s modular syntax structure before producing outputs to compare with GPT-4 and BERT results for measuring interpretability and coherence alongside user comprehension metrics.

Comparison to Natural Languages

Synthesean exists as an opposite system to natural human languages because they naturally contain ambiguous elements from idioms and cultural references and words with multiple meanings. *Synthesean* implements domain-specific rules and modular syntactic structures to minimize semantic uncertainty while providing dual accessibility for human users and machine users.

Key distinctions include: (a) *Word Order*: The word order system of *Synthesean* operates through strict syntactic rules which produce clear expressions and minimize interpretation errors because human languages follow flexible contextual patterns; (b) *Modularity:* The modular syntax structure allows machines to understand the language while keeping human users engaged through its balanced approach between algorithmic precision and cognitive familiarity; and (c) *Separation of Semantic Layers*: Traditional languages combine cultural meaning with grammar and expression while embedding both metaphor and emotion into their grammatical structures. *Synthesean* maintains separate semantic layers because this structure ensures precise meaning preservation throughout various usage scenarios.

The emotional communication gap resulting from this separation requires *Synthesean* to use specialized dialects for compensation. *Emotivese* represents a specialized dialect of *Synthesean* which addresses emotional constraints found in typical AI language systems. The structured emotional awareness system in *Emotivese* allows AI systems to demonstrate empathy through simulated emotional intelligence while staying within *Synthesean's* controlled linguistic structure.

Computational Linguistics and AI Adaptability

Synthesean enables AI-human interaction meaningful by applying its unified linguistic framework combining symbolic reasoning with neural adaptability and cognitive modeling. The dual-focus on structure allows AI systems functional communication to remain both contextually appropriate and ethically sound. The framework is composed of three key elements: (a) *Synthesean* implements rule-based logic to establish linguistic transparency and structural consistency and maintain interpretative standards across different contexts; (b) The system grows by learning from user interactions through real-time processing while adapting its responses within ethical constraints that maintain contextual alignment; it includes structured boundaries to stop miscommunication from undesirable algorithmic drift; and (c) *Synthesean* uses intentional design to simplify complex information while preserving depth, and emphasizes clarity making information accessible and meaningful.

Synthesean functions as a bridge between machine logic and human cognition aiming to establish ethical communication which boosts cognitive alignment. The framework establishes adaptability and clarity to support and encourage critical thinking and cognitive flexibility in AI-human communication.

IMPLICATIONS FOR AI AND HUMAN COGNITION

As AI is increasingly interfering with our everyday activities, a detailed evaluation is needed of how AI language patterns influence human decision-making abilities, learning processes and problem-solving capabilities. With a goal-oriented structure, *Synthesean* promotes structured analysis and focused problem-solving to enhance communication efficiency throughout different knowledge areas.

The heavy reliance on AI-generated linguistic patterns transforms human cognitive processes to more rigid and data-dependent. Human cognitive abilities including creativity, abstract thinking and divergent thinking might decrease because of this shift. Students who depend on AI repeatedly in educational settings will develop weaker problem-solving abilities and critical thinking skills (Zhai & Wibowo, 2024) which restrict their potential for independent thought and deep learning.

Synthesean enhances AI's decision-support role by producing clear, unambiguous language. This precision improves professional communication and reduces interpretive errors, supporting more reliable outcomes in policy and industry. The harmonization of AI communication patterns with human cognitive systems offers organizations potential improvements in their performance across different industries.

The adoption of *Synthesean* as an effective system demands the implementation of comprehensive AI literacy programs. Gabriel (2020) stresses that AI systems need accompanying training and educational programs before deployment to enable users to effectively and ethically work with AI-generated outputs. The lack of proper preparation will restrict both the advantages of language augmentation and its distribution fairness. The wider adoption of *Synthesean* brings forward significant cultural as well as ethical issues. Standardized AI language systems endanger global linguistic diversity since they tend to favor dominant language structures at the expense of minority linguistic expressions. Policymakers must establish governance systems that defend linguistic diversity while providing equal AI communication benefits to all communities and actively work to reduce bias in AI language output. The emergence of algorithmic inequality occurs when AI systems cannot eliminate differences between information access and decision-making capabilities.

The following section discusses advantages and disadvantages of AI-human communication systems by comparing operational benefits of AI use, and the loss of human autonomy and cognitive independence, and points to the importance of the preservation of human linguistic heritage.

SYNTHESEAN AS A FRAMEWORK FOR AI-HUMAN LINGUISTIC EVOLUTION

As AI becomes embedded in everyday communication, the urgency grows for a structured linguistic system—one that both protects linguistic diversity and supports ethical, cognitively aligned interaction. *Synthesean* presents a solution by using its context-based domain-adjustable framework to develop AI language while protecting human discourse complexity. *Synthesean* establishes a system to preserve the balance between artificial intelligence precision and natural language flexibility. *Synthesean* functions throughout multiple knowledge domains to support AI systems which maintain human cognitive emotional and social requirements.

The modifications made by AI technologies extend beyond language functions because they reshape human processes for information processing and interpretation as well as decision-making and meaning construction. AI-assisted communication provides users with fast interactions and better accessibility yet it leads to reduced interpretive depth and potential cognitive rigidity which diminishes human language complexity. The transformation of communication into basic transactional exchanges endangers creativity and complexity because it threatens their disappearance.

Synthesean functions as a protection mechanism against such dangers through its core systemic architecture which integrates ethical communication principles with cultural sensitivity and contextual awareness. *Synthesean* enables clear communication paths that avoid simplification and maintain deep insights to generate comprehensible linguistic patterns which remain ethical and socially aware.

Synthesean requires further empirical research to exemplify its practical value in real-world applications. AI systems should be trained to use *Synthesean* dialects while measuring improvements in interpretability, as well as, adaptability, and semantic accuracy. Research studies could also compare user responses to *Synthesean*-generated outputs against standard NLP outputs. It is anticipated that these research findings will provide an evidence-based aspect to improve the *Synthesean* model and its applications in emerging AI systems and AI-human communication. The framework establishes the foundations for ethical, transparent and cognitively aligned interactions in AI-human communication.

Figure 18. AI-mediated language regulation and ethical protection

Regulatory Focus	Proposed Action	Expected Impact
AI-Language Certification	AI-generated texts reviewed for linguistic diversity	Prevents loss of linguistic variation
AI-Linguistic Audits	Bias detection in automated AI text	Reduces misinformation risks
Human-AI Interaction Standards	Policy enforcement in Education and Industry AI	Ensures accountability

AI governance needs enhancement to establish proper regulation for language transformations caused by AI systems. AI-mediated language regulation needs to prioritize transparency alongside interpretability and ethical protection measures in its frameworks (Bostrom, 2014) (Figure 18): (a) An *AI-Language Certification System* should be created to evaluate AI-produced texts against linguistic diversity Requirements; (b) The implementation of *AI-Linguistic Audits* would enable researchers to detect algorithmic biases which appear during automated text generation; and (c) The establishment of *Human-AI Interaction Standards* through policy guidelines would require AI-generated communication in legal healthcare and educational settings to maintain human supervision. *Synthesean* establishes a basic structure for ethical AI-human communication by solving these governance problems.

Synthesean as an academic and governing approach has commercial potential that can be applied to legal documentation through AI, automated tutoring, and corporate AI communication systems. *Synthesean* when applied to business AI solutions has the potential to dramatically enhance clarity of human-AI interactions which would decrease the chances of misinformation in AI-generated content.

Since AI-generated language will play a significant role in professional and educational and social interactions, it is important to make sure that the advancement of such technologies will not compromise human cognitive and linguistic diversity. *Synthesean* proposes a way of solving the problem of the incompatibility of the machine language and human flexibility to ensure that the machine-generated language remains meaningful, ethical, and relevant to human needs. *Synthesean* creates a setting for human and AI to interact linguistically in a collaborative manner to create a future where AI communication makes language more expressive and inclusive rather than limiting it.

SYNTHESEAN VS. AUTOLECT

A Framework for Language Integrity

Synthesean requires a comparison with *Autolect* during its transition from design to practical use. While *Synthesean* exists as an ethically designed language system which aligns with human mental processes and easy interpretation, *Autolect* exemplifies the uncontrolled development of AI-generated language that uses syntactical correctness to hide semantic confusion and cognitive misalignment. *Autolect* demonstrates coherence at surface-level and frequently contains semantic content that is empty or limited potential for interpretive depth. In this case, in order to optimize the process an intervention is required in the algorithmic probability that produces *Autolect*.

Figure 19. Illustrative Comparison of Synthesean vs. Autolect

PROMPT
"Explain the benefits of AI in education"

SYNTHESEAN (HUMAN-ALIGNED OUTPUT)
"AI can personalize learning by adapting to individual student needs. Through real-time feedback and data analytics, educators can better understand learning patterns and intervene effectively. However, it is essential to maintain critical thinking and human oversight in all AI-mediated instruction."

AUTOLECT (GIBBERLINK-STYLE OUTPUT)
"Adaptive modality synthesis in cognitive learning loops enhances scalar feedback deployment through platformic resonance, optimizing ontological metrics within user-adjusted interfaces. Pedagogic latency is minimized via procedural outputs, suggesting value in decentral intelligence dispersion."

Synthesean emerges as a hybrid AI-human language framework, which combines ethical principles, cognitive functionality and contextual clarity. *Synthesean* maintains meaningful content, enabling reflective thinking, cultural understanding and domain-specific communication. Its design architecture actively promotes both interpretability and human values. *Autolect* is the result of probabilistic text generation systems, syntactically correct but semantically vacant. Machine learning systems communicate successfully in *Autolect*, having been statistically trained, to disregard both coherence, context and cultural sensitivity. Figure 19 illustrates the difference between *Synthesean* and *Autolect*, while the latter may sound technical, it lacks semantic grounding - a hallmark of *Autolect*.

Multiple *Autolect* manifestations are conceptualized here, which demonstrate distinct communicative function deficiencies:

Hollowcode: Hollowcode presents straightforward understanding but completely lacks emotional or cultural significance. The text presents a formal structure and proper grammar, yet it fails to create emotional connections with readers and their cultural backgrounds. The AI condolence message reads "We regret the incidence and have provided the normal official condolences" without expressing human emotions or personal sentiments. The feedback system of *Hollowcode* generates statements about assignment development but ignores student individuality and work quality.

DriftSpeak: human syntax is slowly transformed into machine-friendly syntax. *DriftSpeak* can be identified by its use of overly formal language, repetition, and unusual syntax, which are likely to be derived from the training data rather than from actual human communication. For instance, the statement could be made that, "The student had difficulties with the concept," whereas *DriftSpeak* would say, "Conceptual acquisition is suboptimal compared to baseline expectations."

This kind of phrasing, if constantly exposed to, can cause human communication to become more robotic and impersonal.

Echolex: echoic language that mirrors sense but lacks intention. *Echolex* tends to create statements that look like they are coherent but only replicate linguistic structures without any real meaning. For example, in response to a question on ethics in AI, *Echolex* may produce, "Moral frameworks have to be in tandem with ethical compliance to ensure structural congruence," which sounds meaningful but is devoid of any concrete or practical information. It repeats the argument without real involvement.

Ghostscript: grammatically intact structures devoid of meaning. The outputs of *Ghostscript* are context free grammars that are syntactically correct but semantically empty. For instance, a sentence like, 'The modality of conceptual synergies converges with cognitive pathways in adaptive flux' sounds good but one cannot really tell what it means. This is because *Ghostscript* occurs when AI is overtrained for fluency as opposed to communicative effectiveness. These forms as a collective show a language development without human involvement which threatens the ability to interpret, think critically, and express culture.

Synthesean ≠ Autolect

There are fundamental differences between *Synthesean* and *Autolect* (Table 9) across six critical dimensions:

Origin: Synthesean is developed through human intervention and ethical design principles whereas *Autolect* arises from unmonitored algorithmic operations. *Synthesean* exists as a purposefully designed system which stands in opposition to the uncontrolled evolutionary process of *Autolect*.

Semantic Quality: Synthesean focuses on delivering clear information that remains relevant to specific domains through precise language use. The system maintains language quality by keeping it meaningful and consistent with human interpretation systems. *Autolect* generates output that shows fluent sentences but lacks semantic depth because its statistical pattern recognition methods produce unreflective language.

Cognitive Impact: Synthesean exists to develop reflective thinking abilities alongside cognitive adaptability and analytical reasoning skills. The organized and intentional dialogue structure of *Synthesean* enables users to perform critical and meaningful content engagement. *Autolect* operates through statistical pattern recognition which results in repetitive unreflective language generation. Such systems used for extended periods may reduce human abilities to think critically and abstractly as well as diminish metacognitive awareness. In AI-mediated environments, Synthesean preserves cognitive vitality by sustaining dialogue, meaning, and reflective engagement—qualities often lost in unstructured generative systems.

Cultural Expression: Synthesean maintains the emotional and idiomatic and metaphorical aspects of human language which protects cultural specifics and linguistic details. *Autolect* transforms language into statistical averages and normative structures which results in cultural expression flattening and communication style diversity reduction.

Governance and Ethics: Synthesean implements ethical design principles and transparency protocols and embedded governance mechanisms to support responsible AI deployment. These features enable interpretability, accountability, and regulatory alignment. *Autolect* lacks built-in safeguards which makes it more susceptible to misuse and bias amplification and opaque decision-making processes that create difficulties for maintaining trust and control in AI systems.

Linguistic Risk: Synthesean operates as a collaborative tool through its modular structure to maintain semantic coherence and communicative integrity in AI-human interactions. *Autolect*'s unmonitored human language simulation creates an increasing danger of semantic drift and disorder which could generate incoherent misleading or cognitively destabilizing outputs.

Autolect and the Descent into Nullingua

The typological category of *Autolect* serves as a framework to understand degenerative AI language forms but its fundamental epistemological impact becomes most evident through the conceptual framework of *Nullingua*. *Nullingua* describes the semantic collapse which occurs in AI-generated discourse because the language structures appear correct but fail to transmit meaningful content with ethical value or cultural relevance.

The four types of *Autolect* represent progressive stages towards, what I term here as, *Nullingua*, a state where communicated language becomes more synthetic, with meaning dissolving into patterned noise. *Nullingua* refers to more than an inadequate language, as it represents a post-linguistic simulation generating discourses that function structurally as a language, but ontologically they are empty, where cognitive processes are replaced by algorithmic duplication.

Synthesean offers a fresh conceptual framework for AI-human discourse based on paedagogical and ethical principles which opposes *Nullingua*. *Nullingua* is the extensive threat *Autolect* creates to meaningful communication and meaning construction. *Synthesean* functions both as a desired communication AI-human system and as a dialectical resistance against *Nullingua*'s silent expansion across educational cultural and epistemological territories.

THE SYNTHESEAN PEDAGOGICAL FRAMEWORK: LITERACY FOR THE AI ERA

Students need *Synthesean Literacy* which combines multiple disciplines to develop skills for recognizing and creating AI-generated language while critically evaluating its ethical implications. Students need Synthesean literacy to differentiate between ethically sound outputs and semantically empty forms such as *Autolect.* Students learn to create AI-generated content through formal instruction about prompt engineering and dialect selection and language analysis which enables them to develop human-aligned content. The educational process depends on teachers who demonstrate these practices through support from prompt builders, language integrity rubrics and dialect toolkits. The teaching approach uses Vygotsky's mediated learning theory and digital epistemology frameworks to develop critical awareness and ethical discernment and adaptive communication skills which students need to navigate the changing AI-human linguistic environment.

Synthesean literacy competencies

Achieving Synthesean fluency requires structured educational programs that teach students to navigate, interpret, and ethically co-create AI-generated language. This form of literacy can extend to move past basic output evaluation as it includes comprehension of the impact of AI language on AI dynamics and human cognitive processes.

Synthesean literacy features a pedagogical framework which consists of three interconnected competencies: *Recognition*, *Creation*, and *Reflection*.

Recognition: Student education begins by teaching them to recognize *Synthesean* outputs from *Autolect* outputs. Instructional tools combined with comparative exercises help students recognize signs of linguistic degradation that appear in *Hollowcode, DriftSpeak, Echolex, and Ghostscript.* Students examine AI-generated responses to detect problems with emotional flatness together with contextual irrelevance and cultural detachment. The comparison between *Synthesean* and *Autolect* students strengthens their analytical thinking ability and language awareness skills. Students learn both ethical decision-making and critical reasoning abilities through evaluation justification.

Creation: The education continues into teaching students how to guide AI systems to create content that follows *Synthesean* standards. Students require knowledge about prompt structures that function with dialects which include *Pedagogese* for educational feedback and *Emotivese* for empathetic communication as well as *Legalean* for legal analysis. Students learn prompt engineering abilities through this practice which enables them to understand tone and clarity and ethical framing better.

Students practice creating prompts which leads AI to create assignment feedback while they improve AI outputs to match human communication standards. Students learn to assess the philosophical and ethical aspects of AI-mediated language during the last stage of this process.

Reflection: The final stage includes student participation through critical evaluation of AI-mediated language from philosophical and ethical perspectives. Students analyze the following questions at this stage. The AI technology has changed my understanding of truth in what way? Students analyze the *Synthesean* human values which do not appear in *Autolect*. The final stage examines how language affects human dignity and creative expression as well as cultural identity throughout the digital age. The assessment tools consist of media analysis and structured debates and reflective writing to develop ethical awareness and digital citizenship skills for responsible AI system interaction.

The *Synthesean* pedagogical framework functions as an interdisciplinary system that works across multiple academic fields. Students of literature examine AI-created story techniques while science students evaluate AI abstract clarity and potential biases through multiple *Synthesean* dialect simulations in civics classes. In the modern evolving educational landscape AI language literacy must be established as a fundamental skill at the same level as digital and information literacy.

Educators need training to understand and apply *Synthesean* principles for effective instructional implementation. Professional development workshops will explore both AI language ethics alongside prompt engineering techniques and dialect toolkits usage. The framework applies cognitive development theories that integrate Vygotsky's work about mediated learning together with digital epistemology competency development (Vygotsky, 1978). Students who practice ethical communication will develop the capacity to control the AI world they will face after entering its advanced environment.

The adoption of practical tools based on the *Synthesean* pedagogical framework by educational institutions will provide effective implementation. These tools enable real-world *Synthesean* principles implementation which provides learners and educators with accessible structured AI-human language interaction.

Synthesean Literacy Tools

A set of tools has been developed to support the practical application of *Synthesean Literacy* in educational settings to enable students and educators to meaningfully engage with AI-generated language. These tools translate the conceptual principles of *Synthesean* into accessible resources for prompt construction, output evaluation, dialect training, and curriculum design.

The *Synthesean Prompt Builder* (Appendix A, Figure 20) is an online classroom application that helps users create proper AI prompts through *Synthesean* language dialects. The tool would offer: (a) a dialect selection feature with four options which include *Pedagogese*, *Emotivese*, *Legalean*, and *Analytese*; (b) drop-down menus alongside pre-built templates with step-by-step language patterns; and, (c) instant feedback by evaluating the clarity of statements as well as their ethical content and their relation to the domain.

The *Language Integrity Rubric* (Appendix B, Figure 21) functions as an assessment tool which helps students and educators evaluate AI-created language output. The evaluation framework consists of five essential criteria: (a) *Semantic clarity*; (b) *Contextual relevance*; (c) *Emotional resonance* (if applicable); (d) *Ethical transparency*; and (e) *Domain-specific accuracy*. The evaluation system uses a rating scale with specific descriptions along with relevant examples. The rubric serves two purposes to evaluate student revisions of AI text and to offer formative feedback and facilitate peer-review discussions. The rubric serves as a tool for students to evaluate their AI-written essays during group work when assessing paragraph alignment with *Synthesean* standards.

The *Dialect Toolkits* (Appendix C, Figure 22) consist of printable or digital guides which present each *Synthesean* dialect through: (a) Core syntax and vocabulary features; (b) Sample sentence structures; (c) Ethical use cases and cautions; and (d) Role-based voice guidelines (e.g., academic, legal, emotional). The toolkits assist learners to understand and apply each dialect effectively. The toolkits provide AI prompt "cheat sheets" together with dialect flowcharts and interactive role-play scenarios.

The *AI Language Literacy Curriculum* (Appendix D, Figure 23) functions as an adjustable educational framework that schools can integrate into media studies or language arts or ethics or computer science curricula. A university digital communication program hosts the course with an AI ethics in language module dedicated for students. Students must develop an *Emotivese* and *Legalean-based* chatbot system for mental health support before writing about their ethical challenges.

These tools connect theoretical concepts to practical application which enables educators and students to critically engage with AI-generated language. The systematic integration of these tools creates an AI-literate society which preserves human values while keeping context and following ethical communication standards.

GOVERNANCE, ETHICS, AND THE FUTURE OF AI LANGUAGE

AI systems that facilitate cross-sector language communication require immediate implementation of strong governance systems. Unregulated AI content generation poses serious risks to semantic accuracy, cultural diversity, and ethical accountability. Multiple regulatory measures should be established by policymakers to protect cultural heritage and maintain contextual nuance (Bostrom, 2014). Syntactically correct text generated by AI systems lacks semantic meaning when unregulated thus they enable misinformation while perpetuating biases and diminishing linguistic diversity (Gabriel, 2020; Hendrycks et al., 2020).

The core governance structure of *Synthesean* combines natural linguistic patterns with formal syntactic organization and embedded ethical safeguards for AI-generated communication. Two fundamental instruments form the foundation of this framework: (a) *AI-Language Certification* evaluates AI output for semantic integrity and cultural awareness; and (b) *AI-Linguistic Audits* detect algorithmic biases while establishing accountability systems. These tools enable ethical communication through human oversight in critical domains such as law medicine and education which maintains contextual relevance and moral responsibility.

Synthesean offers a foundation for global AI communication standards by aligning human dignity with principles of interpretability, transparency, and linguistic accountability. The development of future governance models needs to incorporate formal linguistic ethics to create responsible and inclusive AI discourse (Gabriel, 2020; Hendrycks et al., 2020). *Synthesean* has the potential to evolve from its current conceptual state into a regulatory system which protects human control and language diversity in AI communication systems.

CONCLUSION

Meaningful human–AI interaction depends on the design, implementation, and regulation of structured linguistic frameworks. *Synthesean* protects human linguistic systems from damage through its ethical language architecture which also controls unregulated AI language production. *Synthesean* operates as an ethical language architecture that produces human-understandable outputs and preserves cognitive alignment in an algorithmically controlled linguistic space. This framework operates beyond the level of abstract theory because it directly requires immediate implementation. Societies need educational AI literacy programs and ethical language system design from technologists and AI communication regulations from policymakers to determine their direction. The structured syntactic configurations together with modular dialects of *Synthesean* generate transparent educational AI content which adjusts to various cultural environments.

The study in this paper outlines an educational approach for students to develop AI language abilities. The participatory governance of AI mediated communication occurs through prompt-building tools that work with dialectal frameworks and integrity rubrics to provide operational guidelines to users.

Synthesean creates a system which allows users to keep control of language during the present era of autonomous intelligence. The linguistic framework provides interpretable structured communication while the pedagogical model teaches learners and educators ethical AI literacy and the governance instrument supports policy initiatives to protect semantic integrity, cognitive autonomy and cultural diversity. *Synthesean* establishes itself as a future-oriented solution which protects AI-mediated language from becoming meaningless while maintaining inclusivity and human focus.

REFERENCES

Bender, E. M., & Koller, A. (2020). Climbing towards NLU: On meaning, form, and understanding in the age of data. *Proceedings of the 58th Annual Meeting of the Association for Computational Linguistics*, 5185–5198. https://doi.org/DOI: 10.18653/v1/2020.acl-main.463

Bostrom, N. (2014). *Superintelligence: Paths, dangers, strategies*. Oxford University Press.

Boym, S. (2001). *The future of nostalgia*. Basic Books.

Devlin, J., Chang, M.-W., Lee, K., & Toutanova, K. (2019). BERT: Pre-training of deep bidirectional transformers for language understanding. *Proceedings of the 2019 Conference of the North American Chapter of the Association for Computational Linguistics: Human Language Technologies*, 1, 4171–4186. https://doi.org/DOI: 10.48550/arXiv.1810.04805

Floridi, L., & Chiriatti, M. (2020). GPT-3: Its nature, scope, limits, and consequences. *Minds and Machines*, *30*(4), 681–694. DOI: 10.1007/s11023-020-09548-1

Gabriel, I. (2020). Artificial intelligence, values, and alignment. *Minds and Machines*, *30*(4), 411–437. DOI: 10.1007/s11023-020-09539-2

Hendrycks, D., Burns, C., Basart, S., Critch, A., Li, J., Song, D., & Steinhardt, J. (2020). Aligning AI with shared human values. *arXiv*. https://arxiv.org/abs/2008.02275

Marcus, G. (2022). The next decade in AI: Why we need a new approach. *Daedalus*, *151*(2), 110–124. DOI: 10.1162/daed_a_01926

Vygotsky, L. S. (1978). *Mind in society: The development of higher psychological processes*. Harvard University Press.

Whorf, B. L. (1956). *Language, thought, and reality: Selected writings of Benjamin Lee Whorf*. MIT Press.

Zhai, X., & Wibowo, S. (2024). Human cognition and AI-generated texts: Ethics in educational settings. *Humanities & Social Sciences Communications*, *11*, 45. Advance online publication. DOI: 10.1057/s41599-024-04002-4

APPENDIX A

Example of Synthesean Prompt Builder

Figure 20. Synthesean Prompt Builder

PURPOSE:

Help users construct clear, ethical, dialect-specific AI prompts

TOOL FORMAT:

Prompt Builder Template

Component	Description	Example Input
Dialect Selection	Choose from: Pedagogese, Emotivese, Legalean, etc.	Pedagogese
Domain Context	What is the subject or field?	Secondary school biology
Desired Output Type	Essay, summary, policy, dialogue, etc.	Short explanatory paragraph
Ethical Intent	What values should be reflected (e.g., inclusivity, fairness)?	Inclusive language, avoid stereotypes
Tone & Complexity	Target age, readability, tone	Age 14, clear, neutral tone
Final Prompt Example	Synthesized example	"Using the Pedagogese dialect, explain photosynthesis to a 14-year-old using inclusive and simple language."

APPENDIX B

Example of Language Integrity Rubric

Figure 21. Language Integrity Rubric

PURPOSE:

Evaluate AI-generated text for clarity, ethics, and contextual fit.

TOOL FORMAT:

Rubric Scoring Sheet

Criteria	Description	Score (1–5)	Comments
Semantic Clarity	Is the meaning clear and understandable?		
Contextual Relevance	Does the text match the subject/domain?		
Emotional Resonance	Does it reflect appropriate tone or empathy?		
Ethical Transparency	Are values, fairness, or intent embedded?		
Domain-Specific Accuracy	Are field-specific facts and terms used correctly?		
	Total Score		

Scoring Guide: 1 = Poor, 3 = Acceptable, 5 = Excellent

APPENDIX C

Example of Dialect Toolkits

Figure 22. Dialect Toolkits

PURPOSE:

Provide linguistic features, example sentences, and usage guidance.

TOOL FORMAT:

Dialect Summary Sheet (Pedagogese Example)

DIALECT:

Pedagogese

CONTEXT:

Education, tutoring, feedback

CORE FEATURES:

Aligns with Bloom's Taxonomy - Uses scaffolding language - Encourages growth and inquiry.

FUNCTION	PHRASE EXAMPLES
Positive Feedback	"Great progress—you're applying the concept well."
Guidance	"Let's try another way to approach this problem."
Clarification	"In simpler terms, this means..."
Encouragement	"You're on the right track. Keep exploring!"

USAGE TIP:

Avoid technical jargon unless it has been taught.

APPENDIX D

AI Language Literacy Course Module

Figure 23. Language Literacy Course Module

	Module Topic	**Learning Outcomes**	**Activities**
1	Introduction to AI Language	Define AI language and its implications	Readings + Class Discussion
2	Synthesean vs. Autolect	Identify structured vs. unstructured AI language	Text comparison activity
3	Practicing with Dialects (Pedagogese, etc.)	Generate AI content using dialect prompt	Prompt Builder Exercise
4	Ethics of AI Language	Analyze ethical risks and transparency in AI-generated text	Media analysis + Integrity Rubric scoring
5	Evaluating AI-Generated Communication	Apply rubric to assess AI output across different contexts	Peer review workshop
6	Synthesean in the Real World	Explore use of Synthesean in business, healthcare, and law	Case study presentations
7	Designing Ethical AI Prompts	Develop domain-specific prompts that reflect ethical values	Guided prompt engineering task
8	Final Project: Co-Creation with AI	Demonstrate proficiency in Synthesean use and evaluation	Student-led projects + reflection essay

Assessment Types:	**Resources Needed:**	**Extension Ideas:**
Prompt writing and editing	Access to GPT-like AI tools	Invite AI researchers as guest speakers
AI-generated text analysis	Synthesean Dialect Toolkits	Cross-disciplinary units e.g., science + ethics)
Group presentations	Language Integrity Rubric	Synthesean vs Autolect outputs: A Debate
Reflective writing	Case study repository	
Rubric-based peer evaluation		

Compilation of References

Abdulmunem, R. A. (2023). Artificial Intelligence in Education. In Khlaif, Z., Sanmugam, M., & Itmazi, J. (Eds.), *Comparative Research on Diversity in Virtual Learning: Eastern vs. Western Perspectives* (pp. 241–255). IGI Global Scientific Publishing., DOI: 10.4018/978-1-6684-3595-3.ch012

Abou-Khalil, V., Samarasinghe, S., Gaines, B., & Nasser, H. (2021). Emergency online learning in low-resource settings: Effective student engagement strategies. *Education Sciences*, *11*(1), 24. DOI: 10.3390/educsci11010024

Abulibdeh, A., Chatti, C. B., Alkhereibi, A., & Menshawy, S. E. (2025). A Scoping review of the Strategic Integration of Artificial Intelligence in Higher Education: Transforming University Excellence Themes and Strategic Planning in the Digital Era. *European Journal of Education*, *60*(1). Advance online publication. DOI: 10.1111/ejed.12908

ACBSP. (2020) Accreditation Council for Business Schools and Programs, https://acbsp.org/page/membership_list

Adams, D., Chuah, K. M., & Devadason, E. (2024). From novice to navigator: Students' academic help-seeking behaviour, readiness, and perceived usefulness of ChatGPT in learning. *Education and Information Technologies*, *29*, 13617–13634. DOI: 10.1007/s10639-023-12427-8

Adegbite, W., & Govender, C. (2022). How fourth industrial revolution skillsets mediate the relationship between work integrated learning, graduate employability, and future job. *EUREKA: Social and Humanities*, (4), 3–17.

Afolabi, A. (2024). Ethical issues in artificial intelligence adoption in African higher education institutions in Nigeria. *African Journal of Information and Knowledge Management*, *3*(2), 22–33. DOI: 10.47604/ajikm.2735

Ahmed, S., Shehata, M., & Hassanien, M. (2020). Emerging faculty needs for enhancing student engagement on a virtual platform. *MedEdPublish*, *9*(1), 75. DOI: 10.15694/mep.2020.000075.1

Akhoirshieda, M. S., Khalif, K. M. N. K., & Awang, S. (2024). Artificial intelligence in the United Arab Emirates public sector: A systematic literature review. *IAES International Journal of Artificial Intelligence*, *13*(3), 2472. DOI: 10.11591/ijai.v13.i3.pp2472-2481

Alamäki, A., Nyberg, C., Kimberley, A., & Salonen, A. (2024). Artificial intelligence literacy in sustainable development: A learning experiment in higher education. *Frontiers in Education*. Advance online publication. DOI: 10.3389/feduc.2024.1343406

Al-Ammal, H., & Aljawder, M. (2021). Strategy for Artificial intelligence in Bahrain: Challenges and opportunities. In Springer eBooks (pp. 47–67). https://doi.org/DOI: 10.1007/978-981-16-0771-4_4

Al-Ansari, A., Al Mohsen, H., & Coutts, C. N. (2022). Critical Factors in Promoting Sustainable Innovation in Bahrain. *Journal of Sustainable Business and Economics*, *5*(2), 1–21-21–21.

Al-Baity, H. H. (2023). The Artificial Intelligence Revolution in Digital Finance in Saudi Arabia: A Comprehensive Review and Proposed framework. *Sustainability*, *15*(18), 13725. DOI: 10.3390/su151813725

Alhabeeb, A. M. (2015). The Quality Assessment of the Services Offered to the Students of the College of Education at King Saud University Using (SERVQUAL) Method. *Journal of Education and Practice*, *6*(30), 82–93.

Alharasis, E. E., Haddad, H., Alhadab, M., Shehadeh, M., & Hasan, E. F. (2025). Integrating forensic accounting in education and practices to detect and prevent fraud and misstatement: Case study of Jordanian public sector. *Journal of Financial Reporting and Accounting*, *23*(1), 100–127. DOI: 10.1108/JFRA-04-2023-0177

Ali, A. M., Futaih, R. F., Shukur, M., & Al-Orfali, A. K. (2024). Forensic Accounting and Fraud Detection Emerging Trends and Techniques. *Journal of Ecohumanism*, *3*(5), 525–542. DOI: 10.62754/joe.v3i5.3921

Aljawarneh, S. A. (2020). Reviewing and exploring innovative ubiquitous learning tools in higher education. *Journal of Computing in Higher Education*, *32*(1), 57–73.

Allam, Z. (2020). Demystifying the Aspect of Quality in Higher Education: Insights From Saudi Arabia. *SAGE Open*, *10*(1), 1–8.

Allen, L. K., & Kendeou, P. (2023). ED-AI LIt: An Interdisciplinary Framework for AI Literacy in Education. *Policy Insights from the Behavioral and Brain Sciences*, *11*(1), 3–10. DOI: 10.1177/23727322231220339

Almatrafi, O., Johri, A., & Lee, H. (2024). A systematic review of AI literacy conceptualization, constructs, and implementation and assessment efforts (2019–2023). *Computers and Education Open*, *6*, 100173. DOI: 10.1016/j.caeo.2024.100173

Al-Omari, O., Alyousef, A., Fati, S., Shannaq, F., & Omari, A. (2025). Governance and Ethical Frameworks for AI integration in Higher Education: Enhancing personalized learning and legal compliance. *Journal of Ecohumanism*, *3*(8). Advance online publication. DOI: 10.62754/joe.v3i8.5781

Alotaibi, N. S., & Alshehri, A. H. (2023). Prospers and Obstacles in Using Artificial Intelligence in Saudi Arabia Higher Education Institutions—The Potential of AI-Based Learning Outcomes. *Sustainability*, *15*(13), 10723. DOI: 10.3390/su151310723

Alqasemi, S. S., Il-Agure, Z., & Dempere, J. (2023). Towards Standardized AI-Ready Data: A Proposed Framework for the UAE. https://doi.org/DOI: 10.1109/itt59889.2023.10184264

Alshahrani, B. T., Pileggi, S. F., & Karimi, F. (2024). A Social Perspective on AI in the Higher Education System: A Semisystematic literature review. *Electronics (Basel)*, *13*(8), 1572. DOI: 10.3390/electronics13081572

Alshurafat, H., Al Shbail, M. O., & Mansour, E. (2021). Strengths and weaknesses of forensic accounting: An implication on the socio-economic development. *Journal of Business and Socio-economic Development*, *1*(2), 135–148. DOI: 10.1108/JBSED-03-2021-0026

Alshurafat, H., Beattie, C., Jones, G., & Sands, J. (2020). Perceptions of the usefulness of various teaching methods in forensic accounting education. *Accounting Education*, *29*(2), 177–204. DOI: 10.1080/09639284.2020.1719425

Altun, O., Saydam, M. B., Karatepe, T., & Dima, Ş. M. (2024). Unveiling ChatGPT in tourism education: Exploring perceptions, advantages and recommendations from educators. *Worldwide Hospitality and Tourism Themes*, *16*(1), 105–118.

American Board of Forensic Accounting. (2022). Principles of Professional Practice. https://abfa.us/about/principles/

Amerstorfer, C. M. (2020, July). Problem-based learning for preservice teachers of English as a foreign language. In *Colloquium* (pp. 75–90). New Philologies.

Amineh, R. J., & Asl, H. D. (2015). Review of constructivism and social constructivism. *Journal of social sciences, literature and languages, 1*(1), 9-16.

Amin, H. M. G., Hassan, R. S., Ghoneim, H., & Abdallah, A. S. (2025). A bibliometric analysis of accounting education literature in the digital era: Current status, implications and agenda for future research. *Journal of Financial Reporting and Accounting, 23*(2), 742–768. DOI: 10.1108/JFRA-12-2023-0802

Amin, H., & Mirza, M. S. (2020). Comparative study of knowledge and use of Bloom's digital taxonomy by teachers and students in virtual and conventional universities. *Asian Association of Open Universities Journal, 15*(2), 223–238. DOI: 10.1108/AAOUJ-01-2020-0005

Anderson, G., & Arsenault, N. (2005). *Fundamentals of educational research.* Routledge.

Anderson, L. W., & Krathwohl, D. (Eds.). (2001). *A Taxonomy for Learning, Teaching and Assessing: a Revision of Bloom's Taxonomy of Educational Objectives*. Longman.

Anderson, T., & Dron, J. (2011). Three generations of distance education pedagogy. *International Review of Research in Open and Distance Learning, 12*(3), 80–97. DOI: 10.19173/irrodl.v12i3.890

Anjarwati, R., & Sa'adah, L. (2021). Student learning engagement in the online class. *EnJourMe (English Journal of Merdeka). Culture, Language, and Teaching of English, 6*(2), 39–49. DOI: 10.26905/enjourme.v6i2.6128

Annamdevula, S., & Bellamkonda, R. S. (2012). Development of HiEdQUAL for Measuring Service Quality in Indian Higher Education Sector. *International Journal of Innovation, Management and Technology, 3*(4), 412–416.

Arain, A. A., Hussain, Z., Rizvi, W. H., & Vighio, M. S. (2019). Extending UTAUT2 toward acceptance of mobile learning in the context of higher education. *Universal Access in the Information Society, 18*(3), 659–673. DOI: 10.1007/s10209-019-00685-8

Arar, K., Tlili, A., Schunka, L., Salha, S., & Saiti, A. (2025). Reimagining Educational leadership and Management through Artificial Intelligence: An Integrative Systematic Review. *Leadership and Policy in Schools*, •••, 1–23. DOI: 10.1080/15700763.2025.2451982

Archambault, S. G., Ramachandran, S., Acosta, E., & Fu, S. (2024). Ethical dimensions of algorithmic literacy for college students: Case studies and cross-disciplinary connections. *Journal of Academic Librarianship, 50*(3), 102865. DOI: 10.1016/j.acalib.2024.102865

Arshad, I., Bhutto, N. A., Sarki, I. H., & Khuhro, R. A. (2011). Student's Perception about Service Quality level and Significant Determinants of Service Quality for Business Institutes/Universities in Pakistan. *Interdisciplinary Journal of Contemporary Research in Business*, *3*(8), 1062–1077.

Atenas, J., Havemann, L., & Nerantzi, C. (2025). Critical and creative pedagogies for artificial intelligence and data literacy: An epistemic data justice approach for academic practice. *Research in Learning Technology*, *32*. Advance online publication. DOI: 10.25304/rlt.v32.3296

Atkinson-Toal, A., & Guo, C. (2024). Generative Artificial Intelligence (AI) Education Policies of UK Universities. *Enhancing Teaching and Learning in Higher Education*, *2*, 70–94. DOI: 10.62512/etlhe.20

Ayling, J., & Chapman, A. (2022). Putting AI ethics to work: Are the tools fit for purpose? *AI and Ethics*, *2*(3), 405–429. DOI: 10.1007/s43681-022-00045-w

Azam, A. (2018). Service Quality Dimensions and Students' Satisfaction: A study of Saudi Arabian Private Higher Education Institutions. *European Online Journal of Natural and Social Sciences*, *7*(2), pp-275.

Babu, T. A., & Sharmila, V. (2023). Using artificial intelligence chatbots like 'ChatGPT'to draft articles for medical journals–Advantages, limitations, ethical concerns and way forward. *European Journal of Obstetrics, Gynecology, and Reproductive Biology*, *286*, 151. PMID: 37210245

Baird, A., & Schuller, B. (2020). Considerations for a more ethical approach to data in AI: On data representation and infrastructure. *Frontiers in Big Data*, *3*, 25. DOI: 10.3389/fdata.2020.00025 PMID: 33693398

Bankins, S., & Formosa, P. (2023). The ethical implications of artificial intelligence (AI) for meaningful work. *Journal of Business Ethics*, *185*(4), 725–740. DOI: 10.1007/s10551-023-05044-6

Bansal, R., Kumar, S., & Sharma, A. (2023). A systematic literature review on student engagement in online learning amid COVID-19. In *Technology-driven e-learning pedagogy through emotional intelligence* (pp. 166–181). IGI Global., DOI: 10.4018/978-1-6684-7639-0.ch011

Barana, A., Marchisio, M., & Roman, F. (2023). Fostering Problem Solving and Critical Thinking in Mathematics through Generative Artificial Intelligence. *International Association for Development of the Information Society*. https://eric.ed.gov/?id=ED636445

Baskara, F. R. (2024). From AI to We: Harnessing Generative AI Tools to Cultivate Collaborative Learning Ecosystems in Universities. Proceeding International Conference on Learning Community (ICLC), Baxter Magolda, M. B. (2014). Self-Authorship. *New Directions for Higher Education, 2014*(166), 25–33. https://doi.org/https://doi.org/10.1002/he.20092

Baskara, F. R., & Mukarto, F. X. (2023). Exploring the implications of ChatGPT for language learning in higher education. *Indonesian Journal of English Language Teaching and Applied Linguistics, 7*(2), 343–358. DOI: 10.21093/ijeltal.v7i2.1387

Bender, E. M., & Koller, A. (2020). Climbing towards NLU: On meaning, form, and understanding in the age of data. *Proceedings of the 58th Annual Meeting of the Association for Computational Linguistics*, 5185–5198. https://doi.org/DOI: 10.18653/v1/2020.acl-main.463

Berendt, B., Littlejohn, A., & Blakemore, M. (2020). AI in education: Learner choice and fundamental rights. *Learning, Media and Technology, 45*(3), 312–324. DOI: 10.1080/17439884.2020.1786399

Bernotaite, S., & Ottesen, E. (2023). Entanglement of support and governance in digital curriculum instruments: The case of educational reform in Norway. *European Educational Research Journal.* Advance online publication. DOI: 10.1177/14749041231213902

Bhasin, M. L. (2015). An empirical investigation of the relevant skills of forensic accountants: experience of a developing economy. *Available at SSRN* 2676519. https://dx.doi.org/DOI: 10.2139/ssrn.2676519

Bhave, A. V. (2024). Artificial Intelligence In Forensic Accounting: Software Applications and Case Study Analysis. *Bharatiya Shiksha Shodh Patrika*, Vol. 43, Issue 1 (III), January-June: 2024

Biagini, G. (2024). Assessing the assessments: Toward a multidimensional approach to AI literacy. *Medical Education, 15*(1), 91–101. DOI: 10.36253/me-15831 PMID: 38279173

Bian, Q., Ling, X., & Yan, S. (2024). Bridging the algorithmic divide. *Education as Change, 28.* Advance online publication. DOI: 10.25159/1947-9417/17983

Billett, S. (2011). Learning at the site of work. In *The Routledge international handbook of learning* (pp. 246–254). Routledge.

Birla Institute of Technology and Science. (n.d.). *M. Tech artificial intelligence and machine learning*. Retrieved March 15, 2024, from https://bitly.ws/3fVWZ

Blanford, J. I., Bowlick, F., Gidudu, A., Gould, M., Griffin, A. L., Kar, B., & Unwin, D. (2022). Lockdown lessons: An international conversation on resilient GI science teaching. *Journal of Geography in Higher Education*, *46*(1), 7–19. DOI: 10.1080/03098265.2021.1986687

Bostrom, N. (2014). *Superintelligence: Paths, dangers, strategies*. Oxford University Press.

Boym, S. (2001). *The future of nostalgia*. Basic Books.

Braun, V., & Clarke, V. (2006). Using thematic analysis in psychology. *Qualitative Research in Psychology*, *3*(2), 77–101.

Braun, V., & Clarke, V. (2021). Can I use TA? Should I use TA? Should I not use TA? Comparing reflexive thematic analysis and other pattern-based qualitative analytic approaches. *Counselling & Psychotherapy Research*, *21*(1), 37–47.

Breidbach, C. F., & Maglio, P. (2020). Accountable algorithms? The ethical implications of data-driven business models. *Journal of Service Management*, *31*(2), 163–185. DOI: 10.1108/JOSM-02-2020-0185

Brown, H., Lee, K., Mireshghallah, F., Shokri, R., & Tramèr, F. (2022). What does it mean for a language model to preserve privacy? *2022 ACM Conference on Fairness, Accountability, and Transparency*, 2280–2292. https://doi.org/DOI: 10.1145/3531146.3534642

Burmann, C., Zeplin, S., & Riley, N. (2009). Key determinants of internal brand management success: An exploratory empirical analysis. *Journal of Brand Management*, *16*, 264–284.

Calvo-Porral, C., Lévy-Mangin, J. P., & Novo-Corti, I. (2013). Perceived quality in higher education: An empirical study. *Marketing Intelligence & Planning*, *31*(6), 601–619. DOI: 10.1108/MIP-11-2012-0136

Carobene, A., Padoan, A., Cabitza, F., Banfi, G., & Plebani, M. (2024). Rising adoption of artificial intelligence in scientific publishing: Evaluating the role, risks, and ethical implications in paper drafting and review process. [CCLM]. *Clinical Chemistry and Laboratory Medicine*, *62*(5), 835–843. DOI: 10.1515/cclm-2023-1136 PMID: 38019961

Cerri, S. (2012). Assessing the quality of higher education services using a modified SEDRVQUAL scale. *Annales Universitatis Apulensis Series Oeconomica*, *14*(2), 664–679.

Changwong, K.. (2018). Critical thinking skill development: Analysis of a new learning management model for Thai high schools. *Journal of International Students, 11*(2), 37–48. DOI: 10.14254/2071-8330.2018/11-2/3

Char, D. S., Abràmoff, M. D., & Feudtner, C. (2020). Identifying ethical considerations for machine learning healthcare applications. *The American Journal of Bioethics, 20*(11), 7–17. DOI: 10.1080/15265161.2020.1835306 PMID: 33103967

Chen, X., Xie, H., Zou, D., & Hwang, G. J. (2020). Application and theory gaps during the rise of Artificial Intelligence in Education. *Computers & Education, 146*, 103751.

Chimbunde, P., & Moreeng, B. B. (2024). The Sustainability of Curriculum Reform and Implementation Through Teacher Participation: Evidence from Social Studies Teachers. *Journal of Curriculum Studies Research, 6*(1), 83–98. DOI: 10.46303/jcsr.2024.6

Christodoulou, E., & Iordanou, K. (2021). Democracy under attack: Challenges of addressing ethical issues of AI and big data for more democratic digital media and societies. *Frontiers in Political Science, 3*, 682945. DOI: 10.3389/fpos.2021.682945

Churches, A. (2009). Taxonomıa de Bloom para la era digital. *Eduteka. Recuperado, 11*, 1–13.

Cong-Lem, N. (2024). Teacher Agency for Change and Development in Higher Education: A Scoping Literature review. *International Journal of Educational Reform*. Advance online publication. DOI: 10.1177/10567879231224744

Craft, B. A. (2024). When you come to a fork in the road, take it, and the future ain't what it used to be: Lessons in living with ChatGPT. *Research Issues in Contemporary Education, 9*(2), 125–126.

Crawford, K. (2022). Atlas of AI: Power, politics, and the planetary costs of artificial intelligence. *Perspectives on Science and Christian Faith, 74*(1), 61–62. DOI: 10.56315/pscf3-22crawford

Cruz-Benito, J. (2022). *AI in Education*. MDPI-Multidisciplinary Digital Publishing Institute.

Dang, H., Benharrak, K., Lehmann, F., & Buschek, D. (2022). Beyond text generation: Supporting writers with continuous automatic text summaries. In M. Agrawala & J. O. Wobbrock, (Eds.), *UIST '22: Proceedings of the 35th annual ACM symposium on user interface software and technology* (Article 98). Association for Computing Machinery. https://doi.org/DOI: 10.1145/3526113.3545672

Davidyan, J., Huels, D., Brian, W., Gissel, D., & Jodi, L. (2022). Two truths and a lie: Introduction to deception detection. *Issues in Accounting Education, 38*(2), 85–93. DOI: 10.2308/ISSUES-2021-054

Davis, C., Farrell, R., & Ogilby, S. (2010). Characteristics and skills of the Forensic Accountant. *American Institute of Certified Public Accountants, 2010*, 11-26. http://thefraudgroupllc.com/tools/library/documents/forensic.pdf

Davis, F. D. (1985). *A technology acceptance model for empirically testing new end-user information systems: Theory and results*. Massachusetts Institute of Technology.

Desouza, K. C., Dawson, G. S., & Chenok, D. (2020). Designing, developing, and deploying artificial intelligence systems: Lessons from and for the public sector. *Business Horizons, 63*(2), 205–213. DOI: 10.1016/j.bushor.2019.11.008

Devlin, J., Chang, M.-W., Lee, K., & Toutanova, K. (2019). BERT: Pre-training of deep bidirectional transformers for language understanding. *Proceedings of the 2019 Conference of the North American Chapter of the Association for Computational Linguistics: Human Language Technologies*, 1, 4171–4186. https://doi.org/DOI: 10.48550/arXiv.1810.04805

Dewey, J. (1933). *How we think: A restatement of the relation of reflective thinking to the educative process*. D. C. Heath.

Dewey, J. (1938). *Experience and education* (Vol. 14). Kappa Delta Pi.

Dibie, E. U. (2024). The future of renewable energy: Ethical implications of AI and cloud technology in data security and environmental impact. *Journal of Advances in Mathematics and Computer Science, 39*(10), 10–9734. DOI: 10.9734/jamcs/2024/v39i1019734

Dillon, A., Chell, G., Al Ameri, N., Alsayed, N., Salem, Y., Turner, M., & Gallagher, K. (2024). The use of large language model tools such as ChatGPT in academic writing in English medium education postgraduate programs: A grounded theory approach. *The Journal of Educators Online*.

Divito, C. B., Katchikian, B. M., Gruenwald, J. E., & Burgoon, J. M. (2024). The tools of the future are the challenges of today: The use of ChatGPT in problem-based learning medical education. *Medical Teacher, 46*(3), 320–322. DOI: 10.1080/0142159X.2023.2290997 PMID: 38149617

Dondi, M., Klier, J., Panier, F., & Schubert, J. (2021). Defining the skills citizens will need in the future world of work. *McKinsey & Company, 25*, 1-19.

Duhaylungsod, A. V., & Chavez, J. V. (2023). ChatGPT and other AI users: Innovative and creative utilitarian value and mindset shift. *Journal of Namibian Studies, 33*, 4367–4378. DOI: 10.59670/jns.v33i.2791

Dumitru, D., & Halpern, D. F. (2023). Critical thinking: Creating job-proof skills for the future of work. *Journal of Intelligence, 11*(10), 194. PMID: 37888426

Duong, C. D., Nguyen, T. H., Ngo, T. V. N., Dao, V. T., Do, N. D., & Pham, T. V. (2024). Exploring higher education students' continuance usage intention of ChatGPT: Amalgamation of the information system success model and the stimulus-organism-response paradigm. *The International Journal of Information and Learning Technology, 41*(5), 556–584.

Du, Q., & Tate, T. (2024). ChatGPT, plagiarism, and multilingual students' learning to write. *The CATESOL Journal, 35*(1). Advance online publication. DOI: 10.5070/B5.34831

Durtschi, C., & Rufus, R. J. (2017). Arson or accident: A forensic accounting case requiring critical thinking and expert communication. *Issues in Accounting Education Teaching Notes, 32*(1), 89–105. DOI: 10.5555/iace-51350TN

Dwivedi, Y. K., Hughes, L., Ismagilova, E., Aarts, G., Coombs, C., Crick, T., & Williams, M. D. (2021). Artificial Intelligence (AI): Multidisciplinary perspectives on emerging challenges, opportunities, and agenda for research, practice and policy. *International Journal of Information Management, 57*, 101994. DOI: 10.1016/j.ijinfomgt.2019.08.002

Dwivedi, Y. K., Pandey, N., Currie, W., & Micu, A. (2024). Leveraging ChatGPT and other generative artificial intelligence (AI)-based applications in the hospitality and tourism industry: Practices, challenges and research agenda. *International Journal of Contemporary Hospitality Management, 36*(1), 1–12.

Eaton, S. E. (Ed.). (2023). *Handbook of academic integrity*. Springer Nature.

Education and Training Evaluation Commission. (2020), Accredited Institutions, https://etec.gov.sa/en/productsandservices/NCAAA/academic/Pages/OrgsDirectory.aspx

Eitel-Porter, R. (2021). Beyond the promise: Implementing ethical AI. *AI and Ethics, 1*(1), 73–80. DOI: 10.1007/s43681-020-00008-0

Ejjami, R. (2024). Integrative Literature Review 5.0: Leveraging AI and Emerging Technologies to redefine academic research. *International Journal for Multidisciplinary Research, 6*(5). Advance online publication. DOI: 10.36948/ijfmr.2024.v06i05.28756

El Hajal, G., & Rowson, B. (2020). The future of hospitality jobs. *Research in Hospitality Management*, *10*(1), 55–61.

Elendu, C., Amaechi, D. C., Elendu, T. C., Jingwa, K. A., Okoye, O. K., Okah, M. J., & Alimi, H. A. (2023). Ethical implications of AI and robotics in healthcare. *Revista de Medicina (São Paulo)*, *102*(50), e36671. DOI: 10.1097/MD.0000000000036671 PMID: 38115340

Elken, M. (2023). Collaborative design of governance instruments in higher education. *Studies in Higher Education*, *49*(6), 1095–1106. DOI: 10.1080/03075079.2023.2258905

Elkhwesky, Z., El Manzani, Y., & Elbayoumi Salem, I. (2024). Driving hospitality and tourism to foster sustainable innovation: A systematic review of COVID-19-related studies and practical implications in the digital era. *Tourism and Hospitality Research*, *24*(1), 115–133. PMID: 40479339

Ellili, N., Nobanee, H., Haddad, A., Alodat, A. Y., & AlShalloudi, M. (2024). Emerging trends in forensic accounting research: Bridging research gaps and prioritizing new frontiers. *Journal of Economic Criminology*, *4*, 1–17. DOI: 10.1016/j.jeconc.2024.100065

Ennis, R. H. (2015). Critical thinking: a streamlined conception. In Davies, M., & Barnett, R. (Eds.), *The Palgrave Handbookof Critical Thinking in Higher Education* (pp. 31–47)., DOI: 10.1057/9781137378057

Esmaeilzadeh, P. (2020). Use of AI-based tools for healthcare purposes: A survey study from consumers' perspectives. *BMC Medical Informatics and Decision Making*, *20*, 1–19. DOI: 10.1186/s12911-020-01226-w PMID: 32698869

Farazouli, A., Cerratto-Pargman, T., Bolander-Laksov, K., & McGrath, C. (2024). Hello GPT! Goodbye home examination? An exploratory study of AI chatbots impact on university teachers' assessment practices. *Assessment & Evaluation in Higher Education*, *49*(3), 363–375.

Farrell, O., & Brunton, J. (2020). A balancing act: A window into online student engagement experiences. *International Journal of Educational Technology in Higher Education*, *17*(1), 1–19. DOI: 10.1186/s41239-020-00199-x

Feng, K., Zhao, X., Liu, J., Cai, Y., Ye, Z., Chen, C., & Xue, G. (2019). Spaced Learning Enhances Episodic Memory by Increasing Neural Pattern Similarity Across Repetitions. *The Journal of Neuroscience : The Official Journal of the Society for Neuroscience*, *39*(27), 5351–5360. DOI: 10.1523/jneurosci.2741-18.2019 PMID: 31036763

Ferreras-Garcia, R., Sales-Zaguirre, J., & Serradell-López, E. (2020). Competences in higher education tourism internships. *Education + Training*, *62*(1), 64–80.

Figaredo, D. D., & Stoyanovich, J. (2023). Responsible AI literacy: A stakeholder-first approach. *Big Data & Society*, *10*(2). Advance online publication. DOI: 10.1177/20539517231219958

Firdaus, A. (2006). Measuring service quality in higher education: HEdPERF versus SERVPERF. *Marketing Intelligence & Planning*, *24*(1), 31–47.

Firth, D. R., Derendinger, M., & Triche, J. (2024). Cheating better with ChatGPT: A framework for teaching students when to use ChatGPT and other generative AI bots. *Information Systems Education Journal*, *22*(3), 47–60. DOI: 10.62273/BZSU7160

Floridi, L., & Chiriatti, M. (2020). GPT-3: Its nature, scope, limits, and consequences. *Minds and Machines*, *30*(4), 681–694. DOI: 10.1007/s11023-020-09548-1

Fouad, A. M., Salem, I. E., & Fathy, E. A. (2024). Generative AI insights in tourism and hospitality: A comprehensive review and strategic research roadmap. *Tourism and Hospitality Research*, •••, 14673584241293125.

Fowler, D. S. (2023). AI in Higher Education. *Journal of Ethics in Higher Education*, *3*. https://doi.org/DOI: 10.26034/fr.jehe.2023.4657

Francis, N. J., Jones, S., & Smith, D. P. (2025). Generative AI in Higher Education: Balancing innovation and integrity. *British Journal of Biomedical Science*, *81*. Advance online publication. DOI: 10.3389/bjbs.2024.14048 PMID: 39850144

Fu, Q. K., Zou, D., Xie, H., & Cheng, G. (2022). A review of AWE feedback: Types, learning outcomes, and implications. *Computer Assisted Language Learning*, *37*(1–2), 179–221. DOI: 10.1080/09588221.2022.2033787

Fu, Y., Weng, Z., & Wang, J. (2024). Examining AI use in Educational contexts: A Scoping Meta-Review and Bibliometric analysis. *International Journal of Artificial Intelligence in Education*. Advance online publication. DOI: 10.1007/s40593-024-00442-w

Gabriel, O. T. (2023). *Data privacy and ethical issues in collecting healthcare data using artificial intelligence among health workers* (Master's thesis, Center for Bioethics and Research).

Gabriel, I. (2020). Artificial intelligence, values, and alignment. *Minds and Machines*, *30*(4), 411–437. DOI: 10.1007/s11023-020-09539-2

García Botero, G., Nguyet Diep, A., García Botero, J., Zhu, C., & Questier, F. (2022). Acceptance and use of mobile-assisted language learning by higher education language teachers. *Lenguaje*, *50*(1), 66–92. DOI: 10.25100/lenguaje.v50i1.11006

García-López, I. M., González, C. S. G., Ramírez-Montoya, M. S., & Molina-Espinosa, J. M. (2025). Challenges of implementing ChatGPT on education: Systematic literature review. *International Journal of Educational Research Open*, *8*, 100401. DOI: 10.1016/j.ijedro.2024.100401

Gardner, P., & Bartkus, K. (2014). What's in a name? A reference guide to work-education experiences. *Asia Pacific Journal of Cooperative Education*, *15*, 37–54.

Garg, N. (2014). An empirical study on Assessing quality of educational Service using SERVQUAL Model. *American Business Review*, *15*(1), 109–124.

Gasanov, E. I. (2024). The Experience of Using AI in the Forensic Economics: A Scoping Review. *Futurity Economics&Law*, *4*(3), 261–277. DOI: 10.57125/FEL.2024.09.25.15

Gasser, U., Ienca, M., Scheibner, J., Sleigh, J., & Vayena, E. (2020). Digital tools against COVID-19: Taxonomy, ethical challenges, and navigation aid. *The Lancet. Digital Health*, *2*(8), e425–e434. DOI: 10.1016/S2589-7500(20)30179-0 PMID: 32835200

Gavorník, A., Podroužek, J., Oreško, Š., Slosiarová, N., & Grmanová, G. (2024). Beyond privacy and security: Exploring ethical issues of smart metering and non-intrusive load monitoring. *Telematics and Informatics*, *90*, 102132. DOI: 10.1016/j.tele.2023.102132

Gerdes, A. (2022). A participatory data-centric approach to AI ethics by design. *Applied Artificial Intelligence*, *36*(1), 2009222. DOI: 10.1080/08839514.2021.2009222

Goertzen, B. J., Whitaker, B. L., Noble, D. J., Greenleaf, J., & Olsen, R. D. (2024). Are state comprehensive institutions prepared for AI? Not yet. *Teacher-Scholar: The Journal of the State Comprehensive University*, *13*(1). Advance online publication. DOI: 10.58809/CXOM8451

Grassini, S. (2023). Shaping the future of education: Exploring the potential and consequences of AI and ChatGPT in educational settings. *Education Sciences*, *13*(7), 692.

Guan, C., Mou, J., & Jiang, Z. (2020). Artificial intelligence innovation in education: A twenty-year data-driven historical analysis. *International Journal of Innovation Studies*, *4*(4), 134–147. https://doi.org/https://doi.org/10.1016/j.ijis.2020.09.001

Guba, E. G., & Lincoln, Y. S. (1994). Competing paradigms in qualitative research. *Handbook of qualitative research, 2*(163-194), 105.

Guilherme, A. (2019). AI and education: The importance of teacher and student relations. *AI & Society*, *34*(1), 47–54. DOI: 10.1007/s00146-017-0693-8

Hadizadeh, A. (2024). ChatGPT, the end of L2 academic writing or a blessing in disguise? *Acuity. Journal of English Language Pedagogy, Literature, and Culture*, *9*(2).

Halaweh, M. (2023). ChatGPT in education: Strategies for responsible implementation. *Contemporary Educational Technology*, *15*(2), ep421. DOI: 10.30935/cedtech/13036

Hall, A. (2007). Vygotsky goes online: Learning design from a socio-cultural perspective. Learning and socio-cultural Theory: Exploring modern Vygotskian perspectives international workshop 2007, Hsu, C. H., Xiao, H., & Chen, N. (2017). Hospitality and tourism education research from 2005 to 2014:"Is the past a prologue to the future?". *International Journal of Contemporary Hospitality Management*, *29*(1), 141–160.

Haque, M., & Tausif, M. (2020). Managing quality in university framework: Students' perspective. *Management Science Letters*, *11*(2), 627–636.

Haugom, E. (2022). The effect of changing from campus-based to digital teaching on student attendance: A case study of Norwegian business students. *Heliyon*, *8*(11), e11563. DOI: 10.1016/j.heliyon.2022.e11307 PMID: 36411901

Hawanti, S., & Zubaydulloevna, K. M. (2023). AI chatbot-based learning: Alleviating students' anxiety in english writing classroom. *Bulletin of Social Informatics Theory and Application*, *7*(2). Advance online publication. DOI: 10.31763/businta.v7i2.659

Hazari, S. (2024). Justification and Roadmap for Artificial intelligence (AI) literacy courses in Higher education. ScholarWorks. https://scholarworks.waldenu.edu/jerap/vol14/iss1/7/

Hendrycks, D., Burns, C., Basart, S., Critch, A., Li, J., Song, D., & Steinhardt, J. (2020). Aligning AI with shared human values. *arXiv*. https://arxiv.org/abs/2008.02275

Herington, J., McCradden, M. D., Creel, K., Boellaard, R., Jones, E. C., Jha, A. K., & Saboury, B. (2023). Ethical considerations for artificial intelligence in medical imaging: Data collection, development, and evaluation. *Journal of Nuclear Medicine*, *64*(12), 1848–1854. DOI: 10.2967/jnumed.122.264107 PMID: 37827839

Hoi, V. N. (2020). Understanding higher education learners' acceptance and use of mobile devices for language learning: A Rasch-based path modeling approach. *Computers & Education*, *146*, 103761. DOI: 10.1016/j.compedu.2019.103761

Hollister, B., Nair, P., Hill-Lindsay, S., & Chukoskie, L. (2022). Engagement in online learning: Student attitudes and behavior during COVID-19. *Frontiers in Education*, *7*. Advance online publication. DOI: 10.3389/feduc.2022.851019

Holloway, J., & Parcerisa, L. (2024). Teacher collaboration: How conditions of accountability shape teachers' autonomy, responsibilities, and relationships. *Teachers and Teaching*, ●●●, 1–15. DOI: 10.1080/13540602.2024.2436028

Holmes, W., Bialik, M., & Fadel, C. (2019). *Artificial Intelligence in Education: Promises and Implications for Teaching and Learning*. Center for Curriculum Redesign. https://curriculumredesign.org/wp-content/uploads/AIED-Book-Excerpt-CCR.pdf

Holmes, W., Bialik, M., & Fadel, C. (2021). *Artificial Intelligence in Education: Challenges and Opportunities for Teaching and Learning*. Centre for Curriculum Redesign, 43.

Hońko, S., & Hendryk, M. (2024). The Role of AI in Accounting: Insights From Practitioners. *European Research Studies Journal, 27*(2), 989-1003. https://ersj.eu/journal/3863

Hosseini, M., Resnik, D. B., & Holmes, K. (2023). The ethics of disclosing the use of artificial intelligence tools in writing scholarly manuscripts. *Research Ethics*, *19*(4), 449–465. DOI: 10.1177/17470161231180449 PMID: 39749232

Hryciw, B. N., Seely, A. J. E., & Kyeremanteng, K. (2023). Guiding principles and proposed classification system for the responsible adoption of artificial intelligence in scientific writing in medicine. *Frontiers in Artificial Intelligence*. Advance online publication. DOI: 10.3389/frai.2023.1283353 PMID: 38035200

Huang, X., Zhang, J., & Hudson, L. (2021). Factors affecting learning performance in flipped classroom: An empirical study based on RCOI framework. *Review of Education*, *391*(3), 98–122.

Huang, Z., Mao, Y., & Zhang, J. (2024). The Influence of Artificial Intelligence Technology on College Students' Learning Effectiveness from the Perspective of Constructivism — Taking ChatGPT as an Example. *Journal of Education. Humanities and Social Sciences*, *30*, 40–46. DOI: 10.54097/y1x3jj43

Hwang, G. J., & Chen, N. S. (2023). Exploring the potential of generative artificial intelligence in education: Applications, challenges, and future research directions. *Journal of Educational Technology & Society*, *26*(2).

Hyder, I., & Bhamani, S. (2016). Bloom's Taxonomy (cognitive domain) in higher education settings: *Reflection brief. Journal of Education and Educational Development*, *3*(2), 288. DOI: 10.22555/joeed.v3i2.1039

Imjai, N., Swatdikun, T., Rungruang, P., Basiruddin, R., & Aujirapongpan, S. (2024). Empowering generation z accountants in the era of data complexity and open innovation: Nurturing big data analytics, diagnostic, and forensic accounting skills. *Journal of Open Innovation*, *10*(2), 100308. DOI: 10.1080/1097198X.2025.2480972

Impact and implementation of experiential learning: An industry-university partnership case study. (2025). Journal of Applied Learning & Teaching, 8(1). https://doi.org/DOI: 10.37074/jalt.2025.8.1.5

Jarrah, A. M., Wardat, Y., & Fidalgo, P. (2023). Using ChatGPT in academic writing is (not) a form of plagiarism: What does the literature say? *Online Journal of Communication and Media Technologies*, *13*(4), e202346. DOI: 10.30935/ojcmt/13572

Jo, H., & Park, D.-H. (2024). AI in the Workplace: Examining the Effects of ChatGPT on Information Support and Knowledge Acquisition. *International Journal of Human-Computer Interaction*, *40*(23), 8091–8106. DOI: 10.1080/10447318.2023.2278283

Johnson, A. (2023). ChatGPT in schools: Here's where it's banned–And how it could potentially help students. *Forbes*.

Johnson, R., & Christensen, L. (2014). *Educational Research Quantitative* (5th ed.). Qualitative, and Mixed Approaches.

Jurafsky, D., & Martin, J. H. (2019). *Speech and language processing* (3rd ed.). Pearson.

Juskiw, P. (2017). *Assessing the Implementation of Internal Branding Training in the Hotel Industry*. Walden University.

Kaddouri, M., Mhamdi, K., Chniete, I., Marhraoui, M., Khaldi, M., & Jmad, S. (2024). Adopting AI in education. In Advances in educational technologies and instructional design book series (pp. 25–72). https://doi.org/DOI: 10.4018/979-8-3693-7255-5.ch002

Kaiser, K. (2012). Protecting confidentiality. *The SAGE handbook of interview research: The complexity of the craft, 2*, 457-464.

Kaminski, J. (2011). Diffusion of innovation theory. *Canadian Journal of Nursing Informatics*, *6*(2), 1–6.

Kang, D. S. (2016). Turning inside out: Perceived internal branding in customer-firm relationship building. *Journal of Services Marketing*, *30*(4), 462–475. doi:10.1108/JSM-07-2015-0229

Kang, X., & Zhang, W. (2023). An experimental case study on forum-based online teaching to improve student's engagement and motivation in higher education. *Interactive Learning Environments*, *31*(2), 1029–1040. DOI: 10.1080/10494820.2020.1817758

Kanselaar, G. (2002). Constructivism and socio-constructivism. *Constructivism and socio-constructivism*, 1-7.

Kasneci, E., Seßler, K., Küchemann, S., Bannert, M., Dementieva, D., Fischer, F., & Kasneci, G. (2023). ChatGPT for good? On opportunities and challenges of large language models for education. *Learning and Individual Differences*, *103*, 102274. DOI: 10.1016/j.lindif.2023.102274

Kassim, N. M., Bogari, N., & Zain, M. (2013). Service quality of a public university in Saudi Arabia. *The Journal of Learning in Higher Education*, *2013*, 1–18.

Kassim, N. M., Bogari, N., & Zain, M. (2015). Female students' perception of service quality in a gender-segregated college environment. *Social Behavior and Personality*, *43*(6), 921–930.

Khalifa, M., & Albadawy, M. (2024). Using artificial intelligence in academic writing and research: An essential productivity tool. *Computer Methods and Programs in Biomedicine Update*, *100145*. Advance online publication. DOI: 10.1016/j.cmpbup.2024.100145

Khalil, M., & Er, E. (2023). Will ChatGPT Get You Caught? Rethinking of Plagiarism Detection. In Zaphiris, P., & Ioannou, A. (Eds.), Lecture Notes in Computer Science: Vol. 14040. *Learning and Collaboration Technologies. HCII 2023*. Springer., DOI: 10.1007/978-3-031-34411-4_32

Khan, A., Egbue, O., Palkie, B., & Madden, J. (2017). Active learning: Engaging students to maximize learning in an online course. *Electronic Journal of e-Learning*, *15*(2), 107–115.

Khattab, F. (2018). Developing a Service Quality Model for Private Higher Education Institutions in Lebanon. *Journal of Management and Marketing Review*, *3*(1), 24–33.

Kılıç, B. İ. (2020). The effects of big data on forensic accounting practices and education. In *Contemporary issues in audit management and forensic accounting* (Vol. 102, pp. 11–26). Emerald Publishing Limited., DOI: 10.1108/S1569-375920200000102005

Kim, S. S. (2023). Motivators and concerns for real-time online classes: Focused on the security and privacy issues. *Interactive Learning Environments*, *31*(4), 1875–1888. DOI: 10.1080/10494820.2020.1863232

Knoth, N., Decker, M., Laupichler, M. C., Pinski, M., Buchholtz, N., Bata, K., & Schultz, B. (2024). Developing a holistic AI literacy assessment matrix – Bridging generic, domain-specific, and ethical competencies. *Computers and Education Open*, *6*, 100177. DOI: 10.1016/j.caeo.2024.100177

Kong, S., Cheung, W. M., & Zhang, G. (2022). Evaluating artificial intelligence literacy courses for fostering conceptual learning, literacy and empowerment in university students: Refocusing to conceptual building. *Computers in Human Behavior Reports*, *7*, 100223. DOI: 10.1016/j.chbr.2022.100223

Kooli, C. (2023). Chatbots in education and research: A critical examination of ethical implications and solutions. *Sustainability*, *15*(7), 5614.

Kramer, B., Seda, M., & Bobashev, G. (2017). Current opinions on forensic accounting education. *Accounting Research Journal*, *30*(3), 249–264. DOI: 10.1108/ARJ-06-2015-0082

Krathwohl, D. R. (2002). A Revision of Bloom's Taxonomy: An Overview. *Theory into Practice*, *41*(4), 212–218. http://www.jstor.org/stable/1477405

Kruger-Roux, H., & Alberts, R. (2024). Generative Artificial Intelligence Policy for academic literacy in South African Higher education. In Advances in educational technologies and instructional design book series (pp. 1–22). https://doi.org/DOI: 10.4018/979-8-3693-1054-0.ch001

Lankshear, Colin & Knobel, Michele. (2011). New literacies: Everyday practices and social learning.

Larson, D. B., Magnus, D. C., Lungren, M. P., Shah, N. H., & Langlotz, C. P. (2020). Ethics of using and sharing clinical imaging data for artificial intelligence: A proposed framework. *Radiology*, *295*(3), 675–682. DOI: 10.1148/radiol.2020202383 PMID: 32208097

Laupichler, M. C., Aster, A., Schirch, J., & Raupach, T. (2022). Artificial intelligence literacy in higher and adult education: A scoping literature review. *Computers and Education: Artificial Intelligence*, *3*, 100101. DOI: 10.1016/j.caeai.2022.100101

Lawless, B., & Chen, Y.-W. (2019). Developing a method of critical thematic analysis for qualitative communication inquiry. *The Howard Journal of Communications*, *30*(1), 92–106.

Lee, K. (2018). Case Study for the Application of PBL in Engineering School: Focused on an Artificial Intelligence Class. *Journal of the Korea Academia-Industrial cooperation. Society*, *19*(4), 154–160. DOI: 10.5762/KAIS.2018.19.4.154

Lérias, E., Guerra, C., & Ferreira, P. (2024). Literacy in Artificial Intelligence as a Challenge for Teaching in Higher Education: A Case Study at Portalegre Polytechnic University. *Information (Basel)*, *15*, 205.

Leslie, D. (2020). Tackling COVID-19 Through Responsible AI Innovation: Five Steps in the Right Direction. *Harvard Data Science Review*, (Special Issue 1). https://doi.org/DOI: 10.1162/99608f92.4bb9d7a7

Li, J., Zong, H., Wu, E., Wu, R., Peng, Z., Zhao, J., Yang, L., Xie, H., & Shen, B. (2024). Exploring the potential of artificial intelligence to enhance the writing of English academic papers by non-native English-speaking medical students: The educational application of ChatGPT. *BMC Medical Education*, *24*(736). Advance online publication. DOI: 10.1186/s12909-024-05738-y PMID: 38982429

Lim, C. P., Zhao, Y., Tondeur, J., Chai, C. S., & Tsai, C. (n.d.). Bridging the gap: Technology trends and use of technology in schools. https://eric.ed.gov/?id=EJ1016573

Limna, P., & Kraiwanit, T. (2023). The role of chatgpt on customer service in the hospitality industry: An exploratory study of hospitality workers' experiences and perceptions. *Tourism and Hospitality Management*, *29*(4), 583–592.

Long, D., Roberts, J., Magerko, B., Holstein, K. A., DiPaola, D., & Martin, F. (2023). AI Literacy: Finding Common Threads between Education, Design, Policy, and Explainability. Association for Computing Machinery, New York, NY, USA, Article 329, 1–6 https://doi.org/DOI: 10.1145/3544549.3573808

Long, D., & Magerko, B. (2020). What is AI literacy? *Proceedings of the 2020 CHI Conference on Human Factors in Computing Systems*, 1–16. https://doi.org/DOI: 10.1145/3313831.3376727

Loos, E., Gröpler, J., & Goudeau, M.-L. S. (2023). Using ChatGPT in education: Human reflection on ChatGPT's self-reflection. *Societies (Basel, Switzerland)*, *13*(8), 196.

Luckin, R. & Holmes, W. (2016). Intelligence Unleashed: An argument for AI in Education.

Luckin, R., Holmes, W., Griffiths, M., & Forcier, L. B. (2021). *Intelligence unleashed: An argument for AI in education*. Pearson Education.

Lundblad, J. P. (2003). A Review and Critique of Rogers' Diffusion of Innovation Theory as it Applies to Organizations. *Organization Development Journal*, *21*(4), 50.

Lysaght, T., Lim, H. Y., Xafis, V., & Ngiam, K. Y. (2019). AI-assisted decision-making in healthcare: The application of an ethics framework for big data in health and research. *Asian Bioethics Review*, *11*, 299–314. PMID: 33717318

MacCallum, K., Parsons, D., & Mohaghegh, M. (2024). The Scaffolded AI Literacy (SAIL) Framework for education. *He Rourou*, *23*. Advance online publication. DOI: 10.54474/herourou.v1i1.10835

Maguire, M., & Delahunt, B. (2017). Doing a thematic analysis: A practical, step-by-step guide for learning and teaching scholars. *All Ireland journal of higher education, 9*(3).

Mahapatra, S. N., Singh, B. K., & Kumar, V. (2020). A survey on secure transmission in Internet of Things: Taxonomy, recent techniques, research requirements, and challenges. *Arabian Journal for Science and Engineering*, *45*(8), 6211–6240. DOI: 10.1007/s13369-020-04461-2

Mahmood, S. (2021). Instructional strategies for online teaching in COVID-19 pandemic. *Human Behavior and Emerging Technologies*, *3*(1), 199–203. DOI: 10.1002/hbe2.218

Mahrishi, M., Abbas, A., & Siddiqui, M. K. (2024). *Global Initiatives towards Regulatory Frameworks for Artificial intelligence (AI) in Higher Education*. Digital Government Research and Practice., DOI: 10.1145/3672462

Maimaiti, G., Jia, C., & Hew, K. F. (2023). Student disengagement in web-based videoconferencing supported online learning: An activity theory perspective. *Interactive Learning Environments*, *31*(8), 4883–4902. DOI: 10.1080/10494820.2021.1984949

Malik, M. A., Amjad, A. I., Aslam, S., & Fakhrou, A. (2024). Global insights: ChatGPT's influence on academic and research writing, creativity, and plagiarism policies. *Frontiers in Research Metrics and Analytics*, *9*, 1486832. DOI: 10.3389/frma.2024.1486832 PMID: 39583913

Manikeswari, D., Ratnakaram, S., Shaikh, Z. H., Alawi, S. H., & Kumar, A. (2024). PBL in Higher Education: Empowering Students for the Industry Dynamics. [EEL]. *European Economic Letters*, *14*(3), 1137–1140. DOI: 10.52783/eel.v14i3.1873

Manikeswari, D., Ratnakaram, S., & Sirisetti, S. (2024). Psychometric testing - the game changer: A 360-degree view of psychometric testing and its applicability in HR functions. *International Journal of Business Excellence*, *33*(1), 48–75. DOI: 10.1504/IJBEX.2024.139112

Manis, K. T., & Choi, D. (2019). The virtual reality hardware acceptance model (VR-HAM): Extending and individuating the technology acceptance model (TAM) for virtual reality hardware. *Journal of Business Research*, *100*, 503–513.

Marcus, G. (2022). The next decade in AI: Why we need a new approach. *Daedalus*, *151*(2), 110–124. DOI: 10.1162/daed_a_01926

Martin, F., & Bolliger, D. U. (2018). Engagement matters: Student perceptions on the importance of engagement strategies in the online learning environment. *Online Learning : the Official Journal of the Online Learning Consortium*, *22*(1), 205–222. DOI: 10.24059/olj.v22i1.1092

Massaro, D., & Bernstein, J. (2022). Artificial intelligence in literacy. In Elsevier eBooks (pp. 529–542). https://doi.org/DOI: 10.1016/b978-0-12-818630-5.07005-6

Mateus, J.C., Lugo, N., Cappello, G., & Guerrero-Pico, M. (2024). Communication educators facing the arrival of generative artificial intelligence: Exploration in Mexico, Peru, and Spain. *Digital Education Review*. https://doi.org/DOI: 10.1344/der.2024.45.106-114

MBAToday, Accredited Business Schools in Saudi Arabia, https://www.mba.today/schools/saudi-arabia

Means, B., Toyama, Y., Murphy, R., Bakia, M., & Jones, K. (2009). *Evaluation of evidence-based practices in online learning: A meta-analysis and review of online learning studies*. U.S. Department of Education.

Medlin, B. D. (2001). *The factors that may influence a faculty member's decision to adopt electronic technologies in instruction*. Virginia Polytechnic Institute and State University.

Mehta, K., Mittal, P., Gupta, P. K., & Tandon, J. K. (2022). Analyzing the impact of forensic accounting in the detection of financial fraud: The mediating role of artificial intelligence. In *International Conference on Innovative Computing and Communications: Proceedings of ICICC 2021*, Volume 2 (pp. 585-592). Springer Singapore. DOI: 10.1007/978-981-16-2597-8_50

Meng, T., & Lai, I. K. W. (2024). How employee-guest interactions and welcome hospitality create brand attitudes for first-time hotel customers. *Asia Pacific Journal of Marketing and Logistics*. Advance online publication. DOI: 10.1108/APJML-03-2024-0376

Mercer, N. (1995). *The guided construction of knowledge: Talk amongst teachers and learners*. Multilingual matters.

Merceron, K., & Best, K. (2024). Integrating Professional Perspectives for AI Literacy. In Advances in educational technologies and instructional design book series (pp. 300–315). https://doi.org/DOI: 10.4018/979-8-3693-0831-8.ch014

Meyer, K. A. (2014). Student engagement in online learning: What works and why. *ASHE Higher Education Report*, *40*(6), 1–114. DOI: 10.1002/aehe.20018

Miao, J., Thongprayoon, C., Suppadungsuk, S., Garcia Valencia, O. A., Qureshi, F., & Cheungpasitporn, W. (2024). Ethical Dilemmas in Using AI for Academic Writing and an Example Framework for Peer Review in Nephrology Academia: A Narrative Review. *Clinics and Practice*, *14*(1), 89–105. DOI: 10.3390/clinpract14010008 PMID: 38248432

Michel-Villarreal, R., Vilalta-Perdomo, E., Salinas-Navarro, D. E., Thierry-Aguilera, R., & Gerardou, F. S. (2023). Challenges and opportunities of generative AI for higher education as explained by ChatGPT. *Education Sciences*, *13*(9), 856.

Miles, M. B., & Huberman, A. M. (1994). *Qualitative data analysis: An expanded sourcebook*. sage.

Min, H., Nancy, S., & Gursoy, D. (2016). A Longitudinal Investigation of the Importance of Course Subjects in the Hospitality Curriculum: An Industry Perspective. *Journal of Hospitality & Tourism Education*, *28*(1), 10–20. DOI: 10.1080/10963758.2015.1127168

Miranda, J., Navarrete, C., Noguez, J., Molina-Espinosa, J. M., Ramírez-Montoya, M. S., Navarro-Tuch, S. A., Bustamante-Bello, M. R., Rosas-Fernández, J. B., & Molina, A. (2021). The core components of education 4.0 in higher education: Three case studies in engineering education. *Computers & Electrical Engineering*, *93*. Advance online publication. DOI: 10.1016/j.compeleceng.2021.107278

Misra, D., & Stensaker, B. (2024). Balancing control and legitimacy in higher education policy implementation. *Studies in Higher Education*, •••, 1–14. DOI: 10.1080/03075079.2024.2306340

Mohammed, B. O. (2018). Statistical quality control charts for measuring educational service quality at Albaha University, Saudi Arabia, from the viewpoint of students. *Journal of Economics and Administrative Sciences*, *24*(102), 1–23.

Moher, D., Liberati, A., Tetzlaff, J., & Altman, D. G.PRISMA Group. (2009). Preferred reporting items for systematic reviews and meta-analyses: The PRISMA statement. *PLoS Medicine*, *6*(7), e1000097. DOI: 10.1371/journal.pmed.1000097 PMID: 19621072

Molnar, A., Weerakkody, V., El-Haddadeh, R., Lee, H., & Irani, Z. (2013). *A Framework of Reference for Evaluating User Experience When Using High Definition Video to Video to Facilitate Public Services* (Vol. 402). doi:DOI: 10.1007/978-3-642-38862-0_27

Moriau, L., & Angouri, J. (2023). Participatory curriculum development: The case of EUTOPIA, a European university alliance. *Curriculum Journal*, *35*(3), 337–360. DOI: 10.1002/curj.243

Morley, J., Kinsey, L., Elhalal, A., Garcia, F., Ziosi, M., & Floridi, L. (2023). Operationalising AI ethics: Barriers, enablers, and next steps. *AI & Society*, **•••**, 1–13. DOI: 10.1007/s00146-023-01422-w

Morrison, A., & Barry O'Mahony, G. (2003). The liberation of hospitality management education. *International Journal of Contemporary Hospitality Management*, *15*(1), 38–44.

Mounce, P., & Frazier, J. (2002). The effect of forensic accounting education on an accountant's employment potential. *Journal of Forensic Accounting*, *3*(1), 91–102.

Mukhtar, K., Javed, K., Arooj, M., & Sethi, A. (2020). Advantages, limitations and recommendations for online learning during COVID-19 pandemic era. *Pakistan Journal of Medical Sciences, 36*(COVID19-S4), S27–S31. https://doi.org/DOI: 10.12669/pjms.36.COVID19-S4.2785

Murdan, A. P., & Halkhoree, R. "Integration of Artificial Intelligence for educational excellence and innovation in higher education institutions," 2024 1st International Conference on Smart Energy Systems and Artificial Intelligence (SESAI), Mauritius, 2024, pp. 1-6, doi: DOI: 10.1109/SESAI61023.2024.10599402

Murdock, H., & Murdock, D. H. (2018). Association of Certified Fraud Examiners (ACFE). *Auditor Essentials*, 7-10.

Mutawa, A. M., & Sruthi, S. (2024). UNESCO's AI Competency Framework. In Advances in educational technologies and instructional design book series (pp. 75–96). https://doi.org/DOI: 10.4018/979-8-3693-0884-4.ch004

National University. (2024). *Challenges of distance learning for students*. Retrieved March 15, 2024, from https://www.nu.edu/blog/challenges-of-distance-learning-for-students/

Nielsen, J. (1994). *Usability engineering*. Morgan Kaufmann.

Nieuwoudt, J. E. (2020). Investigating synchronous and asynchronous class attendance as predictors of academic success in online education. *Australasian Journal of Educational Technology*, *36*(3), 15–25. DOI: 10.14742/ajet.5137

Nikolic, S., Wentworth, I., Sheridan, L., Moss, S., Duursma, E., Jones, R. A., Ros, M., & Middleton, R. (2024). A systematic literature review of attitudes, intentions and behaviours of teaching academics pertaining to AI and generative AI (GenAI) in higher education: An analysis of GenAI adoption using the UTAUT framework. *Australasian Journal of Educational Technology*. Advance online publication. DOI: 10.14742/ajet.9643

Noh, N., Raju, R., Eri, Z., & Ishak, S. (2021). Extending technology acceptance model (TAM) to measure the students' acceptance of using digital tools during open and distance learning (ODL). IOP Conference Series: Materials Science and Engineering, Nuong, M. D., & Ragavan, N. A. (2023). Digital Future of the Global Hospitality Industry and Hospitality Education: Review of Related Literature.

O'Donoghue, T. (2006). *Planning your qualitative research project: An introduction to interpretivist research in education*. Routledge.

Ogbeide, G.-C. (2023). ChatGPT in Hospitality and Tourism Education and Industry. *The Consortium Journal of Hospitality and Tourism*, •••, 26.

Oh, S., & Sanfilippo, M. R. (2024). University Governance for Responsible AI. *Proceedings of the Association for Library and Information Science Education Annual Conference*. https://doi.org/DOI: 10.21900/j.alise.2024.1706

Ojha, B., Agrawal, A., & Arya, A. (2024). Artificial intelligence integration in higher education. In CRC Press eBooks (pp. 1–23). https://doi.org/DOI: 10.1201/9781003469315-1

Oliver, S. L., & Hyun, E. (2011). Comprehensive curriculum reform in higher Education: collaborative engagement of faculty and administrators. https://eric.ed.gov/?id=EJ1057195

Orey, M. (2010). *Bloom's taxonomy. Emerging perspectives on learning, teaching, and technology*. The Global Text Project.

Osman, A. R., & Saputra, R. S. (2019). A pragmatic model of student satisfaction: A viewpoint of private higher education. *Quality Assurance in Education*, *27*(2), 142–165.

Pandey, A. S., Sharma, Y., Tiwari, A., Chauhan, R., Tyagi, S., & Kumari, J. (2024, May). Ethical implications of AI-powered communication tools. *In 2024 International Conference on Communication, Computer Sciences and Engineering (IC3SE)* (pp. 1857-1861). IEEE.

Parasuraman, A., Zeithaml, V. A., & Berry, L. L. (1985). A conceptual model of service quality and its implications for future research. *Journal of Marketing*, *49*(4), 41–50.

Parisot, A. H. (1997). Distance education as a catalyst for changing teaching in the community college: Implications for institutional policy. *New Directions for Community Colleges*, *1997*(99), 5–13.

Park, J.-H., & Yang, I. Y. (2020). Utilizing an AI-Based Grammar Checker in an EFL Writing Classroom. *Academic Journal of Applied Linguistics*, *36*(1), 97–120. DOI: 10.17154/kjal.2020.3.36.1.97

Parmaxi, A., & Demetriou, A. A. (2020). Augmented reality in language learning: A state-of-the-art review of 2014–2019. *Journal of Computer Assisted Learning*, *36*(6), 861–875. DOI: 10.1111/jcal.12486

Paul, R., & Elder, L. (2008). *The miniature guide to critical thinking: Concepts and tools*. Foundation for Critical Thinking Press.

Pautasso, M. (2019). The structure and conduct of a narrative literature review. *A guide to the scientific career: Virtues, communication, research and academic writing*, 299-310. DOI: 10.1002/9781118907283.ch31

Perkins, M. (2023). Academic integrity considerations of AI large language models in the post-pandemic era: ChatGPT and beyond. *Journal of University Teaching* [3] *& Learning Practice, 20*(2). https://doi.org/DOI: 10.53761/1.20.02.07

Peters, M. D. J., Marnie, C., Colquhoun, H., Garritty, C. M., Hempel, S., Horsley, T., & Tricco, A. C. (2021). *Scoping reviews: reinforcing and advancing the methodology and application. Systematic Reviews*. BioMed Central Ltd., DOI: 10.1186/s13643-021-01821-3

Pichardo, J. I., López-Medina, E. F., Mancha-Gutiérrez, J. M., & de la Fuente, J. (2021). Students and teachers using Mentimeter: Technological innovation to face the challenges of the COVID-19 pandemic and post-pandemic in higher education. *Education Sciences*, *11*(11), 667. DOI: 10.3390/educsci11110667

Pinski, M., & Benlian, A. (2024). AI literacy for users – A comprehensive review and future research directions of learning methods, components, and effects. *Computers in Human Behavior Artificial Humans, 2*(1), 100062. DOI: 10.1016/j.chbah.2024.100062

Prince, M., Felder, R., & Brent, R. (2020). Active student engagement in online STEM classes: Approaches and recommendations. *Advances in Engineering Education, 8*(4), 1–25.

Pu, Y. A., & Barnard, R. (2025). Teacher and Learner Agency for Collaborative Learning. https://doi.org/DOI: 10.4324/9781032643144

Qadhi, S., Alduais, A., Chaaban, Y., & Khraisheh, M. (2024). Generative AI, Research Ethics, and Higher Education Research: Insights from a Scientometric Analysis. *Information (Basel), 15*(6), 325. DOI: 10.3390/info15060325

Rahman, M., Terano, H. J. R., Rahman, N., Salamzadeh, A., & Rahaman, S. (2023). ChatGPT and academic research: A review and recommendations based on practical examples. *Journal of Education. Management and Development Studies, 3*(1), 1–12. DOI: 10.52631/jemds.v3i1.175

Ranade, N., & Saravia, M. (2024). Teaching AI Ethics in Technical and Professional Communication: A Systematic review. *IEEE Transactions on Professional Communication, 67*(4), 422–436. DOI: 10.1109/tpc.2024.3458708

Rana, K., Aitken, S. J., & Chimoriya, R. (2025). Interdisciplinary Approaches in Doctoral and Higher Research Education: An Integrative Scoping review. *Education Sciences, 15*(1), 72. DOI: 10.3390/educsci15010072

Rapley, T. J. (2001). The art (fulness) of open-ended interviewing: Some considerations on analysing interviews. *Qualitative Research, 1*(3), 303–323.

Rashid, M.M. and Rehman, M.Z., (2017). Quality of higher education in Bangladesh: Application of a Modified SERVQUAL model problems of education in the 21st Century, 75(1), 72-91

Rathnakar, G., Pachuau, L., Geetha, T., Prabhuswamy, M., & Praveenkumar, S. (2024). Practitioner Insights on Policy-Driven Shifts in College-Based Education. In Advances in educational technologies and instructional design book series (pp. 91–120). https://doi.org/DOI: 10.4018/979-8-3693-4058-5.ch005

Ratnakaram, S. P., Manikeswari, D., Shaikh, Z. H., Mahapatra, D. M., Mohanty, B. S., & Soni, A. (2025). Wearables and AI-Smart Technologies: Transforming the Education Sphere. In Ul Rehman, S. (Ed.), *Wearable Devices and Smart Technology for Educational Teaching Assistance* (pp. 27–52). IGI Global Scientific Publishing., DOI: 10.4018/979-8-3693-7817-5.ch002

Reiss, M. J. (2021). The use of AI in education: Practicalities and ethical considerations. *London Review of Education*, *19*(1). Advance online publication. DOI: 10.14324/lre.19.1.05

Rezaee, Z., Lo, D., Ha, M., & Suen, A. (2016). Forensic accounting education and practice: Insights from China. *Journal of Forensic & Investigative Accounting*, *8*(1), 106–119.

Rezaee, Z., & Wang, J. (2019). Relevance of big data to forensic accounting practice and education. *Managerial Auditing Journal*, *34*(3), 268–288. DOI: 10.1108/MAJ-08-2017-1633

Riapina, N. (2023). Teaching AI-Enabled Business Communication in Higher Education: A Practical framework. *Business and Professional Communication Quarterly*, *87*(3), 511–521. DOI: 10.1177/23294906231199249

Roche, T., Wilson, E., & Goode, E. (2024). Immersive learning in a block teaching model: A case study of academic reform through principles, policies and practice. *Journal of University Teaching & Learning Practice*, *21*(2). Advance online publication. DOI: 10.53761/5cmd7w70

Rogers, E. M. (2003). *Diffusion of Innovations* (5th ed.). Free Press.

Rožman, M., Tominc, P., & Vrečko, I. (2023). Building skills for the future of work: Students' perspectives on emerging jobs in the Data and AI Cluster through artificial intelligence in education. *Environment and Social Psychology*, *8*(2), 1–24.

Ryan, M., & Stahl, B. C. (2020). Artificial intelligence ethics guidelines for developers and users: Clarifying their content and normative implications. *Journal of Information. Communication and Ethics in Society*, *19*(1), 61–86.

Safdar, N. M., Banja, J. D., & Meltzer, C. C. (2020). Ethical considerations in artificial intelligence. *European Journal of Radiology*, *122*, 108768. PMID: 31786504

Sahin, I. (2006). Detailed review of Rogers' diffusion of innovations theory and educational technology-related studies based on Rogers' theory. *Turkish Online Journal of Educational Technology-TOJET*, *5*(2), 14–23.

Sainath, T. N., Vinyals, O., Senior, A., & Sak, H. (2015). Convolutional, long short-term memory, fully connected deep neural networks. In *2015 IEEE International Conference on Acoustics, Speech and Signal Processing (ICASSP)* (pp. 4580–4584). IEEE. https://doi.org/DOI: 10.1109/ICASSP.2015.7178838

Salas-Pilco, S. Z., Yang, Y., & Zhang, Z. (2022). Student engagement in online learning in Latin American higher education during the COVID-19 pandemic: A systematic review. *British Journal of Educational Technology*, *53*(3), 593–619. DOI: 10.1111/bjet.13190 PMID: 35600418

SAMA. (2020) Saudi Arabia Monetary Authority (SAMA), 56th Annual Report. https://www.sama.gov.sa/en-US/News/Pages/news-595.aspx

Saputra, K. A. K. (2019). Case-Based learning in forensic accounting education. *International Journal for Educational and Vocational Studies*, *1*(6), 545–553. DOI: 10.29103/ijevs.v1i6.1763

Savandha, S. D., Azzahra, A., & Kangas, J. (2024). The Integrated Governance Model for Improving Education Quality (IGMEQ): A comparative analysis of Indonesia and Finland systems. *OPSearch American Journal of Open Research*, *3*(5), 1018–1028. DOI: 10.58811/opsearch.v3i5.126

Schwandt, T. A. (1998). The interpretive review of educational matters: Is there any other kind? *Review of Educational Research*, *68*(4), 409–412.

Schwitzgebel, E., Schwitzgebel, D., & Strasser, A. (2024). Creating a large language model of a philosopher. *Mind & Language*, *39*(2), 237–259. DOI: 10.1111/mila.12466

Selasih, D. & Suranto (2024). Understanding Student Perceptions of Artificial Intelligence Technology: Case Study of Accounting Education Student, Universitas Muhammadiyah Surakarta. *Didaktika: Jurnal Kependidikan, 13*(001 Des), 375-388. DOI: DOI: 10.58230/27454312.1367

Selwyn, N., Hillman, T., Bergviken Rensfeldt, A., & Perrotta, C. (2021). Digital technologies and the automation of education—key questions and concerns. *Postdigital Science and Education*, 1-10. https://doi.org/DOI: 10.1007/s42438-021-00263-3

Selwyn, N. (2022). The future of AI and education: Some cautionary notes. *European Journal of Education*, *57*(4), 620–631. DOI: 10.1111/ejed.12532

Selwyn, N. (2023). *Should robots replace teachers? AI and the future of education*. Polity Press.

Shadiev, R., & Yang, M. (2020). Review of studies on technology-enhanced language learning and teaching. *Sustainability*, *12*(2), 524. DOI: 10.3390/su12020524

Shahrani, A. A., Alhumaidan, N., AlHindawi, Z., Althobaiti, A., Aloufi, K., Al-mughamisi, R., & Aldalbahi, A. (2024). Readiness to embrace artificial intelligence among medical students in Saudi Arabia: A national survey. *Health Care*, *12*(24), 2504. DOI: 10.3390/healthcare12242504 PMID: 39765931

Shalev-Shwartz, S., & Ben-David, S. (2014). *Understanding machine learning: From theory to algorithms*. Cambridge University Press.

Shamsuddinova, S., Heryani, P., & Naval, M. A. (2024). Evolution to revolution: Critical exploration of educators' perceptions of the impact of Artificial Intelligence (AI) on the teaching and learning process in the GCC region. *International Journal of Educational Research*, *125*, 102326.

Shiohira, K. (2021). Understanding the Impact of AI on Skills Development. In: Bonn, Germany: UNESCO-UNEVOC. https://unevoc. unesco. org/home/UNEVOC+...

Shwedeh, F., Salloum, S. A., Aburayya, A., Fatin, B., Elbadawi, M. A., Ghurabli, Z. A., & Dabbagh, T. A. (2024). AI adoption and educational sustainability in higher education in the UAE. In Studies in big data (pp. 201–229). https://doi.org/DOI: 10.1007/978-3-031-52280-2_14

Slimi, Z. (2023). The Impact of Artificial intelligence on Higher Education: An Empirical study. *European Journal of Educational Sciences*, *10*(1). Advance online publication. DOI: 10.19044/ejes.v10no1a17

Sode, M. (2021). Group activities with AI teacher support in PBL education. In *Proceedings of the SEFI 49th Annual Conference* (Vol. 49). https://cir.nii.ac.jp/crid/1010294643612869760

Sperling, K., Stenberg, C., McGrath, C., Åkerfeldt, A., Heintz, F., & Stenliden, L. (2024). In search of artificial intelligence (AI) literacy in teacher education: A scoping review. *Computers and Education Open*, *6*, 100169. DOI: 10.1016/j.caeo.2024.100169

Stansbie, P., Nash, R., & Chang, S. (2016). Linking internships and classroom learning: A case study examination of hospitality and tourism management students. *Journal of Hospitality, Leisure, Sport and Tourism Education*, *19*, 19–29. https://doi.org/https://doi.org/10.1016/j.jhlste.2016.07.001

Su, J., & Yang, W. (2023). Unlocking the power of ChatGPT: A framework for applying generative AI in education. *ECNU Review of Education*, *6*(3), 355–366. DOI: 10.1177/20965311231168423

Su, K. D. (2022). Implementation of innovative artificial intelligence cognitions with problem-based learning guided tasks to enhance students' performance in science. *Journal of Baltic Science Education, 21*(2), 245–257. DOI: 10.33225/jbse/22.21.245

Sun, H.-L., Li, X.-Y., & Liu, R. (2022). The influence of teacher–student interaction on the effects of online learning: Based on a serial mediating model. *Frontiers in Psychology, 13*, 779217. DOI: 10.3389/fpsyg.2022.779217 PMID: 35369265

Sun, Y., & Gao, F. (2020). An investigation of the influence of intrinsic motivation on students' intention to use mobile devices in language learning. *Educational Technology Research and Development, 68*, 1181–1198. DOI: 10.1007/s11423-019-09733-9

Tadimalla, S. Y., & Maher, M. L. (2024). AI Literacy for All: Adjustable interdisciplinary socio-technical curriculum. 2021 IEEE Frontiers in Education Conference (FIE), 1–9. https://doi.org/DOI: 10.1109/fie61694.2024.10893159

Tahiru, F. (2021). AI in Education: A Systematic Literature Review. [JCIT]. *Journal of Cases on Information Technology, 23*(1), 1–20. DOI: 10.4018/JCIT.2021010101

Tang, T., Abuhmaid, A. M., Olaimat, M., Oudat, D. M., Aldhaeebi, M., & Bamanger, E. (2023). Efficiency of flipped classroom with online-based teaching under COVID-19. *Interactive Learning Environments, 31*(2), 1077–1088. DOI: 10.1080/10494820.2020.1817761

Tariq, M. U. (2024). Generative AI in Curriculum Development in Higher Education. In Fields, Z. (Ed.), *Impacts of Generative AI on Creativity in Higher Education* (pp. 227–258). IGI Global., DOI: 10.4018/979-8-3693-2418-9.ch009

Tariq, M. U. (2025). AI-Driven Research Methodologies: Revolutionizing Data-Driven Discoveries in Engineering and Physical Sciences. In Basha, J., Alade, T., Al Khazimi, M., Vasudevan, R., & Khan, J. (Eds.), *Optimizing Research Techniques and Learning Strategies With Digital Technologies* (pp. 97–122). IGI Global Scientific Publishing., DOI: 10.4018/979-8-3693-7863-2.ch004

Tariq, M. U. (2025). AI-Enhanced Project-Based Learning: Revolutionizing Commerce Education With Generative AI. In ElSayary, A. (Ed.), *Prompt Engineering and Generative AI Applications for Teaching and Learning* (pp. 125–142). IGI Global Scientific Publishing., DOI: 10.4018/979-8-3693-7332-3.ch008

Tariq, M. U. (2025). Empowering Patients With AI-Ethical Digital Tools for Health Data Management and Decision. In Pesqueira, A., & de Bem Machado, A. (Eds.), *Navigating Privacy, Innovation, and Patient Empowerment Through Ethical Healthcare Technology* (pp. 197–216). IGI Global Scientific Publishing., DOI: 10.4018/979-8-3693-7630-0.ch008

Tariq, M. U. (2025). Integrating Theory and Practice: Transformative Approaches in Practice-Led Research for Professional Development. In Kwok, S., Yu, P., & Le Corre, J. (Eds.), *Exploring Practice-Led Research for Professional Development* (pp. 419–436). IGI Global Scientific Publishing., DOI: 10.4018/979-8-3693-6376-8.ch016

Tausif, M. R. (2017). Assessing the Quality of Education in Saudi Arabia. *International Journal of Economic Research, 14*(17), 1–8.

Techawitthayachinda, I. R., Deng, Y., Zeng, Z., Liu, H., Chen, Y. C., & Huang, D. An AI-Enable Knowledge Graph and Student's Agency in Productive Struggle During Problem-Based Learning in Cybersecurity Education. Conference Proceeding of The IAFOR International Conference on Education in Hawaii 2022. https://papers.iafor.org/wp-content/uploads/papers/iice2022/IICE2022_62117.pdf

Teixeira da Silva, J. A. (2024). The detection of ChatGPT's textual crumb trails is an unsustainable solution to imperfect detection methods. *Open Information Science, 8*, 202. DOI: 10.1515/opis-2024-0007

Tibor, K. (2024). *From data literacy to artificial intelligence literacy: background and approaches*. Deleted Journal., DOI: 10.3311/celisr.38042

Tomczyk, P., Brüggemann, P., & Vrontis, D. (2024). AI meets academia: Transforming systematic literature reviews. *EuroMed Journal of Business*. Advance online publication. DOI: 10.1108/emjb-03-2024-0055

Traphagan, T., Kucsera, J. V., & Kishi, K. (2010). Impact of class lecture webcasting on attendance and learning. *Educational Technology Research and Development, 58*(1), 19–37. DOI: 10.1007/s11423-009-9128-7

Tubella, A., Mora-Cantallops, M., & Nieves, J. C. (2024). How to teach responsible AI in Higher Education: Challenges and opportunities. *Ethics and Information Technology, 26*(1). Advance online publication. DOI: 10.1007/s10676-023-09733-7

Udell, J., O'Brien, V., Flynn, S., Hooper, H., & Walker-Martin, F. (2023). The practice of sandwich degrees. In *The Routledge International Handbook of Work-Integrated Learning* (pp. 176–189). Routledge.

Ugwu, N. F., Igbinlade, A. S., Ochiaka, R. E., Ezeani, U. D., Okorie, N. C., Opele, J. K., Onayinka, T. S., Iroegbu, O., Onyekwere, O. K., Adams, A. B., Aigbona, P., & Ojobola, F. B. (2024). Clarifying ethical dilemmas of using artificial intelligence in research writing: A rapid review. *Higher Learning Research Communications, 14*(2), 29–47.

UNESCO. (2023). *Guidance for generative AI in education and research.* United Nations Educational, Scientific and Cultural Organization., DOI: 10.54675/EWZM9535

Urmeneta, M. (2023). Reflections on the artificial intelligence transformation: responsible use and the role of institutional research and institutional effectiveness professionals. ˜the œAIR Professional File, Fall 2023. https://doi.org/DOI: 10.34315/apf1642023

Van Acker, B. B., Parmentier, D. D., Vlerick, P., & Saldien, J. (2018). Understanding mental workload: From a clarifying concept analysis toward an implementable framework. *Cognition Technology and Work, 20*(3), 351–365.

Van Akkeren, J. K., & Tarr, J.-A. (2021). The application of experiential learning for forensic accounting students: The Mock trial. *Accounting Education, 31*(1), 39–66. DOI: 10. 1080/09639284.2021.1960573

Van Rensburg, Z. J., & Van Der Westhuizen, S. (2024). Ethical AI integration in academia. In Advances in educational technologies and instructional design book series (pp. 23–48). https://doi.org/DOI: 10.4018/979-8-3693-1054-0.ch002

Van Wyk, B. (2024). Exploring the philosophy and practice of AI literacy in higher education in the Global South: A scoping review. *Cybrarians Journal, 73*, 1–21. DOI: 10.70000/cj.2024.73.601

Vaswani, A., Shazeer, N., Parmar, N., Uszkoreit, J., Jones, L., Gomez, A. N., Kaiser, Ł., & Polosukhin, I. (2017). Attention is all you need. In *Advances in Neural Information Processing Systems* (Vol. 30, pp. 5998–6008).

Vatel. (2023). *Vatel Prospectus* (V. Bahrain, Ed.). Vatel International Business School Hotel & Tourism Management Bahrain. https://vc3.vatelconnect.com/files/sitesecole/brochure/file_1692806821.pdf

Venkatesh, V. (2000). Determinants of perceived ease of use: Integrating control, intrinsic motivation, and emotion into the technology acceptance model. *Information Systems Research, 11*(4), 342–365.

Venkatesh, V. (2024). Paradigm changing metaverse: Future research directions in design, technology adoption and use, and impacts. *Decision Support Systems*, •••, 114307.

Venkatesh, V., Morris, M. G., Davis, G. B., & Davis, F. D. (2003). User acceptance of information technology: Toward a unified view. *Management Information Systems Quarterly*, •••, 425–478.

Venkatesh, V., Thong, J. Y., & Xu, X. (2012). Consumer acceptance and use of information technology: Extending the unified theory of acceptance and use of technology. *Management Information Systems Quarterly*, •••, 157–178.

Vijayalakshmi, D., & Jeevan, J. (2024). Forensic Accounting: Uncovering Fraud with Advanced Analytics. *Library of Progress-Library Science. Information Technology & Computer*, *44*(3). Advance online publication. DOI: 10.48165/bapas.2024.44.2.1

Vijayasarathy, L. R. (2004). Predicting consumer intentions to use on-line shopping: The case for an augmented technology acceptance model. *Information & Management*, *41*(6), 747–762.

Vonderwell, S., & Zachariah, S. (2005). Factors that influence participation in online learning. *Journal of Research on Technology in Education*, *38*(2), 213–230. DOI: 10.1080/15391523.2005.10782457

Vreuls, J., Van Der Klink, M., Koeslag-Kreunen, M., Stoyanov, S., Boshuizen, H., & Nieuwenhuis, L. (2023). Responsive curriculum development: Which factors support breaking through institutional barriers? *Journal of Vocational Education and Training*, •••, 1–29. DOI: 10.1080/13636820.2023.2270470

Vygotsky, L. S. (1978). *Mind in society: The development of higher psychological processes*. Harvard University Press.

Wakunuma, K., Jiya, T., & Aliyu, S. (2020). Socio-ethical implications of using AI in accelerating SDG3 in Least Developed Countries. *Journal of Applied and Natural Science*, *12*(4), 578–586.

Walters, W. H., & Wilder, E. I. (2023). Fabrication and errors in the bibliographic citations generated by ChatGPT. *Scientific Reports*, *13*, 14045. DOI: 10.1038/s41598-023-41032-5 PMID: 37679503

Wang, P. Q. (2025). Personalizing guest experience with generative AI in the hotel industry: There's more to it than meets a Kiwi's eye. *Current Issues in Tourism*, *28*(4), 527–544. DOI: 10.1080/13683500.2023.2300030

Warschauer, M., & Grimes, D. (2008). Automated Writing Assessment in the Classroom. *Pedagogies*, *3*(1), 22–36. DOI: 10.1080/15544800701771580

Weber, J., & Lewis, J. (2021). Emerging issues in artificial intelligence and ethics in business. *Journal of Business Ethics*, *171*(2), 251–267.

Weng, X., Xia, Q., Gu, M., Rajaram, K., & Chiu, T. K. (2024). Assessment and learning outcomes for generative AI in higher education: A scoping review on current research status and trends. *Australasian Journal of Educational Technology*. Advance online publication. DOI: 10.14742/ajet.9540

Werang, B. R., & Leba, S. M. R. (2022). Factors affecting student engagement in online teaching and learning: A qualitative case study. *The Qualitative Report*, *27*(2), 555–577. DOI: 10.46743/2160-3715/2022.5319

Wester, E. R., Walsh, L. L., Arango-Caro, S., & Callis-Duehl, K. L. (2021). Student engagement declines in STEM undergraduates during COVID-19–driven remote learning. *Journal of Microbiology & Biology Education*, *22*(1), 10–1128. PMID: 33884093

Whorf, B. L. (1956). *Language, thought, and reality: Selected writings of Benjamin Lee Whorf*. MIT Press.

Wiles, R., Crow, G., Heath, S., & Charles, V. (2008). The management of confidentiality and anonymity in social research. *International Journal of Social Research Methodology*, *11*(5), 417–428.

Williamson, B. (2019). Datafication of education. In Routledge eBooks (pp. 212–226). https://doi.org/DOI: 10.4324/9781351252805-14

Williamson, B., & Eynon, R. (2020). Historical threads, missing links, and future directions in AI in education. *Learning, Media and Technology*, *45*(3), 223–235.

Woithe, J., & Filipec, O. (2023). Understanding the adoption, perception, and learning impact of ChatGPT in higher education: A qualitative exploratory case study analyzing students' perspectives and experiences with the AI-based large language model. In.

Wood, D., Bruner, J. S., & Ross, G. (1976). The role of tutoring in problem solving. *Journal of Child Psychology and Psychiatry, and Allied Disciplines*, *17*(2), 89–100. PMID: 932126

World Economic Forum. (2023). The Future of Jobs Report 2023. World Economic Forum. https://www.weforum.org/publications/the-future-of-jobs-report-2023/

World Economic Forum. (2025). The Future of Jobs Report 2025. World Economic Forum. https://www.weforum.org/publications/the-future-of-jobs-report-2025/

Wu, Y. (2024). Critical Thinking Pedagogics Design in an Era of ChatGPT and Other AI Tools — Shifting From Teaching "What" to Teaching "Why" and "How". *Journal of Education and Development*, *8*, 1. DOI: 10.20849/jed.v8i1.1404

Xia, Q., Weng, X., Ouyang, F., Lin, T. J., & Chiu, T. K. (2024). A scoping review on how generative artificial intelligence transforms assessment in higher education. *International Journal of Educational Technology in Higher Education, 21*(1). Advance online publication. DOI: 10.1186/s41239-024-00468-z

Yadav, S. (2024). Advancing education with AI-Driven education for diverse learners. In Advances in educational technologies and instructional design book series (pp. 49–80). https://doi.org/DOI: 10.4018/979-8-3693-6130-6.ch003

Yang, K., & Lee, H. (2023). Implementing ethics in artificial intelligence: A model for ethical decision-making in AI applications. *AI and Ethics*, *3*(4), 779–791.

Yeo, R. K. (2008). Brewing service quality in higher education. *Quality Assurance in Education*, *16*(3), 266–296.

Yew, E. H. J., & Goh, K. (2016). Problem-Based Learning: An Overview of its Process and Impact on Learning. In Health Professions Education (Vol. 2, Issue 2). https://doi.org/DOI: 10.1016/j.hpe.2016.01.004

Yu, K. (2024). Utilizing AI in liberal arts education. *Barun Academy of History*, *20*, 221–235. DOI: 10.55793/jkhc.2024.20.221

Zareinejad, M. (2014). Performance evaluation of service quality in higher education institutions using modified SEVQUAL approach with Grey analytic hierarchy process (GAHP) and multiple Grey evaluation. *Iberoamerican Journal of Industrial Engineering*, *6*(11), 271–293.

Zary, N. (2024). AI Literacy Framework (ALiF): A Progressive Competency Development Protocol for Higher Education v1. https://doi.org/DOI: 10.17504/protocols.io.bp2l6dbpzvqe/v1

Zary, N. (2025). AI Literacy Framework (ALiF): A Comprehensive Approach to Developing AI Competencies in Educational and Healthcare Settings. *Preprints*. https://doi.org/DOI: 10.20944/preprints202503.1188.v1

Zawacki-Richter, O., Marín, V. I., Bond, M., & Gouverneur, F. (2019). Systematic review of research on artificial intelligence applications in higher education–where are the educators? *International Journal of Educational Technology in Higher Education*, *16*, 39. Advance online publication. DOI: 10.1186/s41239-019-0171-0

Zegwaard, K., & McCurdy, S. (2014). The influence of work-integrated learning on motivation to undertake graduate studies. *Asia Pacific Journal of Cooperative Education*, *15*, 13–28.

Zhai, C., Wibowo, S., & Li, L. D. (2024). The effects of over-reliance on AI dialogue systems on students' cognitive abilities: A systematic review. *Smart Learning Environments, 11*, 28. DOI: 10.1186/s40561-024-00316-7

Zhai, X., & Wibowo, S. (2024). Human cognition and AI-generated texts: Ethics in educational settings. *Humanities & Social Sciences Communications, 11*, 45. Advance online publication. DOI: 10.1057/s41599-024-04002-4

Zhang, K., Li, L., & Yu, H. (2024). Analysis on concept of AI Literacy according and Future Education to the result of systematic review. *Journal of Lifestyle and SDGs Review, 5*(1), e03293. DOI: 10.47172/2965-730x.sdgsreview.v5.n01.pe03293

Zhang, K., & Liu, X. (2022). Bridging AI technology with ethical considerations: A study of big data in decision-making. *AI and Ethics, 2*(2), 313–325.

Zhang, K., Li, X., Ye, H., Lin, K. J., Chen, S., & Law, R. (2024). How can ChatGPT assist hospitality and tourism education? *Journal of Teaching in Travel & Tourism, 24*(4), 438–448.

Zhang, P., & Tur, G. (2024). A systematic review of ChatGPT use in K-12 education. *European Journal of Education, 59*(2), e12599. DOI: 10.1111/ejed.12599

Zhang, Z. (V.), & Hyland, K. (2022). Fostering student engagement with feedback: An integrated approach. *Assessing Writing, 51*, 100586. DOI: 10.1016/j.asw.2021.100586

Zhang, Z. (V.), & Hyland, K. (2023). Student engagement with peer feedback in L2 writing: Insights from reflective journaling and revising practices. *Assessing Writing, 58*, 100784. DOI: 10.1016/j.asw.2023.100784

Zhao, T. (2023). AI in Educational Technology. *Preprints*. https://doi.org/DOI: 10.20944/preprints202311.0106.v1

Zhou, X., Teng, D., & Al-Samarraie, H. (2024). *The Mediating Role of Generative AI Self-Regulation on Students' Critical Thinking and Problem-Solving*. Educational Sciences. https://www.mdpi.com/2227-7102/14/12/1302)

Zimotti, G., Frances, C., & Whitaker, L. (2024). The future of language education: Teachers' perceptions about the surge of large language models like ChatGPT. *Technology in Language Teaching & Learning, 6*(2), 1–24.

Zopiatis, A., Papadopoulos, C., & Theofanous, Y. (2021). A systematic review of literature on hospitality internships. *Journal of Hospitality, Leisure, Sport and Tourism Education, 28*, 100309. DOI: 10.1016/j.jhlste.2021.100309

Zopiatis, A., & Theocharous, A. L. (2013). Revisiting hospitality internship practices: A holistic investigation. *Journal of Hospitality, Leisure, Sport and Tourism Education*, *13*, 33–46. https://doi.org/https://doi.org/10.1016/j.jhlste.2013.04.002

About the Contributors

Shahnawaz Khan is currently serving as the Head of Applied Research at Bahrain Polytechnic in Bahrain. He holds a Ph.D. in Computer Engineering from Indian Institute of Technology (BHU), India. He has held academic, leadership, and administrative positions in esteemed universities and software industry across multiple countries. His academic experience extends to directing various committees, including those focused on research, faculty development, and accreditation. He has also been actively involved in education quality and accreditation (such as ABET, BQA, NCAAA, and NACC) for multiple esteemed universities across multiple countries. Dr. Khan is a recognized expert in Artificial Intelligence, Blockchain, and Islamic FinTech. He brings nearly two decades of experience in research, teaching, and industry in computer science, and app development. He has co-founded a vocational training institute, and two IT companies and has served as a chief technical officer. With a strong track record in Artificial Intelligence, his research has resulted in over 70 peer-reviewed publications with over 2000 citations, four patents, and seven edited books. He has also served as an editor for several special issues of SCI and Scopus indexed journals. Dr. Khan has supervised numerous postgraduate and graduate researchers and is a frequent reviewer for top-tier journals and conferences. Dr. Khan is passionate about applying AI to solve real-world problems. He leads a team of researchers focused on developing innovative solutions (by applying artificial intelligence) for real-world problems in areas such as Islamic fintech, healthcare and global warming. He is committed to fostering the next generation of researchers.

Philippe Pringuet is an assistant professor in computer science at Bahrain Polytechnic, teaching on multiple courses of the Programming major. Philippe has 15 years experience in education in European and Middle Eastern contexts and is an Apple Certified trainer and a Senior Fellow of the Advanced Higher Education, UK. Philippe led the development of the Bachelor of ICT Programme at Bahrain Polytechnic and in his roles as Head of School of ICT and then as Dean of the

Faculty of Engineering, provided the leadership to guide the ICT and Engineering programmes towards international accreditation with the British Computer Society and the Institution of Engineering and Technology. Personable and energetic academic with 10+ years management experience establishing a new Polytechnic in a multicultural environment. An active participant in National Education Reform, creating and delivering programmes in a Problem Based Learning approach following student-centred principles and, contributor to the establishment of the Labour Market Observatory. Areas of interest include EDUCATION LEADERSHIP, PROBLEMBASED LEARNING, QUALITY & ACCREDITATION, ASSESSMENT & MODERATION, CHANGE MANAGEMEN

***

Md Shabbir Alam is a faculty member in the Department of Economics & Finance at the University of Bahrain. He holds a Master's and Ph.D. in Economics from Aligarh Muslim University, India, and completed a post-doctoral fellowship at ICSSR. With over 14 years of teaching and research experience across Bahrain, Oman, Saudi Arabia, and India, Dr. Alam specializes in development economics, energy and environmental economics, and international economics. He has published more than 100 research articles, including 65+ in high-impact journals, with over 3,500 citations. He is recognized among the top 2% of global scientists in economics and business by Stanford University and Elsevier and also serves as a supervisor for two Ph.D. students. Dr. Alam serves as an editor for one academic book and a guest editor for two upcoming edited volumes scheduled for publication in 2025. He actively contributes as a reviewer, editorial board member, and conference committee participant.

Husain AlMadhi is currently a Teaching and Learning Specialist at Vatel Bahrain. An experienced educator with a diverse background in teaching across primary, secondary, vocational, and higher education levels, his professional interests include innovative pedagogical approaches and the enhancement of teaching and learning practices in diverse educational contexts.

Huda AlNajjar is the Accounting Program Manager and a Lecturer at Bahrain Polytechnic's Business School. Huda holds a Master's degree in Law and Accounting from the London School of Economics and Political Sciences and a Bachelor's degree in Accounting, Business Finance and Management from the University of York. With over 15 years of professional experience, she specializes in strategy consulting, business development, and financial analysis, with a focus on projects involving public and private companies, as well as SMEs. Her research interests include auditors independence, taxation, strategic management, corporate finance and governance and financial regulation.

Constantine Andoniou is an Associate Professor of Education and the Chair of the Department of Education and Social Sciences at Abu Dhabi University. With an extensive academic background, he holds a Bachelor of Education in Teacher Education, a Diploma in Education in Educational Psychology and Sociology of Education, a Master of Education in Philosophy of Education and Educational Sociology, and a Doctorate of Philosophy in Education. With teaching and leadership experience in higher education institutions across Europe, Australia, and the Middle East, Dr. Andoniou actively collaborates with international researchers and industry leaders to bridge the gap between theoretical advancements and practical implementations of AI and digital technologies in education. Dr. Andoniou's research spans across information theory, postmodernism, digital learning theories, digital transformation, and the integration of educational technology in teaching and learning environments. His research focuses on AI integration in education, particularly in examining how artificial intelligence reshapes human cognition, transforms pedagogical practices, and redefines the role of educators. His current research focuses on developing a competency-based framework to equip educators with the necessary skills to integrate AI into their teaching methodologies effectively. A thought leader in digital media and metaverse technologies, Dr. Andoniou has contributed to pioneering research on the intersection of AI, immersive learning environments, and digital storytelling, with published works exploring the implications of digital and AI-driven ecosystems on education, communication, and knowledge dissemination.

Arjunan Balaji is the Assistant Professor at Bahrain Polytechnic, Kingdom of Bahrain. His work focuses on Experience Design, 3D Look Development, Instructional Design, AI driven storytelling, His area of interest is Animation, Graphic Design, UI/UX Design, Human-Centered Design, AI literacy, and Creative AI for higher education. His research area is of Interaction Design, Character Design, Branding, AI in education and Visual Education.

John Philip Cainoy is an English educator at Bahrain Polytechnic in the Kingdom of Bahrain. He holds a PhD in English Language and Literature from La Consolacion University Philippines. With over fifteen years of experience in higher education, he has taught at the Polytechnic University of the Philippines and contributed to curriculum and research development in English for Academic Purposes (EAP) and English for Specific Purposes (ESP). His teaching portfolio includes courses in Academic Writing, Research and Technical Writing, Linguistics, and TESOL. His research interests encompass affect studies, applied linguistics, digital pedagogy, and the integration of artificial intelligence in academic writing, with recent publications focusing on large language models (LLMs) and their implications for English language education.

Namrata Gulati is an Assistant Professor at the Bahrain Polytechnic and delivers courses related to the HRM Major at the School of Business. Her areas of specialization are Performance Management Systems, Rewards and Compensation and Learning and Talent Development as well as core HRM courses, Leadership and Organization Behavior. She has over 20 years of experience in designing and delivering various courses of HRM at different levels and supervising students in their Capstone Project in the final year focusing on various domains of HRM in different sectors/industry. Her areas of research include Compensation and rewards perceptions, Use of AI in HRM and use of AI in Education .

Abid Hussain Jagirdar serves as the Principal of K.H.M.W. (Khairunnisa Haji Munshi Wajid Ali) College of Commerce, located in Jogeshwari (West), Mumbai. He holds a Ph.D., M.Com, and B.Ed., reflecting a strong academic foundation in commerce and education. Under his leadership, the college, affiliated with the University of Mumbai and accredited with a 'B++' grade by NAAC, continues to uphold its commitment to providing quality education to all students and those pursuing higher studies.

Ankita Jena is currently serving as a Medical Device Engineer. Her fascination with design and mechanisms began at a young age, driving her to pursue a B.Sc. in Design and Computing. Outside of her professional work, she is passionate about reading, which continually broadens her understanding and inspires new ideas. Looking ahead, she is dedicated to contributing meaningful insights that enhances the quality of life, guided by her personal motto.

Nithin Kalorth is an Associate Professor at the School of Creative Media, Bahrain Polytechnic, in the Kingdom of Bahrain. With over 15 years of experience in academia and professional training, he specializes in digital society, digital culture, film studies, photography, mobile storytelling, and news design. In the capacity of mobile journalism and digital storytelling trainer, Dr. Kalorth has conducted workshops for organizations including WHO, Kerala Press Club, The Foreign Correspondents' Club of South Asia, IIT Goa, and BITS Pilani, among others. Dr. Kalorth holds a First Rank and Gold Medal in Electronic Media from the University of Madras and a PhD in Film Studies from MG University, Kottayam, supported by the UGC JRF Scholarship from the Government of India. He has contributed to over 40 national and international conferences and has published extensively across journals, books, and encyclopedias. His expertise extends to the editorial domain, with two well-regarded volumes on OTT media indexed on Scopus. In addition to his academic and professional pursuits, Dr. Kalorth is a dedicated mentor and jury head for the Indian School Film Festival (Oman) and serves as a jury member for the Yuva Film Festival (Chennai, India). His work is driven by a passion for digital innovation in storytelling and a commitment to shaping the next generation of media and film professionals.

Devi Manikeswari, a competent and dedicated educator with extensive teaching/ training experience in tertiary and higher education levels. Areas of expertise and research interests include Higher education, HR, OB and Psychometric testing. .

Anuradha Menon is currently the Program Manager for the Foundation Year at Vatel Bahrain, where she oversees program design, delivery, and student academic development. With over three decades of experience in the field of education, spanning teaching, curriculum development, and academic leadership, her professional interests include innovative pedagogical practices, learner engagement, and academic skills development in higher education.

Mohammad Noor Alam, A Doctorate in Commerce, with over a decade of academic experience, specializing in accounting courses. Currently serving as an Assistant Professor at the University of Bahrain, with prior faculty appointments at prestigious institutions across Oman, Saudi Arabia, Afghanistan, and India.

Satya Pavan Kumar Ratnakaram is an accomplished academician currently employed as an Assistant Professor in the Faculty of Business and Logistics, Bahrain Polytechnic since September 2022. Prior to this, he has worked as a Program Manager and IQA member in the Commercial Studies Division, Bahrain Training Institute, Kingdom of Bahrain for more than 16 years. With over two decades of teaching/training/industry experience across three countries, presented/published more than 25 articles in national and international conferences/journals in the field of Accounting, Banking, Insurance, Higher Education, Problem Solving, AI in education, CSR and ESG.

Sabina Ashfaque Shaikh IQAC Coordinator, K.H.M.W. Night College of Commerce Ph.D. (Pursuing), M.Com, B.Ed., PGDHRM, M.Phil Mrs. Sabina Ashfaque Shaikh currently serves as the IQAC Coordinator at K.H.M.W. Night College of Commerce. She is pursuing her Ph.D. from the University of Mumbai and holds multiple academic qualifications including M.Com, B.Ed., Post Graduate Diploma in Human Resource Management (PGDHRM), and M.Phil. Known for her commitment to institutional development and quality assurance, Mrs. Shaikh plays a key role in ensuring the academic and administrative benchmarks of the college are maintained and enhanced. Her work focuses on academic planning, student-centered initiatives, and continuous improvement strategies in higher education.

Zakir Shaikh is an Assistant Professor, Department of Accounting and Finance, School of Business Administration, Kingdom University, Bahrain. Prior to this, he worked more than 28 years in commercial and academic industry. He has published numerous articles in referred journals and presented many papers in various conferences, both local and abroad in the different area of Accounting, management and Islamic Banking and Finance. He has also participated in a variety of seminars, forums, workshops and international conferences. He obtained his Ph.D. (Islamic Banking and Finance) from India in 2018. His doctoral thesis explored the entrepreneurial phenomenon from an Islamic perspective and argued for profit and loss sharing (PLS) contracts as viable alternatives to conventional interest-based financing instruments. He holds Master degree in Commerce, Business Administration & Finance and Control. He is a member of AAA, Chartered Institute of Islamic Finance Professionals (CIIF), Malaysia; Indian Accounting Association; Orissa Commerce Association, India and associated with Accounting & Auditing Organization for Islamic Financial Institution (AAOIFI), Bahrain

Anand Soni is a seasoned educator and researcher at Bahrain Polytechnic's School of Business & Logistics, with nearly 20 years of teaching experience. He holds a Ph.D. in Management and master's degrees in Business Management and Commerce (ABST). He authored the book Business Analytics and Data Science for Decision Making and has contributed to a patent, journal articles, and book chapters. Dr. Soni has co-guided Ph.D. students, supervised master's theses, and helped develop NQF qualifications. He actively organizes academic events and frequently serves as a keynote speaker, reflecting his commitment to research, education, and professional engagement.

Harishma Devi is an independent researcher, with a Bachelor's degree in Design & Computing from BITS Pilani. As a software developer, she is currently dedicated to creating AI/ML-driven solutions.

Muhammad Usman Tariq has more than 16+ year's experience in industry and academia. He has authored more than 200+ research articles, 110+ case studies, 130+ book chapters and several books other than 4 patents. He is founder and CEO of The Case HQ, a unique repository for courses, narrative and video case studies. He has been working as a consultant and trainer for industries representing six sigma, quality, health and safety, environmental systems, project management, and information security standards. His work has encompassed sectors in aviation, manufacturing, food, hospitality, education, finance, research, software and transportation. He has diverse and significant experience working with accreditation agencies of ABET, ACBSP, AACSB, WASC, CAA, EFQM and NCEAC. Additionally, Dr. Tariq has operational experience in incubators, research labs, government research projects, private sector startups, program creation and management at various industrial and academic levels. He is Certified Higher Education Teacher from Harvard University, USA, Certified Online Educator from HMBSU, Certified Six Sigma Master Black Belt and has been awarded PFHEA, SFSEDA, SMIEEE, and CMBE.

Index

A

B

C

D

E

F

H

I

L

N

www.ingramcontent.com/pod-product-compliance
Lightning Source LLC
LaVergne TN
LVHW062221200926
848484LV00006B/1448